THEOLOGY AND TECHNIQUE

THEOLOGY AND TECHNIQUE

Toward an Ethic of Non-Power

by JACQUES ELLUL

Translation by CHRISTIAN ROY
Forewords by DAVID W. GILL and YVES ELLUL
Introduction by FRÉDÉRIC ROGNON
Organizational editing by VIRGINIA W. LANDGRAF

CASCADE *Books* • Eugene, Oregon

THEOLOGY AND TECHNIQUE
Toward an Ethic of Non-Power

Copyright © 2024 Jacques Ellul. All rights reserved. Except for brief quotations in critical publications or reviews, no part of this book may be reproduced in any manner without prior written permission from the publisher. Write: Permissions, Wipf and Stock Publishers, 199 W. 8th Ave., Suite 3, Eugene, OR 97401.

Cascade Books
An Imprint of Wipf and Stock Publishers
199 W. 8th Ave., Suite 3
Eugene, OR 97401

www.wipfandstock.com

PAPERBACK ISBN: 978-1-7252-5977-5
HARDCOVER ISBN: 978-1-7252-5978-2
EBOOK ISBN: 978-1-7252-5979-9

Cataloguing-in-Publication data:

Names: Ellul, Jacques, author. | David W. Gill and Yves Ellul, forewords. | Frédéric Rognon, introduction. | Christian Roy, translator.

Title: Theology and technique : toward an ethic of non-power / Jacques Ellul, with forewords by David W. Gill and Yves Ellul; Introduction by Frédéric Rognon.

Description: Eugene, OR: Cascade Books, 2024 | Includes bibliographical references and index.

Identifiers: ISBN 978-1-7252-5977-5 (paperback) | ISBN 978-1-7252-5978-2 (hardcover) | ISBN 978-1-7252-5979-9 (ebook)

Subjects: LCSH: Technology and civilization. | Technology—Theology. | Church and the world.

Classification: BR115.W6 E50 2024 (print) | BR115 (ebook)

TABLE OF CONTENTS

FOREWORD TO THE ENGLISH EDITION by David W. Gill | vii
FOREWORD TO THE FRENCH EDITION by Yves Ellul | ix
EDITORIAL NOTE by Virginia W. Landgraf | xi
INTRODUCTION by Frédéric Rognon | 1
    1. The status of *Théologie et Technique* in Ellul's oeuvre | 1
    2. The critique of technical theologies | 5
    3. The theological alternative | 7
    4. The dialogue with René Girard and with Gabriel Vahanian | 9
    5. The contribution to the debate about the Judeo-Christian roots of the environmental crisis | 11
    6. The propositional dimension of the ethics of non-power | 12

PRELIMINARY WORKS
INSTINCTIVE AND NON-SCIENTIFIC INTERMEZZO | 17
SITUATION OF THEOLOGY WITHIN TECHNICAL SOCIETY | 25
INVESTIGATION TOWARD AN ETHIC IN A TECHNICAL SOCIETY | 35
    1. What is Technique? | 35
    2. About some traditional ethical mistakes to avoid | 37
    3. Technical ethics | 40
    4. The ethical issues raised | 42
    5. Proposals for an ethic | 44
THEOLOGY AND TECHNIQUE LITERATURE | 49
THE THEOLOGICAL STATUS OF TECHNIQUE ACCORDING TO GABRIEL VAHANIAN | 60

TABLE OF CONTENTS

THEOLOGY AND TECHNIQUE

First Chapter: THE STAKES OF THEOLOGICAL PRODUCTION IN A TECHNICAL SOCIETY | 77

    Introduction | 77
    1. Technique and theology: the traditional positions of theology | 79
    2. Reception of Technique by theologians: Multiplicity and partial nature of the approaches | 83
    3. Technique and transcendence | 86

Second Chapter: SITUATION OF A THEOLOGICAL REFLECTION ON TECHNIQUE | 95

    1. Man, Nature, and the artificial | 95
    2. Technique according to the Bible | 106
    3. The status of Theology in technical society | 126

Third Chapter: LIMITS | 134

    1. In search of limits | 134
    2. On nature and creation | 141
    3. Judeo-Christianity as the negation of limits | 152

Fourth Chapter: TECHNIQUE AND ESCHATOLOGY | 179

    1. Itineraries | 182
    2. History of God, history of man | 191

Fifth Chapter: ETHICAL MEDIATION | 199

    1. The choice of a theological orientation | 202
    2. The discernment of spirits: the spirit of power | 208
    3. The discernment of spirits: the spirit of deceit | 217

ANNEX TO THE FIFTH CHAPTER | 229

Sixth Chapter: ETHICAL REPERCUSSIONS | 236

    1. Critical non-power | 240
    2. The Ethic of Rupture | 253
    3. Immediatized Hope | 259

BIBLIOGRAPHY | 273

Foreword to the English Edition

IT IS A GREAT pleasure to see Jacques Ellul's *Theology and Technique* in print and in an English translation. We have many to thank for their efforts to achieve this success. First of all, we are very grateful to Jean (son), Yves (son), Dominique (daughter), and Jérôme (grandson) Ellul for their great efforts to bring Jacques Ellul's considerable unpublished work into public view. This volume in particular includes many "notes from the family" to help clarify the text. Next, the contribution of Strasbourg professor Frédéric Rognon to this work is extraordinary. His introduction in this volume is absolutely essential reading to understand Ellul's message and its context both within Ellul's own work and on the larger stage as well.

To bring *Theology and Technique* from its French home into an English translation we need first to thank our anonymous benefactor who generously funded the translation work. Going forward, with opportunities to bring many other old as well as recently discovered works by Jacques Ellul into English language publication, we are eager to find others with the vision and resources to help fund these projects. For several years now, the International Jacques Ellul Society (IJES) has promoted and supported translation and publication of works by Jacques Ellul, especially in partnership with Wipf & Stock Publishers, which maintains a large and growing Ellul collection of primary and secondary writings, now including *Theology and Technique*. This long-term project of publications would simply not have happened without the negotiations and hard work of IJES executive director Ted Lewis. Then came the massive labors by translator Christian Roy to create the English text from the French—and finally Virginia Landgraf's painstaking work on preparing the text for publication. It would almost be criminal to begin reading this book without acknowledging this amazing team that made it possible.

As stated above, Frédéric Rognon's introduction is essential reading to more fully understand this book. I agree with Rognon that this might

FOREWORD TO THE ENGLISH EDITION

be Ellul's most important of sixty or so books—because it brings into direct encounter the two major fields of Ellul's lifelong work: his sociology of technique and technology in the modern world, on the one hand, and his robust theology and ethics of the Word of God, on the other. But this is not an easy read. Here are two preliminary notes to ease your way.

First of all, Ellul will often challenge and shake up his readers with bold, unexpected, perhaps even shocking ideas and assertions about technology, the Bible, and many other topics. My experience in conversation with Ellul was that there was always great depth and a rationale for what he said, even when it went diametrically against the "standard" view. But remember also that Ellul said on many occasions that he was never seeking disciples but rather providing people with tools to think out for themselves the meaning of their lives in the world. We need to listen and learn from *Theology and Technique*—but invite it to help us think through our own understanding of the topics.

Second, we need to read *Theology and Technique* for what it is: an unfinished, rough draft. It includes a six-chapter draft of a book Ellul envisioned—along with several "preliminary works" on the general subject that the Ellul family and French editors thought we would like to have included. Some of the material in the six-chapter "book" was published earlier in essay form in journals. The point is to understand that this volume is far from a finished product from the hand of Jacques Ellul.

Back in the 1980s, during my sabbatical in Bordeaux, Ellul shared with me that his editors and publishers rarely if ever pushed back at him as a university professor on the structure or content of his books. He wrote it, submitted it, and they published it. He was responding with sympathy to my very different experience with aggressive, sometimes intrusive, American editors and publishers. But this explains, I believe, why Ellul's books sometimes seem repetitive and redundant in places—and that includes *Theology and Technique*.

With our profound gratitude to the team that has brought us this volume, with awareness of the rough-draft condition of the work, and with confident expectation that Jacques Ellul will once more bring brilliant flashes of light into our understanding, let's plunge into *Theology and Technique*.

David W. Gill, 2021
Founding president of the International Jacques Ellul Society
Oakland, California

Foreword to the French Edition

THIS IS A DOCUMENT that remained unpublished during Jacques Ellul's lifetime, even though it is as a whole datable to the years around 1975.

It is important to properly gauge the state of the manuscript to understand that, for one thing, it is in fact only partially unpublished. For a few passages, sometimes large ones, are articles published during Jacques Ellul's lifetime. It has been possible to excerpt some pages from other documents and to gather them here in view of this book project.

A "body" of six chapters remains only in a manuscript state, consistent with the plan joined to the original folder. But there were also to be found in the latter a few documents (Intermezzo, Bibliography, etc.) that are more like "preparatory documents" to be integrated in order to support the reflection of the future book.

We make the choice of publishing these documents as they are, in such a way that the book is made up of two distinct parts: 1) preparatory documents; 2) the body of the book (six chapters).

This position respects the manuscript's state.

On the other hand, it gives the book the character of an unfinished sketch: the intended plan is not fully respected; many redundancies with sometimes tiny variations in viewpoint give the published text a clumsy character. Transitions between the different themes treated are lacking, leaving the impression of a disjointed puzzle.

Of course, one will find here most of the themes treated by Jacques Ellul in his other books—he abundantly cites them himself—and this may be the reason why Jacques Ellul did not carry the publication effort to its conclusion.

And yet, despite all these defects, it seems to us that this book, as much by the specific scope of its topic as by its roughness as a sketch, brings a definite contribution to reflection, at once stimulating and provocative. It also allows us to take stock of the evolution of mentalities over the last forty years, as much in sociology as in theology. The radicalization of the stances Ellul takes reflects as much the specialist's mastery as the consistency of his commitment, while avoiding any hermetic jargon. Need we add that the stakes seem considerable to us?

For they involve the author's consistency and his credibility at the moment when he initiates a fruitful debate, a necessary dialogue between Christianity and "post-Christian society," or rather technical society.

Actually, Jacques Ellul is here getting back in touch with a Judeo-Christianity that is destructive of myths and ideologies, and thus liberative for our society. At a time when we are starting to wonder about the societal model we have been developing worldwide at the expense of all others, this recentering may be welcome.

We wish to thank all those who have made the publication of this manuscript possible, particularly Willem H. Vanderburg.

Yves Ellul

Editorial Note

THIS BOOK WAS WRITTEN in the 1970s. Nowadays, we expect academic writers to use words and pronouns for human beings that reflect gender diversity. Ellul was not following that convention. In many cases, he used *homme* —"man"—where most readers would assume that he meant also to include women. However, rectifying his language to be inclusive is more difficult than simply substituting "person," "man or woman," "humankind," or some such expression for every instance of *homme*. One of the major themes in Ellul's thought is that individuals are called to resist mass trends. Substituting a plural for a singular expression would do a disservice to that aspect of Ellul's thought. Using "man or woman" consistently would be wordy, describe children and nonbinary people imperfectly, and lose the semantic tension that occurs when the same singular word refers to the individual and the species. Therefore we have chosen to ask forbearance of the reader with respect to the lack of inclusive language in this text, and we hope that future generations of Ellul scholars who are writing texts *de novo* will find creative solutions to these problems.

The French editors chose not to modify Ellul's inconsistencies in the use of capitals, except for "non-power," "Technique," and "God Almighty." They sought to confine themselves to correcting typos and very slightly altering punctuation when it was faulty. While I have kept the capitalization as is, I have modified the punctuation and some of the run-on or incomplete sentences to fit the standards of conventional English.

The French editors have also verified the bibliographical references given by Jacques Ellul, completing and correcting them in some cases; all additions on their part appear between brackets or in notes that are clearly identifiable as Jacques Ellul's. Additional notes from the translator or editor are identified as such.

Finally, you will find a very comprehensive bibliography at the end of this book that is organized into three sections: works of Jacques Ellul cited

EDITORIAL NOTE

by himself or by the editors, works cited and used by Jacques Ellul (often reconstituted by the editors), and works cited by the editors for this work.

Virginia W. Landgraf

Introduction

by Frédéric Rognon

THEOLOGY AND TECHNIQUE is a formerly unpublished manuscript, found among Jacques Ellul's papers after his death, which occurred in 1994. That does not mean that it was written in the last years of his life. The most recent bibliographical reference mentioned in it is that to *The Technological System*, which dates from 1977. This makes it possible to situate the writing of *Theology and Technique* in the final third of the 1970s. Before underlining its innovative contributions, it should be first situated within the whole of Jacques Ellul's oeuvre.

1. THE STATUS OF *THEOLOGY AND TECHNIQUE* IN ELLUL'S OEUVRE

The architectonics of Jacques Ellul's oeuvre, taken as a whole, cannot fail to startle careful readers, if not to leave them rather perplexed. Our author has insisted on several occasions on giving a dialectical account of the inner logic of his thought and, by the same token, of his oeuvre. More or less half of the fifty-eight books published belong to the sociological side: it is about the critique of technical society, organized around a trilogy (*The Technological Society*,[1] *The Technological System*,[2] and *The Technological Bluff*)[3] and unfolding toward all great social and cultural themes (politics, propaganda, violence, social classes, beliefs, the arts). The other half has to do with the theological and ethical side, including a trilogy as well (*To Will and to Do*[4] and the two works that were condensed into *The Ethics of Free-*

---

1. Ellul, *Technological Society*.
2. Ellul, *Technological System*.
3. Ellul, *Technological Bluff*.
4. Ellul, *To Will and to Do*.

dom in English),[5] but also numerous biblical commentaries and works of a clearly confessional nature. These two components "communicate back and forth in a sort of dialectical exchange in which hope is both the crisis point and the solution," Jacques Ellul maintained, adding: "If you only take the theological dimension into account, you miss the element of incarnation. If you restrict yourself to looking at the sociopolitical dimension, you will be constantly running up against a lack of answers and narrowness."[6] None of the books of the sociological side deals with issues of Christian faith and hope, but each of them finds its theological counterpoint in one of the works of the ethical side. Finally, Jacques Ellul held to the idea of a global construction, thought out as a whole in the immediate postwar period, and realized in its complete outline, in such a way that each of the fifty-eight books could be understood as a chapter of a single work, the introduction to which would have been *Presence in the Modern World*[7] while the conclusion would be *Reason for Being*.[8] The coherence of the global editorial structure would then find its base firmly established.

Yet there are exceptions to the rule. We could mention the books that came after what was supposed to be the conclusion of his oeuvre,[9] and which Jacques Ellul himself viewed as a mere "complement."[10] We could recall the works put together and published posthumously by his students without the author ever having considered their publication,[11] and which are therefore beyond the scope of the initial project without in any way affecting faithfulness to its basic insight. We could mention the unpublished works, whose statuses are varied incidentally: *The Ethics of Holiness*, an extension of *The Ethics of Freedom* that Jacques Ellul did not have time to complete, but of which an edition will soon be enabled by significant work on establishing the text; *The Ethics of Love* (or of *agape*), an extension of *The Ethics of Holiness* and the completion of the ethical work (actually a pentalogy, not a mere trilogy), that the author did not even have the chance to begin; a tract on Islam, finally, that, according to his children, Jacques Ellul

---

5. Ellul, *Ethics of Freedom*. This book is an abridgment of Ellul, *Ethique de la liberté* and Ellul, *Les combats de la liberté*.

6. Ellul with Chastenet, *Jacques Ellul on Politics, Technology, and Christianity*, 21–22.

7. Ellul, *Presence in the Modern World*.

8. Ellul, *Reason for Being*, 3–4.

9. Ellul, *Technological Bluff*; Ellul, *Anarchy and Christianity*; Ellul, *An Unjust God?*; Ellul, *If You Are the Son of God*; Ellul, *Déviances et déviants dans notre société intolérante*; Ellul and Nordon, *L'homme à lui-même*.

10. Ellul, *Reason for Being*, 4.

11. Ellul, *Les classes sociales*; Ellul, *La pensée marxiste*; Ellul, *Les successeurs de Marx*; Ellul, *On Freedom, Love, and Power*.

had finished and submitted for reading to a few specialists, before making it disappear.[12] But above all, we have to mention the titles of several published works that do seem to have managed, during Ellul's lifetime, to articulate theology and sociology in their very midst, thus calling into play a kind of internal dialectics that would echo the external dialectics: *Presence in the Modern World*, which first of all presents Christianity as being revolutionary in essence, then shows that technical society is characterized by the dissolution of ends and the unlimited excrescence of means, before asking how to live as Christians in such a context;[13] *The New Demons*, which, in a very different way, describes changing beliefs in technical society from a strictly sociological viewpoint, before calling upon believers, in a kind of afterword or even an annex coming after the epilogue, explicitly entitled "Coda for Christians";[14] *The Humiliation of the Word*,[15] which probes the respective statuses of word and image in Scripture (where the former comes first)[16] and in technical society (where it is humiliated by the latter's triumph),[17] the better to advocate iconoclasm as a liberational Christian stance;[18] *Changer de révolution*,[19] which analyzes with very academic rigor the status of revolution today and the rise of the proletariat in the Third World, before daring to make a confession of faith that is as explicit as it is unexpected.[20] One should add that each of the books of the theological side bears within itself a dialectical orientation, which is not the case of those of the sociological side. One way to phrase this remarkable symmetry would be to say that the sociological always induces despair, and as such calls for the other pole, while the theological pole always pretends to be fundamentally embodied, due to the presence of the other pole within itself.

---

12. This text, now forever lost, would thus have been the counterpart of Ellul, *Un chrétien pour Israël*, while radicalizing the positions defended in the compilations of articles posthumously published as Ellul, *Islam et judéo-christianisme*, and Ellul, *Israël, chance de civilisation*.

13. Ellul, *Presence in the Modern World*.

14. Ellul, *New Demons*, 209–28.

15. Ellul, *Humiliation of the Word*.

16. Ellul, *Humiliation of the Word*, 48–71.

17. Ellul, *Humiliation of the Word*, 112–82.

18. Ellul, *Humiliation of the Word*, 228–69.

19. Ellul, *Changer de révolution*.

20. Ellul, *Changer de révolution*, 289: "I now leave the realm of observation and demand to enter that of personal conviction, of witness and of proposal. I believe. (And it is now a matter of explicit faith.) I believe that in the final analysis, only the Revelation of God in Jesus Christ could provide at once the lever and the fulcrum."

Thus, the schematic outline of the external dialectic between the two sides of Ellul's oeuvre needs to be qualified somewhat. Given this, how do we situate *Theology and Technique* in relation to the rule and to its exceptions? In a sense, one might say that the present work piles on the exceptions: it is, by definition since it is unfinished, posterior to the work presented as programmed and completed. It is related in some ways to the books compiled by the heirs without Ellul's editorial intention being obvious, since it joins six chapters to "Preliminary works," and many passages have been published separately. This somewhat indeterminate status also makes it a potential unpublished work like *The Ethics of Holiness*, and of course, it belongs to the category of the internal dialectic, as its title indicates without any ambiguity. This dialectic as declared already in the work's heading also makes it unique in this way, a kind of *hapax* within the Ellulian corpus.[21] As such, *Theology and Technique* is a work that cannot be categorized, that is situated beyond the twofold taxonomy of Ellul's oeuvre; and yet, by closely articulating internal dialectics with external dialectics, *Theology and Technique* consolidates with utmost acuteness the dialectical character of Jacques Ellul's thought, if not that of his oeuvre, of which it may constitute the keystone.[22]

Nevertheless, if Ellulian dialectics find their completion in it, the order of terms within the book's title is not without significance. Among the publications of excerpts from *Theology and Technique* after Jacques Ellul's death, at least two ascribed to it the title *Technique and Theology*.[23] It is not to be ruled out that this title might have been that of a prior version of the

---

21. We should however point out that, if he did not write other works whose title would announce internal dialectic, Ellul did publish three articles in two collective volumes with explicitly dialectical headings: "Recherche pour une éthique dans une société technicienne" in *Ethique et technique* and "Technique and the Opening Chapters of Genesis" and "Relationship between Man and Creation in the Bible" in *Theology and Technology*. We should note that these three articles are excerpts drawn from *Theology and Technique*.

22. To Chastenet, who was asking him if the metaphor of the single book of which each one of his works would have been a chapter did not ruin the separation of the work into two sides, the sociological and the theological, Ellul answered in the negative by arguing that the two registers subsist in interrelation, "[i]n much the same way as a negative pole and a positive pole interact and then sparks fly between them" (Ellul with Chastenet, *Jacques Ellul on Politics, Technology, and Christianity*, 91). This answer seems to support our rereading in terms of a (dialectical!) articulation between an internal dialectic and an external dialectic; in this respect, *Theology and Technique* would be a parabolic expression of Ellul's oeuvre.

23. See Coulardeau, "*Technique et Théologie* de Jacques Ellul (Avertissement)," tourdebabel.over-blog.org, September 2011; Ellul, "Intermezzo instinctif et non-scientifique," *Foi et Vie* 111, no. 2 (June 2012) 5–13.

manuscript, especially since it is found among one of the subsections of the first chapter, but with a clearly theological orientation.[24] But the final choice turns out to be in tune with the positions defended by Jacques Ellul in numerous texts, to the effect that his dialectics are rooted in conscious theological presuppositions. As he states in *Jesus and Marx*[25] in response to Georges Casalis,[26] no theology can claim to be "inductive"; all theology is deductive, even if it takes worldly realities seriously. Liberation theologies presuppose class struggle, while Barthian theology presupposes biblical revelation. The former identify reality and truth, while the latter establishes between reality and truth a dialectics that only finds its resolution in Jesus Christ. It is with the awareness of these presuppositions that Jacques Ellul approaches the sociological issues pertaining to technological society. And it is in the name of a Scripture-centered and Christocentric theology that he is going to deploy his critique of theological currents conditioned by our era's technical mentality, which constitutes the heart of *Theology and Technique*.

2. THE CRITIQUE OF TECHNICAL THEOLOGIES

The innovative contributions of *Théologie et Technique* in relation to the whole of Ellul's oeuvre are of many kinds: the critique of the theological currents that are dominant in technical society, the theological alternative he opposes to them, the dialogue with René Girard and with Gabriel Vahanian, the contribution to the debate about the Judeo-Christian roots of the environmental crisis, and finally, the propositional dimension of the ethics of non-power.[27]

The critique of the theological currents that Jacques Ellul views as being determined by technological society raises from the outset the issue of our author's relationship to Marxist-type analyses. If theology is the product of technical infrastructures, are we dealing in Jacques Ellul with a quite classic Marxist approach? It is here that the Ellulian posture must be assessed in all its uniqueness. We know that, contrary to a stubborn commonplace,

---

24. See Chapter 1, section "Technique and theology: the traditional positions of theology," below, pp. 79–83.

25. Ellul, *Jesus and Marx*, 118–52.

26. Casalis, *Correct Ideas Don't Fall from the Skies*.

27. This notion of "non-power" is a neologism created by Ellul, in order to distinguish the biblical concept of ethics from secularized "nonviolence," deprived of its spiritual foundation, and which still aims at efficiency, hence at a certain power.

Jacques Ellul was never a member of the Communist Party,[28] that he has ruthlessly stigmatized Marxist Christians,[29] and that he has always criticized Marxists for dogmatically repeating the words of Karl Marx without taking into account the considerable mutations that have taken place since the middle of the nineteenth century and that have made us go from capitalist society to technical society. Yet Marx's analyses have never ceased to intensely stimulate the Bordeaux professor in his critique of the modern world, to such a point that, if he always presented himself as a "Marxologist," a specialist of Marx, and having taught his thought for over thirty years, he has gone so far at least once as calling himself a Marxist.[30] In order to grasp the subtlety of Jacques Ellul's relationship to Karl Marx, it is however necessary to recall the definition our author gave of "Technique": he understood by this "the main preoccupation of our time; in every field men seek to find the most efficient method."[31] In other words, the concept of "technique" now encompasses very broadly the whole of "techniques" and hence of techno-economic infrastructures in the Marxist sense, since it includes immaterial, notional, and axiological elements, among others. Efficiency as the supreme value, to which every other value and every end are sacrificed, constitutes one of the crucial vectors of "Technique" in the Ellulian sense. It is thus this complex of technical means, of technical representations, and of exclusivist exaltation of efficiency in all areas (economics, work, politics, transportation, food, leisure, communication, arts, education, ethics, the most everyday way of living . . .) that, in Jacques Ellul's eyes, determine contemporary theologies. We are thus far from a mechanical application of the Marxist scheme; by transposing to technical society the methodological arsenal of Karl Marx, Jacques Ellul has integrated the fact that any investigator immersed in this society, and lacking an exterior fulcrum that transcends the system, cannot escape the grip of technical conditionings in his own investigation, and he escapes it all the less as he figures himself exempt from it. The supreme paradox is that liberation theologians of Marxist inspiration

---

28. See Guillebaud, "Mort de Jacques Ellul: Un précurseur impénitent."

29. Ellul, *Jesus and Marx*.

30. "Marxologist yes, but not only. I would say truly Marxist insofar as I have not found a thought or a method that would better allow me to understand the world in which I live. Marx, no question, has profoundly steered my interpretations." Ellul with Guillebaud, "Jacques Ellul ou la passion d'un sceptique," *Le Nouvel Observateur*, July 17, 1982, 14.

31. Ellul, *Technological Society*, 21. Ellul adds: "In other words: Wherever there is research and application of new means as a criterion of efficiency, one can say that there is [Technique]" (Ellul, *Technological System*, 38). [Joachim Neugroschel's translation had rendered *technique* as "a technology"—ed.]

are the last to know where they are speaking from, even as they constantly ask themselves this question!

Jacques Ellul issues an unambiguous verdict against various modern theological currents: due to their unacceptable drift as soon as they enter the technical universe and collude with it, theologies prove agnostic, acritical, and hyperpolitical, establishing a radical continuity between human history and the kingdom of God. In doing so, they serve as an ideological endorsement conferred upon this closed system that is technical society. The positions he most takes to task over this are those of Teilhard de Chardin[32] and Harvey Cox,[33] but also those of death-of-God theologies, political theologies, and World Council of Churches documents. They were dominant on the theological scene in the 1960s and 1970s. The intellectual context having changed a lot over the last thirty-five years, there might have been grounds to fear a certain obsolescence of these critical analyses. The link that Jacques Ellul makes between the technical system and contemporary theological research remains relevant, however, since the influence of technical ways of thinking over mentalities has become if anything even more pervasive. Ellul's critique would therefore deserve to be extended and applied to the most contemporary theological currents of a postmodern type, be it postliberalism, Radical Orthodoxy,[34] and, *a fortiori*, prosperity theologies, not to mention religious movements (Pentecostal and thaumaturgical in style) marked by a technical search for efficiency, which, through the technicization of prayer, border on the identification between the God of Jesus Christ and the figure of Santa Claus.

3. THE THEOLOGICAL ALTERNATIVE

Jacques Ellul is not content to deconstruct technical theologies by bringing to light their servile conformism to the mentality of our time; he also counters them with an alternative. One will not be surprised to learn that it is rooted in biblical revelation. The Scripture-centeredness had already been forcefully stated from the very first page of the first volume of his ethical work, *Le Vouloir et le Faire*: "[T]he criterion of my thought is the biblical

---

32. Charbonneau, Jacques Ellul's faithful friend, has devoted to Teilhard de Chardin's theology a particularly incisive critical study: *Teilhard de Chardin, prophète d'un âge totalitaire*.

33. Ellul developed an extremely early critique of the secularization theory defended by Harvey Cox in a 1963 article ("Le Sacré dans le monde moderne," *Le Semeur* 61, no. 2 (1963) 24–36) and in a 1973 work (*New Demons*).

34. Translator's note: In English (italicized without capitals) in the original text.

revelation, the content of my thought is the biblical revelation, the point of departure is supplied by the biblical revelation, the method is the dialectic in accordance with which the biblical revelation is given to us, and the purpose is a search for the significance of the biblical revelation concerning ethics."[35] One could therefore lodge against *Théologie et Technique* the same complaint directed against *Le Vouloir et le Faire* in its time: does not the raising to the absolute of "biblical revelation," promoted to the status of hypostasis, lead our author to dispense with the hermeneutic task? This critique remains valid, but one should nevertheless take note of the innovation introduced at this price among various theological currents: for Jacques Ellul reverses the usual perspective, by questioning our time and our society, but also our technical way of moving within a technical context, starting from the scriptural given. Our author therefore counters the scientific exegesis of the Bible with the questioning of scientific and technical society (and its mentality) by the Bible itself.

Jacques Ellul's theological references are well-known, i.e., Karl Barth in his first period (which he has even been known to invoke against the mature Karl Barth!).[36] One should say more precisely the Kierkegaardian Barth, the Bordeaux professor having as often acknowledged his intellectual and spiritual debt toward the Copenhagen philosopher as toward the Basel theologian. The Kierkegaardian vein implicitly comes into view in the title of the first of "Preliminary works": *Instinctive and Non-Scientific Intermezzo*. This is a thinly veiled allusion to Søren Kierkegaard's *Concluding Unscientific Postscript to the Philosophical Fragments*.[37] It is, however, meant as an *Intermezzo* and not a *Postscript*, that is, a transition between various investigations, both theological and sociological, rather than, as with the Dane who knew his days were numbered, as the completion of an oeuvre. Nevertheless, Jacques Ellul still keeps a critical distance toward the Kierkegaardian Barth, whom he takes to task for a certain naïveté toward the technical phenomenon; a focus on grace could well lead to a disembodied theology. Jacques Ellul therefore remains fundamentally free in relation to his intellectual and spiritual debtors (Søren Kierkegaard, Karl Marx, Karl Barth). He stands apart from three theological postures vis-à-vis technique: neutrality (technique is *adiaphora*, a category in which he puts the Barthian orientation), pessimism (technique is sin), and optimism (technique is the

---

35. Ellul, *To Will and to Do*, 1.

36. Ellul, *Living Faith*, 124; "Aimez-vous Barth?," *Réforme*, no. 2143 (May 10, 1986) 7.

37. Kierkegaard, *Concluding Unscientific Postscript to "Philosophical Fragments."* One may recall that Ellul had already titled the introduction to *Reason for Being* "Preliminary, Polemical, Nondefinitive Postscript" (Ellul, *Reason for Being*, 1).

will of God). Evidently, the path between these three postures is a narrow one. The only relevant and credible theological alternative to indifference, technophobia, and technophilia consists in building a theology which, while rooted in biblical revelation, nonetheless takes the technical phenomenon into account as what it is: not as a neutral element of which one might make good use or a bad use according to the level of ethical consciousness; not a Satanic power, sinful by nature; nor either a means given by God to man in order to contribute to his creative work and complete it. Technique is ambivalent in itself; one definitely cannot ever disentangle its beneficent effects from its destructive ones. Technique is not the fruit of sin, but the product of the situation in which sin has put man, namely, the reign of necessity. Technique is man's new environment, which has replaced the natural environment,[38] and from which one can only take a distance by leaning on a transcendent fulcrum that is exterior to the technical system. Technique is man's new sacred, of which we are all idolatrous devotees, as long as we do not forcefully desecrate it. Such are the theological presuppositions that Jacques Ellul assumes to lay the groundwork for an innovative theology, one that is faithful to its scriptural source and fully embodied in the most contemporary realities, those of modern man's technical condition.

4. THE DIALOGUE WITH RENÉ GIRARD AND WITH GABRIEL VAHANIAN

One of the most original features of *Théologie et Technique* has to do with the dialogical dimension of Jacques Ellul's thought, as he sets down his positions here in relation to those of René Girard and of Gabriel Vahanian. Toward the first, Jacques Ellul expresses all his esteem, before advancing a correlation of their positions by way of the theme of pride, "another face of the spirit of power." This brings our author to make a link with technique, as the embodiment of this spirit of power in our society: such is the very expression of the "underground" that Dostoevsky wrote about,[39] read anew by René Girard,[40] and thus read anew by Jacques Ellul.[41] The latter can al-

---

38. The threat that the substitution of the natural environment by a technical one represents for the survival of mankind leads Jacques Ellul to advance a striking reversal of Hölderlin's famous dictum ("Where the danger is, also grows the saving power"): "the means that were his own defense have come to endanger him" (p. [104]). Translator's note: my own translation says "meager" where Rognon says "own."

39. Dostoevsky, *Notes from Underground*.

40. Girard, *Resurrection from the Underground*.

41. On the theme of suicide, present in Dostoevsky, reinterpreted by Girard, Ellul's rereading, oriented toward planetary suicide by way of exponential technical growth,

ways be criticized for overinterpreting the respective works of the former two. But then one will recall that the Bordeaux professor forcefully pleaded in favor of the reader's freedom and responsibility, to the point of plainly stating: "it is by 'betraying' me that one is most faithful to me!"[42] Such an "unfaithful faithfulness," practiced by Jacques Ellul with respect to his predecessors, and which he invites his readers to practice with him, most certainly constitutes one of crucial keys to reading how he positions himself intellectually.[43] But this Ellulian interpretation of René Girard's work also has the other great virtue of considerably enriching the file on the articulation between the two bodies of thought. Jean-Claude Guillebaud, as editor to both men, and indebted to them for having "become a Christian again," as he testifies in his intellectual and spiritual autobiography,[44] regretted he had not managed to enable them to meet: despite a few exchanges he was able to provoke, René Girard, according to him, "would prove absolutely impermeable to any critique of technique and to any ecological approach."[45] Convergences remain between them, however, as would be confirmed by the issue of the review *Ellul Forum* devoted to the comparison of the two bodies of thought.[46] An interview of René Girard by David W. Gill, president of the International Jacques Ellul Society (IJES), allows us to realize the extent of the convictions they share.[47]

The enrichment is at least as remarkable when it comes to the dialogue between Jacques Ellul and Gabriel Vahanian (1927–2012). The relationship between the two men has always been marked by ambivalence, and *Théologie et Technique* is no exception to the rule. Jacques Ellul starts by praising Gabriel Vahanian as the instigator of a "theological advance which I deem decisive" (p. 73), as he "has been the first to establish the theological Status of Technique" (p. 69), before pointing out his analytical deficit by arguing that he "fails to answer the question of Technique" (p. 73). What our author

---

proves as clear-sighted as it is bold, since it takes place prior to the apocalyptic turn in Girard's thought.

42. Ellul and Nordon, *L'homme à lui-même*, 144.
43. Rognon, *Jacques Ellul*, 351–71.
44. Guillebaud, *Comment je suis redevenu chrétien*.
45. Rognon, ed., *Générations Ellul*, 173.
46. "René Girard and Jacques Ellul," special issue, *Ellul Forum*.
47. David W. Gill, "Conversation with René Girard," in *Ellul Forum*, no. 35 (Spring 2005) 19–20. "I am mostly interested in his views as a sociologist of religion in the modern world. By contrast, I am an anthropologist of religion interested in the contact and opposition between archaic religious phenomena and Christianity. But I find in Ellul many ideas that I share with him completely. In some ways I am trying to do something similar to what he has done" (19).

particularly takes the theologian to task for is that he has overlooked the radical discontinuity of the technical phenomenon with the advent of technical society, that he has failed to make a distinction between techniques and technique, when the quantitative change is so considerable at the turn of the twentieth century that it necessarily induces a major qualitative change. Jacques Ellul thus finds in Gabriel Vahanian a blindness similar to that of an Emmanuel Mounier who, in *Be Not Afraid*, attacked the "active pessimism" of technophobic catastrophists, contrasting it to the "tragic optimism" of Christians.[48] His thesis was grounded in a certain anthropology, for according to Mounier, man is a creator of artifice, and "barely doing violence to the words," "*artifice is man's nature.*"[49] If Ruskin and Bernanos are explicitly targeted by the polemical charge, it is clear that Jacques Ellul and Bernard Charbonneau, who have chosen dissidence within the Personalist movement in the years before the war already, are directly concerned.[50] The somewhat unexpected filiation that Ellul establishes in *Théologie et Technique* between Mounier and Vahanian (p. 70) leads us to think that in the eyes of the Bordeaux professor, Gabriel Vahanian's work is included in his critique of technical theologies formulated above. This verdict is all the more interesting as this articulation of homage and critique answers, in a kind of chiasmus or of mutual dialectic, to the praises[51] and the reproaches[52] expressed elsewhere by Gabriel Vahanian toward Ellul's thought.

5. THE CONTRIBUTION TO THE DEBATE ABOUT THE JUDEO-CHRISTIAN ROOTS OF THE ENVIRONMENTAL CRISIS

Through a review of a book by Carl Amery, *The End of Providence*, Jacques Ellul implicitly wades into the debate on the roots of the environmental crisis, and this in a very stimulating way. We all know Lynn White's classic thesis, developed in his 1966 article "The Historical Roots of Our Ecologic Crisis," spelling out how the Judeo-Christian tradition was largely responsible for it.[53] In other texts, the Bordeaux professor has contributed to this

48. Mounier, *Be Not Afraid*, 11, 90–91.

49. Mounier, *Be Not Afraid*, 19.

50. Rognon, "Les racines personnalistes de l'écologie radicale," *Entropia*, no. 14 (Spring 2013) 187–99.

51. Vahanian, "Jacques Ellul, un homme d'amitié," in "Le siècle de Jacques Ellul," special issue, *Foi et Vie* 93, no. 5–6 (December 1994) 1–8.

52. Rognon, ed., *Générations Ellul*, 303–10.

53. This thesis was again recently the object of a publication: Bourg and Roch, eds.,

debate by defending Christianity in a rather unilateral way, in a largely apologetic mode. This point was incidentally one of the stumbling blocks between Jacques Ellul and Bernard Charbonneau. For the latter held a much more nuanced and ambivalent position, viewing Judeo-Christianity like the *pharmakon* of ancient Greece, as being both the poison and the counter-poison, the cause of the planet's devastation and the sole remedy for it.[54]

In *Theology and Technique*, Jacques Ellul defends a position that is almost as dialectical as that of his friend, albeit in a different mode. He starts by acknowledging that Judeo-Christianity has sought to desacralize the world, which, through the negation of limits that this movement has induced, might have led to the environmental disaster we are experiencing; but he establishes that the desacralization process has failed, the sacred being a kernel that is almost impossible to "root . . . out in man" (p. 153). He further states that Christianity has been subverted by its Hellenization, and that since the concept of "Nature" took the place of that of "Creation," "the environment can only be given over to the excessiveness of the means of exploitation" (p. 152). He then notes that if Christianity has had no effect on Nature for fifteen centuries, never ceasing to be invaded and never itself conquering, "it is rigorously anti-Christian elements that were at play" in the civilizational ruptures of the sixteenth to the eighteenth centuries (p. 234). But above all, Jacques Ellul maintains that technique, which he conceives as a cutting off from God, has not been influenced by Christianity, but that the latter justified it a posteriori. Thus it is that our author, without yielding anything of his apologetic orientation, enriches the debate with a much more mixed argumentation than that of protagonists in frontal opposition.

6. THE PROPOSITIONAL DIMENSION OF THE ETHICS OF NON-POWER

The most innovative contribution of *Théologie et Technique* without a doubt comes down to the pages devoted to the ethical impulses to be set into play in technical society. For Jacques Ellul develops, much more than in his own writings, the propositional, "positive" aspect of his theological and ethical convictions: what a theology of conflict and rupture, an ethic of transgression and non-power, and a "prophetic" posture would concretely consist in.

Crise écologique, crise des valeurs?

54. Rognon, "Bernard Charbonneau et la critique des racines chrétiennes de la Grande Mue," in *Bernard Charbonneau*, ed. Cazenave-Parriot, 108–16.

INTRODUCTION

As he had already done in *Presence in the Modern World*,[55] Jacques Ellul is careful to refrain from giving excessively precise guidelines that his readers might convert into another legalism, yet, he remains sufficiently concrete to elude any theoretical speculation. This is a subtle dosing at which our author seems to be a virtuoso, as he knows how to throw man back to himself and to his responsibility after having led him to the sharpest and most corrosive self-critique.

Jacques Ellul thus mentions four main thrusts of ethics: non-power, freedom, conflict, and transgression.[56]

Non-power is not powerlessness; the latter comes down to not being able to do, whereas the former consists in the renunciation of doing everything one might have the capacity to do. Jacques Ellul gives examples in the areas of personal life, institutional systems, the economic sphere, and scientific research. What he does not yet call the "precautionary principle" could apply at each of these levels, not in a dogmatic way, but with the intention of rediscovering the meaning of the threshold and the limit, that is, of freedom.

The freedoms that technical society lures us with are futile and superficial; in reality, technical fate has taken the place of natural fate. By transferring all sacredness onto the vector for desacralization that is technique, man has been alienated by his very means of liberation. True freedom is, on the contrary, exercised in the choice to increase or to decrease power, to venerate or to desecrate the technical sacred. As long as this choice is not conceivable, alienation reigns supreme.

The ethics of freedom imply a reconsideration of conflict as a survival value for mankind. Now, the computer excludes tension, *dissensus*, negotiation. As long as there is life, there is conflict, and it is a matter of instilling it when sclerosis threatens.

Finally, an ethics of transgression and of profanation consists in reducing technical objects to useful objects, but devoid of any meaning beyond that usefulness, and certainly undeserving of our devotion or of the sacrifice of our human relations or of our spiritual life. It is not a matter of giving up on living in the technical universe, but of ceasing to serve the technical sacred, to bring technical objects back to our service.

Here, in *Theology and Technique*, Jacques Ellul lays himself bare of all the Cassandra rags in which he has all too often been rigged out, to testify

---

55. Ellul, *Presence in the Modern World*, 98–99.

56. In *Autopsy of Revolution*, Jacques Ellul added a contemplative dimension of ethics: "It would represent a vital breach in the technological society, a truly revolutionary attitude, if contemplation could replace frantic activity." See Ellul, *Autopsy of Revolution*, 285.

to his hope: "If everyone obeys [his calling], the technical system is changed by this very fact" (p. 203); "if Christians enter this ethical path, then a mutation of the technical system may take place" (p. 272). It is by adopting the posture of the prophet of blessing rather than of doom that Jacques Ellul ends and signs what is no doubt his most bracing work of all those he had the good fortune to write.

PRELIMINARY WORKS

Instinctive and Non-Scientific Intermezzo[1]

WE MAY NOW ATTEMPT, taking into account the road already travelled, to find a point of meeting and conjugation. But by happenstance, if indeed it was so, just when I had completed the whole of this essay, I was given to read R. Girard's book *Resurrection from the Underground*. I very much liked R. Girard's thought in his book *Violence and the Sacred*,[2] but the latter did not in principle have anything to do with my investigations. It was about literary criticism. But then I came across this remarkable essay about Dostoevsky discussing the underground psychology, the underground metaphysics, and finally pride, and at once there emerged the relationship between pride and Technique that appeared as a meeting point between Bible study and eschatological investigation.[3]

Pride is another face of the spirit of power. But this term is no longer accepted in ethics, philosophy, psychology, or psychoanalysis. Too colored by Christianity and the idea of sin, pride is no longer fashionable. Yet Girard did not hesitate to put it back at the center of the problem of man and to make it an "operative concept"(!) again, through the "double" and the "underground," making it possible to go even beyond what Freud had thought. I will not be taking up all of it here, but only what is useful.

Pride is neither a fault nor an attitude. It is characterized from the outset by two tendencies, two orientations in its relation to the Other, a duality of appearance and reality. Pride is necessarily a certain taking possession of the Other, an effective but complex domination: "In the underground world the Other exercises a force of gravitation that one cannot conquer except in opposing it with a pride denser and heavier, around which this very Other

---

1. Already published in *Cahiers Jacques Ellul* 2 (2004) 107–13, and later in *Foi et Vie* 111, no. 2 (June 2012) 5–13 [note by F. Rognon].

2. Girard, *Violence and the Sacred*.

3. Girard, *Resurrection from the Underground*, 13–50.

will be constrained to gravitate. But in itself pride weighs nothing for it is not; it does not acquire density and weight, in fact, except through the homage of the Other."[4] The link to the other is complex and indissoluble. For pride at once leads one to want to distinguish oneself from others but to realize that one cannot manage it. It is fascinated by the Other, but with a view to fascinate and dominate him. It implies a worship of self that then transforms into a worship of the other. These are, one might say, the three main facets of the contradiction of underground pride.

> Underground pride, strange thing that it is, is a banal pride. The most intense suffering proceeds from the fact that the speaker does not succeed in *distinguishing himself* concretely from the persons around him. Yet he becomes aware of this failure little by little ... All underground individuals believe they are all the more "unique" to the extent that they are, in fact, alike ...[5]

One cannot distinguish oneself from the other while one has a passion for him. As a result, the Other-self exerts a fascination on the proud man of the underground, so much so that by wanting to worship oneself, and to the very extent of one's revolt against God, one is sent back to the seducing Other, for at the bottom of this relationship of the Master and the Slave, of the seducer-seduced, of the Slave King, of the sadist-Masochist, of the proudest one who is by the same token the most humiliated, there is the refusal and the negation of the relationship with God. "The Self whose vocation is to divinize itself refuses to recognize the fearsome problem that the presence of others poses ... still it must prove to itself its superiority."[6]

> Here the question really is *who* will be the heir, the only son of the dead God. The idealist philosophers believe that it is enough to respond in terms of the self or subject to resolve the problem. But the Self is not an *object* alongside other selves, for it is constituted by its relation to the Other and cannot be considered outside of this relation. It is this relation which the effort to substitute oneself for the God of the Bible always corrupts. Divinity cannot become identified either with the Self or with the Other; it is perpetually part of the struggle between the Self and the Other. Sexuality, ambition, literature—all intersubjective relations—become burdened with this underground battle.[7]

---

4. Girard, *Resurrection from the Underground*, 31.
5. Girard, *Resurrection from the Underground*, 21.
6. Girard, *Resurrection from the Underground*, 44.
7. Girard, *Resurrection from the Underground*, 43.

But the proud one cannot get away from the fascination of the Other, since he only exists as proud through this commensuration to the other, and "everything that the proud desire leads them, after all, to prostrate themselves before the *Other*."[8] Ultimately, this is the absolute Other: Satan.

⌘

The second great dimension of this pride is its double face of appearing as a power that brings together, when in reality it is a power that scatters and divides. This is incidentally a theme immediately related to the previous one. Pride is contradictory in its essence, split, torn between the Me and the other. And this is why Girard makes the theory of the double an explanatory key to the psyche, more basic than the Oedipus complex. There is a beautiful passage on the illusion of morals of harmony between the general interest and particular interests: morals of harmony, between various egotisms, are generated by pride itself, which *always* presents itself (and how true it is in politics!) as a point of coming together, of union, of concord, whereas in reality, there is only rupture and division. "Indeed, the proud wish to be accused of egotism and gladly accuse themselves of it in order better to dissimulate the role that the Other plays in their existence."[9]

In the same way, pride demands distinction, differentiation, autonomization, but at the same time produces, indissolubly, indistinction, the blurring of relations and confusion. It is even by playing on this indistinction that it can get taken for a power that brings together. Likewise again, finally, it is the juxtaposition of opposites that defines the underground spirit, a juxtaposition without any way out, without any solution: union without reconciliation.

Such are the great themes, without explicating them in detail, of pride and the underground Spirit. The reader may well ask at once: "But what does all this have to do with Technique?" The relationship is as close as can be, for Technique represents exactly those very features of the underground spirit which will lead us to say that *in our society*, Technique is the expression, the embodiment, the demonstration of this underground spirit. But we are indeed talking of Technique as it has *become* in our time, playing a role similar to that of Money in previous societies.

We can take up again the two themes of pride, along with their implications. The technical aspect is "the external face of a structure whose

---

8. Girard, *Resurrection from the Underground*, 63.
9. Girard, *Resurrection from the Underground*, 18.

internal face is the hallucination of the double."[10] Technique is the product of a spirit of power that can be translated as pride. It produces indistinction between men, affects everyone the same way, and prevents man from distinguishing himself from others. If that is not to occur, his only way to distinguish himself, to appear different, is derived from the technical object itself. It is thanks to consumption, to the use of power objects, that man distinguishes himself; the one who has a Jaguar is not the same man as the one who has a Citroën 2CV.

But this process of distinction is at the same time that of indistinction. That is to say, this man is necessarily driven by pride, since everything to do with the objective management of his life is technicized alike to everyone. The technical process is abstract, anonymous; it does not recognize anyone but produces a human magma (all things that have been discussed a hundred times in other terms), and precisely because it makes distinction impossible (or else by the use of the technical object, hence by a stronger integration), it provokes underground pride which grows all the more as the difference is increasingly inaccessible.

Thus Technique produces underground pride and at the same time feeds on it; it is on this foundation, for instance, that advertising succeeds. It dangles the prospect that if a new technical progress is achieved, then there will be, there, a possibility of difference. We are faced here with a basic driver of this development, which to my knowledge had never before been brought to light.

Thus we have a twofold structure: the objective one of Technique that exactly reproduces the inner structure of pride, with the seemingly contradictory movement of everyone having to enter the same process, and of yet having to try to differentiate oneself through Technique. The latter answers pretty much exactly to man's will, examined above, to worship himself, which drives him toward the other. It is the situation of what has been celebrated as that of adult man, come of age. Currently, it is Technique that enables man's elimination of God, which is not even any longer a revolt. It is no longer necessary to struggle any more; technical power has replaced that of the Creator.

But this has not changed anything about the unfolding of pride. On the contrary, the more man alone is the victor, the more he is split between the impossible divinity of the Me and the fascination of the Other. I believe it is fundamentally this that explains the association between Technical growth and the development, e.g., of charismatic or dictatorial political powers. Technicized man needs this alienating other, which he uses at once

---

10. Girard, *Resurrection from the Underground*, 21.

INSTINCTIVE AND NON-SCIENTIFIC INTERMEZZO

as a model and as an object of execration. He prostrates and detests; this is a product of the sacred of Technique.[11]

Finally, Technique juxtaposes opposites without any possible fusion, a "union without reconciliation,"[12] of which we have seen that it is exactly the character of the underground spirit. And it just so happens that Technique encompasses everything, but without any synthesis, without any reconciliation. It turns our world into a vast collection of objects, of machines, of methods, without any coherence nor basic relationship. This is why it can be analyzed as a system, but not as a civilization. The pieces of the puzzle fit, but without any relation but a mechanical one.

It is impossible to overstress the fact that Technique is not, and cannot be dialectical, that it produces *opposites* but without ever reconciling them nor moving on to a new stage. Technique has no history or organic existence; it excludes anything qualitative, spiritual, or anything in relation to growth in truth. This is why there can be at once system and chaos,[13] an extreme rationality and the development of irrationality. Within this vast production of objects, of things that add up without ever attaining a synthetic harmony, Technique becomes the appearance of a unity (for everything is held together within the system's iron maiden), whereas in reality, it indefinitely produces ruptures and splits. It has cancelled all forms of human sociability and blown apart the natural setting within which man had achieved his breakthrough, his history—exactly according to its own process, by virtue of which it divides human and social unity into fragments that can be reduced to data for problems that Technique will then solve one by one.

One has to realize that this is no accident we will be able to change, or that could have turned out otherwise; the mechanism of blowing apart and fragmenting human and social "nature" is the very basis, the very condition for the possibility of the development of Technique. And while this is happening, we may celebrate Technique as the great bringer together, mankind having become one big village (McLuhan),[14] long-range relations having blissfully replaced petty short-range relations (Ricoeur),[15] men having developed solidarity on a shrunken planet (Fourastié),[16] communication

---

11. See Ellul, *New Demons*.

12. Girard, *Resurrection from the Underground*, 33.

13. Translator's note: Here as elsewhere when these two concepts are paired, Ellul is alluding to his friend's book: Charbonneau, *Le système et le chaos*.

14. McLuhan, *Understanding Media*.

15. Ricoeur, "Socius and the Neighbor" [note by the family].

16. Fourastié, *Le grand espoir du XXe siècle* [note by the family].

haven been made universal, etc.—exactly what we have encountered with the underground spirit: the appearance of a bringing together that covers up the reality of a blowing apart.

This realization is possible only on the condition, of course, of being willing to view Technique outside of the pious discourse according to which Technique has increased man's freedom, multiplies his possibilities for choice and action, develops knowledge, eliminates the great scourges of mankind (starting with famine), gives man mastery over the universe, and is the answers to all of man's desires and anxieties. These things are all, of course, partially true, but strictly superficial and corresponding exactly to Technique's *mask*, to what it "gives us to see," to that for which it wants to be taken; and we fall back in Dostoevsky, with "The Grand Inquisitor."[17]

Finally, Technique has allowed man to change stones into bread. And he is very happy. But he does not understand why he is not yet in Paradise after this miracle. He has no idea of the price he has already paid to get there. And now, the mask must be lifted. But fearful men cling to the ever-so-beautiful promises of this Santa Claus (as described by the majority of our Western and Communistic intellectuals) that their beliefs and superficiality have brought forth.

↭

There thus exists a fundamental relationship, not an accidental one (or a simplistic one according to which it is out of "pride" in the traditional moralistic sense that man has engaged in science, etc.), between underground pride and technical growth. We can then draw three consequences from this theologically.

The first one is that Technique forces man into the underground. It places him in an objective situation such that what was described as an exceptional case by Dostoevsky (*The Eternal Husband*,[18] Raskolnikov,[19] *The Possessed*)[20] becomes, at a mediocre level incidentally, everybody's lot. Technique has generalized, vulgarized, banalized, and democratized the underground spirit. It is now by the millions that Raskolnikovs and the Possessed can be counted. And it is the objective technical structure that produces

---

17. Philosophical tale by Dostoevsky, in *Brothers Karamazov*, 246–64 [note by the family].

18. Dostoevsky, *Eternal Husband and Other Stories* [note by the family].

19. Main character of Fyodor Dostoevsky's novel *Crime and Punishment* [note by the family].

20. Dostoevsky, *Possessed* [note by the family].

INSTINCTIVE AND NON-SCIENTIFIC INTERMEZZO

them, in an ambiguity without any way out, an insoluble lie, a desperate search for oneself in the other, of unity in rupture. Is it not striking to see the ease, the wantonness, the incoherence of ruptures in our society: divorces, parents-children, generations, races, nations? Never before has society been so fragmented or human relations so fragile and inconstant than since we have understood ourselves within the network of technical norms. It is as though the rigor of the organization is compensated for by the incoherence, instability, and impermanence of interpersonal ties, exactly as the anomic character of society exactly matches the universalization of objectifying structures.

We must not confuse, as people usually do, this instability of human relations and this anomie with freedom! The underground spirit—ambiguity, insoluble lies, hopeless division and contradiction—is what Technique forces man to adopt. An example is Dumitriu's startling *Incognito*,[21] which exactly shows how the Technique of the dominant Communist party (in Romania), a technique of organization and mutual control, produces this underground spirit. There is no better description.

Generalized Technique gives the same result, more neutral and less obvious because it is less mixed up with ideology. Man is locked within a network of ruptures and contradictions from which he can only get out by personally accepting this impossibility. A network of ruptures may well sound like a daring image. By way of comparison, let us consider the predicament of a man on the ice of a lake just as it is thawing. Everywhere the ice is breaking up and ruptures are happening, in a network, and man finds himself exactly a prisoner of this network.

But then we must not forget that the instigator of ruptures is the Diabolos, the divider, and the devil is nothing but a divider. And this is even why he will be vanquished in the end. *Any kingdom divided against itself...*[22] But as long as history lasts, it is never quite obvious. The technical Kingdom is exactly this kingdom divided against itself. Technique indefinitely produces doubles, duplicates, replicas; that is even one of its features. And Girard is profoundly right to remind us that between the double and the devil, there is not a "relation of identity but a relation of analogy. One moves from the first to the second in the way in which one moves from the portrait to the caricature."[23] The devil parodies, but he is the fruit of a parody, which is that of Technique (the parody of the natural). "There is no break in continuity, no metaphysical *leap* between the double and the devil."[24] The latter is

21. Dumitriu, *Incognito*.
22. Matt 12:25.
23. Girard, *Resurrection from the Underground*, 67.
24. Girard, *Resurrection from the Underground*, 67.

perfectly present in the technical system, but his peculiarity is that he is not present within it as devil!

We may sociologically, psychologically note the effects of Technique by speaking of division, anonymity, artificiality, etc., but it is always as observations of isolated facts; the producer is never pointed out. Besides, who would still be naïve and childish enough to talk of the Devil! and to point him out! Yet this is exactly the only way to exorcise him. It is when the Devil is pointed out, when he appears as unveiled Devil in any given work, without ambiguity, when he is objectivized (hence Romance sculptors' need to point him out), that his power is defused. But as long as we are content to shrug our shoulders when faced with such medieval beliefs, while seriously studying the effects, then a free hand is given to the Diabolos, the universal Divider, Father of lies and sovereign parodist.

These reflections obviously lead us to raise the issue about technical reality, of the discerning of spirits, which we will attempt below. But first, there is one last theme for meditation that we can sketch, by following again the analysis of Dostoevsky by Girard. It is that of suicide.

In the radical recusal of Christianity on account of its unsatisfied promise of freedom, on account of the illusory desire for immortality, the only way out is suicide; the point is to annihilate this desire for immortality, and to possess the infinity of freedom in the total acceptance of finitude. It is "redemption in reverse," on the path of nihilism. Now it happens that Technique at once shuts man up in his finitude, gives the false impression of fulfilling the need for eternity, gives man the possibility of total suicide, but cannot manage to get rid of the God of Christianity, and of the promises of the freedom and the resurrection that are found in Christ. It is not Technique that can do it. Only man can. Technique places him in a situation where he absolutely has to eliminate this God, but the death of God is for man to decide. And the only possible way is the death of man himself.

Make no mistake about it; it is sometimes said that because God is dead, man too must die (and in a very specific sense, this is also what Foucault says).[25] Again, it is said that, after the death of God, man's situation is that of being in the absurd and despair. The actual process of the underground mind is the reverse: man must commit suicide so that God dies. It is an inversion and parody of the death of Jesus Christ. It is deemed necessary, and Technique places him in this position. God must die, and Technique puts in the hand of man the absolute weapon to accomplish his project. Therein resides the actual scope of mankind's risk of collective suicide.

---

25. Foucault, *Order of Things* [note by the family].

Situation of Theology within Technical Society[1]

We now need to consider the problem from another perspective and by going through the detour of faith. It is that of the relationship between conduct, behavior, practice, and faith, and secondly the consequences that this might have for Theology.

There is a very banal traditional way of considering the "practice-faith" relationship. Firstly, faith dictates, provokes, brings with it, induces a certain practice, a certain attitude in life, a certain lifestyle. It is the whole ever-renewed problem of Ethics. What are the consequences of the faith for life? People also try to objectify it, to formulate a Christian ethic that can be specified from the doctrine. It is likewise the relationship mentioned in the Gospels between faith and works, between the tree and the fruits.

It follows from this as a corollary that "bad practice" supposes an absence of faith, a bad faith, a doctrinal error. You can tell the tree by its fruits; that much is clear. Hence the importance of works, not in the least to ensure salvation, but as a sign, an index of the truth, validity, and authenticity of the faith and the correctness of the interpretation that is given of it from a theological viewpoint.

Finally, still in the same line, one can also (and it is an extension based, I believe, on a misinterpretation of the thought of Pascal) hold that conduct can induce faith. There is a practice recognized as Christian; apply this practice, even without "having the faith," observe this commandment, and by dint of living as though you were Christian, faith will come; you will become an actual Christian. Kneel down, and consequences will follow.

I would like to take things in an exactly opposite sense, firstly, because it is almost never done; secondly, because what we are going to describe is the most frequent situation in a secularized society; and finally, because that directly ties in with the question of Technique. We need to consider the

1. Already published in *Cahiers Jacques Ellul* 2 (2004) 113–21 [note by F. Rognon].

opposite situation, according to which "bad"[2] practice, bad conduct, bad behavior cause first the blowing apart and the distortion, then the withering away, and finally the disappearance of faith. And this is going to translate into a theological explication, for the one who finds himself in this situation does not generally recognize that he has "lost the faith."

The evolution is then as follows: a man who acknowledges being a disciple of Christ, who believes in the Gospel, who wants to live in faith, finds himself in a condition such that he acts exactly counter to the Word of God. Immersed in a violent world, he behaves, for instance, like other people, according to violence. Once or a hundred times, he will acknowledge he is a sinner. He will confess his sin. He will repent. But it is not genuine repentance, *Metanoia*, since he does not change his practice. He remains so involved in this situation and in this conduct that he does not modify his life. This takes us into the casuistic category of "habitual sinners." But he cannot indefinitely bear this contradiction between this conduct and this faith that sends him back to the biblical reference. There then takes place a twofold evolution: first a deformation of faith to put it in agreement with this practice, then a theological explication of this process which, starting from practice, leads to a new formulation of the faith. At the personal level, faith has hardened, become cold, habitual, with the elimination of any direct relationship with God, of prayer, for instance. That man no longer feels any urge to get to meet with this God, but he can no longer recognize that his conduct was "bad"; he is assured of this conduct. He becomes convinced by social models, by his environment, also by the impossibility of changing, that it is this conduct that is correct, and that consequently, the faith that was accusing it and the theological formulation of faith that put it into question are false. We have a number of biblical texts that indeed indirectly describe for us this process according to which conduct, practice condition the destruction of faith.

But, one may object, why should the former one be true and this one false? For the twin reasons that a destructuring of the relationship with God takes place and that there is a process of self-justification. Now I establish on my own what relationship I want to have with the God of Jesus Christ. In other words, I have destructured, due to my conduct, the relationship that had been established by God and expressed in the faith relationship. On the other hand, I have established a new system that justifies me. I am no longer justified (rendered just from outside by Jesus Christ), but I declare myself just. I establish an interpretation of Scripture and of faith that says I

---

2. I say "bad" in the very straightforward sense of: not in conformity with the consequences of faith, not in conformity with the Model of Jesus, not in conformity with the Word of God in Scripture.

am right, but it is I who *assure myself* of this validity, contrary to the whole of the biblical message.

These two transformations are not an *intellectual* affair; it is an existential process, a fundamental one, that only then provokes the intellectual explication. Man cannot feel condemned indefinitely, indefinitely in contradiction with his own conduct, and he can no *longer* accept that he is justified exclusively by grace in Jesus Christ. This is the destructuring of faith.

But why? Because if faith turns out to be incapable of informing life, the latter, in its persistence, its duration, provokes a conversion of faith. There cannot be indefinite disharmony. I keep assuming that the man in question does not declare himself, as a result, and for this reason of conduct, of practice, non-Christian and an unbeliever. No, he wants to remain in the faith. But the indefinite contradiction is intolerable and insoluble, since the conduct cannot be changed, cannot become a harmonious and consistent consequence of faith. One therefore has to go upstream and come back to the source. One has to reject what one had thought to be faith and its content, since they are proving powerless, and, on the other hand, they are in contradiction with what I am living. One has to remodel this faith and the theology of this faith precisely so that there is coherence and that this faith is said to condition this life. With this inability to live the faith is then established the ideological relationship proper, according to which the notion derived from the faith is nothing but the reflection (and the veil) of practice, itself dictated by the sociological context.

Under these conditions, we do find, not only an inversion of the process to which we are used theologically, but actually a deconstruction, a disintegration of the faith, since the latter assumes first the acknowledgment of Jesus as Lord (of life and the world). When we speak of a deconstruction of the faith, it is exactly insofar as the role of Jesus is now completely changed once this reversal has taken place. Instead of being the stranger who frees me, who justifies me and who establishes himself as Lord of my life's freedom, he becomes a means that I use to posit myself as justifier and origin. I begin my total experience of life through my practice. I become the effective owner of my faith, which I interpret as I please and which makes me master over Jesus Christ.

This is all the more remarkable as in many current guises of this mutation there ever recurs a concern, a preoccupation, not to assert ownership over the faith and to respect the Gospel's independence. People even harshly criticize the bourgeois notion according to which one "has the faith"; this criticism is correct, but the reversal of posture rests on an unconscious and simplistic subscribing to the nonexistence of the transcendent.

Faith is thus dependent on my own *praxis*. It is even nothing but that. We will need to come back to this issue. Let us just keep in mind as a conclusion that behavior becomes a key element of the structuring of faith, and that "morals" is indeed not an appendix, a consequence, but at the very center of revelation. It is not for nothing that when God reveals himself, he gives a "law" *at the same time*! In this orientation, one therefore disdains and depreciates all that may belong to the realm of spiritual experience, of the naïve knowledge of revelation, of mystical amazement, of the possibility of a miracle, everything of which I am not the master and which must now be neutralized by psychological means or a theological disdain for the "wondrous."

A second aspect needs to be considered. Faith also assumes the formation of an original (in both senses) relation with God and the world: original, because it is already about a new creation, and faith amounts to going through a new birth. The latter did indeed take place for the man of which we speak, but it has failed to produce any consequence, and we may then say that *in truth*, it is stillborn. But the one who has gone through this new birth and who has acknowledged the truth of revelation cannot hold it to be null and void (since it did take place! it was accomplished!). From that moment on, the process we have been describing in broad outline is set in motion.

But the behavior, the practice that we adopt and that becomes the point of departure of the whole process of reconstruction of a personality that encompasses faith and uses it, that integrates it and immanentizes it, may originate in a purely personal experience, but will most often be sociological in origin. The classic case which we traditionally think about is that of the adulterer who cannot free himself from the woman with whom he is committing adultery, of the drunkard who cannot free himself from alcohol, etc. This is the order of individual "sin."

In a society that has strong social norms, this man is solitary; he will admit to being a sinner, and either he will henceforth refuse to consider himself a Christian, or he will remain torn between his faith which accuses him (it is his faith, his *conscience* that accuses him and not God) and his conduct that he cannot manage to change. He therefore does not set into motion the process of deconstruction of the faith from conduct, because he is solitary. On the contrary, in a society where social control weakens, where acculturation is not taking place, where anomie is on the increase, this man will no longer find himself as an isolated case; he finds himself in a situation that is becoming ever more general, and hence, the process aimed at escaping from the condition of being torn *can* be set in motion.

If now we introduce in this anomic society a set of behaviors that become "normal" and that have nothing to do with the revelation of God in

Jesus Christ, then of course there will occur a fairly generalized abandonment of belonging to Christianity, but those who remain and purport to be Christians then find themselves in opposition not only to themselves, but also to the prevailing social model. And if they adopt this conduct, they doubly experience a condition of being torn, a contradiction almost impossible to bear. There will thus be call for effecting this revision of faith and of its theological expression.

But let us be very careful: we are not talking about the platitude people go on about, according to which the formulation of the faith in the Old and the New Testaments is the expression of a certain culture; since culture has changed, we must undertake a review of everything that was said at that time—a sociocultural matter and an intellectual process. This is not what is true. What is *true*, in actual truth, is that the behavior issuing from faith seems impossible to us; the faith seems contradictory to the environment, and we *feel like* conforming. The origin of this opinion is a matter of *praxis* and of behavior and does not take into account the fact that the faith has *always* seemed *impossible* to live (all of the Bible attests to it!), and that it is in no way a cultural matter. We carefully hide our desire to be conformed, our will to reunite with the social body and its dominant movements, and we make up the aforementioned theory, but it is only secondary; it is an ideology, a veil of this deeper reality. The cultural and the change in culture are but a pretext to avoid the conflict of faith.

If we look at our society as a whole, we can speak not so much of political opinions, but really of the global passion for politics. We can talk of the passion for and worship of Mammon, of money, of the primacy of desire, of the eroticization of all relations, of moral indifference (situational morals, morals of ambiguity, etc.). These and many other factors[3] are typical of our habitual behavior. It is this behavior that appears normal to us.

So it comes about that for the one who still declares himself a Christian, the contradiction is such between what this society holds to be just and what faith makes us discover in Scripture that it is necessary to recast the faith and to reinterpret Scripture. I need not here, on the topic of Technique, examine these various orientations, all of which happen to derive more or less from its primacy. But I do need to see the effect, what is peculiar to technical society in this respect.

Technique is first of all, let us not forget it, itself a practice. It is not a matter of raising the issue of a conflict of values, nor of an ethical conflict.

---

3. I have analyzed a number of these trends in my study on Hope [*Hope in Time of Abandonment*] inasmuch as they produce despair.

THEOLOGY AND TECHNIQUE

I have shown elsewhere[4] the existence of a specific ethic produced by Technique, and likewise as a value, the one that prevails is that of efficiency. But this is not the question here. The latter is due to the fact that Technique is in itself a conduct, a *praxis*, and *nothing else*. It is a *How to do*.[5] It dictates a given behavior in all areas. If one wants to do something, one has to do it following the technical model and with technical means. There is no choice. (And it is a great illusion of Marxists when they speak of choice, of the establishment of a *praxis* in conformity with Marxist theory.) This practice does not derive from anything other than itself, Technique, which *is* a self-conditioning practice. It cannot bear any outside intervention which, indeed, could only result in making action less technical, and of necessity less efficient. There is no possible relation between a technical action and Christian faith, Marxist theory or any given ideology.

Now, technical action is not limited to *one* aspect, one accidental operation; it covers the totality of our life. We go without interruption from one technical operation to another, without even generally realizing that they are technical actions, defined by a certain method, which has become so natural that we no longer perceive it as technical, and involving the totality of our outer being, the totality of realms of action, of expression and of communication: it is in fact the totality of our works, of our behavior, of our practice that is subjugated, conditioned by Technique.

Christians may no doubt seek three avenues of retreat. The first one, which has been used, generally speaking, in any case, since the eighteenth century, is the separation between the exterior and the interior. What is conditioned by Technique is behavior, thus the exterior; the interior (the soul?) is free, and Christianity has to do with the interior. We must resolutely fight this foolishness; faith implies an external expression that is lived and specific. There is no inner conversion without a change in conduct. The separation between the interior and the exterior is one of the great cowardices and hypocrisies of Christianity.

A second trick of the same kind is the division between public life and private life. One accepts that Technique rules over public life, work, participation in society, etc., but once I am at home, in my house, with my family, Technique no longer has anything to do with it. (Let us note that this corresponds to the position of Marxists toward "religion," a purely private affair, from which no political or public consequence is to be derived.) Here again, it is a blatant lie. First of all, it is not true that someone who is conditioned by Technique for 80 percent of his waking time magically ceases to

---

4. Ellul, *To Will and to Do*.
5. Translator's note: In English in the original.

be when he gets home (what about the TV?). Here again, Revelation gives rise to consequences of the political type, in economics, toward work, etc., that simply cannot be separated from the others. "Unfortunately," in fact, Technique covers the totality of behavior, but Christianity (if it is taken seriously) too: and it is the conflict between these two totalities that cannot be resolved by a separation of areas, one reserved for Technique and the other for the expression of faith.

Finally, a third trick needs to be dismissed: Technique belongs to matters of indifference from a theological standpoint: (*adiaphora*);[6] there is no judgment to be made on this issue, since it pertains neither to good nor to evil, nor to the person's religious aspect. This will very soon take on a new scope: any area won by Technique enters the category of matters of indifference, since Technique itself belongs to it. In other words, anything that is reduced to being nothing more than a technical operation ceases to be Christianity's concern. This has been said time and again about science: wherever the light of science reaches, Revelation is no longer needed.[7] But this is even truer of Technique: now it is enough to answer that wherever man's life is at stake, Revelation is at stake. There are no such things as neutral matters. There are no such things as indifferent actions. Everything is relative to man's life and environment and never leaves them untouched. "Moral conduct" does not exist in itself, no more than spiritual life; they exist in their embodiment in the environment, and the latter has become technical. There is thus no indifference to be entertained, and no way out is possible. Either action is Technique, or it is inspired by something else, a belief, an ideology, a politics, and among other things, Christianity. But the conflict is inevitable.[8]

Now, what is the mode of behavior commanded by Technique? What are the features of technical practice?[9]

First of all, it is agnostic. That is to say, it has no claim to knowledge; it does not derive from knowledge; it is not interested in knowledge. It

---

6. A Stoic concept used to refer to morally "neutral" things, which are neither prescribed nor forbidden [note by the family].

7. And again recently by Barreau, *Religious Impulse*, which suggests that the religious instinct be reoriented toward a transcendental absolute, toward the questions that science does not answer, since for him "no transcendence is to be invoked where science is enough," which is a peculiar idea of a "transcendence ... object."

8. I have confined myself to *very succinctly* reminding readers of these three points because I have treated and demonstrated them, particularly in my books on Ethics.

9. I mean by this the attitude of technicians and users, not that of researchers, of the "technoscientists." And this is why I can say that this practice does not derive from knowledge: one need not have knowledge to drive a car or make a washing machine work; it is enough to practice.

does not know. It is agnostic because what counts is, on the one hand, the correctness of the operations performed, and on the other hand, efficacy, obtaining the effects anticipated. It aims no further. It does not derive from an elsewhere. Behavior will therefore be rigorously circumscribed in its conduct without going beyond that. It is enough to consider the attitude of all users of a technical device; it is obviously an attitude that is indifferent to any truth whatsoever. It is enough to consider as well the behavior of those who apply technical methods; they are strictly agnostic. This is due to the fact that Technique is essentially concrete. It provokes a behavior that can only concern concrete things, what can be counted and be measured (including the unconscious, the psyche, beauty . . .). It only measures values according to the concrete, and even more precisely according to the means created in application in the concrete.

Technique produces a behavior that is constantly situated in the present by getting rid of any dimension of the future. There are only two conceivable forms of the future: the extension of technical action as such (hence the success of these forecasts when it comes to extrapolations), which is a simple repetition, or else the leap into a No-place, a Utopia, but of which one knows that this No-place is precisely not just spatial; it is also what will never take place!

This is a feature of agnosticism: it situates itself of necessity (out of necessity!) in the current. In short, to say that the behavior caused by Technique is agnostic is also to say that it is indeed behavior in a pure form, without admixture of anything else. The existence of this behavior, which is becoming dominant in our society, which is being inculcated in our whole way of life and by our devices, calls into question the possibility of a behavior issuing from faith, hence, according to the process that we have been analyzing above, the work of recasting of faith and of Theology in an elsewhere.

The Theology that corresponds to this practice issuing from Technique will be an *agnostic* theology (we know nothing of God, nor, of course, of the truth of a hypothetical revelation), a *concrete* theology (turned toward the ascertainable real, as we are only interested in knowing if we can effectively act upon this or that situation, so that the whole realm of the spiritual, of prayer, etc., must be gotten ridden of), and a *horizontal* theology (the level of my technical practice is necessarily that of human height, and there is nothing else anywhere).

The second great feature of this practice is that it is "noncritical." Technique can only be criticized by an external device. It is beyond criticism. It can be overcome or replaced only by another technique that is more advanced, more progressive. Technique never criticizes itself. It never tolerates any external criticism. The process of progress is not critical, because it is not criticism we are doing when we ascertain a given result that can be of this or that level of efficiency, of adequateness to its means. We are alluding here to an intellectual operation *upon* Technique, but when it comes to technical behavior, induced by Technique, there can be no prospect, no possibility of criticism. Provided that that behavior and practice are in agreement with Technique, with the imperative of use, with the "directions for use," everything is all right. In this, this behavior is, like Technique itself, perfectly integrated. That is to say, it has its reason within itself, it is constituted as a unity, with an inner unfolding, and its destination is integrated as well. There can therefore be no point from which an effective and *consistent* critique could be performed.

Conversely, to the extent that no critique is possible, technical behavior is a skeptical behavior; nothing can *happen*, no unforeseen change. It is "abnormal" that a piece of equipment would not function as it should. It is inadmissible for the organization to be slow, inefficient, etc. The scandal that is bureaucracy for us is but the face of our skeptical technical behavior. For to be sure, in this universe, there can be no miracles, but neither can there be chaos. Those who speak of such an event as chaos are retrograde pessimists, obeying suspect motives—just as much as those who refer to the possibility of miracle. As an integrated system, Technique can conceive neither of the one nor of the other. And if our intelligence can conceive them, however, at the level of our behavior, we act and practice as good family heads, convinced that the system has to last, and utterly skeptical about anything that might upset it.

When we then adopt this noncritical and skeptical behavior, theology is again compelled to conform. It will as a result become a . . . *critical* theology! But critical of itself! Not even critical of Technique! How would that be possible? What refuses criticism of Technique is not our intelligence, but our total adherence to this practice. And if theology is in conflict, then it comes up against our practice that demands a critical process within a theology given by skepticism.

It then becomes a theology of *subjectivity*: faith as a purely subjective affair, for there can be nothing, there cannot be anything other in the way of objectivity than Technique. Technical practice alone is objective; everything else is reduced to the vagaries of the subjective, and is therefore of no consequence at the level of practical implications, since the subjective is strictly self-enclosed, until such time as it can be purely and simply gotten rid of. Reducing faith to subjectivity, resurrection to the apostles' belief in resurrection, and the lordship of Jesus to the current action of Christians amounts exactly to preparing the way for the total shedding of theology and the Church (under cover of adapting to the conditions of modern man—a feat of stupendous blindness!).

Finally, it is going to be a *political* theology. Why? Because one is looking for the area in which one can reintroduce the unpredictability of human conduct and the possibilities of choice. These are utterly excluded by technical practice; they do not mean anything, quite simply, from the standpoint of a behavior induced by Technique. But theology cannot give up its assertion of unpredictability and of a grip on the real. At the same time, it is skeptical, no longer believing in heavenly intervention nor in our action through prayer. Thus all that remains is politics! In so doing, theology falls victim to both political illusion and theological illusion! It becomes doubly illusory. It has replaced heaven with Politics—and can hum along in dead earnest on the margins of the real.

To sum up: Technique as the dominant force in our society induces an agnostic and noncritical behavior. This behavior is wholly generalized in the Western world; technical practice is universal there. Those who continue to identify as Christians also have, like everybody, this technical practice. Since they cannot tolerate this contradiction (for no consistency is possible between the works of faith and technical practice), and since they refuse to criticize technical behavior (which is not possible anyway), they reconstruct a theology according to their situation, a theology whose role will be justification and compensation, and which will become wholly satisfactory to them. It will have the six features that we have noted (agnostic, concrete, horizontal, critical, subjective, political). And one does recognize in it the features of the dominant theological currents of our time. I believe I have thus explained exactly why this current (so-called modern) theology is what it is, in what way its orientations do not correspond to any properly theological necessity, and what is their complete absence of meaning.

Investigation toward an Ethic in a Technical Society[1]

1. WHAT IS TECHNIQUE?

TO AVOID ANY MISUNDERSTANDING, it may be useful to remind the reader of what I mean by Technique (which is often wrongly called: Technology).[2] Technique cannot be conflated with the machine, nor with a collection of machines, methods, and products. Technique is no longer a secondary factor that is integrated in a nontechnical society and civilization. It has become the dominant factor in the Western world. Our society can best be described as a technical society. All other factors are dependent on Technique. Technique is no longer an incomplete, happenstance mediator between man and the natural environment. The latter is totally dominated and used (in Western society). It now constitutes a complete fabric replacing nature.

Technique is the complex and complete environment within which man must live, in relation to which he must determine himself. It is a universal mediatrix, producing a generalized, totalizing mediation which claims to be total. A concrete example is the city. The city is the place where Technique is exclusive of any natural reality. Outside the city, there remains the choice between the urbanization of the countryside or desertification (nature being then subjected to technical exploitation carried out by a population that is very small in number). This is a reminder that Technique truly is the Environment in which modern man is located. This technical environment entails on man's part a complete revision of his old modes of

---

1. Already published in *Ethique et technique*, ed. Sojcher and Hottois, 7–20 [note by the family, completed by F. Rognon].

2. See Ellul, *Technological Society* and *Technological System*.

behavior, but also of his values, of his traditions, of his morals, of his intellectual or physiological abilities.[3]

On the other hand, Technique constitutes a system in the strict sense of the word,[4] i.e. a whole whose factors are closely interrelated, in such a way that:

- each element only takes its meaning, its significance through the whole;
- any modification of an element has repercussions on the whole and modifies it, and any modification of the whole modifies the elements or their relations;
- there is a privileged, if not exclusive relationship between the elements of the system, excluding whatever is outside the system. Technique should now be conceived as a whole. The features of the technical phenomenon are Autonomy, Unicity, Universality, and Totalization. It obeys a specific rationality. The features of technical progress are self-increase, automatism, the absence of ends, causal progression, the tendency to acceleration, disparity, and ambivalence. Nevertheless, Technique lacks one of the essential features of any organic whole, namely, feedback. It is not yet able to control its mistakes and dysfunctions, to exert a feedback on its source and to modify itself. However, it may be that we are now witnessing the progressive constitution of such feedback.

The ethical problem, that of man's behavior, can only be considered in relation to this system and not to such and such a particular technical object. It matters not that we learn to use "well" or "according to the good" such and such a technique; each one can only be interpreted by the whole. If Technique is an environment or a system, the ethical problem can only be put in terms of this totality. Particularized behaviors and choices no longer have any meaning. It is thus a total reversal of our habits or of our values that is being called for; it is either the rediscovery of an existential ethics or of a new technology.

---

3. See Friedmann, *Sept études sur l'homme et la technique* (Paris: Gonthier, 1966).
4. See von Bertalanffy, *General System Theory* (New York: G. Braziller, 1968).

2. ABOUT SOME TRADITIONAL ETHICAL MISTAKES TO AVOID[5]

The ethical problem with respect to Technique is most often put by considering it a mere neutral tool. Man has Technique (in general) at his disposal much as he has his car. He can make good use of this car. This can entail two factors: either using it according to the laws of the car itself (correctly and in conformity with the mechanism itself, so as to make it perform as much as possible and damage it as little as possible), or using it to do good to someone (picking up a hitchhiker). He can use it wrongly. The same two aspects are present; he can damage his machine or cause an accident. He can also, thanks to the car, want to do evil (murder someone). The car is a simple neutral agent that depends exactly on the user's decision. The car will not start on its own. Nor will the computer take the decision to program itself.

But even by remaining at this level, things are not so simple; the fact of having and using a car changes the driver. He is not the same person when he drives a Mercedes or a Citroën 2CV. He is not the same in his family and at the wheel. The tool induces a set of behavioral as well as psychological consequences.

But in addition, there is no comparison between the fact of *having a technical tool* and *being in the technical system*. The latter is neither neutral nor mastered by man. The system has its own laws of operation that produce a set of consequences that man can only confine himself to registering. There can be no question of changing the system, unless one accepts a total regression (*Zero Growth*,[6] for instance). Technique is not neutral; it has its own orientations, implications, and conditions of operation. It modifies the totality of man and of his environment.

Another aspect, very common, deriving from the one above, is the conviction that man must establish ends and that Technique is but a set of means to achieve these ends. Here again, one holds that man has (or is called to have) mastery over the phenomenon and that all that is needed is to impose the correct ends upon it. It is true that Technique is only made of means; it is a set of means (something we will have to come back to), but with the twist that these means now obey their own law and are no

---

5. In any case, traditional ethical concepts and constructs appear to me to be nowadays completely devalued by the development of this new environment for man, insofar as any morals up to now has been conceived by considering man's relationship to the social body, considered as his normal environment. Furthermore, the total growth of techniques completely rules out the possibility of a "pure morals," and even utilitarianism no longer has any ethical meaning if it is situated within the technical environment.

6. Translator's note: In English in the original.

longer subordinated to ends. Besides, one must also distinguish between ends (values, for instance), objectives (national ones, for instance), and aims (immediate: the researcher seeks to solve a given problem). Science and Technique evolve according to aims, rarely and accidentally according to more general objectives, and never according to ethical or spiritual ends. There is no ground for comparison between the proclamation of values (justice, freedom, etc.) and the orientation of technical development. Those who are specialists in values (theologians, philosophers, etc.) have no influence on specialists of Technique and cannot, for instance, ask that such and such research or existing means be forbidden in the name of a value.

One very significant aspect of this inability is the ever more common tendency according to which the scientist or the technician turns into a moralist; it is starting from Technique that an ethic is proposed that is consonant with this system. Likewise, when people speak of the (genetic, chemical, electric) possibility of fundamentally altering man, of manufacturing him in test tubes, of sticking electrodes in his brain, etc., they do not ask what type of man they want to create. And when this question comes, it seems obvious that it is the scientist or the technician who decides what type of man is to be created, just as when, right now, people propose changes in education to adapt it to techniques. The great weakness of this teleological position is that it ignores a crucial law of the development of Technique, which is that Technique develops following a causal process and never following a teleological process.

When we adopt one of these first two ethical orientations, people always say that it is man who must make good use of Technique or impose ends on it, but they always neglect to ask themselves: *which man?* Is it just anyone? Is it every passerby, every workman, any everyman who might master Technique? Is it the politician? Is it the mass? Is it the scientist and the technician? Is it the community? Is it humanity? Technique is beyond politicians for the most part, and every scientist only knows a tiny particle of the technical apparatus. How could he alter the whole? As for the community or the class, they know absolutely nothing (if indeed they exist at all as a specific entity) of the problem of Technique as a system. Finally, there have regularly been attempts to name "Panels of the Wise" (for instance the Seven Sages of Europe) who have done nothing but show their impotence, as well as intergovernmental commissions of international treaties (the experience of institutions aimed at avoiding the proliferation of nuclear weapons is enlightening in this respect, as is the impotence of official bodies in charge of fighting pollution). Who is the man who should impose ends on the technical apparatus or take it over? Nobody knows.

But we also must not neglect the fact that human beings are already altered by the technical phenomenon themselves. When a child is born, the environment where he finds himself is a technical one; it is an "already there." His whole education is oriented toward his adaptation to the conditions of technical life (teaching him how to cross the street at the red light), and his upbringing is aimed at preparing him to get a technical job. Man is psychically altered by consumption, by technical work, by the news, by television, by entertainment, etc. (currently the proliferation of computer games), which are all technical. In other words, one must not neglect the fact that it is this man, preadapted to Technique and altered by it, who would be entrusted with mastering and reorienting Technique. It is clear that he will not be able to do it in an independent manner. He is no longer an independent subject in relation to a neutral object. He is a subject determined by the object, and often the object of the technical process himself.

This is why the two classic orientations of ethics (an individual ethic and a social ethic) seem obsolete to me, as is the distinction between a fundamental ethic and a special ethic. We are no longer dealing with an ethic of choice, for instance, which would be possible. And if people have been able to describe the ethical situation as a situation of choice, in the technical environment, we are no longer dealing with this situation. Choices and orientation of techniques take place according to technical criteria and not by virtue of a human decision deliberated following a choice between several non-predetermined possibilities. Likewise, the resort to values (except if one is a "realist" and believes in the existence of values in themselves, metaphysical, transcendent, and active in themselves) is meaningless, since the values defined by traditional societies no longer have anything in common with the use of techniques.

Another ethical orientation that seems excluded is the *adiaphora* theory. There are specific ethical questions (e.g. sexuality, the relation with the other) and then there are plenty of indifferent areas where no ethical issue arises: these are the *adiaphora*.[7] Thus it used to be said: gluttony is an ethical issue, but what we are going to eat, or should eat, is a matter of total indifference from an ethical standpoint. For two centuries, Technique was thus considered to be one of those "indifferent matters." After all, what do morals have to do with a motor or a calculation technique? And from there, it was a slippery slope to giving authority to the various techniques, without judgment! Each technique in itself is indeed indifferent.

Finally, another ethical orientation toward Technique is that of adaptation. Technique is reality. Man must adapt to reality. And this is grafted

---

7. Cf. note 6, p. 31.

unto the whole ideology of the fact: Technique is the Fact. Man must adapt to the fact. What prevents Technique from functioning better is the whole stock of ideologies, feelings, principles, beliefs, etc., that man still carries in himself and that derive from his traditional situation. We must (and therein lies the ethical choice!) get rid of all these survivals and lead man to a perfect adaptation as a result of which he will be able to draw as many advantages as possible from Technique. Adaptation becomes a moral criterion. But this leads to the following question.

3. TECHNICAL ETHICS

We are witnessing the appearance of a new Ethic in our society that I have referred to as being a technical ethic because it derives exactly from the technical environment and it directs man toward service to this environment.[8]

Technical morals display two basic features: they are a behavioral morality and they are a morality that excludes any moral *problematic*.

Behavioral morals are exclusively interested in behaviors, seek to produce an orthopraxy, and challenge the validity of issues of intention, feelings, ideals, and debates of conscience. The interesting or worthwhile behavior must not be chosen in terms of moral principles, but according to precise technical rules (for instance what B. F. Skinner calls "Freedom" or "Dignity").[9] Man must be psychologically adapted in order for Technique to produce its best effect.

This leads to an exclusion of the problematic of good and evil, an open morality, or else morals of ambiguity.[10] Technique does indeed exclude ambiguity. The good is clear. The worthwhile environment in a technical universe evidently imposes itself, and we are witnessing an identification between the personal moral decision of the good and social material development. There is a confusion between the good and happiness (well-being).

Technique, on the other hand, has itself become a value. Technique appears to the average Western man to vouchsafe future good and happiness where techniques ensure the necessity of behavior conducive to this progress. Technique carries our hopes (thanks to technical progress cancer will be defeated, etc.). It gives a meaning to life (which is just what was

---

8. In Ellul, *To Will and to Do*.

9. B. F. Skinner (1904–1990), American psychologist, founder of radical behaviorism. His position is that human behaviors are determined by the effects they produce. Two significant books: *Science and Human Behavior*; *Beyond Freedom and Dignity* [note by the family].

10. Simone de Beauvoir, *Ethics of Ambiguity*.

questioned in May 1968). And the common attitude consists, whenever there are drawbacks to the use of techniques, in declaring that this is not due to Technique, but to the fact that man does not know how to use it: implicitly, this means that it is man who produces evil, and therefore that Technique is the good. It is the desirable value and deserves that man sacrifice himself for it (the Martyrs of Science).

From there, a whole system of values is constituted.[11] Jean Fourastié and Jacques Monod have tried to show how science entailed a certain virtue on man's part, and that it is from the starting point of that virtue, henceforth scientifically founded (since science is founded in and of itself), that the whole of ethics can be reconstructed.[12] This virtue is that of intellectual honesty.

But when it comes to Technique, there is no systematic intellectual construction of a scale of values. We see the spontaneous creation of what corresponds to the system's functioning: normalcy, efficiency, success, work, professional conscience, devotion to the collective work; such are the main values of this technical ethic from whose standpoint all behaviors are judged in our society. All concur in favoring the most complete adaptation of man, on the one hand, to machines, instruments and processes, and, on the other hand, to his technical environment. Adaptation, obtained by a variety of psychological techniques, comes into play with respect to the attitude in production, in consumption, and toward the various technical bodies. The social misfit corresponds exactly to the old "immoral individual" of traditional societies. The only good perspective that is open and promoted is that of adaptation, whether one speaks of the "Man-Machine" dyad or one contemplates creating a Kybert.[13]

However, society continues to proclaim a traditional morality. We all know that for Karen Horney, it is the cause of the "neurotic personality of our time."[14] The opposition between the principles, values, and morals taught to children and the actual behavior demanded of the adult is a contradiction. "The Churches preach humility, charity, and poverty yet finance industrial development programs. Socialists have become ruthless

---

11. Whose "situation" relative to what we have called by this name until now will be examined later. These are values subordinate to Technique, whereas until now value was superordinate.

12. Fourastié, *Essais de morale prospective*; Monod, *Chance and Necessity*.

13. The word is used in Ellul in the sense of "mutant," translated by Bromiley as "a changed humanity." Ellul, *Technological Bluff*, 18 [note by the family].

14. Karen Horney (1885–1952), psychoanalyst, and author of *Neurotic Personality of Our Time*.

defenders of industrial monopoly" (Illich).[15] But this basic discordance tends to be erased by the creation of a technical morality.

Technical morality tends to devalue other ways of conduct (be they wasteful, inefficient, nonpurposive, slothful), other values, and other virtues (love, faithfulness, goodness, etc.). But, gradually, we are witnessing a remarkable fact: the integration of some of those behaviors in the technical system itself, by which we mean the frantic growth of computer "games." Play behavior is integrated. But this morality drives back into the realm of the frivolous and the inefficient what might make it possible to give a meaning to man's life. It cannot stand any other meaning than itself. It is totalitarian and exclusive. But it has never been formulated in this authoritarian way. It is not systematized. At least we do not have that impression, because no philosopher or moralist has done it. But it is in effect formulated, not as *morality*, but as a behavioral imperative by a whole slew of psychotechnicians (for instance B. F. Skinner and others). We cannot, under these conditions, consider a conciliation, a "rough compromise," between two moralities. What prevails is a morality based on the behavior necessary for Technique. Under these conditions, those who claim to support another ethical orientation are tolerated as survivals or else find themselves obligated to engage in a conflict, not directly with Technique, but with the ideology of Technique, technical beliefs, and morals.

4. THE ETHICAL ISSUES RAISED

If the issues raised by Technique come down in the final analysis to a question of power, it is because man can do practically everything that such issues arise as, for instance, the exhaustion of the world's resources or the multiplication of risks,[16] or, on the other hand, exponential demographic growth or the infinitely murderous character of wars. Each of these factual problems displays a purely technical aspect and an ethical aspect. It is the characteristic of all the difficulties we are experiencing. Specific ethical problems all derive from this situation. It is thus a matter of power. But the latter has a twofold character. First, it is extrinsic; it is not part of man and not incorporated into him, but it is a power that resides in the new human environment. Secondly, it has to do exclusively with means. It is a disproportion of means that finally provokes the crisis.

15. Illich, *Tools for Conviviality*.
16. See Salmon, *La Société du Risque*. [It would seem that the reference is really to Ulrich Beck's book *Risk Society*, note by the family; or else see Jacquard, *Endangered by Science?*, suggestion by F. Rognon].

Ethical reflection must therefore situate itself first at the level of power. Now, we have here a first factor, a fundamental one; it is the contradiction between power and values. Any increase in power always translates as a questioning, a regression, or an abandonment of values. Of course, this proposition is not objectively and scientifically demonstrable. It is experiential and pragmatic in nature. When a State accepts juridical limitations and a constitutional framework enshrining values, it is because it has little power, or accepts that it will be so, or is willing not to use all the power it could use. When a State becomes effectively all-powerful, there are no more respected values. It is entirely illusory to claim that power can be put at the service of values, and that by increasing power, values will be better defended. This is thoroughly idealistic and unreal. In reality, the growth of power erases values, except those that serve this power.

But if there are no more values, commonly believed and received, there are from then on no more limits nor reference points. The destructuring of values results first in man's inability to effectively judge and appraise his action. At that moment, the rule that imposes itself becomes "Everything that can be done must be done." Why not use torture or the concentration camp? There is no predetermined limit. Power entails an "always more," "always further." At what point should one stop? One finds neither an inner limit nor an outer limit. Every time, it is only one more step to take. It is the constant escalation of power and demoralization that go hand in hand. And since one has taken the previous step, why not this one? To judge one's action, to impose limits and a meaning, one must have a set of values that are irreducible and indisputable. Of course, if one subscribes to the ideology of power, one must at the same time firmly declare that there no longer is any ethical problem, and even that there no longer are any ethics, and even that man does not need them anymore. But one must also know what one is doing; specifically, one has to wonder whether man will be satisfied that nothing has any meaning, and that nothing can serve to attribute a meaning to what one does. But this problem of power does not exist *in itself*; it is inscribed in the phenomenon of the growth of means.

All ethical research can then only refer to the order of means. We can set aside the "Ends-Means" problem, because it seems that more and more thinkers are in agreement about the impossibility of currently dissociating the two. It is no longer a case of good ends that can be reached by just any means. The end is already contained in the means that Technique puts at our disposal. Bad means absolutely corrupt all the most excellent ends. Power and the breadth of current technical means totally cover the field of our thought, of our life, and leave no place for extra-technical ends. It is thus a matter of remaining in this universe of means, and this is where we have to put ethical issues and to seek the adequate behavior. Otherwise, we enter the path of escape, ever more common nowadays: escape in religiousness, in mysticism, or being enclosed in rock music, etc.

5. PROPOSALS FOR AN ETHIC

In view of the above observations, we might say that an ethic for a technical society could only be characterized as an ethic of non-power, of freedom, of conflicts, and of transgression.

But before going over these four points, it would seem important to recall that there are many authors who, using different terms, go in the same direction. When Bertrand de Jouvenel asks that modern man practice friendliness (an art of living whereby one starts by seeking what might suit the neighbor, and never uses extreme means),[17] Georges Friedmann speaks of Wisdom,[18] Ivan Illich of Conviviality,[19] Jean Fourastié of personal discipline (which he unfortunately sees realized in the scientific mentality),[20] Edward Goldsmith,[21] etc., in each case it is about a reduction of power, a discovery of what is more essential for man to live in this universe, and each time it is a moral quality that allows one *not to use* all means possible. Man is called to grow on the moral plane as well as to judge his means. After having criticized Bergson and the "soul supplement"[22] so much, there are many today who come back to it, at least provided it is correctly understood.

An ethic of non-power—the root of the matter—obviously means that man accepts not to do all that he could do. Now, there is no longer any project, nor are there values, nor reasons, nor divine law that could be opposed from outside. We must therefore tackle the inside and assert the impossibility of living together, and probably of living at all, if one does not practice an ethic of non-power. It is the basic option. As long as man is going to be oriented by the spirit of power and toward the acquisition of power, toward indefinite growth (of production, consumption, etc.), nothing is possible.

It would be a systematic and voluntary seeking for non-power, which of course does not mean the acceptance of powerlessness (non-power is in no way powerlessness!), of fate, passivity, etc. (but this is not the danger

---

17. De Jouvenel, *Arcadie*.
18. Friedmann, *La puissance et la sagesse*.
19. Illich, *Tools for Conviviality*.
20. Fourastié, *Essais de morale prospective*.
21. Goldsmith, *Small Is Beautiful*. [This book is actually by Ernst F. Schumacher; note by the family.]
22. Bergson, *Two Sources of Morality and Religion*.

we are exposed to!). On the contrary, for today "fate" is "always more technique"! This ethic of non-power is inscribed precisely at all levels.

- As much in the personal use of technical means (not seeking to outrun others, to be first, to rev up one's car or to set the radio at full blast, etc.).
- But it is also in institutions that this is inscribed. Institutions that tend to develop power by placing competition at the base of social organization are to be rejected, and this will mean as much certain pedagogical methods (contests) as the Olympic Games, as the economic system of free trade or on the international market of the greatest competitiveness! In each case it is a matter of proving efficiency and hence of cultivating power, and hence of going in the direction of the technical system and of the devaluation of any possible morality.
- But it is also in scientific research itself that the ethic of non-power comes into play (for instance, in what Illich calls radical research, that must provide the criteria that make it possible to determine the harmfulness threshold of a tool and to invent tools that optimize the balance of life).[23]
- It is again in politics that this is inscribed (penalization of the powerful, protection of minorities, of the weak and the exploited, *a priori*, etc.).

An ethic of non-power entails the establishment of limits. One needs to refer here to Illich's remarkable analysis concerning thresholds (which are imposed by necessity to continue to survive) and limits (which are the boundaries that a human group gives itself between what is to be done and not to be done). The setting of limits is always constitutive of society, as it is of culture. The unlimited is the negation of the human, as it is of culture. There is no human group that can exist as human in the unlimited of whatever kind (an absolute regulation as well as an absence of regulation).

But this will be tied to a decisive global stance in the area of all technical applications: "the *a priori* of non-intervention." That is to say, every time the scientist and the technician are unable to determine with the greatest accuracy the global and long-term effects of a possible technique, we must without fail refuse to initiate the process of that technique. We are here dealing with a central ethical rule if we want to maintain any possible life and any possible society. But this decision as well as the setting of limits (which

---

23. Illich, *Tools for Conviviality*.

has corresponded to the ancient "sacred") are due to freedom; it is when man has learned to be free that he is capable of limiting himself.

It is obvious that these indications about the fundamental root of ethics leave whole the question of its possibility and of the "how" of this conversion to non-power. However, it is important to underline that this mutation is not impossible, since it is tied to the search for meaning that seems to me very characteristic of modern trial and error.

The second aspect of this ethic is that of freedom. The power of means ensures no freedom to man. The man of technical society has no freedom (even though I know perfectly well all the discourses on the topic: freedom with respect to primal needs, with respect to dangers, diseases, the natural environment, freedom of choice, of consumption and motion, etc., which are correct). The freedoms of which one speaks are superficial appearances. Fundamentally, man is alienated in the technical system, which has substituted technical fate for the old natural fate.

Man is called to constantly free himself from what compels and determines him. But then he was determined by natural and later sociological (cultural) forces (and he has used Science and Technique to free himself from them); now he is alienated by what was once the means of his liberation. Now there is only liberation insofar as, on the one hand, one aims at the current factors of alienation, and where, on the other hand, one can either recuse them, use them, or divert them. Freedom consists in being able to say yes or no when faced with a possibility. Now, we have shown that, in the present situation, it seems that no mastery can be exerted on the technical system. Technique, as a system, currently represents for man the world of necessity in which he finds himself embedded and which purports to spare him the ethical problem itself by claiming to be located outside the field of ethical choices and situations. Liberation can then only consist in recusing it, in driving it into an ever-narrower realm.

But then we exactly get back here to the ethic of non-power; it will be, as we were saying, in the establishment of limits that freedom is exerted. If, on the other hand, choice is the ethical situation par excellence, if it is in and through this choice that freedom is expressed, the fundamental choice that is placed before us is indeed the one having to do with increasing or diminishing power, production, means, etc. Next to this one, all other choices (freedom to choose the color of one's car, or where one will go on vacation, or the brand of one's computer) are perfectly futile and superficial!

Now, the fact is already there: the malaise of modernity, the "ill-being," the rebellion or apathy of the young, suicidal tendencies, express the global fact that modern man is suffering in his total being of unfreedom, of increasing constraints. But he does not know yet whence this oppression comes to him. He accuses anything, secondary factors. He struggles like a blind man. The decisive fact here would be a coming to consciousness that would take the ethics of freedom to the level of the possible and the achievable, and not just of the desirable.

The ethic of non-power and of freedom is creative of *tensions* and *conflicts*. But we are here dealing with an essential feature of ethics in a technical society. Technique tends to demand a concordance, a unity; it is unifying, and this disappearance of conflicts is even presented as a virtue. But as we know, human groups in which tensions and conflicts disappear are groups that become sclerotic, that lose their ability to change and to resist attacks, as well as the ability to evolve.

We are here dealing with a fundamental question, that is, the substitution of technical progress (with its uniform and linear mode) for the former type of human progress (which always occurred in a conflictual and multidimensional fashion). Technical progress is nowadays disastrous for the human group as such, because the effect of sclerosis (or else entropy) necessarily continues to happen. A human society exists only through the successive negotiations of contradictory positions. Yet, for instance, computer-assisted decision-making excludes Negotiation.

If we want human groups to continue to exist, if we want man to have a specific play in a human environment, we have to call upon a conflictual ethics, one that is productive of tensions, and to question the uniformity of big units, of big organizations produced by and necessary for technical progress. Conflictuality is a survival value, for the whole of mankind.

But we are obviously talking about conflictuality as a "true image" of the possible, negotiated, mastered, that does not tend to the pure and simple destruction of the group, to its pulling apart. We are not talking about a nihilism, but about the production of tensions calculated within human groups so that these cannot shut themselves, become enclosed, become perfected (any perfected society is dead), but recover an ability to evolve by themselves, and without reference to the evolution of Technique. To be sure, we do not pretend to exhaust all the content of this ethic!

Finally, another trait of ethics in a technical society would be Transgression. This may appear to be in contradiction with the ethics of limits as expressing freedom. This is not at all the case. For it is not a matter of transgressing limits that do not yet exist to enter the unlimited, but of the transgression of the rules and limits produced by Technique and resulting in alienation (for instance, we must consider the concept of growth as a limit).

It is essential that we make no mistake about the direction of transgression. When it is mentioned nowadays, it is mainly the principles and taboos of eighteenth-century society that are in the crosshairs. Entering the unlimited by using drugs, transgressing sexual taboos, family relations, paternal or marital authority, politeness, or honesty—all these are not true acts of transgression, for they are going exactly in the direction of Technique. It is what Technique has already undermined, sometimes destroyed, which eroticism, for instance, claims to transgress. The whole enterprise of destruction of so-called taboos is in reality a mere translation of the technical real.

Transgression must deal with the real. The real is Technique itself. It will therefore take the shape either of a demythicization of Technique, or of the recusal of technically based action imperatives, or of the questioning of the conditions imposed on man and groups so that Technique can develop. It will again be the "desacralization" of Technique, the critique of the illusions of progress, the calculation of the real "costs" of any growth, etc.

Transgression with respect to Technique will take the shape of the destruction of the beliefs that man invests in Technique, and of the reduction of Technique to being no more than productive of random and pointless objects. It thus entails the search for an external meaning on behalf of which transgression operates and which thereby de-signifies Technique.

Such are, it seems to me, the great orientations that can be made out of a significant Ethics for man as situated in the technical world.

Theology and Technique Literature

WE NEED TO MENTION the quarterly Review of the World Council of Churches, *Anticipation*, which began to appear in 1970 and is now at its twenty-second issue.[1] It is not directly focused on theological reflection on Technique, since its aim is the search for a Christian social thought in view of the future, but the issue of Science and Technique comes up fairly often. We may then cite as the most interesting contributions: Musahkoji, "Technology and the Cultural Revolution," 1970;[2] Gilkey, "Technology, History and Liberation," *Anticipation*, 1974.[3]

One entire issue to set aside is that of November 1974, on *Science and Technology for Human Development*.[4] It is the report of the Bucharest conference (in preparation of the Nairobi Assembly), focusing on the ambiguity of the future and Christian Hope. It doesn't bring anything very new, but at least the issues are correctly framed.

However, the issues on nuclear power are extremely disappointing (1975), merely presenting anew what one finds here and there.[5]

---

1. *Anticipation: Christian Social Thought in Future Perspective*, a publication of the WCC's "Church and Society" Department, Geneva, which appeared from April 1970 (no. 1) to July 1983 (no. 30). This review became the *Church and Society Newsletter* [note by the family].

2. Kinhide Mushakoji, director of the Institute of International relations of Sophia University in Tokyo, "Technology and the Cultural Revolution," *Anticipation*, no. 3 (1970) 8–13 [note by the family]. We thank Anne-Emmanuelle Tankam and Andreas Waldvogel, respectively the archivist and librarian of the WCC, who have given us the references needed for writing several of the following notes.

3. Gilkey, "Technology, History and Liberation" [note by the family].

4. Special issue: World Council of Churches, "Science and Technology for Human Development," *Anticipation*, no. 19 (1974) 8–13 [note by the family].

5. Francis and Abrecht, eds., "Facing up to Nuclear Power," *Anticipation*, no. 20 (1975), and World Council of Churches, "Report on Nuclear Energy," *Anticipation*, no. 21 (1975) [note by the family].

Of course, studies on ecology and environmental perils are many, but without any great originality, since they are generally very dependent on MIT. Studies by Birch are solid.[6] But the theological thought is shallow. As surprising as this might seem, there is practically no new view of Technique issuing from theological thought, nor any renewal of the latter by the technical "challenge."[7] The relationship remains wholly external and in classical terms.

Curiously, the documents produced by the WCC for the last ten years seem to me to be a step backward compared with, for instance, the study by Howe and Todt, *Peace in the Scientific and Technical Age (Background information 1966)* that laid good theological starting bases.[8] Worthy of note is the excellent study by Gruson on the theological problems caused by technological options (December 1973), but it is almost the only one![9]

As for innovation, in spite of its title, this review, in conformity with the tradition in the Churches, largely lags behind in relation to the studies that are done elsewhere! For instance, the issues raised by the computer for Christian faith have not even been raised yet!

꘎

The *Nairobi assembly* of the World Council, in December 1975, has tackled, with the Churches' usual belatedness, the issue of Technique and science. But we see at once how the issue was badly framed. It is liable to all the criticisms we had made about the 1966 Bossey meeting; no progress in the understanding of Technique has been made. We find again the listing of "issues," without any coming to consciousness of Technique's global character. The question of "social responsibility" is raised about technical development, which is totally obsolete. People wonder what the relationship is between the two "revolutions": the one caused by the scientific and technical explosion, the other by the demand for social justice and liberation.

I will say that all the questions raised are belated and fragmentary, and that there has been no progress in the theological understanding of the

---

6. Charles Birch, chairman of the faculty of biological sciences of the University of Sydney [translator's note: he actually held the Challis Chair as a professor from 1960 to 1984], is the author of a lecture on our societies' ecological responsibility, "Creation, Technology and Human Survival," *The Ecumenical Review* 28 (1976) 66–79 [note by the family].

7. Translator's note: English in the original.

8. Howe and Todt, "Peace in the Scientific and Technical Age" [note by the family].

9. Claude Gruson, "Theological problems raised by technological options," *Anticipation*, no. 15 (1973) 22–29 [note by the family].

issue. To be sure, Professor Birch's report is excellent, but I need not take it into account because it confines itself to repeating notions that are already very widespread, and as for the wishes of the assembly, I am obliged to say that they are pious wishes, without any kind of progression in theological thought nor of devising of means to get them implemented.

Of course, one finds, as usual at the WCC, the adoption of American concepts that lie around more or less everywhere, like that of *Technological Assessment,* and recommendations are made on very general issues, for instance, alternative energy.[10] We are again witnessing the confusion between Technique and Science, and the theological questions that are put show nothing but the feebleness of theological imagination! I know very well that people will tell me an assembly of this magnitude is not a working colloquium, and that we have to take into account the international character and the actual level of the people, but then, in a research paper, one is permitted to precisely not take such platitudes into account. Let us just take stock of the inability of these great assemblies to invent what can move, in truth, the Christian people.

The papers presented at the *International Conference on Ethics* at a time of expanding technology, at the *Haifa* Technion in March 1975, are among the most important ones on this issue.[11] To be sure, one finds most of the commonplaces, for instance Steg describing what is in fact a *technical*

---

10. [Translator's note: In English in the original.] "Technology Assessment (TA) is a class of policy studies which systematically examine the effects on society that may occur when a technology is introduced, extended, or modified. It emphasizes those consequences that are unintended, indirect or delayed." Definition drawn from Coates, "What is Technology Assessment?" *Impact Assessment* 1, no. 1 (1982) 20–24 [note by the family].

11. This is the international symposium "On Ethics and Current Technology Related to Social Problems" that took place in Haifa and in Jerusalem in December 1974, and that issued in the Mount Carmel "Declaration on Technology and Moral Responsibility" in 1975. The proceedings were published in Kranzberg, ed., *Ethics in an Age of Pervasive Technology.* They are followed by the text of the "Mount Carmel Declaration." We heartily thank Lior Porat, from the Haifa Technion, who has given us the elements needed to put together the notes pertaining to this symposium. Technion: the Israeli Institute of Technology, Israel's oldest university, founded in 1962, in Haifa, on the heights of Mount Carmel [note by the family].

ethic,[12] Thring representing the idea of the "*Creative Society*,"[13] many blithely confusing Science and Technique, and Buber-Agassi, in *Moralité dans l'industrie*, asserting—and rightly so—a demand for quality in work life and for meaningful work, but this remains a pious wish![14]

Others have unwittingly asserted Technique's primacy (Kahneman, about the decision-making process),[15] or again the creation of a Scientific or Technical ethic (important: Bunge, who as I see it comes closest to this construct).[16]

Certain texts, however, are crucial, such as that of Kurzweil on heteronomous Ethics,[17] the important study by Gordis on the understanding of Science and natural Morals in a Biblical perspective,[18] and the interesting approaches of Tribe on the Environment[19] and *Technological Assessment*.[20]

12. Léo Steg (1922–2004), director for twenty-five years of the General Electric Space Science Laboratory in Philadelphia, is the author of "The Social Responsibility of Scientists," in *Ethics in an Age of Pervasive Technology*, 158–59, and editor of an opuscule, "Should We Limit Science and Technology," *Journal of the Franklin Institute*, Sept. 1975 [note by the family].

13. [Translator's note: In English in the original.] M. W. Thring (1915–2006) has written, among other things, "Towards a Creative Society," *Electronics and Power* 19, no. 21 (1973); and "Lost in the Fog," *Ethics in an Age of Pervasive Technology*, 15–16 [note by the family].

14. Judith Buber-Agassi (1924–2018), professor of economics and sociology in Tel-Aviv, in the USA, in Canada, etc. wrote "Morality in Industry," in *Ethics in the Age of Pervasive Technology*, 174–76. Prior to this, she had written an article that is currently online, "Toward a Rational Work Ethic" [note by the family].

15. Daniel Kahneman, American-Israeli psychologist and economist, Nobel Prize in Economics, is the author of "Human Engineering of Decisions," in *Ethics in an Age of Pervasive Technology*, 190–92, and wrote with Amos Tversky "Prospect Theory," *Econometria* 47, no. 2 (March 1979) 263–91 [note by the family].

16. Bunge, "Technoethics," in *Ethics in an Age of Pervasive Technology*, 139–42; *Etica y ciencia* [note by the family].

17. Kurzweil, "Why Heteronomous Ethics?," in *Ethics in an Age of Pervasive Technology*, 68–71 [note by the family].

18. Robert Gordis (1908–1962), a rabbi belonging to Conservative Judaism, has taught the Bible and Jewish philosophy at the Jewish Theological Seminary in New York for forty years. During this symposium, he gave a lecture entitled "Science, Natural Law and Ethics, a Jewish Perspective," in *Ethics in an Age of Pervasive Technology*, 83–106, which is summarized in *Technology and Culture*, 22, no. 2 (1981) [note by the family].

19. Doubtless Lawrence H. Tribe, "Technology Assessment and the Fourth Discontinuity," *Southern California Law Review*, 46 (1973) 617–60; "Ways not to Think about Plastic Trees," *Yale Law Journal*, 83, no. 7 (1974) 1330–31; "From Environmental Foundations to Constitutional Structures," *Yale Law Journal*, 84 (1975) 545–56 [note by the family].

20. Translator's note: In English in the original.

Likewise, many correct questions have been put (Lieberman: Do we do just things, or do we do things correctly;[21] Jonas on the Possibility of an ethic in a period of generalized fear),[22] but we remain with the question! The very useful and enlightening analysis of Dubois asks what ancient ethics and spiritualist philosophy could bring to the development of ethics in technical society. It is a text at once cautious and deep.[23]

We can hardly consider as a theological reflection the otherwise interesting book of Norbert Wiener, *God and Golem* (a study of certain points about which cybernetics and religion come into conflict), for Wiener's understanding remains theistic, and hardly goes beyond traditional religion. The technical work of man seems to him to be a parable of that of God, who made man in his image, as man makes the computer in his image. Man remains the locus of the creation of moral judgments and values. Now, Wiener will say, we cannot live and conceive a society without making these judgments and effect choices in view of values, something which the computer is forever incapable of doing. But he does not broach the question of whether by any chance these ethical and theological functions might not be radically devalued by technical multiplication.[24]

We must take into account a brief but surprising study by John Warwick Montgomery, *Computers, Cultural Change and the Christ*, where we see Christian orthodoxy (in the narrowest sense) take hold of the computer. The latter can be a wonderful instrument at the service of Christians. The computer causes a true revolution that must be at the service of the central doctrine of the Christian faith, redemption through Christ. The spread of Christianity rests on communication; now, the computer is the ideal instrument of communication. Revelation entails a radical choice between a yes and a no; it cannot tolerate ambiguity or dialectics. Now the computer, by virtue of the binary system, is based on the law of noncontradiction. There is thus a concordance. This being the case, how do we put the computer at the service of Christ? By using it for a nonambiguous spreading of precise information. Above all, the computer is the device par excellence

---

21. Lieberman, "Broadening Engineering Education—The Technological Imperative", in *Ethics in an Age of Pervasive Technology*, 160-61 [note by the family].

22. Hans Jonas (1903-1993), German historian and philosopher. His paper at the Technion was published as "Heuristics of Fear," in *Ethics in an Age of Pervasive Technology*, 213-21. His most famous book is *Imperative of Responsibility* [note by the family].

23. Dubois, "What Ancient Ethics Can Contribute," in *Ethics in an Age of Pervasive Technology*, 78-82; "Ethique ancienne, philosophie spiritualiste et technologie," *Revue thomiste*, 75 (1975) 418-31 [note by the family].

24. Wiener, *God and Golem, Inc.* For him, "the machine [...] is the modern counterpart of the Golem of the Rabbi of Prague" (95) [note by the family].

for apologetics. We must pare down all of philosophical and theological thought, add up all criticisms, objections, responses, etc., and the computer thus puts at the disposal of everyone throughout the world the means for a universal apologetics, the spread of the faith being based on the knowledge and refutation of contradictions. This is a rather startling view of the message, but in effect, it situates rather well the skewering of theology when it enters the technological universe![25]

Among the investigations undertaken at the request of Churches, we may cite:

Cameron P. Hall, *Human Values and Advancing Technology: A New Agenda for the Church in Mission*,[26] which I haven't been able to look into, and the books of Hans-Ruedi Weber, *Experiments with Man*, and *Man in his Living Environment: An Ethical Assessment*, which are decent investigations, but which hardly advance knowledge of technical reality nor the theology of the question.[27] We find again in it an ethical concern without any real theological foundation (and much closer to a humanist ethics), and a way of putting the issue that is quite classical.

A more sizeable note obviously has to be devoted to the proceedings of the Conference of the "Church and Society" Department in 1970.[28] This conference gathered a large number of specialized scientists, a small number of sociologists or philosophers of Technique, and theologians. As we have often said, the comparative principle is the only one that can be satisfactory in such matters, so the breakdown was satisfactory. But from the start, we see there were four basic givens stated at the outset that would distort the whole thing:

- "Human values can be exalted or destroyed depending on the use we will make of technique" (the issue of the good or bad use that we have shown, as early as 1950, to be a total mistake when it comes to Technique).

- A complete confusion between science and Technique (what is specific to the technical phenomenon was almost never understood,

---

25. Montgomery, *Computers, Cultural Change and the Christ* [note by the family].

26. Hall, ed., *Human Values and Advancing Technology* [note by the family].

27. Weber, *Experiments with Man; Man in his Living Environment* [note by the family].

28. Gill, *From Here to Where?* [note by the family].

people constantly speaking now of science, then of technique without any distinction!).

- The search for a solution to the divorce between Science and Faith, an effort to overcome the indifference or even antagonism between Christianity and the sciences. It was thus a matter of reducing antagonisms, and at no time did the idea of a dialectical process dawn. The dialectical idea of interrelation was totally alien to this conference, which was thus in a complete impasse.

- Finally, specialization was strictly maintained. Each scientist or technician was called to speak from the standpoint of his science, of the "dangers" and positive aspects of his specialty, and to review the research. We therefore remain within the framework of what we may consider to be precisely the first decision to put into question: that of specialization. We sometimes remain completely beholden to the viewpoint of modern science in what is often recognized as its principal error. And hence, at no time did the assembly advance toward a global understanding of Technique. The idea of a technical system never occurred to it, not even as the study of the technical system. We thus remain at the level of platitudes about this or that excess of diversified specialized techniques, which is a false way of putting the issue and can lead to nothing.

Such are the four basic, irreparable errors that make the proceedings of this conference quite useless. We will however be more specific at both levels, the technical one and the theological one.

In the technical realm, people of course got caught up in the discrimination between good and bad techniques (with the greatest uncertainty as to on what basis this judgment was made). They listed "issues of concern," those that are to be found exactly anywhere. There was no need to gather an assembly of scientists and Christians to pile up these platitudes: the environmental problem, pollution, the "P Bomb" [population bomb], genetics, urbanization, computers, etc.—in other words, the "dangers" or "drawbacks" of the application of sciences—according to the simple criterion: does it risk destroying humanity or values? At no time did people get out of listing mode.

And of course, starting from this way of putting the issue, we witness every time the debate between those who believe in it and those who do not. There are those who have total confidence in science to resolve everything and those who have the impression (but it never goes beyond the impression!) of not knowing where we are headed. All of this is complicated still by the political-social sensitivities of Third World representatives who refuse to position the issues of Science and Technique other than to evaluate them in terms of the advances needed for their own country, and who therefore refuse in advance to take into consideration the collective dangers of the application of Techniques. This viewpoint, which is the most banal one in all conferences on the topic, seemed even exacerbated (instead of being brought down to a reasonable size) because the delegates in question were Christians.

Whenever people chanced to leave the realm of science to enter that of Technique, we of course witnessed the glorification of the raising of living standards (think of the awful life of our grandparents, and of the comfort, the convenience, the information, etc.! Urbanization and industrialization have been affirmed as a liberation of man). The only issue is to improve technology: wider dimensions, going beyond the provincialism of national planning, reducing armaments, and the abuses of private consumption. It can only be a development of Technique; this is a basic given. We have to facilitate the transfer of complete technological systems, to help the Third World technicize itself by developing the local use of raw materials, to increase the means of communication, etc. In other words, Christians are merely pushing in the direction in which Technique is going on its own. Likewise, people become enthusiastic about the computer: it must be applied everywhere, in the social and cultural areas, and of course (this is likely the Christian character of this reflection!) in the Church; the computer can surely facilitate the organization of Churches. People never exit from platitudes about computers. Let us consider three of them. If there are abuses, it is the legislator who must intervene and limit them (by defining, for instance, rights to privacy; it does not occur for even a second that the legal system is totally inefficient for this kind of issue!). The computer is after all nothing but a mechanical slave, an extension of human intelligence that limits itself to enlarging man's choices. We can impose our will and our values on it. How simple it is! But this is totally false.

Finally, we get to a work program for the WCC: to examine the ideological assumptions and the agreements that have favored technical development (introducing democracy in decision-making processes), to study the diversity of possible forms of Technique according to different societies to serve men in a positive sense. Great conviction then: we can orient Technique as we want; we have to do it in view of democracy and the Third World.

If we now proceed to the theological reflections, we can discern those that are sprinkled in the speeches of scientists and what the theologians bring. But from the outset, we have to note that the kickoff given by Eugene

Carson Blake, general secretary of the WCC, started the whole conference in a wrong direction. He defines the "true" questions as follows: Which discoveries of science and Technique threaten or favor man's flourishing? In what does the end of existence consist in the technological era? The results are moralism, the absence of a global view of Technique, the criterion of man's flourishing (?), and the subservience of ends to Technique. Blake accidentally shows his ignorance of the actual problem when he "condemns" the analysis of those who show that an improvement of the situation of the peoples of the Third World can hardly be expected for at least a generation on account of the environmental crisis. There is no attempt to find out if it is true or not; he simply "condemn[s] this *kind* of analysis," thus any analysis that might contradict his ideological prejudices.[29]

This being said, the two great basic assumptions, implicit but ever-present, are the following.[30] First, the fact being a given, there can be no question of arguing with it (this always comes up; genetic engineering is a fact—therefore . . .). It is never a matter of questioning the fact from the standpoint of truth. On the contrary: biological discoveries being what they are, what new ethics does this produce? Everything is subservient to the force of things and the law of facts.[31] It is an eminently technical mentality, but I fail to see how it is Christian.

It is true that this was compensated for by the other basic assumption, in total contradiction: man remains lord and master of doing as he pleases with the technical tool (if that were true, one fails to understand why the WCC has shown itself so coy, conformist, and actually subservient to the scientific imperative!). We have already seen that the computer is but a perfectly servile device, one that does whatever man wants. Given this, everything is resolved. And more specifically, this makes it possible to *totally* shrug off the problem, that of Technique as well as that of Theology, by stating, which was a big keynote of this conference, that in any case science and Technique are dependent on the political options of those in power.

---

29. Words by Rev. Eugene C. Blake, in his welcoming address opening the preparatory conference, in Gill, *From Here to Where?*

30. Other than the overall assumption that the Church must seek to express the incarnation of Christ in the struggles of the world and the transcendence of God over our systems: correct, but something that was decidedly left aside.

31. Translator's note: *la force des choses* ("the force of things") is a French idiom for the pressure of necessity as "the way things are" and go in the world. Not coincidentally, Ellul's friend and intellectual mentor Bernard Charbonneau used this phrase as the title of the thousand-page, single-spaced outline of his thought he wrote down during the war, many parts of which he would develop into books a couple of decades later. This background should be kept in mind whenever Ellul uses the term, sometimes emphasizing it, since it is clearly fraught with meaning for him.

Phew! In that case, we are saved: change the government and all problems are resolved. One is left dumbfounded before such simplistic reasoning, such ignorance of the reality of Technique and Politics!

From these two premises, two stances are derived, equally false: the first, that Technique must be "oriented," be given roles to fulfill, while we are always free, of course, to formulate goals (but Technique's causal development process is ignored); and the second, that it really all comes down to a matter of morals. One constantly reaffirms the importance of man's responsibility, of his dignity, of his improvement of service, etc. These moral notions are probably true, but they do not get beyond the traditional humanistic level and found empty hopes upon sheer vagueness.

Finally, theologians were meant to speak up, but alas, the fact is that they practically did not say anything. The team's two "gurus" were Teilhard de Chardin[32] and Harvey Cox. The Church must actively collaborate in the development of science and Technique in view of the future. Technology is a fulfillment of God's plan and a modern form of divine judgment. There is the possibility of a repentant and creative human response. We learn that man, machine, and nature together form a *living* organism—(again Teilhard). As for Cox, his paper heralded *The Feast of Fools*.[33] I have sufficiently critiqued it elsewhere. In other words, we remain stuck with the greatest poverty for lack of analysis of Technique and of new theological reflection.

Of course, there were also incidentally accurate reflections, by Zen on pollution in the Third World,[34] by Kerr on the danger of genetics,[35] by Kuin on the opposition between wealth of having and fullness of being,[36] by Parmar on the ideology of power contained in any technique and the fact that power is never neutral,[37] by Dumas on the existing gulf between "science and faith" (an assembly of futurists is not necessarily an assembly of men

---

32. Extensively cited by W. D. Marsch, professor of social ethics at the University of Münster; see Gill, *From Here to Where?* [note by the family].

33. Cox, *Feast of Fools*. He maintains here a thesis opposite to the one he had defended a few years earlier in *Secular City*, for he announces a rebirth of the religious with a return to more affective and spontaneous modes of thought, and he wonders about the effects of "this anti-technological neoromanticism" on the Church's position toward the world [note by the family].

34. Muhadam Taufick Zen, professor of geophysics and vulcanology, director of the geophysics laboratory of the Bandung Institute of Technology [note by the family].

35. Warwick E. Kerr, from the University of São Paulo [note by the family].

36. Pieter Kuin, former director of Unilever in the Netherlands and visiting professor at Harvard Business School [note by the family].

37. Samuel L. Parmar, professor of economics at the University of Allahabad and president of the working committee of the "Church and Society" department [note by the family].

who hope).[38] There was also a good analysis of the calling into question of Democracy due to Technique.

But these interesting points cannot hide the mediocrity and the banality of the whole affair. No, we do not find there the smallest embryo of theology in relation to Technique.

---

38. André Dumas, theologian, in Gill, *From Here to Where?* His lecture would be the object of an article in *Réforme*, Sept. 26, 1970, and would appear in André Dumas, *Prospective et prophétie* [note by the family].

The Theological Status of Technique According to Gabriel Vahanian[1]

I.

WITH THE WORKS OF G. Vahanian, we are dealing with a perspective totally different from the one presented here.[2] But this theological study is of such importance in my eyes, since on the one hand it is the only original one on the question (infinitely more so than that of Moltmann, who totally failed after the excellent beginning of his *Theology of Hope*),[3] and on the other hand it performs a basic critique of the usual rehashing (particularly of articles published by the WCC), that I think I ought to devote a whole paragraph to it.

It is extremely difficult to summarize G. Vahanian's theses because his books are very complex and very dense. And yet, I will try to say how I understand this theology, before I sketch the elements of a critique that prevents me from totally subscribing to it.

It seems to me that there are three basic pairs to be brought out from the outset.

Man and the human: up to now there has been a process of hominization, but this does not fulfill the higher project; man is not yet man. There is

---

1. Untitled document. Title proposed by the family on the basis of the last sentence of the first part.

2. List established on the basis of Vahanian's thesis report, in 1977, where Ellul draws up an inventory of the following works that he takes into account: *Death of God*; *Wait Without Idols*; *No Other God*; *God and Utopia*; and four articles published in the series of hermeneutical colloquia of the Istituto di studi filosofici of Rome edited by Enrico Castelli: "Idéologie et Eschatologie"; "En ce jour-là"; "Sécularisation, Sécularisme, Sécularité"; and "L'expérience de Dieu" [note by the family].

3. Moltmann, *Theology of Hope* [note by the family].

an overcoming of our current situation to be done, toward what Vahanian calls (without defining it, but he is right in this, he is not called upon to establish an abstract outline of what man *should* become!) the human. We are thus in the process of this creation. And this is characterized, among other things, by the distance and the relation between this human and the Wholly Other: for the God of Jesus Christ is truly the other, but this God and man are not opposites, contradictions, such that where God is, man is not, nor is there any identity: God and man are set in a relation (an existent one) of alterity. Each is what he is, radically, but not without the other. So that man is the very condition of God. This is fulfilled in the incarnation. But it is in terms of this relation that man is called to become more, the new man, who does not fall from the sky, but who is fulfilled through successive projects, as many approximations of the human.

The second pair is *the Novum and the Eschaton*. The *Novum* seems to me to have a mainly human dimension: it is the Newness that man can cause to appear, and which derives neither from Nature nor from History, able as they are to express necessities, to produce consequences that are precisely not the *novum*. The latter is the specific feature of man who is able not to obey the Nature of things, the Force of things, and to create novel situations. It is a liberation from the chronological, the technical, the topological, the artificial. This *Novum* is located first in the imaginary, but in an imaginary that seeks to become concrete.

The *Eschaton* is "the ultimate" which on the one hand puts into question everything that has claims to ultimacy, and on the other hand does not correspond to an ultimate in the "*ultima necat*" sense;[4] it is not a "posterior," or the equivalent of the end of the world, but an ultimate that is constantly present over the course of a life, and which must be lived in faith. The latter is always and of necessity "eschatic."

But this *eschaton* is also a realization of the *Novum*. The relation between the first and the second pair is that the true *Novum* will in the final analysis be man's advent to the human. It is situated in relation to the *Eschaton*, as man is situated in relation to God (relation of alterity). As for eschatic faith, it is the attitude of the believer who is not waiting for the end of the world, but who anticipates Christ's return here and now. This *eschaton* therefore belongs neither to Nature nor to History, but in each of them produces a *Novum*. In other words, the *Novum* is indeed the invention of man, but it is only truly possible in terms of the *eschaton*. "Without *eschaton*, no *novum*."

---

4. Fragment of the inscription placed on Roman clock faces: *vulnerant omnes, ultima necat*; namely: they [hours] all wound, the last one kills [note by the family].

And the knowledge of the *eschaton*, eschatology, is expressed in three forms: there is an eschatology of the Father, aimed at the other world (the restoration of creation); an eschatology of the Son, which has to do with the world's reconversion; and an eschatology of the Spirit that announces the end of the world. Consequently, we are dealing with a theology which, on the one hand, does not make of eschatology an appendix relating to the end of history, and, on the other hand, refuses any notion of a lost paradise, of an apocalypse (in the traditional sense) and of a historicization of the *eschaton*. For what is most important is the rigorous link between the work of each person of the Trinity, the constitution of the human environment, and ethics.

- To the work of the Father corresponds an eschatology of Nature where the polarity of the *eschaton* and the *novum* appears under the guise of creation and calling (hence a corresponding ethics).

- To the work of the Son corresponds an eschatology of history, where the polarity of the incarnation and redemption is expressed in a destination of (redeemed) man that does not close history, but opens an availability for the future, which produces an ethics of responsibility.

- To the work of the Spirit corresponds an eschatology of the project, that leads up to the fact that God is everything in all (pleroma) and that man has put on the new man (resurrection), which as an ethics gives freedom.

Finally, the third pair is *Theology of Salvation, Theology of the Kingdom*, but while the first two tend to institute a relationship, and to show a dialectical movement, here we are in a critical position, of "either-or." Vahanian believes that theology has gotten mired in a theology of Salvation, in a perspective dominated by "the fall," "sin," salvation. All this not only reduces to the individual, to individual adventure, the cosmic work of the Father in the Son, but also locks up within a historicization, and within a periodization, what is of the order of eternity.

Nothing is explained by the fall, but everything must be seen in the perspective (and the reality) of the Kingdom. For the dominant feature according to which everything must be thought is the institution of the Kingdom. The civilization whose symbolism is centered on the notion of Salvation, Vahanian says, implies that everything is founded on "man-in-view-of-God" (or God understood as the advent of man), hence on a future-tense man. By contrast, the civilization whose symbolism is centered on the Kingdom of God implies the human as the event of God, hence it is "God-in-view-of-man," and God in the present.

The theology of salvation was suited to a static and fragmentary society or civilization. The theology of the Kingdom is the only one that is fitted to a rapidly evolving, globalizing civilization. The Christian, who has always sought to be present to the world, is present in a different way in one case and the other. In the first one, faithfulness to Transcendence had as a consequence the primacy of salvation as a presupposition of the reign of God (the kingdom had to *follow* the proclamation of salvation). Nowadays, the terms have to be reversed in view of the same faithfulness: the believer's inscription in the world can only occur in view of the reign of God as a presupposition of salvation. That is to say that for Vahanian, salvation is not eliminated, but is situated in relation to the already actual presence of the Kingdom. (Thus, whereas the theology of the Fathers called Jesus "Lord and Savior," classical theology erased the Lord little by little to emphasize the Savior's role; with Vahanian we emphasize in the opposite direction, in line with orthodox theology, but also that of Cullmann for instance.)[5]

It seems to me that it is in terms of these three "pairs" that Vahanian's reflection on the world as it is today and on Technique is organized.

We have not yet spoken the two keywords of this body of work: Utopia (and Utopianism, which is not the same thing) and Technique. That is because both of them are situated in relation to the framework we have attempted to elucidate.

Utopia, Vahanian tells us, is "what might take place precisely where there is no place" (and it is one of the main forms of responsible protest). Consequently, utopia corresponds to the project that man might have of a future to be built. It is reflective of man grappling with the human, man seeking to realize the human, a situation that expresses God's own condition. And this utopia has in sight the *Novum*, the unexpected, the unforeseen, the Unconditioned: what breaks with the conditionings of History and Nature, i.e. of Economics, of Politics and the Sociological. It has in sight the new world (but nowhere is it said that it can reach and accomplish it), this world that is characterized by the invention of the human by man. And hence, Utopia cannot fail to meet with eschatology, since the latter also has in sight the new world where man can effectively be the new man. And this process calls forth the union of the *Novum* and the *eschaton*, which fulfills the Pleroma.

---

5. Cullmann, *Christology of the New Testament* [note by the family].

Utopianism appears where the human bursts forth here and now. It is what is at stake in the dialectical pair "*Eschaton—Novum.*" But this utopianism only appears in its full light when it starts from the revelation that the Old Testament gives of God as creator. God is not an "absolute," but is in view of man, himself in view of God; this creaturely man is other, hence free, and utopianism expresses the authentic part of man. And finally, Utopia is the reconciliation of Transcendence and immanence, in a "to be said," a "to be made to say," that is, the invention, the innovation of being. It is expressed in the utopianism of Faith, which makes it possible to live now the eschatology of the incarnation.

But if we can be in agreement about all this, one has to understand then that utopianism only exists for Vahanian in its *relation* to faith, and not just any faith, but expressly the Christian faith. No utopia is acceptable without this relation, but what does not appear clearly is the point of knowing if this relation must be explicit, and again if ultimately any utopia implies this relation. In addition, utopianism is not a set of fanciful ideas, which is to say that utopianism is established in *relation* to something real, already existing. Utopianism is established in *relation* to Nature (man coming out of natural fate), or in relation to history (man coming out of historical conditioning), or in *relation*, now to Technique. But utopianism is itself constitutive of Nature, of History, and of Technique, exactly insofar as on the one hand these are constructions of man, and on the other hand, the three of them are in search of a *Novum*, but taken in themselves, the *Eschaton* is missing.

It is then a matter of positing the relation between Utopia and *Eschaton*. Vahanian elucidates this, almost always in ternary formulas. He will say for instance that if man is the event of God, Utopia is the event of the Kingdom, and the *Novum* is the event of eschatology. And here we have to replace the word "Project" in the formula that we have already cited with the word "Utopia"; to the work of the Father answers an eschatology of Nature, to the work of the Son, an eschatology of History, to the work of the Holy Spirit, an eschatology of Utopia that refers to the Pleroma and the Resurrection. Thus, conversely, it is possible to say that the *Eschaton*, as principle of creation, is constitutive of Nature (which is not a ready-made given), that as principle of redemption, it is constitutive of History (no objective reality either), and that as principle of pleroma, it is constitutive of Pleroma.

But if Utopia, the invention of man, is an indispensable dimension, we must not however overestimate it and attribute to it a place or a greatness it does not have. Man is not to put himself in the place of God, and Utopia in the place of the Kingdom; we must here reproduce this "relation of alterity" which, as we have seen, Vahanian institutes to denote the God-Man relation. He will thus say that Utopia is to the Kingdom what Nature is to

Creation, History to redemption, or the Flesh to the Spirit. It is a relation of *radical alterity*, but a *relation*, neither contradiction, elimination, exclusion. The Spirit can only become incarnate in flesh, even if the latter "has desires contrary to those of the Spirit."

Thus Creation, the work of God, can neither be known as such nor understood. It is indispensable that man work out a concept, that of Nature, that provides him with a framework to read creation, etc. And Utopia, bearing, expressing man's project, can be the expression of the truth of the already present Kingdom, for the reality of the new man (already created in us) must open up to new patterns of the human: precisely those that can be formulated in Utopia.

And now, let us move on to *Technique*. We have already said that according to Vahanian, we must not try to understand Technique from the fall, but in the perspective of the Kingdom, which points to the original goodness of creation. He therefore totally rejects one of the perspectives I adopt here.

Technique, as an enterprise of man, manifests the very reality of man, and this from the beginning. Indeed, for Vahanian, there are no differences: Technique is one, it is the same twenty thousand years ago and today. For Technique takes its standard not in imagination as compensation for the failings of the real, but in the imaginary that perfects the fullness of the real. It is the discovery of what man is in himself. And the effects of this Technique that we see are finally excellent. Technique develops artifice, but we must not forget that everything is artifice, since man's first step. It externalizes man. It makes him mobile. It forces him to let go of his obsolete traditions, and hence to go forward along the path to self-creation, and in particular the traditions of "anthropocentric rationality." It enjoins man to invent himself, to invent new lifestyles, to discover a new meaning.

Critiques of Technique are captive to ancient concepts. Vahanian rejects criticisms of efficiency (would it be bad in itself?) and of automatism. This idea of automatism is drawn from a mechanistic understanding of the laws of Nature, and this automatism has an economic and social meaning far more than a technical meaning, as should have been the case if Technique were tied to automatism.

Thus, Technique does not jeopardize humanism in the least: it is on the contrary today the sole "reservoir" of humanism, the "framework of its rebirth." Technique is born with man and cannot destroy him; Technique exists only from the moment when man becomes aware of the fact that he *is* a body, as much as he *is* a soul. And Technique appears to the body as religion does to the soul (this is not from Vahanian, but I think we can go that far). It is constitutive of the human. The process of humanization is no more endangered by technical civilization than it has been either by messianist humanism or by the humanistic naturalism of old. Man tends to be more man. This has happened by way of many enterprises, for instance by flowing into the mold of history or of nature; now this march goes on through technology. In other words, Technique, which has been a path of hominization, now tends toward the human. It is the great means of realization of the human. It is what enables us to be present to the invention of the world; it reproduces, discovers . . . the human.

And this is why Vahanian constantly slides back and forth between Technique, period, and the technique of the human, without it being possible to perceive exactly if any technique is necessarily a technique of the human, or if there are techniques and a Technique of the human, or finally if Technique might one day become a technique of the human. In the final analysis, it is even nothing but a technique of the human: "inscribing" the human in what is not human, inscribing him in what is alien to him. This is what is at stake in techniques of the human and what is at stake in technical society. Critiques confine themselves to wanting to continue the previous state, but precisely in the theological perspective in which Vahanian situates himself, the weight of the old must be abandoned.

But we must hasten to add that humanization does not automatically derive from Technique. It is only possible that Technique would make man face the demand for the human and draw him into a new adventure of alterity. But in any case, in Vahanian's eyes, one can speak of technique only from the moment when man invents himself and makes himself, and conversely, one can speak of technique wherever man invents himself and makes himself. But techniques are themselves inscribed in wholes of different types that are an always religious universe. Thus it is that techniques have been situated in a mythological universe, but now they are situated in a universe whose keynote is technological; and in all these cases, Vahanian insists on underlining that the problem of Technique is a religious one in nature. Technique does not exist by itself, but only in relation to this universe. This then leads to positing the problem of the relation between Utopia and Technique.

I could say "broadly speaking" that on the one hand Technique frees man from the constraints of Nature and of History, and thus makes him available for a *novum*, this *novum* that is just what is announced in Utopia. It is the means for the actualization of the techniques of the human, and these are the possibility of causing the hominid to tip over into the human. There is thus a precise complementarity. Techniques of the human are in themselves any humanization process that is triggered in the name of a utopianism of human reality. Humanization does not consist in realizing a utopia, like some kind of program, but is the utopia consisting in the realization of man that anticipates the human. And utopia appears at the same time as what prevents Technique from creating an unlivable world. "We can now better define this utopianism of the human reality by stating that it consists in the 'new man' who transcends the dialectic of man and the human, of hominization and humanization, and, likewise, of flesh and spirit, of art and artifice. It assumes the form of a technique set in motion by the necessity of making a clean sweep of everything in man which appears to be only a residue of the human."[6] We thus have a close relation between this Utopianism of human Reality and the process of the technique of the human.

But the play of utopia is not thereby completed. For just as there has been a utopianism of nature, and one of history, so the function of the imaginary in man also creates a utopianism of Technique, which gives it a meaning and an end. And as always, it is necessary to establish the theological relation: thus, the utopianism of nature seeks to express the notion of redemption, and the *utopianism of technique* seeks to express the notion of pleroma.

This coincides well with the fact that on the one hand, Technique is totalizing and universalizing. But what matters here is that theologically situating Technique thus of necessity places it in relation with the *eschaton*, and thus with the end of Time. The technique of the human is thus, in short, the actualized possibility of an event of the *eschaton*, and as we have seen that faith in Jesus Christ is necessarily eschatic, there is a correlation between faith and Technique. Technique challenges traditional faith, puts an end to the "mythological" understanding of transcendence, gets rid of the assumptions by virtue of which God is the object of a human experience, but does not exclude the possibility of "articulating" the transcendence of God, in the form of God's radical alterity, of which man will be the guarantor, but by being truly "himself."

Technique thus marks the birth of a new form of expression of the Christian faith (or I would rather say: the demand for this birth!) and the negation of traditional Christian religion. This transcendence demanded of God is no longer conceived from a speculative standpoint, but must be lived at the level of what Vahanian calls liturgy (service), namely: the political,

---

6. Vahanian, *God and Utopia*, 96.

ethical, social, cultural level. The Transcendence in which the revelation of Jesus Christ leads us to believe is no longer an "attribute" of God, by which God distinguishes himself from man, but a "work," where, the word having become incarnate, God collaborates with man and man with God.

This transcendence does not exclude God from the world, for the incarnation has taught us that this God, creator and father of Jesus Christ, only concerns this world. And yet, we know the countless biblical texts against "the world." Vahanian then has here a formula that is particularly strong: "If God reigns, it is neither on this nor on another world, nor on (or from) the end of the world, but on a world that is *other*." (And Technique, by decentering man from his traditional world, brings him to situate himself in relation to an other world.)

It follows that Christian faith in this God (defined by Vahanian as the reality of man who is man only insofar as he is the new man) is geared toward iconoclasm and eschatology: iconoclastic, it denies any idolatry (without for that turning into a profanation of the world); eschatological, it involves the reign of God when it gets involved in the world. But by getting involved in the world as involving the Kingdom, it is no longer sacralizing: "Neither profanation nor sacralizing, faith is above all the crucible of the human." Such are at it seems to me the basic features of this theological investigation about Technique.

I leave aside certain consequences, actually much hazier, about the liturgy and the ecclesial mutation, which are indispensable (Vahanian goes so far as to say that if ecclesial revolution fails to happen, the technical adventure will have been a failure), but where Vahanian's work reaches its limits. I will however mention as an example the analysis of "rationality—quantitative." Vahanian constructs this analysis pertaining to Technique again following his ternary model: Nature, History, Utopia.

- The rationality where nature is converted into a technique of the human is above all a metaphysical reality: quantity is measured in terms of substance and has the organism for model. A primitive period of society, economic scarcity, and the predominance of the ideology of evil and sin correspond to a utopia of abundance and a view to the end of the world, the passage beyond time.
- The rationality where history is converted into a technique of the human is above all an ideological rationality relative to which quantity is measured in terms of freedoms and has the social contract as its model. It is Reason that reigns (and no longer the "end"). History finds a meaning, which is Progress. Paradise is foreseen on earth. Abundance is possible.

- But there is a third stage, and a third possible attitude: the rationality in which it is the imaginary (fiction, utopia) that is converted into a technique of the human; then we necessarily have a technological rationality, in which quantity is measured and is expressed in terms of organization, and this is going to be formulated as Utopia. Now, in going here from the organism to the organization, there is a voluntary decision of man that modifies the real (remarkably, it is by rationalizing the imaginary that we get to the greatest grasp on the real), and thanks to Technique, it is no longer quantity that is problematic, but quality. And quality is no longer conceived in terms of "here below/ the beyond" (the abundance of the heavenly paradise), but in the here and now, in the presence of the kingdom. Technique, as the vector of the human, destroys the ideologies from which past generations have lived.

One can then glimpse fairly clearly the relation in all this: Technique—Utopia—Kingdom of God—Transcendence—*Eschaton*. I believe that in so doing Vahanian has been the first to establish the theological Status of Technique.

II.

And yet, despite the force of this construction, the theological exactness of the interpretation, the intellectual seduction of the synthesis, I cannot fully subscribe to it.

A first level of criticisms can be easily dismissed, but I will put them forward nonetheless: Vahanian is being easy on himself when he attributes to the terms he uses an entirely different meaning (which he has the honesty of giving in a glossary) than the one that is usually accepted.

- Utopia is not "what might take place precisely where there is no place."
- Myth is not "what technique takes over from."
- Technique is not "art as the art of living, the method of the human, and the application of science, which have to do with man in his whole being."

That is to say that, if we accept the (not quite arbitrary!) definitions that Vahanian gives, the construction holds. But some of his definitions are peculiar to him, and on the other hand they are strictly abstract. Of course, any philosopher, theologian, scientist, and even anyone can give a word a definition that is peculiar to him. Let us grant that designations are arbitrary. But when one takes words that have such a potential, such an intellectual and emotional charge, such a past as Utopia or Technique, one is not really quite free to make them say something else than what is necessarily evoked in the reader, at the risk of grave misunderstandings.

But I have said that these attributions of meaning are not wholly arbitrary: for Vahanian essentially starts from etymology. Now the danger here is that of disregarding the whole history and sociological weight of a word. Utopia is not what Vahanian says, but the long intellectual and sociological journey of utopias from Plato to science fiction, as Servier and Laplantine have described it.[7] When I say utopia, I am not referring to what might take place where there is no place, but to imaginary, authoritarian, closed, static, and regressive systems aimed at formulating a kind of socioeconomic paradise on earth. Now, from this point, none of what Vahanian says works.

And this leads to the other critique: the definitions are perfectly abstract and do not refer to anything actually real. Technique is not art, "as the art of living." I have several times tried to describe what Technique truly, concretely was today. It has nothing in common with what Vahanian is talking about. It is not a technique of the human in the sense he means it. It presents very specific features. And I have to reject once more the myth formulated by Mounier over thirty years ago and taken up by Vahanian, that Technique, from the first broken stone up to now, remains the same thing.[8] Vahanian's declarations on Technique do not correspond to any current reality.

Of course, that means that his theological construct does not apply to reality. In other words, he correctly resolves the problem he has set himself with the data he has chosen, but not the question that technical reality poses to us concretely today.

To be sure, one may declare, as many theologians do: "What you see and describe as reality is but an appearance; if you look deeply, Technique is indeed what we were saying beyond changes in the circumstances. In spite of and contrary to all your observations, technique is what I declare and not what you see." This is a little reminiscent of Sartre's famous dictum—which I have often cited—who, in a discussion with physicists, annoyed by their analyses, had proclaimed something like this: "As a philosopher, I know much better than all physicists what matter is."

---

7. Jean Servier (1918–2000), ethnologist and historian, *Histoire de l'Utopie*; François Laplantine (1943–), philosopher, researcher in ethnology and anthropology, *Les trois voix de l'imaginaire* [note by the family].

8. No doubt a reference to the lecture by Mounier, "Christianity and the Idea of Progress," in *Be Not Afraid*, 65–108 [note by the family].

But this is a very dangerous attitude. It reminds me of the debates of the 1930s and 1940s about the State when a positive theology of the State was being worked out based on texts about the Authorities, and where theologians absolutely refused to take into account the reality of the Hitlerite or Stalinist State, of the enormous growth of the modern State in general, etc., and answered that these accidents could not be taken into account by theology. They only neglected, among other things, that the State, properly so called, is an exclusively modern reality, and that one is not entitled to call a State just any form of political power. Biblical texts about Authorities apply (as I was trying to show around 1935) to people who are wielding political power, but not to the State!

Likewise, for Technique, there is no need do to a metaphysics of Technique, because that is the projection into the past, and in heaven, of a perfectly unknown reality. Which means that references to previous thought are inadequate. Technique is not an entity, an "ens"[9] that one can insert in a metaphysics, or if one presents it as Vahanian does, then one at least needs to explain why it is not that concretely, why, for instance, one can in no way declare that the modern technical system is a technique of the human. This central criticism having been done, there remain many specific criticisms; I am going to deal with three of them.

First of all, Vahanian starts from the idea that societies that came before technical society lived in scarcity, penury, and that it is scarcity that explains a certain theology. But this is incorrect. Fortunately, modern studies, from a historical and ethnological standpoint, show that traditional societies are not societies of scarcity; famine was almost unknown in them, aside from exceptional climate crises.[10] Scarcity only appears with urban concentration (in India), with the systematic exploitation of resources (in some areas of the Roman Empire for instance), or with explosive population growth (China). But it is mainly from the conjunction of these three factors, plus industrialization, that scarcity develops. Europe becomes more and more unhappy and in penury between the fifteenth and the late nineteenth centuries. And we must not project this on traditional societies that have been, at their level of course, societies of natural abundance. China only experienced tragic famines in the nineteenth century. Previously of

---

9. Refers to Being par excellence in scholastic philosophy [note by the family].

10. The critique of the thesis of scarcity in primitive societies might be clarified by the work of Sahlins, *Stone Age Economics* [note by F. Rognon].

course, a famine might accidentally occur, but this was not an endemic and generalized situation. In other words, the theology that Vahanian explains in this way has entirely different foundations.

Another point I have felt uneasy about is the confusion between a world that is other and that is rightly applied to the Reign of God and then ... the new world prepared, generated by technicization. It is not the correlation that disturbs me, but the fact that one could consider technical society as Other. It is not Other: it is indeed a novelty in relation to all that has been done and is known in human history, but there is no relation of alterity; it is a systematization that locks man up in a perpetual Same and prevents precisely any exit toward an other world. There is a radical rupture between technical self-increase and the alterity of God.

Finally, this causes our opposition to appear: Vahanian is seeking a certain concordism between the process of the technical "*novum*" and the divine *eschaton*. I for one see only rupture, basic contradiction, relation of opposites by violence and conflict. And I can only see that if one seeks the *Novum*, today it can only be in relation to the technical system. This is an obsolete view that consists in saying that Technique has introduced newness in relation to nature or history; it has replaced them, but is now part of the old world in relation to which the absolute newness of God is to be asserted. It is with respect to technique that critique must come into play, and no longer in relation to Nature or History. It is toward Technique that one needs to be iconoclastic, and it is what is radically challenged by the presence of the *eschaton*.

And this leads us to a third critique: Vahanian maintains that Technique must not be situated in relation to the "fall," in an infralapsarian situation, but on the contrary in relation to the original excellence of creation.[11] But here we have a difficulty between dogmatic theology, which can indeed support this and brilliantly demonstrate it as Vahanian does, and biblical theology that has to refrain from going beyond the texts.

Now, the texts are extremely clear. I will not come and repeat what I have written above. All techniques are explicitly tied to the situation of the fall, of man's revolt against God and an autonomy expressing the refusal of God (music, forge, city, etc.). There is an obvious opposition here between a systematic theology and a biblical explication.

But it must be underlined that starting from the *eschaton*, conceiving the *eschaton* as being present (something with which I am in complete agreement) need not eliminate the *initium*, and substitute for this infralapsarian

---

11. *Infralapsarian*: coming after the fall; *supralapsarian*: coming before the fall [note by the family].

initium a supralapsarian "Reschit"![12] On the contrary, it is indeed this contradiction between the *initium* of revolt and the recapitulation of grace that gives its whole meaning to the incarnation. This is what I have tried to show in *The Meaning of the City*.[13]

And in this same area, I feel rather uneasy about the total elimination of sin, the fact that Technique seems unscathed by sin. If this is the case, what are we to make of the spirit of power and domination that characterizes it? Now, to suppress this means at once failing to consider the risk of the technical adventure and completely devaluing grace (where sin abounds, grace is superabundant); but what does the Reign of God still mean apart from Grace?

This being said, there remain his main points, which represent a considerable contribution: the necessity of the *novum*, and the dialectics between the latter and the *eschaton*; all the consequences of Transcendence and God's radical alterity (with the other World, the theology of the pleroma, the relation of alterity, man as condition of God, among other things); the eschatic and iconoclastic character of the Faith; and the ternary interpretation of Nature, History, Technique (but I would prefer, as far as I am concerned, to put here: *Society*; then we would have a genuine consistent process). For all this, this work represents a theological advance which I deem decisive. But it fails to answer the question of Technique as it is today in this world.

---

12. *Reschit*, Hebrew word and *initium*, Latin word: beginning [note by the family].
13. Ellul, *Meaning of the City*.

THEOLOGY
AND TECHNIQUE

1

The Stakes of Theological Production in a Technical Society[1]

INTRODUCTION

I WAS MEANT TO come to this point, where the two series of works I have conducted until now, theological and sociological (about technical society), apparently parallel and unrelated to each other, join up. And from this point on, it will appear, clearly I believe, that all my theological writings were conceived in terms of a critique of the world in which we are, and that all my books about technical society (all the others) were the search for the real given in which the revelation may—or may not—be inscribed, in a life that claims to be Christian.

My aim here is not to judge Technique from a theological viewpoint, nor to say the absolute truth about Technique, nor to inscribe it within a beautiful construction, where everything finds its place. Theology no longer has an eminent discourse, as we well know—and if I wrote a text entitled Linguistics (or Structure) and Technique, I would immediately meet with general approval, since Linguistics has replaced triumphant Theology, with the same mistakes. One of my intentions is thus to show that, still, Theology continues to have something to say on the topic of the technical system and on technical society. And something probably decisive, penultimate, radical, and topical. More topical than any other discourse.

---

1. The title and subtitles of this chapter were suggested by the family.

Then, and this for those who consider themselves Christians, one must not forget that theology can only be an inducement to action. How could we neglect that Christian faith totally entails a practice (without being reducible to it!)? Consequently, the point is really "who to be" in such a society, which of course cashes out as a "what to do." So that one should not be reassured if one arrives at satisfactory theological formulas, at an elucidation of Technique out of Theology. It is quite clear that this is unimportant unless it issues in the concreteness of an experience that is inspired by it. There is no theological truth in itself. There is no possession of a truth.

There is light and force, daring and project, the discernment of a spirit, meaning from a transcendent that reveals itself, and that is all that theology can provide us with. It does not replace living. Turning theology into an intellectual game or a substitute for what can be experienced is betraying it. I therefore totally reject the modern discourse on theology that terms it an ideology of the ruling class.

To speak in this way, one obviously has to start by rejecting the very possibility of a Transcendent that reveals itself. And to be sure, it is legitimate when one is in no way faithful to Jesus Christ to reject it, and in this case it is true that Theology as such has nothing to say to the one who cannot listen—who literally no longer has an ear because his ear is totally stopped up by the world's clamor. But it is not legitimate to adopt this attitude if one still claims to refer to Jesus Christ, because he is nothing without the Transcendent, who is absolute Being, wholly present and become (in Jesus Christ alone) immanent. Thus, the small traditional comment on ideology has no other basis than a parroting faith, a commonplace that seems like a scientific truth in our society and that will be as forgotten tomorrow as the *Organon*[2] or the *Defensor Pacis*[3]—in any case, the issue would be, at the end of this investigation, to know if someone who invokes Jesus Christ has something specific to be or to do in this specific world that is Technique, and what. But this can only come from a properly theological reflection about Technique.

---

2. A set of logic treatises attributed to Aristotle [note by the family].

3. Work by Marsilio of Padua (1324) about the temporal power of the papacy [note by the family].

THE STAKES OF THEOLOGICAL PRODUCTION

1. TECHNIQUE AND THEOLOGY: THE TRADITIONAL POSITIONS OF THEOLOGY

I must first briefly recall, in order to dismiss them, most of the interpretations theologians give about Technique. There are, it seems to me, three currents.

One of them is simply uninterested in the issue, not understanding how there could be a theological problem. It is, I might say, the most frequent attitude among professional theologians. Deep down, they are interested in traditional philosophical problems on the one hand, and on the other hand in what the Bible (also read through traditional glasses) evokes. The modern world is not their problem.

An erudite and charming theology professor asked me twenty years ago, when I was giving a few lectures in a Theology Faculty, what my courses were about. When I told him, "the Big City," he looked at me with amazement and childlike wonder, exclaiming, "That is extraordinary; really, how can one give classes on the city? And what does this have to do with our students?" We are no longer there, but there are still many theologians (and in spite of appearances, it comes down to the same thing) who see Technique as belonging to neutral objects—*adiaphora*—about which there is no positive or negative judgment to be made, that do not raise any theological issues nor ethical ones. Technique is neutral; man may use it as he sees fit. I will not take up again the debate I have waged against this idea since 1950, or, again, how in the first Barthian line, one will say that grace alone matters and that Technique is not worth getting so worked up about, since "Grace is stronger."

Today a theologian will less easily say this, but, however, he will always find himself in a more comfortable position to debate issues that have philosophical content. One will easily conceive the debate about communism, or abortion, or structuralism, or any political problem (the Bible speaks directly about political power!) as something worth a theologian's interest and having an opinion about. He is on *his* ground (on the condition of bringing others to it!), but Technique! He thinks that theology has nothing to say, without realizing that this simply means that theology then has nothing to say to the man who is living today in this society, which also means that his message is exclusively heavenly, and that there is thus a radical treason of the Incarnation.

The two other currents can be termed, it goes without saying, the pessimistic and the optimistic. And I am compelled to say that they seem to me equally superficial, as incompetent as, for instance, the countless arrangements which we have been witnessing for twenty years to make compatible, and sometimes identify, Marxism or communism and Christianity! Simplicissimus!

The pessimistic current is elementary; it seems to have been dominant half a century ago. Either one holds, in seemingly strict Calvinist observance, that Technique is the fruit of sin, hence necessarily bad; or one ascribes to Technique a kind of apocalyptic value (it leads to the end of the world); or it belongs to "this world," as it is judged by the Gospel of John. In all those cases, it is opposed to salvation, to grace, to love, and the only possible attitude would consist in fighting it or doing without it.

It is too easy to declare that this is but a reflection of anxiety about the new, of looking back to a former time, of the incapacity of Christians to enter today's world. We can leave this aside, for this orientation is practically no longer maintained, except among ecologists.

By contrast, the other current, the optimistic one, is thriving more and more. It is then a matter of justifying technical development in various ways and of showing that it corresponds to the will of God, that if there are accidents, they are never more than accidents: Technique is essentially good and just. I will mention a few examples of these orientations.

To give honor where honor is due, we have to start with Teilhard de Chardin. He places technical evolution within a cosmic perspective. We know the general pattern: unity is the function and the criterion of cosmic becoming. Starting from a scattering, matter becomes more concentrated in stages: earth, biosphere, noosphere, etc. In this evolution, society has its place: starting from the organization of society, the future of the human species is accomplished in the Word of God. There, mankind escapes the earth, and starts to commune with God.

In this evolution of society, human scientific and technical progress, and then the very movement of life are continuous; they follow the same evolution toward more spontaneity and more organization, simultaneously. There is more spontaneity because there is a movement going from the accumulation of unstable energy toward personalization and more organization because there is a spontaneous movement of unification of personal centers. This double movement manifests the Spirit; it is thus progressive.

In this scheme, Technique has an eminent role. Today, one can recognize four effects. At the level we have arrived at in our history, Technique gathers and organizes scattered materials, enables population growth (which is an end in itself through the necessary densification), generates great social units, and causes communion between men. It therefore has a unification function once mankind has matured enough for sociological unity. Such is its first function. The second is to constitute a new matter, as an intermediate between raw matter and animated matter. It causes inert matter to participate in the ascension toward God. The third is that starting from both these premises, one can see appear a system of lines of force, and Technique is today the great agent favoring precisely the evolution toward growing states of organization and consciousness. Finally, today, with techniques of communication, information, etc., it is the decisive phase of technical socialization, of co-reflection, of unity through information, that *leads to* the maturation of the Spirit, an ultrahuman issuing from Technique, in view of building up the cosmic Christ. Technique is then a tool of spiritualization. Right now, thanks to Technique, a new kind of life is beginning; socialization (as allowed and caused by Technique) *is* the progressive concentration on a planetary scale of the potentials scattered in a suprapersonal unity. Through this movement, and in the very process of technique, man becomes christified.

We may take another example of these theologies of justification, no doubt less broad, but that had more successors in the end, that of Mounier.[4] It seems to me that we find in it two roots. First of all, the notion of progress is consonant with Christianity; history has a meaning. The movement of history is going toward something better, and this movement is the very movement of man's liberation. Now, progress today is taken up by Technique, which is a decisive moment of said liberation. Man is the author of his own liberation. Any development of man's activity is necessarily positive, since Christ has become incarnate. And if man's future is necessarily positive, the same must be true of Technique, since the latter is but the extension of man's body into the body of the world.

But the other line of theological inquiry in Mounier refers to man's created nature and to the function that is attributed to him by God. Man has a demiurgic function. Thanks to Technique, man becomes co-creator along with God of a new world. But at the same time, man creates himself; he breaks out of limits and becomes adolescent. He is called to take on new responsibilities that do not exceed his nature, but on the contrary exactly correspond to this nature! Technical activity forces man to play the role toward creation which God intended for him. It is the famous "parry to Narcissus."[5] Thanks to Technique, man leaves self-contemplation and enters his own realization.

---

4. Mounier, *Be Not Afraid*. This work includes three lectures given between 1946 and 1948 at UNESCO, at the Rencontres internationales de Genève, and at the Semaine de Sociologie: 1) "In an Hour of Apocalypse"; 2) "The Case against the Machine"; 3) "Christianity and the Idea of Progress" [note by the family].

5. The expression is from Mounier, *Be Not Afraid*, 63: "Technical activity, like work, is a weapon against narcissism." It allows man to find access to the impersonal, thereby tearing him away from the affective forces of romanticism and self-centeredness [note by the family].

Around these two major orientations, we will have the development of countless propositions that are hidden in it, but not made explicit. God's creation is not something finished, accomplished; it is a set of virtualities that God was putting at man's disposal. And he had to exploit these materials, to "explicate" these virtualities; and it will be precisely through Technique—he thus "realizes" the old world and hence God's intention.[6] On the other hand, man himself was something unfinished, unfulfilled; as long as he was in a genetic relationship with the creator, he was not the one God wanted as a counterpart, meaning that it is from the moment when he claims his autonomy and acts through Technique that man at last becomes the image of God. Moreover, it is only with the rupture with God that man's history starts—*Felix culpa!* And through this history, there has always been a discovery of the human condition as such. Technique produces humanization. It is thanks to it that man becomes a mature adult.

Finally, two other orientations may be briefly recalled. Matter as worked through by Technique is the material support of the new creation, for any matter fashioned by technical work has been primed for spiritualization. In other words, through technical work, the kingdom of God is prepared, as this matter better reflects the divine image. The history of Technique is at once human and divine, and thus every technician has his function to prepare the Kingdom of God. One could say from that perspective (Laloup and Nélis) that the more grace abounds, the more Technique progresses.[7] Every Machine is one more stage on the way to the "consummation" of any thing, that is, its fulfilment and its perfection. The last current has a more ethical connotation: Technique bears a kind of challenge to the perfection of man. It entails a development of his responsibility, of the sense of communion, a restoration of the body's validity.[8] It entails the obligation for man to reveal

---

6. The composite of commonplaces on these matters is now a given. Created in the image of God, man was made to (?) dominate Nature (?) and subdue it thanks to his intelligence (?) He is not God's competitor but his collaborator (?) If man progresses it is thanks to science and he acquires a considerable mastery that has deep theological significance (H. Fesquet).—One can of course always say anything, but this composite that rejects wholesale the whole message of the Bible, that totally ignores the reality of Technique, these excessive simplifications of a few complex hypotheses turned into truths of the faith, all this strikes me as highly improper. There is no need to search and to reflect to come to this point! A pure discourse of justification of current society! [The question marks are the author's own.]

7. Laloup and Nélis, *Hommes et machines* [note by the family].

8. This is found in Catholic writings of 1955; it is not only today, contrary to what Fernando Belo, in *Materialist Reading of the Gospel of Mark* believes, that the importance of the body is being discovered in Christianity!

himself as a free being, to make choices, and to pass value judgments. Thus Technique, by this other way, forces man to be a man.

To be sure, I will not carry out a critique of these theories, of these theological explanations. Such is not my purpose. I will confine myself to making three remarks. In all this, we are talking more of religion or spirituality, wishes and gnosis, than about theology. Furthermore, what characterizes all these systems is a profound lack of understanding, not to say ignorance, of what Technique actually is. Finally, it cannot escape even the most superficial glance that we are dealing with efforts to justify, in a religious way, the situation as it is.

In short: since Technique is the world in which we are, there must be a way that God has his place in it; there must be a way that we, Christians, can assert our relation to this world—and so we try to show that all this is indeed in accordance with God's will. It is the traditional process of 90 percent of theological activity since the fourth century. If the fierce condemnation on the part of cenobitic[9] or puritan types may be viewed as the sign of a psychological disease, inadaptation, paranoia, or prenatal anxiety, these pseudo-theological justifications may just as well be viewed as the sign of a sociological disease, a basic fear of disagreement and being singled out, or neurosis. In both cases, we are in any case dealing with a complete absence of relation to the real. I leave their truth aside. This brief reminder at least delimits certain points beyond which we ought to situate ourselves and gives the example of what may not be done. Alas, things are more complicated than these nice composers of symphonies would have us believe, and it is not in a clear and succinct judgment, provided with grounds, that the truth of the matter can reside.

2. RECEPTION OF TECHNIQUE BY THEOLOGIANS: MULTIPLICITY AND PARTIAL NATURE OF THE APPROACHES

Many authors have already tackled this issue of the relation between Technique and Theology, seeking to found Technique, to explain it theologically, and to understand it. But it seems that for all the studies I have read, almost without excepting a single one, one can make a common criticism. To be sure, their authors are good theologians, but they actually have no idea of what Technique is. They do not carry out any rigorous and complete analysis.

9. Cenobitism is a form of monastic life; unlike hermits, cenobites live in community [note by the family].

Some will deal with one aspect: for instance, the computer or telecommunications, or industrial mechanization. We will then have studies on the computer and Faith, or social reactions to mechanization. Others keep the vague, general idea of Technique one finds pretty much everywhere; they adopt commonplaces without really knowing what it is about.

Others still adopt a very self-assured viewpoint on Technique, which is that of a certain ideological current. Many theologians thus refer casually to the analysis of Technique done by Marxists or even Communists, or to the conclusions of the MIT and the Club of Rome, which goes to show to what extent these theologians have purely and simply succumbed to fashion. They *start* dealing with the central issue of our society when it is brought to the level of commonplaces by MMC[10] (Cultural Mass Media) and everyone is talking about it. It is very striking that in the review of the World Council of Churches especially devoted to this issue of technical society (*Anticipation*), there is practically no reference to the authors who have actually attempted a real analysis of the technical whole (Mumford,[11] Friedmann,[12] Simondon,[13] for instance). There is thus no global understanding of the phenomenon. Without knowing what one is talking about, one turns out to be very sensitive, for instance, to social consequences. It seems that the human is situated exclusively at that level.

Now I believe I have shown, by devoting twelve books to the study of technical society and the technical system, that we are dealing with a body which it is extremely difficult to come to know. But if one wishes to carry out a serious theological study, it is still better to know what one is talking about. All these articles are made pointless by their lack of an object. It is true that people sometimes go about it differently, by way of dialogue and comparison between scientists or technicians, and then theologians, which is excellent in some regards.

But one has to realize that the scientist, who knows very well the object of his work and his methods, does not necessarily know what science is as a sociological or psychological phenomenon. No scientist could have written

---

10. Multi Media Communication [note by the family].

11. Lewis M. Mumford (1895–1990) was an American historian who specialized in the history of technique. He wrote, among other books, *Technics and Civilization*; and *Myth of the Machine* [note by the family].

12. Georges P. Friedmann (1902–1977), a philosopher by training, is known above all as a sociologist of work. He was particularly interested in man's relations with the machine in industrial society. He wrote *La crise du progrès*; *Industrial Society*; *The Anatomy of Work*; and *La puissance et la sagesse* [note by the family].

13. Gilbert Simondon, French philosopher and author of *On the Mode of Existence of Technical Objects* [note by the family].

Weber's analysis or that of Kuhn.[14] The technician is even less capable. This is for two reasons.

- The first is that Science has been a topic of ever-more precise reflection and studies for over three centuries, especially the last hundred and fifty years, whereas those on Technique are still at the first faltering steps. The best specialists of the analysis of Technique are still at the stage of first hypotheses. Thus a scientist might be aware of works on science that have begun with Descartes and then the *Encyclopédie*,[15] but no technician knows the basic works on Technique taken as a whole; they are too recent!
- The second reason is that the scientist, in spite of his specialty, is an intellectual and may, accidentally, turn science into his research topic, with uneven results (thus Rostand, Jacob, Monod),[16] whereas the technician is, to an even higher degree, a practitioner and a man of action. He never reflects about Technique, barely on his own technique, and then only to perfect it. Thus the dialogue method is fruitful, for specialized sectors, between scientists and theologians (who incidentally are almost immediately going to veer off into metaphysical issues), but it is useless between technicians and theologians; they belong to different universes. There is no meeting ground. And since neither one of the two groups has a global understanding of Technique, they can hardly have a basic research relationship. They therefore remain at the level of opinions.

In this area, I would like to underline three common mistakes shared by almost all of these works by theologians on Technique. The first one is that they approach the question under its philosophical aspect, that is, its permanent one. There have always been techniques; man is a technician. What there is to search for, to understand, or to elucidate is that feature. Technique is a permanent phenomenon, and without asking oneself any other questions, it is the technical fact in itself that one will be considering. In other words, one will reason theologically, indiscriminately, on the technique of Australopithecus breaking the first *pebble*[17] as on that of the

14. Thomas S. Kuhn (1922–1996), American philosopher, historian of science. He is known above all for his work *Structure of Scientific Revolutions* [note by the family].

15. Of Diderot and d'Alembert [note by the family].

16. François Jacob (1920–2013), biology researcher, Nobel Prize winner in 1965 with Jacques Monod. Among his works: "L'évolution sans projet"; and *Possible and the Actual* [note by the family].

17. *Pebble* [translator's note: in English in the original]: a flint nodule used in prehistoric times to make weapons and tools [note by the family].

computer. For all theologians, there is an identity between ancient and modern techniques. It is Technique and that is all. They fail to ask why the question never occurred to theologians before the last few years. The problem of work was always raised, never that of Technique. It is true that in many of these studies, Technique is almost immediately reduced to work, a very secure commonplace. They are thus quite ignorant of what is specific to Technique in our society (and I am saying Technique, not some of *its* consequences) and so cannot say anything about it from a theological standpoint. They fail to realize that there have been two radical upheavals, that of the late eighteenth century that would give rise to industrial society and that of 1939–1945 that gives birth to technical society, and that there is strictly nothing in common between the Technique of our developed world and all that mankind has known for two million years. They fail to realize that there, more than anywhere else, the famous play of the quantitative and the qualitative is at work.

The second reproach I would make against almost all these studies is that they are almost never theological; they almost instantly come down to moral issues. It is a matter of behavioral issues, and hence people talk at an ethical level; now, to be sure and as we will see, there is indeed a set of ethical issues, but there are first some basic theological issues. Rare are those (like Vahanian for instance) who have situated Technique in an eschatological perspective. Most often therefore, people will be content to pass judgments about Good and Evil on Technique, to sort out good and bad techniques, which proves that they have no idea what they are talking about, but conditions the attitude that is the object of my third critique.

Almost all these studies have a political orientation (and particularly those of the World Council of Churches); they are implicitly and sometimes explicitly beholden to the conviction that everything can be resolved by a political path—be it regime change (Technique ceasing to be harmful in a socialist world), or a new political orientation (making Technique serve the Third World, instead of making it an instrument of domination). In all these cases, people think with the certainty that everything is a matter of politics, and that thanks to politics we will master and change Technique. This is why these many studies will be of little help to us.

3. TECHNIQUE AND TRANSCENDENCE

In finishing this introduction, I would like to raise a basic theological issue that I will not otherwise need to debate. I would like to formulate it as follows: the technical system in its effective current reality makes the

Transcendent unavoidable. Is our God only the Jesus of Nazareth who walked on our earth, who was poor, who knew all of man's hardships and *thereby*, thereby *only*, showed us who God is? As is sometimes said, this is a God who is wholly immanent and who is weak. We know all the explanations about religion and the God of the gaps. I will not take them up anew.

But I would like to take up the question in a very different way. If one knows what the technical system is,[18] one is compelled to understand it as something totally global. That is to say that, on the one hand, it is a totality, and on the second hand, that it covers, alters, qualifies the totality of aspects of human, social, political, intellectual life, of human relationships as well as of artistic research, and it turns *all of them* into something else. Finally, it absorbs, recycles, and assimilates all that is born outside of it. All acts and thoughts of protest end up being turned in favor of the technical system and finding their place in it. The *fear*, so frequent among the young, of being "recycled by the system" is the expression of reality (they are only mistaken in the way they refer to the system, when they think it is capitalism). The technical system is what is totally global, unavoidable, and unassailable.

Therefore, if we accept to be reduced, spiritually and in "religion," to the sole and exclusive horizontal relation (following Feuerbach),[19] this brings with it some important consequences. First, there is no reference point that would make it possible to cast judgment on this system. The reference to Jesus of Nazareth is *nonexistent*, for he has not been anything but a possible model in a nontechnical traditional society, but there is *no* common measure with what we know. He can neither be a model, nor a reference point, nor an inspiration—Nothing. In its globalness, the technical system excludes what was prior to it, and which has become perfectly meaningless and *obsolete*. As for our time, the technical system absorbs all that is outside to make it a part of the system (which is happening for instance with the tragedy of Third World countries, that find there their true new slavery). There is no outside reference that might exist, least of all the life or conduct of Christians.

Secondly, still keeping the hypothesis of an atheistic Christianity, no more is there—and this is a consequence of the first point—any possibility of a critique. If no reference point outside the system can be imagined, one cannot have any view *upon* this system from the point of a nonintegrated perspective, and as a result, no critique can be carried out, first in terms of this view, and then according to different criteria. And this is why, in fact, the studies I am criticizing are readily to be situated within the system

18. And I have no choice but to refer to my own works!
19. Feuerbach, *Essence of Christianity* [note by the family].

in question! There is no possibility of a critique in either sense: neither of putting into question, nor of division. To carry out a critique of either kind, one has to be outside what one is criticizing oneself (self-criticism is the obvious fact of an external thought that penetrates you and forces you to put yourself into question!). One needs to have a fulcrum, another scale of values, an external instrument of analysis to do this critique. The surgeon who performs the removal of a tumor and makes this "critique" cannot be inside the patient. Now, the technical system in its globality excludes any other scale of values as another viewpoint, making it strictly inoperative. And it assimilates instruments of analysis and criticism by placing them in the now classic dilemma: either they can be efficient, and then they are necessarily technical, and they partake of the technical system, reinforcing it by criticizing it—or they remain outside of technique, and for that very reason are inefficient and worthless.

The third consequence, still keeping the hypothesis of the death of God (of the transcendent God, etc.), is that this world is henceforth without an opening, without any way out, either in its present condition or in its historicity. There is no other possibility than to enter the technical path; there is no prospect of having any life that is different. The hippie experiment is a recurrent phenomenon without any significance. One cannot open this world from the inside toward something else. Technique has truly subdued everything; it is gradually closing. It is literally becoming the equivalent of a *Fatum*, of *anankê*, of fate, of destiny. On the one hand, nothing can make it vary in its logic; on the other hand, it indefinitely totalizes itself through its very contradictions (for, of course, it includes thousands of internal contradictions, but which make it progress). Likewise, when it comes to the future, no hope is possible, for everything is determined by the play of the technical system. I do not want to say that this system works well, but that it works on its own; it can lead to catastrophe, but nothing can prevent it from working.

There is no other way out than these two possibilities: on the one hand, the system does not work well and produces chaos, with unimaginable losses (see Roberto Vacca and what Bernard Charbonneau would lean toward),[20] for everything will be practically annihilated due to the system's very globality; on the other hand, the system works well, and this would be something equivalent to the brave new world (which I was inclined to believe in my first study on Technique), but with a consequence as catastrophic as it is final, as what is going to be produced will not be a kind of normalized, stabilized, artificial paradise, indefinitely reproducing

---

20. Vacca, *Coming Dark Age*; Charbonneau, *Le système et le chaos* [note by the family].

THE STAKES OF THEOLOGICAL PRODUCTION

itself, but will be real entropy, producing second-degree chaos in its turn. These two ways out are strictly tied to the globality of the technical system; there is strictly nothing else to hope for in the future. Such are the three consequences of horizontal theology.[21]

If a hope is still possible, if there is any prospect that man might still live (it is true that we have a growing world of thinkers, structuralist philosophers, and linguists and behaviorists who accept with a light heart the disappearance of man—being in this perfectly consistent with the technical system they best express), if there is still meaning to life and history, if there is a way out aside from suicide, if there is a love that is not integrated in Technique, if there is a truth that is not useful to the system, if there is at least the taste, the passion, the desire and a hypothesis for freedom, one must realize that this can now rest nowhere but in the Transcendent, and very specifically, in the Transcendent as it is unveiled in Christianity. That is the Transcendent that reveals itself in such a way that it can be understood and received by man, the Transcendent that is said in the word, but that remains no less Transcendent for that. A pure Transcendent, remaining the unknowable object of negative theology, is also perfectly nonexistent for man, and if he were to intervene, it would then (and only then) that one would be dealing with the famous *Deus ex Machina*.

But what Jesus Christ reveals to us is not just the example of Jesus of Nazareth, nor his permanent presence in the poor. It is precisely the Transcendent, who has drawn near to us. A classic and banal theology? To be sure! But there is no other. For any other theological discourse is strictly reduced to nil by Technique. Only the pure Transcendent, because it is exterior and strictly unassimilable, whatever the extension of the technical system, provides us with a different reference point, vantage point, critical apparatus. It alone makes it possible to carry out a critique of the system. It alone makes it possible not to get locked up inside the dilemmas of Technique on the one hand, inside moral evaluation on the other hand. Of course, all this is not guaranteed or given in advance. It is not something easy, for at this level of analysis, we are not to expect the Transcendent to intervene as such. It is obviously *we* who are supposed to make do with this, to act, but it is the possibility for our intervention to take place, without which no human action with respect to the universally global is possible. In other words, the Transcendent is not first, at this level, *what does*, but

---

21. And this conveys the extent of the superficiality of so-called liberation theologies or Revolution theologies, that no doubt start from generous good intentions, but that evolve in total ignorance of our world's real (and not dream) condition. Of course, these are theologians who claim to know the real condition because they know the Third World's concrete destitution. But they are far from having understood its reason.

simply the condition for us of *a doing* (still in relation to this universally global). It is the presupposition without which the very idea of extraneousness with respect to modern Technique is not possible. Those who, from a philosophical or theological standpoint, believe the opposite, or rather, do not even raise this question nowadays, but who, when they see my statement, will fail to see its importance, only show thereby that they have no idea of what the reality of the technical milieu today is.

But, people may say, this God who is then necessarily transcendent in the condition indicated is not so different from the gods of Nature, of the time when Nature was the environment in which man found himself. There too, a transcendent god was needed who would allow man to fight nature, to have an external reference point so as to be able to precisely situate himself in relation to him and win the certainty that he could survive and dominate the hostile world of nature. I would tend to agree. And I can already hear the triumphal chant saying: "So your Transcendent is a pure 'religious' and has nothing specifically Christian about it."

Before answering, I would however want to make two observations. The first is that the technical environment is a voluntary and abstract artificial system. Hence the Transcendent God must be consciously heard, clearly recognized as the transcendent, and of a nonspecialized universality. The second is that the technical system, precisely as a creation of man, comes from inside man, demands heartfelt adherence on man's part, and develops the means of inner possession; man is manipulated from the inside as he has never been in the course of his history. His adherence to the natural world was spontaneous, immediate; his adherence to the technical world is now produced by transformation techniques. An equivalent to the old gods of Nature is therefore totally insufficient. What is needed is a transcendent that is really transcendent and not just believed to be so by man. What is needed is a transcendent that does not leave this brain and this heart, failing which it would be absolutely nothing more than the reflection of the technical system itself. One could say that the gods of Nature, also understood, for some, as transcendent, were also just reflections of the natural world; so I will remind the reader that, rather surprisingly, the god of Israel, for his part, was not that. He was really different from the others. And now, it is this same God who, as Transcendent, absolutely does not coincide with the technical environment, and because he is not the *product* (even necessary, even indispensable in order to survive as man) of man's heart and mind, he alone is in a position to fulfill the office of salvation in this time.

But there is a second axis of reflection. We have said that it is obvious that this transcendent must at the same time be the one that reveals itself, so that we are no longer dealing with a Transcendent as a hypothesis that man posits in order to have an external reference point from which a critique would be possible. If a critique is felt as necessary, and man then gives himself the means of fulfilling it, just as a geometer posits a point outside of his figure so as to, starting from it, trace the needed line (but one then forgets if one makes this comparison that this geometer is not *in* the figure!), this Transcendent remains a purely human hypothesis. Already at the end of the previous point, we had noted that this transcendent cannot, to play the role of providing critique, be a pure fiction, a hypothesis that disappears once the conclusion is known. Now, and how could it be otherwise, with the movement of revelation, we are dealing with a Transcendent who acts, and thus *is* in itself.

Because the Transcendent reveals itself, this means that this world, as closed as it is, can never actually be closed, it cannot fulfill itself, it cannot perfect itself, close itself in a total system. This technical world is exactly subject to the story of Babel, there too, a city built to enclose human totality (including its gods). A universal city—and a world from which the transcendent was to be eliminated: the walls of Babel were meant to exclude this God, maybe leaving him a door. But now it comes about that precisely because he is the God who reveals himself, he declares, "Let us go down and see . . ."; and then, Babel bursts.[22] The opening comes from the outside.

And in the same way, while we, willy-nilly, can only continue the movement that tends to perfect, develop, improve the technical system and so continue to close the system that keeps us prisoners, while we cannot carry out any opening, any breakthrough from inside, now it comes about that we receive the assurance that the one who is inassimilable, impossible to recycle, will proclaim: "Let us go down and see . . ."

From then on, if we hear this word, and if we believe in this God of Jesus Christ, Transcendent, Father, and already come, we can conceive a hope, we can live a hope, whatever the situation of the world in which we are. An opening is always possible. Thus a meaning can be received, discovered, and given. Thus there is a possibility of a history to *make*, a history other than that of Technicization, of man's inscription in the technical world. This is a history that is no longer mechanical and necessary, but on the contrary to be invented, and a history that does not end in catastrophe, whatever the guise of that catastrophe. Because there is a Transcendent that can indeed come and upset the givens, it is still possible for man to make a history of his own, without being radically defined, circumscribed, carried by a *Fatum*. But this is exactly the only guarantee, the only possibility.

---

22. After Genesis 11:7 [note by the family].

Here we must answer one last objection: do we not find here the *Deus ex Machina* who, intervening from outside, is going to resolve everything? The God of the gaps which we locate in this transcendent because we cannot resolve our own problems and which we entrust with resolving them in our place? It would be tempting to do this conflation, but unfortunately it is totally impossible. One must first realize that *all* theologies that reduce God to this world are in reality instances of ideological conformity to the sociology of this world. Why is there this exclusion of the Father God, of the Transcendent, of the Unheard-of, of the Creator, of the one who can intervene through miracles and wonders, of the vertical orientation? It is exclusively, and I do mean *exclusively*, i.e., excluding any other reason and foundation, because the technical system convinces us that there is nothing beyond itself.

This should take us into another path of investigation, which after all is not without reference to "*Technique and Theology*," namely: what is the status, the role, the function of theology in a technical society? I have touched upon it incidentally in some of my books (*The New Demons*, for instance), but it would be worth making a systematic study of it, and then one would realize that this modern theology is the exact reflection, the ideological product of Technique, meant to help the latter to fulfill, close, and perfect itself. Affirming a Transcendent in relation to Technique is today the way of nonconformity.[23]

23. As for the famous argument, ever-repeated, according to which, if one wants to proclaim the Gospel to today's man (called irreligious!), if one still wants to be able to talk about Jesus Christ, one must abandon all the "religious" concepts and vocabulary of yesteryear and, in particular, no longer talk of Transcendence (evidently excluded by science), it is particularly stupid under an appearance of reason. First of all, there is no doubt than man has always desired to be told things that pleased him, that suited him, that did not risk putting him in disagreement with himself, nor in conflict with his milieu! How could it be otherwise? Formerly plunged into a world not of his making, he needed to be talked to in "supernatural religious" terms because that fitted with his experience (and neither the God of Israel, nor Jesus Christ fitted!). Today, because he is plunged into the mechanical world he has manufactured, he needs to be rid of the Transcendent; it goes without saying. But by obeying this demand, we are doing strictly nothing more than what the producers of ordinary religious language have always done. This is the religious discourse that modern man expects. It is this that causes neither contradiction nor drama; it is not only a question of being able to communicate. It is in effect revelation's adaptation, fitting to the cultural and technical environment, hence its elimination!

As for the other side, according to which science has shown the nonexistence of the Transcendent, one has to be very naive; science started out by positing as a premise, as a hypothesis, as a basic given, this very nonexistence. It has made its way all along by ignoring it. And, at the end, it finds again what it had posited at the beginning. But nothing has been "proven." Everything resides in a set of assumptions (that make the scientific process possible) producing *beliefs* (Monod is typical of this kind

THE STAKES OF THEOLOGICAL PRODUCTION

Do not conform to the current age; this is now what we are supposed to do. But there remains one last step. This Transcendent is not a *Deus ex Machina*, nor a God of the gaps because, as we know very well, it reveals itself, meaning that it manifests in all sovereignty, by a free action, unforced and in our eyes uncertain, and without any necessity—in other words, even if we fully believe in this Transcendent, we have no guarantee. There is no mechanism in place. There is no liberation that comes into play automatically. He *may* intervene.

And on the other hand, all we know about it, in Jesus Christ, is that he loves his creature, his creation, and that he comes to liberate and save. We therefore *think* that he will intervene—and we live in this hope, are driven to *act* ourselves in this *love*. But if it is true that we must act ourselves, it is absolutely not sufficient that we have the conviction of a transcendent that would be illusory and purely subjective. The subjectiveness of faith cannot suffice in this instance and replace the objectiveness of the Transcendent.

I do not enter the terms of the debate between Bultmann and Barth; being philosophical, this debate is infinite—but here we are not doing philosophy. I am tempted to take up again the quarrel that Marx led against the young Hegelians when he said: since the latter think that revolution by the Idea is the revolution, and they attack private property at the philosophical level, thereby thinking they have done everything, they end up making an idea of revolution, and destroying an idea of property, even as the economic-legal reality of private property remains as is and the condition of the exploited has not changed in any way.[24] Likewise, we are not dealing with a purely subjective phenomenon that puts us into question; the technical system is terribly objective, real, exterior to us. And it is this—not the idea that we have of it nor the impression that we get of it, nor some small individual drawback—that we have to master or to fight against according to the case. The idea of a Transcendent reduced to my subjective faith, of a Risen one living only in the heart of his disciples and then in ours, may give me the inclination to do it, but assuredly no sufficient possibility. I will then have the impression of having liberated myself, but nothing more.

It is a matter, *in this event* (I am not going beyond), of a Transcendent who objectively, effectively intervenes and on his own. But it is never a matter of anything except a pure possibility. Nothing ever forces him to do it. And when we read the biblical story at the beginning of the liberation of the people of Israel out of Egypt, we indeed see that this God goes silent for

---

of procession! [in the sense of theory; note by the family]), nothing more. And we have seen elsewhere to what extent modern man is religious, but religious in a non-Christian way and unable to tolerate the Transcendent. This is something else.

24. Doubtless Marx, *Critique of Hegel's Philosophy of Right* [note by the family].

centuries, between Joseph and Moses, and for generations the people he has chosen are going to weep, cry, call out, suffer, certainly not understand why this God is not coming—and then one day, God remembers. One day, he has turned toward Israel. One day—nobody knows why. So there is no historical certainty, nothing mechanical about this decision. We are perfectly given over to our problem and our fight. But the faith in the possibility of the sovereign God's decision, a faith that rests on the knowledge of the fulfillments of his promises, on the reality of his presence in Jesus Christ (but indeed the presence of the Transcendent in Jesus Christ, without which he is nothing more than an interesting example of a certain ideal of humanity): this faith gives something to live from because the game is not over.

The game is not over, not because the technical system is not closed yet, nor because I can still intervene; no, we can say, "The game is not over, because the Transcendent, *for his part*, can intervene!" And in this latitude, in this play that exists in the pieces of the puzzle, I however can inscribe myself as a living person. Thus, this Transcendent is already now creative of newness, even within the technical environment, and this newness is the effective hope that he causes to be born. But it is truly an external creative act. It is not a natural spontaneous production of my belief or my ideology. Such is, I believe, the first theological element that the technological system forces upon us.

It is from this first given, a fundamental one, that the rest of these developments are built, even if I do not constantly refer to it. Finally, for those who do not accept this Transcendent as ultimate reality, beyond our knowledge and our experience, it then has to be admitted that there is strictly no other future than the technical end, in all senses of the word, and the end of the human, in the sole sense of elimination.

2

Situation of a Theological Reflection on Technique[1]

1. MAN, NATURE, AND THE ARTIFICIAL

I DO NOT PROPOSE to start here with an anthropology, still less with a theological anthropology, or a biblical one. I would like to say (but it is not quite true!) that I will begin with an anti-anthropology. I cannot base myself on a philosophy, be it of essences or of existence, for none of them seems decisive to me. I would be very tempted, out of laziness of mind, a need for clarity and security, to accept the idea of a constant human Nature, but I see as a historian or sociologist so many diversities (nonessential to be sure, but still radical!) and contradictions, that I do not know what this nature boils down to. I could start by defining it, and declaring that everything that goes against it is unnatural, but I have always been loath to cast such arbitrary moral judgments. And I feel caught between the recognition of an effective common ground between all humans (along the lines of: all humans have two arms and two legs) and the realization that it is so poor and insignificant that I don't really see what it could be useful for. Then there is the idea that almost everything is variable and that man makes himself and does not preexist with an immutable given, as experience confirms, and then how do we understand the genesis and effective creation not of an empty potentiality, but of a being existing before God and fully armed![2]

 1. The title and subtitles of this chapter were suggested by the family.
 2. Translator's note: likely an allusion to the Greek myth of the goddess Athena's birth out of Zeus's brow as an adult in full armor.

It seems to me that we may attempt to start from at least two observations that are rather generally accepted in anthropology, prehistory, sociology—namely, that man is a peculiar animal from the start, peculiar in that he was physiologically less well-adapted to a given environment than all other animals. He is not exactly adjusted to the natural environment. His hand is far less precise, efficient to cut than a lobster claw, his leg much less exactly calculated to run than the leg of the leopard or the deer. But if he is less perfect in his structure, he is polyvalent. He can on the one hand become integrated (to varying degrees) in the most diversified environments—on the other hand perform tasks, each less perfect, that are infinitely more varied than any other animal can handle. In each case, it will be less well than the animal, but he survives where the animal disappears. Take a cheetah to Greenland, it dies. Man becomes an Eskimo. Take a polar bear to the Kalahari, it dies. Man becomes a Bushman. And in his lack of perfect adaptation that expresses an almost infinite adaptability, man is never totally in harmony with the environment in which he finds himself. The animal is always in perfect harmony, wondrously fitted to the role it has to play in such an environment. But when a glaciation occurs, warm-weather animals disappear; man buries himself in caves and uses fire. The animal thus takes part in a given general equilibrium, where it plays exactly its role, whereas man appears as a predator, and a parasite. He is always a little exterior to this natural environment, intervening in it by disturbing it. He behaves as a parasite, often using the wrong way what the animal would use correctly. He is not a necessary and cohesive element for a given environment; he does not belong to the wondrous environmental equilibrium that exists between given flora and fauna.

This leads to the second feature we must acknowledge in man. From his origins, and precisely because he is in this situation, man seeks to explore the environment, to make it suitable for him, and what is more, to annex it. From the outset, man has sought to develop the environment in which he lives (and this is what is referred to by the famous remarks according to which we can only be sure of dealing with human bones when they are accompanied by tools, however elementary these may be). I think it is a very superficial and insufficient view that has led people to talk of *Homo faber*, or to believe that man invented tools to strengthen his defense, improve his hunting, etc. These inventions that build on each other and always go in the same direction are actually ways for man to have a grasp on the environment. He seeks to alter this environment to make it favorable to him. Man is first and foremost a developer. We were saying a little before that, taken to an unfavorable world, he "adapts" (while always remaining less adapted than the native animal), but it is not only he who adapts. He also adapts the

SITUATION OF A THEOLOGICAL REFLECTION ON TECHNIQUE

environment to himself, so as to be able to survive. He is a developer; he can create another order than the one that existed before him. Because of this, he disturbs the natural order, and he does not respect it, although, to be sure, he cannot do just anything.

But the question is then: if he cannot do it, is it because he lacks the means to do it or because he is so well integrated in the natural order that he cannot ontologically transgress it? Without a doubt in my eyes, it is the first proposition that is the right one. Everywhere man can concretely succeed in creating a totally artificial environment, he does it (the city): if this is indeed man's place in relation to any environment, we therefore say that there is not for man a natural order that imposes itself to him of necessity, and that man, wherever he appears and exactly within the limits of his means, creates a different, artificial order, one that situates itself in symbiosis with the natural order that at times it deeply disturbs, and at other times it replaces.

One needs to understand that had it been otherwise, that is if man had remained exactly in a status of nature, obeying exactly the laws of the environment, he would have disappeared as being everywhere less well adapted than animals. But, one could say, it is not only conformity to the environment but also conformity to animal nature. Man is after all an animal like the others: there is a common nature, and this is the one we need to consider. If it were so, one would have to admit that in reality, man would have never taken off from his animal status. He would have gone through the same cycles indefinitely and started again the same experiences. He has an "animal nature," it is obvious, but what is most remarkable is that, just as he appeared as a developer of his environment, likewise he purported to escape animal identity. There too, it was a question of life and death. He tends to go beyond what his animal structure imposed to him as limits, to compensate for whatever was a weakness in him. This means therefore that animal nature is not a model for man either. He is a man precisely because he is going to do something other than what the animal would have done. There again, it is transgression and not imitation, identification, adaptation.

Let us note incidentally that this comes into play in very different senses. For a long time, man's common animal base was presented to us as an aspect of nature to be respected, an unbreakable given (and this belonged to the *Natura* of Roman jurisconsults) to lead us to some kind of moderation, of respect. But today, other behaviors come to be legitimated; we have been able to read, for instance, that since dogs are spontaneously and indistinctly attracted to both sexes, this justifies bisexuality in man. The search for the "Natural," with an animal model, to destroy morals, taboos, etc., has become a "revolutionary" attitude, whereas this defense of what is natural was traditionally reactionary. The good innocents who justify their cravings and their glandular secretions in this fashion fail to realize that they exactly negate themselves in their totality, instead of attaining an authenticity!

Man has distanced himself from the animal in such a way that there is no longer a spontaneous animal nature that might represent a limit for man, nor an animal behavior that might in any way serve as a model. Man cannot be founded on animal nature since it just so happens he has transgressed it. That the way of this transgression is diverse and variously interpreted is obvious, but it seems to me that in any case this may boil down to the establishment of a meaning attributed to acts and behaviors. It is because man has considered such and such a gesture and given it a meaning other that the one it concretely and immediately held that he split off from animality.

A lot has been said over the last few years about the experience of death, but the experience of one's own death is only known through, on the one hand, the death that one gives to another, and on the other hand, the refusal of the death of those near to us. And the first case is symptomatic. The animal kills, and it eats, and everything ends there. Man asks the question of this death and of the meaning of the act he has performed. Now this is closely related to the status of man as developer that we were speaking about earlier. He is that not by instinct (of what?) nor by reaction, nor by imitation, etc., but simply because he asks the question of the meaning of what he risks and what he *must* do to survive. This is why the apparently triumphant dogma of materialisms (matter precedes consciousness) is absurd: if man had simply been originally what Marx or Skinner describe, he would have instantly disappeared.[3] Man worked because the awareness of the environment was having its effect; he changed this environment, whatever name one gives it. What makes man is not the tool, but the idea of making a tool.

Having this idea of something artificial implies infinitely more than what we think. This implies that each event, each gesture also take on meaning. In other words, acts can remain naturally the same in animal terms. The sexual act, birth, death, and suffering are all animal acts. But man ascribes them a value and orientation and situates them in a continuity, an order, that makes them other. The rites, taboos, prescriptions, prohibitions, morals, myths, magic, graphic representations, *carmina*[4]—all this is what causes man to transform the natural animal act into a human act. Take that away, and man literally disappears. There does not even remain the animal, since

---

3. Skinner, *Science and Human Behavior* and *Beyond Freedom and Dignity*.

4. Translator's note: As a specialist of ancient Rome, Ellul is referring to *carmina*, plural of the Latin word *carmen* for song, hymn, charm, spell, ritually chanted for religious or, more often, magical purposes.

man is the weakest of all animals. If he works and defends himself, it is not due to some mysterious vital drive, to some defensive instinct of the species, but because he ascribes a meaning to what he does.

This comes into play at every level. Benveniste has rightly written, "Using a symbol is the capacity to identify the characteristic structure of an object and to identify it in various contexts. It is that which is *peculiar to man* and which makes man a rational creature."[5] This operation of symbolization is not just intellectual but encompasses the whole of "Nature and Man." Man is a developer; man distances himself from the animal because he is a symbolizer. He superimposes on the whole of animal behavior a symbolic whole.

Thus we see a second degree of the order wanted, invented by man. On the natural order of environmental equilibria, he superimposes an artificial order, produced by his equipment. On the natural order of animality, he superimposes an equally artificial order, the symbolic one. The same sexual, "family," nutritional, etc. reality becomes—effectively, totally (and not in an illusory fashion!)—other. One can then no longer take nature nor the animal as a model. Man creates an artificial human universe, from the origins. Had it not been this way, again, he would have disappeared. And it is because this universe exists that he will be able to accomplish "what no beast in the world" will. This happens both positively and negatively. He will dedicate himself in the extreme, go beyond the limits of any natural resistance, and invent, like no beast in the world. And he will destroy, slaughter, and torture, like no beast in the world.

But is there not at least a specific nature of man, so that it is precisely by this nature that he was thus led? I am afraid I have to say that what seems to me to characterize this being that is a stranger in every place, strange in every environment, is just that he does not have an immanent nature of his own. We have seen that he is maladapted and undetermined from the outset. He invents himself according to times and places, and there is neither an ideal prior model from which we would have fallen, nor an ideal model to come which we would have to realize, nor a kind of ground common to all mankind (which would be rather small, incidentally, given the incredible diversity of mores and morals). He sets a rule that can be taken for natural, but he transgresses it so hugely that one cannot know whether man is not the antithesis of this rule. Take the commandment "You shall not kill," to which we will return, and which is indeed basic. But precisely, man kills, indefinitely and in all forms. Is his "nature" to set this rule or to kill?

---

5. Benveniste, *Problems in General Linguistics*, 23 [note by the family; emphasis Ellul's].

THEOLOGY AND TECHNIQUE

Each time one has wanted to find a natural principle in man—reason, sociability, religion, work, etc.—one finds the exact counterpart that seems just as natural. Why would man not first be a being of fancy and folly, a nature that makes society and challenges it (as he has recused environmental equilibrium), a transgressor and violator of holy things, a sloth—this is just as "natural." It is as though what is proper to man is precisely deviation, the recusal of rules he sets according to nature or decision.

In any case, nowhere is there any evidence of such a nature. The rules he sets, as we have seen, are artificial in relation to the natural and animal environment, and if they are in conformity to his own nature, here he is now constantly transgressing them, and this precisely because they are artificial!—and he discerns and knows it full well.

The major mistake then, about this point, on the part of theologians, has been to believe that God's will was ultimately the Natural in man. Either that God had imposed a certain prefabricated nature, inherent in his creation—or that the law of God, made explicit for the Jewish people, was identified with a nature. Both reasonings are false. It is quite impossible to identify the God of biblical Revelation, who is precisely Non-Natural from every point of view, with any kind of nature. It is impossible that the law *revealed* as an astonishing truth to a chosen people corresponds to a latent common nature. It is no less impossible that the God whose only revelation (in the Old and the New Testaments) is that he is the liberator would have, as it were, predetermined a nature at this summit of creation that is man, having a specific calling of love and worship that both presuppose freedom. In other words, that God did not create a human automaton, endowed with natural mechanisms producing expected effects; he created a freedom, which of course immediately opens the field to indeterminacies. So what we were trying to discover above about man being indeterminate, maladapted, etc., seems to me to correspond to the biblical God's creative will, which in no way establishes an order for man nor an order in man, but institutes a freedom, a being of freedom, with the chance that goes with it.

Man is therefore not endowed with any model nature, with any preestablished moral consciousness, with any compulsory and determining Nature. He is one undetermined. It is exactly to the extent that he answers in this way to his calling that he is, becomes, makes himself man—but he can also not answer it! In other words, he only lives in the artificial. He reworks and produces the environment that he needs in order to live as an artificialized nature. He transcends his "animal" nature in a symbolic order (of the imaginary) and only realizes his human being by producing this artificiality. Consequently, we must say that man is indeed a denatured animal, but this not in the least in a pejorative sense, for it could not be otherwise; he could

SITUATION OF A THEOLOGICAL REFLECTION ON TECHNIQUE

only become man by ceasing to be fitted to a nature. He does not have a model nature. And due to this fact as well, there is no point in seeking a human paradigm. There can be none, except in this very creation, in those successive inadaptations.

But it is necessary here to specify that when I ascertain this concordance between this view of man taken by a number of current studies, and then what theology can say about it, I in no way mean to reinforce, still less to prove the one by the other, nor to say that theology is right since certain orientations of human sciences lead to the same result, nor to provide these with a complement of certainty through theology. This has no value. We are dealing with two levels of ascertainment and methods. I will confine myself to taking stock of the coincidence, at least at the level of some current knowledge and some theological interpretations—as I know very well that all theology does not play out that way! We have known, and still know, a massive theological affirmation of the fixedness of the human species, of the existence of a permanent nature, etc. Of necessity, the question can arise of knowing if, in the final analysis, theology is not talking rubbish, according to the circumstances or the sociopolitical or intellectual currents in which the theologian is immersed. I have often dealt with this question elsewhere. I will limit myself here to say that this idea of a God who creates a free creature is fundamentally biblical, and represents a fairly general tendency in theology, but the same consequences are not always drawn from the concept of creation and that of freedom. It is here that the difficulty begins.

One must of course emphasize from that point on that society is an artificial phenomenon. It is not because, as soon as man exists, we find him in society that the latter should be viewed as his nature, as founded in nature. The existence of a society was, like the use of tools, a *sine qua non* solution of man's survival in a hostile environment. But we need not seek to fuse this society into some human Nature, a nature that would for instance be "sociable" (which does not mean anything). That would again be seeking to give qualitative precedence to the "Natural": for something to be legitimate, it would have to be founded in Nature, to be natural. On the contrary, we know full well that there has never been a primitive society; as soon as man exists as such, he is in society. As soon as society exists, it is not the indistinct, shapeless horde where the physically strongest prevail; it is an artificial, complex arrangement, entailing a symbolic network, a set of common beliefs, a hierarchy of combinations. Society is always and from the beginning a structured whole whose invention is not due to a natural expression, but to a deliberate search of an artificial type.

But there again, we have an evaluation problem to do, for a system that might have been quite acceptable when the social body was limited in quantity and in means of action can become intolerable by growing fast and giving itself extremely powerful techniques. There is no comparison between a "primitive natural" and a "civilized artificial," only the comparison between two equally cultural and artificial forms of society.

Thus what we have explicated leads us to reject the famous opposition between the Natural and the Cultural; nowhere and at no time is there a Natural in man. The Natural or Nature is what allows man to live, to survive, what provides him with the raw material of his history and his activity, at the same time as it endangers him. The Natural is the challenging of man by circumstances, his constant negation. Nature is what tends to eliminate this predator, this parasite, so as to regain its equilibrium. Man *is not* of Nature. He is *within* this nature, which is something else altogether.[6] He uses it, but it is hostile to him. He *does not have* a Nature that would entail that there is a concordance between his "natural" environment and himself. He is a wanderer and a traveler on this earth; he no longer has a happy, wholesome place of which he would partake. Man is thus, from his origin, an artificial. He is a producer and produces his own art; he is wholly cultural. What subsists of nature in him (for one should not misinterpret here; I do not claim that the body, digestion, sexuality, birth and death, etc., are not "natural"!) is only of value to the extent that it is integrated within a set of myths, only has a *human* quality to the extent that it receives meaning from symbolic activity.

Hence this can in no way serve as a measure or a limit or a model or a norm. One absolutely cannot look at human "nature" to find what one should do in such a case, or to know if man disobeys by acting in such a way. This man, artificial since he is that, who has as it were instituted himself, does not have an outside reference point to know what is allowed or not. The only problem is therefore that of *meaning* and of the *measure* of what he is and of what he does. In theological terms, I would say that it is the eschatological problem and that of limits—which we will be studying in the next chapters. Now, for man, neither this meaning nor this measure

---

6. Here again, I could find a coincidence with the biblical narrative. It is exactly what is written in Genesis 3, as a consequence of Adam's rupture with God: the one who was the summit of creation, its supreme flower, and whose role was to lovingly manage this creation in total communion, broke the wholeness of this order and of this unity as a result of his own rupture with God. He then ceases to be the glory of this creation, the expression of this love, to become a stranger to it. The earth will produce thorns; it will be hostile to him. He will have to work it, to work against it to force it to produce. And the most eminently natural acts, Birth and Death, become hard, painful, frightening. In other words, all that is of Nature is now turned against man, who is a stranger in this realm that was meant for him. This is nothing but a statement of how man no longer belongs to Nature, nor Nature to man.

can come from Nature. It is here that we find most misinterpretations. How could nature provide on its own a framework to that which has no point in common with it? This illusion could be entertained as long as man's means were so weak that, for instance, Nature ended up winning almost every time. One could then think that this was the limit imposed—by God or by the all-powerful order of things. But now we see that the growth of our technical means radically challenges nature, risks annihilating it, and likewise allows a total, brutal, violent manipulation of human "nature," which shows that there is there neither permanence, nor anything inviolable, nor a sacred realm. Man is totally transformable into almost anything; the Whole is a matter of Means. That is the tragedy. So long as means were limited, the limit imposed itself of itself; it *was* the weakness of the means.

Today, we realize there is no longer anything outside this enterprise that might oppose it. The limit must therefore be sought elsewhere than in an existing being as an outside obstacle. And since everything is a matter of Means, and these means are created by man in his specifically human activity, this means that the limit can only be found by this man himself, can only come from him.

Thus, the whole theological problem does not come down to knowing whether man has a nature in agreement with Technique, but is exactly the problem of means in themselves, and of knowing if man has any reason not to carry on to the end in the elimination of nature, which would most assuredly mean his own elimination. But the problem of this coming to consciousness entails here a reversal that seems almost superhuman: how can we admit that what has until now allowed man's survival in a hostile environment, what has made it possible for man to become man, could become what would produce the elimination of the environment and the production of an antihuman?[7] The ever-invasive, aggressive forest, covering cultures, everywhere springing from the soil that man has painfully cleared, this forest was his ceaseless, implacable enemy. And man has become over five hundred thousand years the tree's adversary. How can we hope, now

---

7. This is the permanent problem of the quantitative and the qualitative. It is known to be the fierce attitude of Chaunu (*Histoire quantitative, histoire sérielle*) whose historical works I otherwise admire so much. Chaunu proves that any society has progressed in civilization when there was a growth of its components, and conversely, that a decline is absolutely inevitable when there is a decline in population. Hence, we must not be afraid of numbers and we must continue to favor population growth. He refuses to do the reversal, no doubt for theological reasons as well. But how can one fail to realize that the excess of power reverses the situation? In a very simple way: let us take an empty liter measure; I fill it with water. And if I fill it to three quarters I will have a better supply of water than if I fill it at one and a half. But if I continue to pour water in when it is full, I am wasting water; there is a reversal point in everything.

that technical means risk producing the total elimination of the forest, that man would convert in the etymological sense and become friendly toward the tree now that he has decisively won? How can we believe that the means that were his meager defense have come to endanger him?

One could give numerous examples. Another one: man has only survived by dint of the multiplication of his children: "increase and multiply"—it is the condition of survival. How can we hope that all of a sudden, now that technical means ensure a total victory of the human species, man would totally reverse his understanding of the possibilities of survival, and understand that this multiplication is precisely the absolute risk for him?

Under these conditions, it is not, therefore, from a theological standpoint, God who is going to intervene to prevent this or that. We are to expect neither a repressive action, nor a delimitation in itself by God of two realms (one natural and legitimate, the other artificial and reprehensible), nor the revelation of a clear, explicit will of God about these issues, showing us with the obviousness of a divine will what is allowed and what is forbidden in the here and now[8] of our situation. All these are but lazy and illusory expectations.

But no more is it possible to trace a constant, permanent border between a Natural and an artificial. We know in particular the entirely futile character of the search carried out for so long for a distinction between needs that are natural to man and artificial needs. The more their origin and content were rigorously narrowed down, the more people got convinced that so-called natural needs (which of course have a physiological base) are deeply cultural and artificial. A simple example: food. It is obvious that man needs to eat—a natural need. But one strictly cannot stop there. He does not eat just anything that would be physiologically useful or acceptable to him. He *only* eats what the world in which he has lived has taught him to eat; a food that is considered exquisite here is held to be foul and useless there. There is thus no such thing as a clear, original, natural need to eat. One does not "eat" in the absolute; one eats *something*, and this something is artificially determined.

We can generalize this. Finally, there will no more be any judgment to make about the artificial on the basis of the natural. The latter is not a

---

8. Translator's note: As elsewhere, Ellul uses for "here and now" the Latin phrase common in French, only here he adds capitals: *Hic et Nunc*. It is worth noting that this happened to be the title of the small but influential review that was a key channel for the reception of Barth in French Protestant thought in the 1930s, when Ellul was drawn to its circle of young Personalist Barthian thinkers (e.g. Denis de Rougemont, Roland de Pury, Roger Jézéquel, Albert-Marie Schmidt, and Henry Corbin, before he moved on to Islamic studies). The phrase "here and now" frequently used in Latin by Ellul is thus an echo of a Barthian slogan of his generation.

positive, good value, such as would allow us to gauge, appreciate, and as the case may be, condemn the artificial. It is incidentally remarkable that it is exactly in the historical period of the extreme development of techniques that the word artificial has taken on a negative connotation and entails a kind of pessimistic value judgment. We therefore need not ask ourselves what God demands or condemns with respect to Technique, nor what Nature allows or forbids (Nature does not speak!). To be sure, we can measure how much techniques endanger the environment in which we are called to live, whether this environment be that of society or that of the "natural given" (air, water, earth, etc.). But these are appraisals of a scientific, technical, sociological, environmental, etc. nature. And this belongs to an artificial and cultural type of activity that man has precisely *always* taken on insofar as he entered this artificial way. But this is not theological in nature.

What would be theological is, for instance, the motivation leading man to launch upon this search. What certainly is theological is, on the one hand, man's relation to his technical equipment, the situation of man within creation, man's responsibility before God toward this creation and other men, and, on the other hand, the evaluation of the meaning that the human enterprise has in God's eyes. Once more, none of this amounts to theologically privileging a Natural against an Artificial. One would have to admit a Nature equivalent to the original creation, intact. Now the Bible never stops telling us that it is not the creation as God gave it. And, for instance, we know very well, in Romans 8, that the creation as a whole "fell" following Adam's rupture, that violence and destruction entered it, that it has become at once enslaved and fractured, and that it awaits in suffering the moment of its reintegration.

The artificial is tied to the being of man; it is our environment; we have to be willing to live in it. It is indeed true that that question did not arise as long as the so-called Natural environment was dominant, and I have described often enough the opposition between the totally artificial environment of the city and that of the country (also artificial but starting from natural givens). But I would prefer to speak of a second-degree artificiality to describe our condition. Man has transformed the natural into an artificial for his own use.

Now it comes about that our modern action consists in reducing this very artificial into reworked elements. It is obvious that chemistry, with the creation of absolutely new bodies, is an example of choice. We are on the eve of an irreversible deviation from matter, for instance. We are constantly using products that do not exist in Nature. Now, we are still living with the belief in a naturalness that has ceased to exist.⁹ And we cannot in this respect play the part of regret and a return to the past. Likewise, our instruments enable a mutation of man, a mutation of *"poiesis,"* a falsification of values. We are no longer creating *anything but* objects and events that leave the realm of naturalness; they are therefore dangerous. But I cannot view them as "false" or "counterfeit." They become that if they are used for what they are not, or against the use intended for them. They become that when they get taken for Nature.¹⁰ This is where falsification starts.

But it is not according to a natural evaluation that we are going to be able to appraise it.¹¹ And falsification must be properly distinguished from artificiality. It is on this point that we will need to seek what a theological direction might be. Our reference therefore cannot be of a natural type, but of necessity the locus of Revelation, which is to say, the Bible. This is not a question of literal interpretation of the texts nor of first-degree quest for what the Bible might be saying about Technique; this we are going to do quickly in the following section as a work item. But it is obvious that for the *current* situation on the one hand, if, on the other hand, one has understood the consistency that exists between the being of man and his technical activity, it can only be a theological reflection both more global (relative to the Whole) and topical: what is there to say about techniques at this moment of our evolution, of our history, of our society?

2. TECHNIQUE ACCORDING TO THE BIBLE

Technique according to the first chapters of Genesis[12]

It is always a rather distressing issue to realize the influence that sociological currents, the "world's" climate, have on theological thought, the expression

---

9. See on this point the remarkable studies of Dorfles: "Intenzionalità e mitopoiesi nelle tecniche odierne," and "Mythe de la naturalité et les transformations fruitives" [note completed by F. Rognon].

10. See Ellul, *Technological System*: Technique as Nature.

11. One can see that I agree here with some of the theses of Edgar Morin, in *Le Paradigme perdu*, according to which, over the course of evolution, such a relation of interdependence has set in between social development and biological brain development that, even if there ever was a primal, original nature, it has become perfectly fused with culture; nature has merged with the sociocultural. "Man is a cultural being by nature, because he is a natural being by culture." It is not a play on words. I believe that this corresponds to the best possible ascertainment of the human real.

12. French original published in *Foi et Vie* 59, no. 2 (March-April 1960) 97–113 [then translated into English and published as "Technique and the Opening Chapters of Genesis" in Carl Mitcham and Jim Grote, eds., *Theology and Technology: Essays in*

of the Church's faith. Nowadays we are possessed by the Myth of Work, amazed by the greatness of technical works, and now seeing the Church, like everybody else, granting work pride of place in her thought, starting to justify it along with Technique. Because Technique is a great work of man, we must find a way to legitimize it. Because work takes up nearly all of man's life, and becomes his reason for living, we must show it to be holy. To be sure, the issue is never consciously put in these terms. But one is compelled to note that it is only now that theologians are striving to legitimize technique and work, that they are doing in their own area with their own method what everyone is doing, that factual circumstances have altered their thinking. This is all the more serious for being unconscious.

Whereas it used to be commonplace to teach that work was a consequence of the fall, belonged to the world of sin and was only pain, there is now mostly an emphasis on the fact that work existed in Eden already, that it only became painful after the fall (which is correct). The biblical texts being put forward are obviously rather scarce. There is mostly, in chapters 1 and 2 of Genesis, 1:28: "Be fruitful and multiply, and fill the earth, and subdue it; and rule over the fish of the sea and over the birds of the sky and over every living thing that moves on the earth"; 2:15: "And Jehovah God took the man, and put him into the garden of Eden to cultivate it and to keep it"; and, additionally, Psalm 8:7: "You have given him dominion over the works of your hands; you have put all things under his feet."[13] On this basis it is claimed that work is not a consequence of sin, but that "work is the destiny prescribed to man by the Creator. It is the sign by which God attests that man is his collaborator." These lines by H. Mehl-Koehnlein[14] are nuanced, and it might be possible to admit this notion of collaborator (provided it is not based on 1 Corinthians 3:9, which is a totally improper application to material work of a text referring to witness), but less easily the idea of an association to the work of creation (?).

But it is a slippery slope, where one soon gets to this, for instance: "According to God's design, there is a cooperation of man with creation. Man is in the world to fulfill, complete, perfect the work of creation and make it usable for him."[15] And we take one more step: "To cultivate means

---

Christian Analysis and Exegesis (Lanham, MD: University Press of America, 1984), 123–37, note by F. Rognon]. Here, pp. 106–19.

13. Editor's note: Ps 8:7 in the Hebrew is Ps 8:6 in the English.

14. Mrs. Herrade Mehl-Koehnlein is the author of a book on Saint Paul, *L'homme selon l'apôtre Paul*, and the entry "Travail" in *Vocabulaire biblique* [note by the family].

15. Rondet, in *Lexikon für Theologie und Kirche*. [The reference appears to be wrong. This encyclopedia mentions three times (vol. 3, p. 300, vol. 5, p. 318 and vol. 8, p. 1296) the Jesuit Henri Rondet (1898–1979). A professor of dogmatics at Lyon-Fourvière

THEOLOGY AND TECHNIQUE

to generate new creations ... man has the faculty to create. This is why he is truly in the image of God."[16]

One thus finds in Protestant theology the idea often expressed in Catholicism that man has a demiurgic function, that he completes creation, that he creates as it were beside God. "If man liberates certain created virtualities, if he enriches his stay with wondrous instruments, it is because God wills it ... He rejoices at the progress of his work, ... at the gradual realization of the possibilities that He has mysteriously hidden within creation, ... in other words, God is the Creator of Techniques ... The technical operation is sacral; by laying his hand on the created to transform it, man puts his hand in that of God."[17]

This idea was also strongly expressed by Mounier.[18] And all of this was drawn from these two verses of Genesis.

Needless to say, as the above text shows, whoever says work says technique; the assumption of work into the garden of Eden leads to an assumption of Technique. Adam was an inventor and a technician in Eden, as someone once retorted to me: "If Adam received the order to cultivate, what was he doing it with, if not with tools?"

It seems to me that this whole set of ideas seriously misjudges what the Bible tells us of creation before the fall, of what we can make out, without ever succeeding in truly knowing it, since in our sinful situation we cannot understand what Adam was before the rupture. We just have to try to make it out, by humbly respecting the biblical text without straining it.

We have here a first certainty: the creation as God made it, as it came out of his hands, is *perfect and complete*: "God saw every thing that He had made, and behold, it was very good" (1:31); "God ended His work which He had made" (2:2). Provided we take these texts as they are, we must then recognize that God's work is fulfilled, that it is complete, that there is nothing to add to it.

That does not mean that this is a static situation where nothing changes; there is indeed change according to the inner rhythm of creation as it is shown to us. There is no imaginable progress, no alteration coming from a third agent. What would progress mean, since everything is perfect? Is it possible to go to another stage of perfection? That would mean that the

---

from 1932 to 1951, and then from 1960 to 1970, he is especially known for his teaching on grace. Note by the family.]

16. According to a note on the website www.jesusradicals.com, this quote from Henri Moussiegt is drawn from an article in *Réforme* that appeared in 1959. This piece of information could not be verified [note by the family].

17. Laloup and Nélis, *Hommes et machines*.

18. Mounier, *Be Not Afraid*.

work of God was not perfect. Is it possible to add to it and to exploit hidden possibilities? That would mean that God's work was not completed—that God rested before being finished. What could it mean to cooperate in creation? That man as creature is co-creator? To say that it is as creator that man is in the image of God is to have a peculiar idea of the image of God! It is a simple absurdity that is nowhere mentioned in the Bible.

What is meant by the idea that man completes creation? With what? What complement needs to be brought to what God himself declares perfect and completed? What is meant by the idea that man makes "usable" for himself the goods of creation? It would be a peculiarly incomplete and absurd creation where there would be numerous things, but unusable by the one God institutes as king of this creation. When God gives him the grass and fruits to eat, it does not seem that man need make an invention to render them usable. The term given is very clear: God *gives*—man has nothing to do with it; man receives, period. It may be that God calls man to a certain collaboration, but it is not creative. It is only a matter for man to fulfill the will of God, to inscribe himself within the order, to be God's counterpart. Such is this collaboration which has nothing to do with work as we can imagine it. Man works in this creation, without completing it, without unfolding it, without causing anything new to arise, living only within this perfection; himself perfect, he has nothing to invent, for his invention could only be a lessening of this completed work. He has nothing to begin, nothing to earn, nothing to develop. He simply is: no progress in the sense of improvement, but to be sure progress in the sense of a walk, in the humblest sense of the term.

Any other conception is a glorification of man, with a glory that is due only to God. In the theory of man's demiurgy, there reappears the ever-reborn temptation to want to attribute something to man which does not seem due to God, to make of him more than a creature, to grant him an initiative, a greatness outside and beyond what God grants him, to give an honor back to man! Alas, in this good intention, it is always an honor that one takes away from God.

Yet, in Eden, man is indeed called to work. It is indeed a matter of cultivating the garden, but at once we see this work through our knowledge of work, which is from the fall. Perforce, we see a work aimed at production, a work that is creative of forms and values, a work without which nothing would be—so that, starting from this conception of work, we are perforce led to the idea of a work that creates, that adds to creation (before I worked, there was nothing: afterwards there is my work), a productive work, hence a technical work. But this is but the transposition into Eden of the work we know after the fall.

Is there anything else we can say? To be sure, there is at least one clear indication in Genesis: trees and plants produced abundantly, according to their species, each having within itself its own seed (1:11–12). No other cultivation is needed, no care to be added to it, no graft, no plowing, no concern; creation spontaneously brought man what he needed, according to the very order of God who had said: "I give you . . ." And the counterpart proof of this is precisely to be found in the fall's condemnation: creation will refuse to give man its fruit, will produce thistles and thorns, and he will then have to perform work that is not only painful, but *productive*. This is the big difference (3:18–19).

There is indeed work without necessity (Adam will not die of hunger if he ceases to work), a work without purpose, without production. It is not a work to obtain a surplus, to earn a living, to produce, it is a work for *nothing*; the fruit, the product, what is necessary for Adam's life, is freely given by God—not in exchange for a work, a duty, an obligation, but truly freely—without a relation of necessity with work. There is no causal link between this work and this product that is only part of the order of creation. It is not a useful work; it is also a free work. So why then does Adam work? For this one reason that should seem to us compelling and sufficient: because God told him to, Adam obeys God in freedom, disinterestedly, and in this obedience is included work, free action, which is hardly different from play, and which includes no possibility for self-glorification, no product which Adam could refer to himself.

One should also note that, aside from cultivating, the text says "to keep." And it is the same problem—Adam does not need to keep against someone or something. There is no danger, no bear that is going to come and slit throats in the herd, no boar that is going to come and lay waste to the harvest. Adam is entrusted with keeping this garden against nothing. (One should not speak of the serpent, for, here, it is not the garden that Adam was meant to protect, but himself, and more than himself, Eve! It is absolutely not the same issue.) Yet Adam is entrusted with keeping—here again, freely, because God gives him this function, and Adam is not to ask the reason or justification. He acts as a master steward, because the Eternal puts him at the head of his creation, and as a master steward, he keeps and cultivates, even if there is no necessity, even if there is no threat.

Such is the order that God establishes, and this order, including this cultivation and this keeping, is perfect. There is nothing to add to it; nothing in it can be lost. God can rest in the dialogue with his creation, presented to him by the head of this creation, as an offering and as a royal image of free love.

SITUATION OF A THEOLOGICAL REFLECTION ON TECHNIQUE

※

Man works; therefore he needs means. A technique is needed to cultivate, people say, thus tying technical invention to the very situation of Adam in Eden, to the order of work, to the demiurgic function. And while we are at it, we cannot leave aside the current situation of technique, which is indeed creative, which indeed puts the world in a new situation, which radically alters all relations. In the current view (of the world of the fall), one may indeed speak of demiurgy. But justifying it by a so-called Edenic situation is a different matter. To say that Technique could exist in creation before the fall seems to me tantamount to committing another grave mistake about what Scripture, once again, allows us to glimpse.

God's creation was an *universum*, a whole, a unity. We now know only the fragments of this broken mirror, but, coming out of the hands of God, this mirror was intact. It was one. We always imagine a system of relations similar to the ones we know today, maybe only more perfect, taken to the absolute. Now, what we know is a system made of pieces and bits; it is fragmentary relations, mendings, clumsy assemblies of scattered units that tend to autonomy. We obviously start from the individuality of each fragment and we think that, from there, we can restore a whole. In creation, there was nothing of the sort; it was itself, as a whole, unity. It was not a synthesis, since a synthesis presupposes separate elements that come together, but indeed the one as a whole.

The relation within this creation, was, as within the Trinity, an immediate relation of love and knowledge. There could be no mediate relations between Adam and creation, since he inwardly belonged to this *universum* (in the etymological sense of what is turned toward unity), nor between Adam and God, since he was the image of God, which is to say that the relation of love was perfect between them. And in a world without division, without any mystery, it was not useful to reestablish bridges, ties. In a world where the relation was a direct one, it was not useful to resort to means of any degree of sophistication in order to act. In a world where the communion of all things and harmony prevailed, there could be no place for coercion or a mediated subjection. For by the same token no distinction was possible between means and ends. Adam alive was in communion with his only possible end, and there was no means to be used.

I have tried to show how in Jesus Christ, it was the means that were reintegrated into the end,[19] whereas in creation, this distinction has not been established yet. Everything was truly a whole, and the fullness of God

---

19. Ellul, *Presence in the Modern World*.

filled all things, while wisdom played before him.[20] What end is to be pursued under these conditions and by what means? What meaning can still be attached to the notion of means when everything is given in the unity of being?

Therefore, if we glimpse what can justify this unity of creation with its Creator, we understand that there cannot be, for instance, property in Eden. Universality is handed over to Adam to manage it, but there is no particularized thing that Adam might appropriate to himself. It is only when the unity of creation is broken that things separate, that each element assumes a particular destiny, and that there then is a relation of man with individuated things. It is only then that a particular relation is established that may be termed property. If we understand what this wondrous universality is, we understand in exactly the same way that there cannot be Technique, no manner of Technique, of any kind—for Technique is only ever a set of means—and the search for the most efficient means, and these two elements are radically excluded. There cannot be any means in a world where all relations are immediate.

In the same way that Adam had no need to institute religion or magic to settle his relations with God, because he spoke to God face-to-face, and that there were no protocols, nor sacrifices, so Adam had no need to use procedures to come into contact with nature, to use plants, to lead animals. He was in communion with this whole to which he belonged while ruling it, and he had no method to follow, no Technique to apply, because he had no coercion to use, no need to overcome, no more than he had to defend himself against a threat or coercion. This whole world of techniques in all its applications is completely foreign to Eden.

What is more, if we consider that Technique has only one goal, efficiency, we must ask what a search for efficiency can possibly mean in a world of communion and free gifts. We have seen in particular that, when it comes to work, it could never be technical, because its aim was not to produce, to coerce earth into giving it a fruit it would have refused him. Insofar as it was freedom, disinterestedness, ease, play, there was no technique to be applied; that would mean a direct contradiction in terms. There could be no question, at that point, of making the earth produce more than what it was spontaneously producing, since in this *universum*, the idea of a "more" is wholly alien.

We have an idea of this situation in the story of the manna, where each received daily what he or she needed, but where conservation methods and techniques to keep some, to have more, were utterly useless. Efficiency,

---

20. See Proverbs 8:30 [note by the family].

SITUATION OF A THEOLOGICAL REFLECTION ON TECHNIQUE

more, property, reserves, are all notions tied to Technique, but without any meaning in relation to Eden.

Let us note, additionally, for those who cling to their idea of technique in Eden and say that, to cultivate it, some tool must have been needed, that one should then not stop halfway, for, alas, our text not only says "cultivate," but "cultivate and *keep*." We are then forced to conclude that if Adam needed a tool to cultivate, he therefore also needed a weapon to keep; both are identical. If then Adam's work is the starting point, the justification, the initiation of Technique, his mission to keep is the starting point, the justification, the initiation of the police and the army. Does this seem improbable? It is no less and, if we reject the weapon, we must also reject the tool.

But, people also say, Adam was entrusted with ruling over creation; now, precisely, in today's world, it is Technique that is the means of this domination, it is thanks to his inventions, it is since he is in possession of a true technical apparatus that man can *truly* rule over this creation, and consequently obey God's order. Now, since he had received the same order in Eden, the way had to be the same. (Always the same vice, which is to try to imagine Eden starting from our situation.) Let us leave aside the means; let us only think of what was, what this domination of Adam before the fall might have been.

We have a perfectly clear example of it when God has "all animals come to Adam" to see how he would call them so that any living being bear the name man would give it, "and man gave a name to all animals" (Gen 2:19–20). It is hard to understand by what aberration people have claimed to draw from such a text the origins of science and Technique! "That assumes the recognition of species, hence observation, the source of science. Knowing is one of man's first callings, he puts in it all the resources of his spirit . . ." Let us wonder at the ambiguity of the terms: knowing, no doubt, but in the biblical sense which has nothing whatsoever to do with scientific knowledge. Spirit? Certainly, but in the biblical sense, which has nothing to do with scientific intelligence. It is such shifts that radically distort the meaning of the text of revelation. As for saying that this act of naming is at the origin of science, this betrays a tragic misconstrual of Adam's act.

Already in the phrase quoted, it is said: "Recognize the species," that is to say, distinguish them. And this is indeed the first mechanism of scientific and technical intelligence, which is one of division, of separation, of analysis. Language in the service of science is partitive language, whereas biblically, giving a name is exactly the reverse phenomenon; it is a recapitulative fact. To assign a name is to discern a spiritual reality, assign a spiritual value, trace a role, a destiny; it is to establish a relation for God. To give one's name is to reveal oneself in one's whole being, put oneself at the disposal of the one to whom one speaks, and grant one's truth (and not reality). We are, biblically, in the presence of a spiritual fact that has nothing in common, no point of relation with the intellectual operation of science. It is a fateful misconstrual of the text that allows one to liken them. When Adam gives a name to a plant, he will not be calling it crucifer, because it displays such and such a sign, and the plants displaying such a sign belong to such a family, etc. He attributes a destiny to fulfill before God. Master of creation, by and for God, he presents it thus to God by naming it. For he is free to do so. God happens to leave him the initiative and freedom in this global relation with the whole of this world ("to see how he would name them"!). But it is an act where man is not outside, a *deus ex machina*, a scientist who observes: he is himself involved in this play of creation in which he confers on each animal both its place and its role!

But let us reflect further; it is also an act of domination. He thereby asserts himself as the Master. It is thus not by using or coercing that he is the Master, but by naming, that is by speaking. He uses speech—like God; Adam, the image of God, speaks as God has spoken. His speech, far from being scientific language, is an extension of God's speech. And just as God creates through his speech ("God says and things are"), so does Adam manifest his mastery, his domination through speech. He needs nothing more than this sovereign speech, which expresses both God's love and his power. It is not by a technique that he cultivates, that he keeps, that he dominates; it is by speech alone—exactly like God who does not create by technical means, but by his speech. There is no relation of exploitation, use, subordination; speech is the expression of spiritual superiority, of direction that yet leaves the other intact (which Technique never does) and free to decide. Before the fall, there was thus for Adam no other form of domination over the world, and his language is not an intellectual operation of analysis, but knowledge as communion, participation, love.

To properly grasp the unheard-of difference, before and after the fall, of this situation of domination, it is enough to compare what God says to Adam and what he says to Noah. To Adam, he says, "Fill the earth, and subjugate it; and rule over all the animals."[21] To Noah (after the flood and in the midst of the attempt to recover a just humanity before God), he says, "Fill the earth. The fear and the terror of you shall be in every animal of the land . . . with everything that moves on the ground; they are given into your hand."[22] The distance is enormous; it is, I might say, the whole distance between Adam's speech and the fall's technique. Instead of rule without

---

21. Gen 1:28.
22. Gen 9:1–2.

means, and in communion, there is now fear, the fear of animals around man who dominates them by his technical means. Animals no longer come; they flee. They are no longer loved in the freedom of creation, presented to God by Adam in praise; they are delivered into the hands of man. On the one hand, speech, on the other hand, hands; it is here that we truly witness the insertion of Technique.

If it is not untrue to consider Technique as having its starting point in an order of God, who assigns to man his domination, it is not from the creation given to Adam, but from the order of the fall. Adam dominates and so does Noah, but not in the same way, nor under the same conditions, nor with the same meaning.

☙

In reality, the first time that the Bible talks very clearly of Technique is about Cain. Nothing was stopping it from talking about it with respect to Adam as well. The three descendants of Cain are the one who raises herds, the one who plays music, the one who forges instruments or iron and brass—three techniques.[23] And the Bible explicitly says that they begin there: "He was the father of those who . . ." I do not think it is quite by chance (and, of course, one must also take into account that this might be an etiological myth of the specialty of Ken'ite blacksmiths, but this would in fact change nothing to the truth). We need not dwell on this text, but we may try to understand why the Bible talks to us about Technique only after the fall and in Cain's situation. We have seen why Technique is an impossibility in Eden, but the fall causes a radical break; the *universum* that had been created is shattered.

> a) Adam is no longer in direct communion with God. He hides, the rupture is consummated between them, and, starting from this rupture between God and man, all other ruptures ensue. Adam and Eve separate (Adam accuses his wife—what break could be greater?). They are no longer one, but two. Man and animals separate (Eve accuses the serpent). They learn fear and shame: "Then the eyes of both of them were opened, and they realized they were naked."[24] That is to say exactly that the relation between the elements of creation is now completely turned upside down; instead of unity, of communion, there is now an I and a Thou. There is the gaze of the Other, which is a

23. Gen 4:20–22.
24. Gen 3:7.

stranger's gaze, and that is laid on me. There is that I am under fire from the Other's gaze, which is now a loveless gaze, without understanding, unwelcoming, but only coldly perceptive (there is that science which perceives the objective reality of things and that sees that I am other; this gaze now turns everything into an object; the other has become an object for me). The mirror of creation is shattered. The *universum* is broken. Then, means are needed: means to try to hold together the pieces, means to establish new relations in this relationless world.

b) Now mediators, intermediaries are needed, because distance has been established between God and man, between men, between man and matter. There is no longer any immediate contact. Everything has become mediatized. In particular, in his relation to God, man is going to institute religion, at once as a screen between them and as a means of approach. Thus arise the sacrifices of Abel and Cain.[25] In his relation to nature, man creates Technique. We are then launched into the world of means, in their endless, unbridled multiplication. It is important to understand that the proliferation of means which characterizes our time is not some kind of progress incipient in Adam's situation in Eden.

c) It has become necessary precisely because the Edenic situation no longer exists! In this broken universe, also, the word no longer has any virtue. Our language is no longer the same as that of Adam. It is no longer the extension of the embodied Word, having spiritual power, initiating force—*Words, Words!*[26] There is no longer in language any but the most distant reflection (and, to be sure, fortunately, this reflection is indeed there), and the word can still be a sign (it can still refer to the Word!) of that of God, but on the one hand, because it is degraded, because it is the word of sinful man, because it is the word of man separate from God, from the Living One who gives power to the Word, and on the other hand, because it falls in a broken world, in a universe of rupture, of disobedience and refusal, it can no longer be the instrument this lost Adam needs. It is no longer up to the task of establishing bridges between the fragments of the world, bringing to obedience what is steeped in rebellion, or, even when it expresses the truth, of determining the destiny of things; Adam equipped with his word alone is perfectly helpless in this world. He needs other weapons, other means. He must still ensure his domination, but he needs new means for this. It is here that he must invent, and these means will no

25. Gen 4:3–4.
26. Translator's note: In English in the original.

SITUATION OF A THEOLOGICAL REFLECTION ON TECHNIQUE

longer be those of communion, but those of coercion, of division, of use, of exploitation.

d) Here is where Technique is to be situated. And it cannot be otherwise in the situation where Adam is placed by the very order of God: "Cursed is the ground because of you ... It will produce thorns and thistles for you ... by the sweat of your brow you will eat your food,"[27] in addition to the serpent's work: "I will put enmity between you and the woman."[28] Thus the world becomes hostile to man, doubly hostile. Nature, which produced everything in abundance for Adam's nourishment and joy, becomes a nature that refuses itself, barren and rebellious. There was no need to have a tool in Eden, because one had everything. But now, Adam is in a world that does not give him anything freely, a world that closes itself at his touch, a world that, of its own accord, only gives him useless things. As a result, Adam must vanquish, must coerce this nature that only gives him thorns and thistles. Adam will compel it to deliver its wheat, its fruits. But for this he needs to wound the earth, to open it with his plough, to search it and to unveil it. He must wound the tree and prune it and graft it. Thus Adam finds himself in a relation of struggle; he dominates through his means, that is, through his technique, which cannot be an instrument of love, but of domination.

e) Likewise, the world has become hostile through the powers of aggression it holds against man—the wild beast, beginning with the serpent. Man is now forced to defend himself against what attacks him, and now other means are necessary—weapons, for instance (for why should technique be reserved for tools? Weapons are the sign of no less originary a technique!), but above all the whole of Technique. A good specialist of these issues could write that Technique was a "protective sheath that man sets up around himself!" (Leroi-Gourhan).[29] It is true that Technique is at least as much a set of means of protection as a means of domination. But in either case, what characterizes this instrument is its efficiency.

f) The only thing that marks out Technique is efficacy! That is an absolutely new concern, that makes sense it this world that refuses itself and attacks but would make absolutely none in the garden of Eden.

---

27. Gen 3:17.

28. Gen 3:15.

29. Leroi-Gourhan, *Evolution et techniques*, vol. 2, *Milieu et techniques* (Paris: Albin Michel, 1945) [note by the family].

Now Adam has to succeed. What does success mean in a world of the freely given, of the gift? Now Adam is placed in a *truly* new situation. He knows the necessity of which the facts we were recalling above are but aspects. He had lived in freedom; his work was freedom, play, childhood. He was free to be himself before his Creator who was his father. He was free from every restraint, of any obligation. He only knew this freedom, along with its complement of respect for God's will, respect in a free love and a free dialogue. There was no law, but an order, the very order of God's freedom.

But from the moment Adam separates himself from this God, when his freedom is no longer love, but choice between two possibilities (and as for us, we only know that freedom, which is always a choice between two possibilities, and we characterize freedom by the possibility of choice, but let us not forget that this is now no more than the freedom of the world of the fall, of heaviness and of death), from that moment, Adam goes from the world of freedom to that of necessity. When he no longer draws his life from loving communion with God, he lives within the order of law. He now knows what ought means; he now knows that an implacable order rules his destiny, that his universe is the one where everything falls, is truly that of gravity, anxiety, fall. Everything is now necessarily regulated; fatality becomes the sign of his life. He is subject to a play of all manner of laws: physical and moral, biological and sociological, that are but facets of the same necessity.

And in this universe of necessity under which he is forced to bend, it comes about that man learns to use this necessity, to use cunning with it, or to turn it against itself. He learns to know and decipher the laws of nature to modify his own condition. It is by submitting to these laws that he succeeds in dominating them; it is by discerning them as necessity that he succeeds in living in their midst, in subsisting as a man who has kept at the bottom of his heart the memory of and the aspiration to freedom. But, when we write this, we have done nothing more than describe the process of Technique, itself guided by science. It is a means of subjugating necessity by bending to it. But in a world where there was no necessity, what did this mean? Thus, whatever the angle by which we approach Technique, we realize that it can only be a phenomenon of the fall, that it has nothing to do with the order of creation, that it is in no way a consequence of Adam's calling as willed by God, but necessarily of the situation of fallen Adam.

SITUATION OF A THEOLOGICAL REFLECTION ON TECHNIQUE

⚐

And now, there remains for me to beg the reader not to make me say what I am not saying! I am not saying that Technique is a fruit of sin. I am not saying that Technique goes against God's will. I am not saying that Technique is bad in itself. I am only saying that Technique is not an extension of Edenic creation, that it is not an obedience of man to a calling that would have been given him by God, that it is not the fruit of Adam's first nature. It is the product of the situation in which sin has put man, inscribed exclusively in the fallen world, and belongs exclusively to the fallen world. It is a product of necessity and not of man's freedom.

There[30] remains now for me to add a concluding remark: it is obvious that, from a biblical standpoint, the problem of Techniques does not stop with this origin. This is all the more as, we must always recall, biblically, it is not Genesis that gives the meaning of a reality, its meaning, but on the contrary, it is its end. There is here a misconstrual that must be fought against ever anew. Many theological currents base themselves on the events of the beginning to appraise the value of a given reality. This attitude comes either from traditional mythical thought (with which biblical thought is equated), or from historicism, which claims to explain succession by precedent and seeks causes, or by a metaphysical thought based on origins, etc. It has thus been maintained that the story of Creation was given biblically as a point of departure, that the story of the fall was the origin story of the fallen world, and that we had to draw the consequences of these premises. The movement of biblical thought is absolutely not that one. In the Old Testament, everything is rigorously based on the promise, that is to say, that what matters is the promise received today and that is absolutely bound to be fulfilled. In the New Testament, everything is rigorously based on the resurrection and the presence/expectation of the Kingdom; past events that are given to us are there neither to give a first cause, an origin, nor to fix, to establish with rigor an assured situation. They are there exclusively to elucidate and found the promise, and in the New Testament, to elucidate and explicate the Resurrection and the Kingdom.

In other words, as it were, the creation story is not a story aimed at explaining us how the creation took place, nor even what is its meaning; the story of the "fall" is not there to explain to us the origin of Evil, a stupendous misinterpretation that keeps on being committed, it must also be said, insofar as these stories are separated from the rest of the text and that they are taken as separate blocks. We must keep in mind that in any case,

---

30. The manuscript resumes [note by the family].

they are historically *late* writings, belatedly introduced, whereas the Jewish people already had an interpretation of its history and was certain of the value of God's promises. They are not stories introduced in imitation of the cosmogonies of neighboring peoples (which the Jewish people had known for a long time and could have introduced much earlier). We must also keep in mind that these Genesis texts are very seldom quoted, very rarely in the OT's later writings, as well as in the NT.

In reality, they would become fundamental starting with the invasion of Greek thought in Christianity, starting from a substantialism of origins and a causalism that is not biblical. They are there solely in relation to the certainty of God's promise, of the Election of Israel aimed at all. What are these stories then? They are solely a referral, starting from the Promise, toward the one who made it, the one whose will is creative of life and order, the one with whom man had a filial relation that had to be replaced by that of the Covenant and the Promise because the filial relation had been broken. But they must be read in this light of the Covenant and the Promise and in no other!

Likewise, for instance, the story of the original Birth, of the Nativity, is not what should be read first, but only after the resurrection (exactly as it has also been written), meaning that the Nativity is the confirmation, the explication of the Resurrection; so it is not that: "There was a begetting by the Holy Spirit and a virgin Birth; therefore the one born thus had to rise again." On the contrary: Jesus is risen, which assumes the presence in him, attested throughout his life, of the very creator of life, which means that he was a new creation, not beholden to the limits of human birth.

Now it is crucial that we know whether we are *starting* from the origin or the end. In one case, you are put under a fate of mechanisms and causalities. Starting from this first cause, everything unfolds relentlessly. In the other, you know that you are going toward a fulfillment, toward a new creation whose first elements are already given in the present, but with two hitches: on the one hand, the pathways are obscure, and man is responsible for this historical path; on the other hand, the present situation is disastrous, and one has to wonder why.

Having set down these few reflections, we shall say that the origin of Techniques that we have tried to recall does not place them within an accursed fate. The attempt is simply to tell us what the experience of Technique is. And the mistrust will continue, as for instance many texts remind us that the altar of the Eternal must be made of raw stones uncut by iron—as though the involvement of Technique made impure what was supposed to serve God. However, we are not dealing with an obligation, and Technique is on the contrary placed very high for the building of the Temple. Hiram

SITUATION OF A THEOLOGICAL REFLECTION ON TECHNIQUE

was an able technician and beloved of God for that. Architecture as well as sculpture, weaving, etc., all find themselves legitimized by the service of the Lord and the building of his Temple. Having said that, we are hardly more enlightened.

To re-situate Technique in its full biblical dimension, I must refer to what is the most perfect product of the combination of all Techniques: the city. I believe we may apply to Technique in general all that I have tried to show as theological meaning issuing from the Bible for the City. For the latter may, for the ancient era as for the modern era, be entirely identified with Technique. The city is at once the product, the site, the gathering, the culmination of all Techniques—be they commercial or building techniques, be they administrative or aesthetic ones, be they sanitary or sociological ones, be they bank techniques or industrial ones, be they military or research ones. Relatively speaking, the city was the same thing, displayed the concentration and model of all Techniques; there are cities only where there are the most sophisticated techniques. Technique can only develop in this totally artificial environment. Consequently, what the Bible tells us about the City must be understood and interpreted for Technique.

I will therefore allow myself to recall in a few brief pages the main conclusions to which I had arrived for the city.[31] The guiding thread of any reflection on the City from a biblical standpoint is in the origin that is shown to us. Man is created in a garden, Eden, set by God in the natural environment. God makes a nature for man and finds that it is in this world of trees, of plants, of animals, of rivers and seas that man should be most at home.[32] The other "origin," which is that of the city, is joined to Technique, since it is Cain who founds the first city as a challenge against God, as a refusal of the situation that God makes for him: that of a wanderer upon Earth, with the protection and the promise of God as only guarantee, protection, salvation. Cain prefers to give himself a security, a more tangible insurance. He refuses the condition of a wanderer. He wants to root himself. He refuses God's protection and ensures his own. He builds walls and shutters himself within. From there will also come weapons and techniques. The City thus becomes at once man's place from which God is excluded and the place man makes for himself, the expression of man's "nature." Man has

---

31. The details of this whole study are to be found in my book *Meaning of the City*. I apologize to readers who may already know this study, but I had to also throw light on Technique in this way. They may skip the following few pages.

32. This is obviously the origin of the conviction that "Nature" is good, and that man finds his model in Nature, which is in no way the meaning of the biblical text. The creation has nothing to do with the concept of a Nature. All that is said here is meant not to throw light on the Man-Nature relation but on the God-Man relation.

chosen to live there rather than within the setting that was given to him by God. There he invents an original world in which the first creation has no part. Man determines for himself a new origin, recusing the one God had set; he is himself the creator of another world, one where his opposition to God becomes concrete. Technique is one of its expressions. Those are the two points of departure (which are recurrently shown to us and not as historically, sociologically given genuine points of departure).

Now, the point of arrival, the end point of human history in God, is the appearance of the perfect City—the heavenly Jerusalem that comes down from the sky. The final object of the promise is thus a resurrection in and for the City—in other words, there is no recreation by God of Eden; Paradise is not a Garden. This is in contrast to all other mythologies where the end, the fulfillment, is a return to the beginning, to the origin, to a lost golden age. Biblically, there is nothing of the kind, in contrast too to all crude interpretations that people have of the biblical text itself.[33]

This has incalculable implications. It entails two major theological consequences. The first is thus that God does not impose upon man the place of his choice. Once again, we find here the God who wants his creature free, even in rupture, in disobedience, in revolt and insolence. Man decided he would live in the city; God accepts this decision of man and indeed promises him that he will live eternally in the City brought to its perfection. The other consequence is that the place that man has created through his revolt, in his refusal of God, to defend himself against God, to exclude God, becomes the place of election, of reconciliation, where God will be all and in all. In other words, in the most concrete and the most historical way, God forgives beyond all revolts, not just in a spiritual and inner manner, but in a fashion that is embodied in man's work.

A set of possible understandings arises from these two major theological consequences. It is obvious that over the course of history, the cities of men remain marked by this first meaning: the city is the place of war, of hatred, of the spirit of power, of noncommunication, of pride, of the exploitation of man by man. All this, point by point, is taken up and shown by countless biblical texts. And as a result, it is under God's curse—condemnation falls on it ever anew, not as such, but for all that it represents and signifies. And yet, all is not condemnation; it is also (without this changing its nature) the place where the Promise lies. As dramatic, as tragic as its fate may be, there is yet the slim purple thread woven into the weft, and that runs, carrying grace. There is the promise upon all the cities which are

33. Again recently, in Fernando Belo's commentary, *Materialist Reading of the Gospel of Mark*, we find the blithe assertion that, as in all mythical stories, the Bible shows us a return to origins with Paradise, a return to Eden. This is an absolute misconstrual.

blessed in Jerusalem. This remains secret, hidden, mysterious, understandable only to the one who turns to the Eternal to understand and receive the blessing. The rest, the apparent side of history, carries on in this mixture of violence, greatness, progress, and wars.

Thus we are not going from progress to progress, from cities that are less good to better ones, to triumphantly end up, after sufficient evolution, and in a natural fashion, in the heavenly Jerusalem. The latter comes after the absolute rupture, what is known as the Last Judgment. There is a break in History, a final condemnation of the City taken to the absolute, in the great Whore, Rome. There is literally an annihilation (reduction to nothing) of the absolute City, and in it of all Cities. It is through this annihilation that the perfect City is then *given* to man by grace.

There is no continuity; there is a *taking up* and an *assumption*. This means that on the one hand, in the "judgment," God does not cancel man's work, but takes it up, integrates it for the new creation. On the other hand, God fulfills the intention, the expectation, the desire of man. That is to say, in the course of History, man has never succeeded in realizing the perfect, ideal, fulfilled city that he wishes; God is going to give him what he has been looking for through all of History.

There is thus a double fulfillment: that of God's promise consecrating the reconciliation and the communion between God and Man, and that of man's project at the same time brought to its perfection and shorn of its harmfulness. Thus, God assumes the whole of human History and of Man's works. He makes it his own history. He does not create the final, perfect city from nothing, but from the very work of man. Without it there can be no heavenly Jerusalem—since it is man who invented the city. It is human discovery and innovation that are for God the given elements of this perfection. Hence in the multiplication of loaves, the five loaves and two fishes brought by the disciples. But the passage from one to the other occurs through the Lord's absolute. Finally, in this act, God assumes not only man's innovation, but also his revolt; the fruit of revolt that is absolutely bad is taken by God for himself, it is thereby turned into reconciliation. This is what is meant by the traditional theological link of the assumption of the human condition by Jesus. Such is, schematically summed up, the theological meaning of the City according to the Bible.

Now, it must be possible to exactly transpose this for Technique. In other words, the latter which is historically under condemnation, which is the Witness of man's greatness, of his power, but which produces the human disaster, is not destined for nothingness and damnation. Technique has exactly the same meaning. It is promised to the same assumption and the same taking up, because it is the means of man's work.

And here we must end with this crucial remark: Technique before God has no reality *in itself*; it is only relative to man. It is good insofar as it produces good for man. It is bad insofar as it produces evil for man. It is good insofar as it is an exaltation of God's creation. It is bad insofar as it expresses man's *hubris*, his spirit of power, his search for his own glory. And the two qualifiers "good," the two qualifiers "bad" are in exact relation one to the other. This technique is viewed by God only in its relation to man. This means that because God loves man above all expression, because he has decided to save him at the price of his own abandonment, at the price of his own death in Jesus Christ, then also he loves man with his works, because man—man beloved of, saved by God—is not the naked being, shorn of his history and of his works. It is the man produced by this history, the bearer of *all* his works (not just moral ones!), who is loved, saved, destined for eternal life. God's love for man with all his works includes Technique too, as a major work of man.

The point of a theology of Technique is therefore not to know its final destiny; we know it very simply. Nor is it to know if it is blessed, in conformity with God's will, or accursed. The only problem is on this earth, in the course of this history, as we await the realization of the promise, in the in-between of our birth and of our death. What does Technique represent? What can we do or say about it? How can we attempt to master it, to orient it? This is essentially, and even when considered theologically, a spiritual matter, on the one hand, and an ethical one (in the widest sense), on the other. Such is our only problem.

For if people used to easily draw from the "fall" the consequence of a radical loss of humanity (and here of Technique), and the vision of a total hell, we must not draw from the act of God fulfilled in Jesus Christ the consequence of such an obvious and assured salvation that there is nothing left to do on Earth. And, as far as Technique is concerned, we must not draw from the final fulfillment by the grace of God the consequence that is at its *source*; the fact of this assumption forbids one to declare that Technique is damned, rejected, worthless, and to refuse to participate in it. But no more is it possible to say that it is actually just (even if it justified by grace, along with man), nor that it can be subscribed to unreservedly: for it is indeed *condemned*—only what is condemned can be reprieved! It remains in the stream of history, the work of a spirit of power that is the reverse of the spirit of Jesus Christ. It is at the service of a man who, to put it simply, remains a sinful man. It expresses a fatality in his development and not a freedom. It manifests, in its very enterprise, that technical man deems himself part of a world without salvation, without savior, and without answer.

SITUATION OF A THEOLOGICAL REFLECTION ON TECHNIQUE

Likewise, because we have understood the amazing value of the promise, the meaning of the final "recapitulation," we are not allowed to reassure ourselves about the final outcome. We cannot say, "Since everything ends well anyway, we can continue the technical enterprise as though nothing was the matter; we are free to do anything with Technique." Taking this attitude would be to ensure that the promise remains unfulfilled, for it would mean taking God's word in vain (hence no new creation would be possible any longer; the only way out would then be nothingness). We should not forget that this God who forgives remains a sovereign God, who remains totally free, and grace remains pure grace. One cannot therefore entertain any speculation on his promise for our autonomy in the course of history.

There thus arises the question of man's *full* responsibility with respect to Technique. Man is called in judgment by that *too*. That puts him at the center of the problem of the "Good," in its full sharpness, because Technique is an objective and collective fact. It is not a matter of intention nor of virtue or of individual behavior; that a man behaves *well* toward Technique says absolutely nothing about the global phenomenon. What is more, we are not to believe that Technique is justified in itself if it is used for man's material, bodily good. The problem, as we have said, is ethical, but this does not mean moral. It is first fundamentally spiritual, for beyond the two questions raised above (limits and eschatology) arises the still more crucial issue of how we can go about turning Technique, this instrument of revolt, of autonomy, of the spirit of power, into, here and now already, in the course of this history, as figure and prophecy, an instrument that makes God's glory appear in the midst of men.

The ways of exercising this responsibility are obviously tied to historical circumstances and cannot be defined once and for all, remaining identical. There cannot be any permanent, repetitive solution, nor a codification of a good use of Technique. Conversely, there cannot be any present pessimism about Technique, since the final answer belongs to the God of Jesus Christ, whose work and promise we know. Between these two orientations, let us at least say that we are called to become aware of the fact, and of taking the question raised with total seriousness, for there is a total risk which corresponds to the question raised by Jesus Christ: "When the Son of Man comes, will he find faith on the earth?"[34] Nothing in man's Nature guarantees his continued existence, and also, it must be taken seriously in a total way because there is an increase in suffering, of anxiety in the whole of mankind. This may correspond to the prophecy of Ecclesiastes: "For with

---

34. Luke 18:8.

much knowledge comes much sorrow."[35] The very fact, as we have seen, of the rupture for the creation of the new Jerusalem, and of the Recapitulation of the works of man, of any life, of the whole of history, means there is no progress. There is no calculable advance toward the Kingdom of God, as though more of it were built today than two thousand years ago. There are advantages and drawbacks to Technique which are very difficult to weigh against each other, and from which it is impossible to derive the idea of a progress. And this absence entails a new answer every time, invented, taken by man in a present decision. What the Christian may have deemed to have been the right attitude toward Technique yesterday can in no way be of use to me today. But no more need I judge him for his decision from the standpoint of my present one.

We are thus challenged by Technique (which is constantly evolving, which constantly invents new situations for man, and which is today on an altogether different scale from all that has preceded it) to invent what Christian life might be in and relative to this environment, to discover how to restore an end to this body of gigantic but aimless means, and no doubt to know its meaning and its place before God, but in view of and solely relative to the current behavior that, collectively, we might have to adopt.

3. THE STATUS OF THEOLOGY IN A TECHNICAL SOCIETY

Logically, one should not only be looking at Technique from the standpoint of Theology, but also at the Status of Theology in Technical Society. We will leave aside commonplaces on this topic, namely for instance that Theology, not having the status of a science, has lost its interest, its raison d'être; that Theology is obviously not the science of sciences; that modern man, no longer having any Christian reference, is no longer interested in Theology; that Theology no longer explains anything about what present man lives, feels, etc.; in other words, that is has no point nor legitimacy. This is too simple.

What seems important to me is instead this: we continue to do Theology (even if it concerns few people), but the question is then to know *which* theology. There are some great mutations. At first sight, one will think of political Theology, of the reconciliation between Christianity and Marxism, of Liberation Theology or of Revolution Theology, of the Theology of Culture. In all cases, we are talking about a kind of reconciliation of this or that work of man with Revelation. And we can then say that there is nothing original, nothing new there, since this has constantly been the temptation

---

35. Eccl 1:18.

SITUATION OF A THEOLOGICAL REFLECTION ON TECHNIQUE

since the fourth century, be it with the philosophy, the art, or the scientific knowledge of the time. But the concern and incidentally, as strange as it may seem, the method to achieve it are the same.

But there is a much deeper, more essential transformation, I might say an essential reversal of Theology, sometimes involuntary, sometimes conscious. This reversal was initiated by Bultmann, by Tillich, and by Bonhoeffer's prison letters, but of course they have not gone all the way, have not drawn all the consequences. Now, currently, it is done. In order to do it, people usually refer to Nietzsche and Freud (much more than Marx, who is not useful for the project), secondarily to Blanchot,[36] Bataille, etc. I could say that this new theology is characterized by its disinterest in the object of Theology, on the one hand, and by its refusal of the past on the other.

The rejection of the object means that this theology no longer talks of God. It no longer pretends to be turned toward, still less inspired by God. God is dead, but we are still doing a Theology, but not even that of the death of God, which is passé. This Theology enters the philosophical way of Lacan, Deleuze, Guattari,[37] etc. Therefore, on one hand, there is no reality, and on the other, there is no object of knowledge. It is a matter of de-realizing Theology. This current is not even that of the old negative Theology (we know nothing about God; we cannot say anything about him, other than that this God exists), for it is simply without interest whether God exists or not. Precisely insofar as God could be an object, a reality, etc., has no legitimacy, value, or meaning of any kind for this theology.

This philosophical current is no longer interested in the object of a knowledge, but in the knowledge of that object, that is to say, it is knowledge, the process of knowledge, identity that is *alone* being considered, that alone becomes an "object" of knowledge. Of what? It matters little. In other words, it is the process of theological knowledge that is being considered, and of course, what is then emphasized is language, since this is the locus of all knowledge. Language itself becomes Theology's Theme, and not the real, or man, or God.

When we say language, there could still be some confusion, since a Christian might promptly translate this as a Theology of the word; this is certainly not the case. This would be to "make God speak," whereas, not being an object of Theology, he has nothing to say. There is no word of God. Nor is the object of Theology this word; enough of logocentrism, people will say! No, it is only about human speech in its practice. Hence, modern

---

36. Maurice Blanchot (1907–2003), novelist, literary critic and philosopher, friend of Georges Bataille [note by the family].

37. Félix Guattari (1930–1992), psychoanalyst and philosopher, student of Lacan, and then collaborator of Gilles Deleuze [note by the family].

Theology, in its first aspect, no longer speaks of God, but deals with our discourse about God. It is totally de-realized. And what is rather important to underline is that after the subject has been eliminated, it is obviously normal that the object too be eliminated. There is no speaking subject any longer. But neither are we speaking *about* or *of* something. Knowledge only refers to the fact of speaking.

The second aspect of this theology is its total rejection of rootedness in the past; there can be no question of a creed, nor of a deposit of the faith, nor of a tradition, nor of a continuity of the gospel, nor of a design of God ... The past is necessarily, absolutely dead. There is no reference to retain from it, particularly since, as is often said, after Marx, Nietzsche, and Freud, one can no longer think as before. Also, because all of Theology has been idealist until now, a break must be made in order to make it materialist. Finally, because it was inspired by a certain philosophy and we have radically changed philosophies, it can thus from now on only be oriented toward ... what? I cannot say what the future is, since theologians also recuse this future logically derived from the past, or again this conception of time as divided between past, present, future, which, they figure, does not correspond to anything.

But it is a "hope theology" that is a projection. We think we can breathe, and find something in common (as above with the Word of God), but this is not in the least the case, for we are not talking about a theology *of* hope! It is a hope theology that recuses all that has been able to be said up to now about this hope within the framework of a classical theology. We are again here dealing with a language, hope being the metaphor that celebrates our "believing." There is no content to this hope; we are talking about an opening unto a given or a forgiven, the entrance into a wandering, into the discovery of an impossible that can only be glimpsed from afar, as an expression of man's desire in the final analysis. And hope Theology will be "the metaphor of a metaphor."

But this hope then brings us to a third feature of this theology: it is a theology of gospel-like practice. Not an ethic nor a practice of works! That would be another misconstrual. For an ethic would assume commandments or a reference to a Word of God, etc., all things one is rejecting, but there is nothing but a practice, valid in itself, that is the sole reality, never given in advance. It is a practice that has nothing to do with the "moralizing pleas of individual conscience," for practices taking into account the sites and levels where our society's life actually plays out (here nonetheless political liberation theologies are being recycled!).

And this practice must be the response to a call made to me by the other (not the neighbor! for, people will say, the concept of the neighbor still assumes a relation of individual to individual), which is the criterion of what I have to do. Gospel-like practice has no other legitimacy than being a response to this call, and theology can only be a theology of *this* practice. (Let us still note in passing, and without using this as an argument, that the other on the one hand and politics on the other have a reality. After having told us that we had to abandon any idea of objective reality... But no doubt I haven't understood anything.)

Now, what seems to me quite crucial is that this theology with its three axes is the theology directly inspired by, or what is more, necessitated by technical society. At a time when Marxists are introducing some "play" in the relation between ideology and productive forces, I will be more rigorous on this point: this theology is an ideology that is purely the image and reflection of Technique. For what is very interesting is first to note that the theologians who speak abundantly of society will speak of capitalism, imperialism, the Third World, communism, etc., but never about Technique. They don't know. Their discourse only has to do with political superficiality.

The result is that they are unable to answer a question that has become the obvious to which all have to pay their dues: "Where is the speaker speaking from?" If they raise this question, they will promptly say, "From a capitalist, bourgeois, academic, etc. place," which situates the problem at its most elementary level. It is as though a man in an elevator said that he is speaking from a small wooden platform framed by three glass panels, etc. They fail to see that they are speaking from a technical society that has to such an extent become their environment, their being, their brain, that they are no longer able to see it.

Now, their theological discourse pompously based on Nietzsche, Freud, Artaud, Bataille, Lévi-Strauss, Lacan, etc., is the discourse of Technique, as banal as any cliché. These theologians absolutely do not know *from where* they take their discourse! It is enough that we go over the three points mentioned. Starting with the last one, the simplest one: it all comes down to a practice. To be sure: this is exactly what Technique is and does and the considerable mutation it has brought about. It is a practice. This is all it is. It devalues all else. Only the efficiency of means matters; that is practice. All those who want to make of practice the criterion of everything today are obeying technical ideology, purely and simply. They are entirely steeped in the seriousness of practice, bringing about the vanishing of values, of the subjective, of the individual, etc., etc., etc., all that which philosophy gives form to. They are in general agreement about holding that philosophy speaks with some delay relative to the event (Hegel's famous owl),[38] but in

---

38. According to Hegel, the philosopher as "scribe of the Absolute" can never anticipate the manifestation of this absolute, he can only reflect after the fact: "[I]t is only

this case, the theologian fails to ask relative to what he is late and to what he gives form. He fails to realize that his primacy of practice was imposed to him by the technical world as the sole criterion of validity for thought.

The second point, the erasure of the past for a projection toward a realized impossible, is exactly the same as the approach of Technique. The past no longer holds any interest, because it is a past prior to the technical advent. It cannot be taken into account because it has nothing in common with what we experience and know today, but what constitutes the break is the application of techniques. The past no longer has any continuity with our present (hence the rejection of the idea of a deposit of faith). Everything has changed, through Technique alone. That toward which one is oriented, which is pompously adorned with the term "desire," is what is achievable by Technique. For today's man desires nothing else.

And when we are told about hope toward an impossible, it is in fact a "metaphorical" image for the technical operation, for it is not an actual impossible (to which we will need to return), but something "presently impossible, but achievable tomorrow." Now this is exactly the technician's position. Technique delivers us from the Wondrous (we no longer need a Flying Carpet, nor magic words; all that fairy tales dreamed about is realized by Technique), which Theology takes advantage of by abolishing the wondrousness of miracles and therefore, as well, miracles themselves, with all that this entails. This technique constantly situates us in this attitude of mind: the not-yet-possible, achieved tomorrow. This is exactly what this hope Theology corresponds to, which has nothing to do with biblical hope but with a human process that remained hypothetical, for instance in Bloch's analysis of hope,[39] but through Technique, this hope has taken on a concrete dimension.

The final point is the disappearance of the object in favor of a knowledge of knowledge. This is what is most important and must be examined at several levels.

First of all, it is quite clear that this so-called civilization of objects, of things, in which we live, is very secondary in relation to the civilization of *processes*. Let us consider how much the objects provided to us are made to be used quickly, thrown away and abandoned. "Consumer" products are devoid of interest: what is interesting is at the first level the performances they allow us to accomplish (the car for instance); at the second level, the

---

when actuality is mature that the ideal first appears over against the real and that the ideal apprehends this same real world in its substance and builds it up for itself into the shape of an intellectual realm . . . The owl of Minerva spreads its wings only with the falling of the dusk." Hegel, *Hegel's Philosophy of Right*, 13 [note by the family].

39. Bloch, *Principle of Hope*.

processes used for making them. The goal is not to obtain such and such a new object, but to implement such and such new technical system. The object vanishes in a formless jumble of things that pass and fade away. What remains is the passion for *How to do*.[40] In intellectual terms: only the process of knowledge, not its object, holds any interest.

But let us go further. The more Technique becomes powerful, efficient, dominating, the more what it applies to loses any interest. We can do practically anything; the reality upon which we act no longer has any value. Friedmann has showed it at length; the worker no longer needs to know the material, since his machine can do anything with the material in question.[41] Technique has a *total* hold on reality, so there is no point in pretending that this reality is still one. The only reality is Technique itself, precisely! That is the procedure, the process, the agent of action. And we translate that in intellectual terms by saying that the object of knowledge does not exist, but that discourse itself has become reality. Technique forces us to abandon the idea that there is an object of knowledge, because the object on which it is applied is itself erased.

But this repudiation of an objective reality incidentally produces an interesting effect. Insofar as they repudiate this reality, our theologians cannot see the reality that surrounds and inspires them either; they do not see Technique, because it would still be an object, which they negate and whose possibility they recuse. This impotence leads them to this situation which we saw above, that they also do not know *from where* they speak, *who* inspires their discourse! It is a question without any interest, of course, since only discourse in itself is interesting! What wondrous camouflage of technical power: they are really using what the ideologues of false consciousness had been accused of by Marx! By cutting loose from the object and the past, this theology glories in being a theology that is not fixed, but "wandering," not superficial, but "as an abyss"; it recuses whatever is dogmatic and whatever claims to express a truth (in any case, we have seen that what matters here is not truth but "expressing"). There is no content of faith, for the way of believing fashions what we believe. There is not a confession of faith, but a functioning of faith (and the analysis will of course be made that the objectivity of faith functions in order to reassure oneself about belonging to a group and a justification of what one is), etc.

What is lacking in such a deep critical theology is simply to realize that *everything*, strictly everything that is stated in it, is literally dictated by the functioning of the technical system. The values and faith contents

---

40. Translator's note: In English in the original.
41. Friedmann, *Industrial Society*; see note 11, p. 84.

that are put into question are put into question neither by a science, nor by a philosophy, nor by a progress of conscience, but by the very functioning of Technique. If Theology is wandering, it is in a wandering produced by the shaking of certainties due to Technique alone. What is challenged by this wandering happens to be what Technique challenges (the existence of extrinsic values, the possibility of something transcendent, historical continuity, the project preexisting method, etc.). And one then has to wonder whether theology has any other function than to ratify the situation in which the theologian is being put. For these modernist theologians reproach classical ones for this (and rightly so), but they are doing exactly the same thing. Their critique focuses, on the one hand, on the past and the theological expressions of the past, actually abolished by the new situation, and on the other hand, on conformism relative to a reality with respect to which they are wrong, taking for the last word of revolutionary analysis the critique of the bourgeoisie or of imperialism. But they forget to criticize what is truly conditioning them, for they do not even know. And it is this ignorance, this lack of clear-sightedness, this replacement of reality with a discourse about reality that is explicitly called Hypocrisy in the Gospel.

There remain two remarks for us to make. First of all, these theologians constantly speak of the famous epistemological shift or Copernican reversal performed starting with Freud and Nietzsche. But they are not aware that this actual shift is not the result of a philosophical change, let alone a theological one, but of the rupture caused by the rise of Technique. This is what actually devalued the old ways of understanding and knowing; this is what put into question the old certainties. It is the computer that caused the explosion of linguistics. And theologians pick up the pieces by trying to remake a discourse that would correspond to this real, to that shift. After all, Galileo and Copernicus were not philosophers, nor even scientists; they were good technicians, skilled experimenters, using all the new instruments available!

The last remark is that if man is no longer looking for *what* to know, but for the process of knowledge, if he claims to only grasp discourse about . . . (without concern for: about what!), this involuntarily signals his resignation, for this means that he *himself* no longer has any grasp on the real. What has grasped, what influences the real, what dominates it is something other than this man. It is the universal mediation through Technique. The Medium has replaced not just content, but the possibilities of mastering it. Man gives up on something other than understanding the medium. There is no longer any real; all there is left is processes. It is Technique that has become at once *the real and the process*. It is a process that covers all the real. It is the real inasmuch as it is process. The theologian hence limits himself to giving up, explaining that such is the new true god, brought back to faith in this.

It is obvious that a rigorous analysis of the technical system forbids us to enter into such a theology of conformity to the system. Those who then think they are at the cutting edge of progress, those who can only burst out laughing when the objectivity of faith, Transcendence, the specifically Christian, etc. are mentioned, and who are in reality mere ideological appendages of the technical system, will hold the view that theological propositions based on something transcendent, or critiques made from a Word of God, are retrograde, reactionary, etc. This is simply because they will not have understood their own situation in a society they know nothing about, and how much these propositions are a hundred thousand times more revolutionary than their drifts, their expenditures, their desires, and their outbursts!

I do not pretend to answer these questions in the following pages, because we are talking about a very long-term work that only began yesterday. I try at least to outline the first elements of a response that should not be delayed too long, or else the human technical adventure may end in a historic catastrophe (only historic to be sure! But that does count for something!) without precedent, because it may be the final one (historically, yet again!).

3

Limits

1. IN SEARCH OF LIMITS[1]

An essential question: can man do everything or is he limited?
A question that needs to be multiplied:

- Does "Everything" mean Anything, indiscriminately or the maximum possible?
- Does "Can" mean: what is possible to him, or what is allowed for him?
- Does that mean then that there are forbidden areas? Forbidden because man does not succeed in having access to then (in which case, science and Technique will maintain: we cannot *yet* reach them, but tomorrow...) or forbidden because (morally, religiously) he must not have access to them; or because there is an absolute obstacle, insuperable by any means whatsoever, God.
- Is it man who sets the limit, in which case he can move it, or is it Nature (in which case it is neutral), or is it God? But is this God the All-Powerful Lord who freezes realms and imposes on the sea, "You will reach to that point, but not beyond"? Or the Lord Jesus Christ who places us in our responsibility, as a liberated man who can know, love, will what God has chosen as the best possible, but who can also, because God respects his independence, do the very opposite, being

---

1. Subtitle suggested by the family.

then only given over to the risks this entails, and from which God finally saves him, just not temporally?

Here are the issues. And even if we manage to know that there are limits, that certainly does not tell us *what* they are, nor *where* they are set. And in a biblical theology that purports to be faithful, we absolutely cannot produce a legalism, that is, formulate, clearly, as a Law, a discrimination between a Good and an Evil, a catalogue of limits, a fixed geography of allowed places and prohibited places. Besides, that would be of no use when dealing with the technical process!

One doubtless needs to recall here two traditional theses in order to take them into account, but also to show how relative they are.

For some, man is limited, by nature. He has the experience of his limit, be it that of the reach of his senses and his forces, or that of the length of his life. It is on the experience of this indisputable limit that we need to base the limit of Technique. In other words, the limit would be traced by the very ability of man's being to take on, understand, use Technique. Somewhat as in the Middle Ages the tenure attributed to a serf was gauged by the quantity of land he was able to circle within a day's continuous ploughing.

But this measure and this conception which are the great humanist rule, and very legitimate for a number of things (for instance the limit of the property acceptable in the faith) do not mean anything when it comes to Technique: for the latter is precisely what man has invented in order not to be set within his own "natural" limits. He has given an extension to his senses, which no longer have any limits; he has multiplied many times his physical power, which no longer has any limit; he has launched upon a cumulative work which, as a moving work, appears to give him permanence: Technique is precisely the recusal, by man, of his condition of being limited. He has wanted to get out of his natural limits in this way. Purporting to have Technique fit into them is tantamount to negating it in its totality. And I do say in its totality: it is not enough, for instance, to discriminate between human-scale techniques and others, allowing for the spinning of wool and for hand-weaving, while one recuses the manufacture of artificial industrial fabrics. This is very tempting, it is the first naïve reaction. One may prefer certain technical procedures while putting technical gigantism into question, but one has not understood that this is not where the problem lies.

Technique in itself is something other than the accumulation of such and such a procedure, of such and such a device; it has a specific reality, and it is with respect to that that we have to make a decision. Now one aspect is precisely the power of unlimited growth, starting from the first lineaments. Whether we want it or not, these foundations exist, and it is perfectly useless to pretend not to deal with them to return to medieval techniques. Technique is in itself the unlimited that, precisely, man has passionately desired in order to get out of the limits of his body. It is wholly inadequate to pretend to come back to these limits in order to have Technique fit into them; this is indeed, as we see it, the negation of the whole of Technique.

Now, I believe that on the one hand this is unthinkable, and on the other hand this is not theologically correct either. If God, as we have seen, has taken the decision not to cancel man's history, what right would we have to decide that in the name of this God, we must cancel this work of man—and with it, all thinkable civilization? For, and this is here the crux of the difficulty: the unlimited growth of Technique puts into question and rapidly risks destroying all civilization. But the negation of this technique (its reduction to the limits of the individual human) is the negation of all of civilization, and even of all of history, since nothing in the work of man has been done without this technique.

The second traditional thesis, very fashionable these days, consists in saying that from the origin there were limits to man's enterprise over nature.[2] These limits essentially came from the sacred character of the world, of Nature, of the environment. Whatever was sacred could not be manipulated, used, destroyed at will by man. A sacred wood could not be cut, a sacred spring could not be used for the tanning of skins or the washing of wool . . . Surrounded by a sacred universe, man knew himself to be limited in his enterprises. He might have techniques, but he could not use them just anywhere nor in any way. To this, one needed to add the extraordinarily restricting character of ritualizations. Techniques entered these frameworks and had no possibilities for expansion. The unlimited remained a virtuality, but prohibitions remained more powerful.

And so it comes about that Christianity intervenes in this equilibrium, by desacralizing the world, deritualizing religion, and negating magic. It brings things down to being only things; it refuses the limits of a sacred that it manifests as imaginary; it kills the gods of the forest, the earth, and the waters, and, as a result, it puts all things at the disposal of man who can, from now on, use "nature" as he sees fit, without limits imposed from the outside. Why should one respect what is now no more than matter?

And we must here pay heed to Bernard Charbonneau's call-out: by spiritualizing God too much, by making him radically heavenly and Transcendent, man was necessarily pushed away toward Matter, his action

---

2. And which we find again in detail as we critique Carl Amery's book *Das Ende der Vorsehung*, French translation: *Fin de la Providence*; see Annex to Chapter 5, pp. 229–35.

materialized, man's material instinct liberated.³ The more transcendent and spiritual corresponds to a more materialistic and immanent. Christianity has separated what the ancient world, and the traditional world, had carefully joined, balanced. From that moment on, man may seek the most efficient means and use everything without limits and without shame. The unlimited is inherent to Christianity itself, perhaps not the Christianity of theologians, but Christianity as experienced by the masses of the faithful, and producing effects that were not so much spiritual (having to do with holiness), but concretely historical ones.

All this is partially correct. There is no denying the desacralization produced by Christianity.⁴ Neither is there any denying Christianity's influence in the development of Science and Technique. But the question is to know whether, as we shall see below, Christianity has been the only factor; whether, as we are going to examine, we are not actually dealing with the substitution of one set of limits for another. But it remains true that the things of this world are in Revelation only things, without anything more.

This being said, and in the search for limits, one crucial remark at least needs to be made: the famous limits coming from the sacred are artificial creations of man. I will refrain from giving an opinion on the existence in itself of a sacred. But I am only looking at its expression in the human world and in society. Can we say there was just *recognition* of something that existed in itself, or the *expression* by man of a reality that was experienced as necessary?

The fact that the phenomenon is universal does not mean that the sacred preexists man, but only that, placed in comparable life conditions, man has survived in part thanks to this discovery of the sacred, belonging to the symbolic, the social imaginary. And actually, if desacralization, in certain periods, could occur, it is because we are more in the realm of an expression than of an objective recognition. It seems to me that man has

---

3. Translator's note: Ellul is probably referring chiefly to Chapter 6, "Nature and Christianity," of Bernard Charbonneau, *Green Light*, where his friend also discusses at length Amery's book *Das Ende der Vorsehung*.

4. Which I have studied at length in my article "Actualité de la Réforme" in *Protestantisme Français*, 1942 [actually "Signification actuelle de la Réforme," in *Protestantisme français*, ed. Marc Boegner and André Siegfried (Paris: Plon, 1945), 137–65; note by the editor]. See also the annex to Chapter 5 on Amery's book devoted to this issue, pp. 229–35.

instituted the sacred. Elsewhere I have explained its use and meaning.[5] The sacred takes over the world in which man lives, and assigns a meaning to it. It therefore draws limits. And we know that one of the functions (much more than a consequence) of the sacred is even the delimitation of a sacred realm, characterized by sacrality, absolute defilement, and purity, and a realm of the profane—with, in between them in some cases, the realm of the *Sanctus*, which prevents the relation to the sacred.

As a result, it was obvious that technical activity, even when it too was referred to a sacred, could not dent the reserved realm. There were absolute limits. However, it was always possible to transgress them by magic—it too a technique. But it could not be conceivable that the world be entirely covered by the technical network, nor that a complete freedom of development be left to it. The boundaries of the sacred, the reserved realm, were not left at the individual's free disposal. Even set up, invented by man, these borders were not arbitrary and subjective. They were endowed with objectivity by the absolute belief in the existence of an objective sacred and by the group's adherence. Everyone believed in that sacred, defined, determined by experiences, traditions, myths, etc., and this belief produced an inevitable attitude of respect.

And this had exactly to do with *limits*, since the sacred had been instituted precisely to establish this map of the world where man could find his bearings, thanks to these limits and the reference points. The very object of the sacred is the limit. We must keep this in mind if we want to understand the radical difference of perspective in which Judaism and Christianity will situate themselves. But aside from the belief, the conviction that one became *sacer*, defiled, accursed if one laid hands on the sacred, the pressure of the entire group also worked toward the objectification of the sacred. The belief was collective, and as a result, the social group was steeped in the belief that it would be radically jeopardized if the sacred was violated. The transgressing individual was then sanctioned, excluded, in order to reestablish equilibrium within the group. Thus, limits had an objectivity—taking into account, it goes without saying, that when we say that this sacred was instituted by man, we do not mean that there is a moment when men gather to decide in common, in a clear, rational, conscious, and arbitrary way what is going to be sacred and what is going to be held as profane. It is obvious that things never happened in this way. It is the same problem as with Rousseau's famous social contract.

But the fact remains that though they are not voluntary, deliberate, arbitrary, these limits drawn by the sacred in which one believes are

---

5. Ellul, *New Demons*.

nevertheless artificial. They belong to this grasp man has on the world, to his first attempt to organize it. It is indeed true then that, secondarily, this delimitation protected the natural world. It was not only a protection of man against the world's aggression, not only the acknowledgment of man's powerlessness to physically act upon the world, but also a protection of nature against man's hold.

And this led to a certain equilibrium, more or less harmonious: after all, I readily grant that the sacred has been the major factor preventing the exploitation of nature by man, the unleashing of hubris, the opening of something unlimited. But one should not forget that, conversely, the sacred has been a factor of man's enslavement. It produced terror in man. Living in a universe that was steeped in sacredness, man found himself under attack from two sides: from the natural forces that jeopardized his physical existence and from the supernatural forces that jeopardized his existence as a man. The sacred is *fascinans et tremendum*, to be sure, and in relation to it, man lives in constant and paralyzing terror.

We should not in our day and age, because we see the very negative consequences of the technical unlimited, provoked in part by the disappearance of the traditional sacred, fall into another Rousseauism and yearn back for the happy time when all natural forces were endowed with a sacred power. To invest Nature with sacredness was on the one hand to give it meaning, and at the same time to hope that one could act upon it by the appropriate means of the sacred, since the material means to intervene were lacking. It was to respect it in its deep originality. But, on the other hand, it was giving oneself over to the terrible adventure that every natural phenomenon was much more frightful because it expressed not the random play of blind forces, but a terrifying will, a wrath, a hatred, a passion that needed to be appeased by any means. The sacred ensured a protection of nature, but doubtless to man's benefit and detriment at the same time. We have now come out of this situation, for better or for worse. But we must constantly recall that we have come out of an artificial situation to enter another artificial situation.

Let us start from another viewpoint. Let us briefly go over some of Konrad Lorenz's theses on aggression.[6] We know his demonstration, which I hold to be very sound despite many discussions, sometimes based, it seems to me, on misunderstandings.

6. Lorenz, *On Aggression* [note by the family].

The point that interests us here is the following one: it seems that in each animal species, spontaneous, innate aggression, which is also expressed toward representatives of the species, is nonetheless curbed so that it does not go to the extreme and cause the destruction of the others, which would rapidly lead to the destruction of the species. There is, possibly for the need to preserve the species, a self-limitation of the means of destruction. These innate, hereditary brakes, that are symbolically expressed in a great variety of ways (exactly as aggression itself is also expressed in part symbolically) obviously relate exactly to this aggression, or rather even to the natural means at the disposal of the instinct for aggression. In other words, the more powerful are the means of destruction inherent in the physiology, the morphology of a given species, the more rigorous, active, and rapid are the brakes. Obviously, the brakes for the conservation of the species must be more powerful in the tiger than in the rabbit.

Here appears man's peculiar problem: naturally, morphologically, his forces are limited, his natural aggression has few natural means to express itself. He is actually not very dangerous for his fellow humans (and still less for wild beasts!). He thus has inhibition reflexes in proportion to his weak forces, and as a result, slow and relatively inefficient brakes to aggression. Now what radically alters this relatively satisfactory natural equilibrium is the invention of weapons by man. He makes up for his weakness with artificial means of aggression that rapidly multiply his power by ten. But the inhibition reflexes adapted to his "nature" do not; they remain slow and weak. What used to be consistent with a certain morphology is not altered, because what alters man's power does not get inscribed in his morphology, but remains exterior to him, a pure artifice that does not change his structure, an external means.

It is then that there occurs a remarkable phenomenon: man gives himself limits. He artificially puts a brake to his power from the moment when the latter is no longer limited by the play of reflexes. Man, who again deliberately situates himself within the artificial, gives himself rules he must not transgress under pains of seeing his species disappear.

It is in particular the famous declaration "Thou shalt not kill" that fits this pattern.[7] It has been said, I believe rightly, that man truly became man when he set this rule; it is here that, in a crucial way, he separates from the animal world and truly appears wholly other. No animal ever invented the setting of voluntary limits to his action. There too, and by another path, we thus find again the mechanism of taboos, of prohibitions, which are "what is peculiar to man," and we should be aware that the deliberate negation

---

7. Exod 20:13.

of taboos, the (modern) fact of ridiculing them, of abolishing moral, traditional rules is not a return to a Natural human stage, but is purely and simply a negation of man, tending to his elimination. For if we abolish the "Thou shalt not kill," since the means of destruction have not stopped growing, the annihilation of the species is going to happen very rapidly.[8]

2. ON NATURE AND CREATION[9]

One will never say enough how much damage has been done by a fair number of the first Christian theologians when they infused the Greek thought of their time into biblical concepts, when they transposed Jewish thought into Hellenistic forms, when they covered the existential and dialectical originality of the Bible with a metaphysical and logical interpretative system. We know enough problems such as Time and History, Soul and Spirit. I would like to briefly take up again here another theme, already studied elsewhere: Nature and Creation.

It seems that man (we are obviously dealing with Western man!) feels the unbearable, intolerable, unacceptable character, intellectually as much as at an existential level, of a world that is not closed, of a world that does not include its end within itself. He feels an unquenchable thirst for settling in a world whose beginning and end he grasps, and if he does not yet grasp them, he needs at least the certainty that nothing happens before or after, supposing that there can be a before and an after, which, as we have abundantly been shown in recent years, are cultural concepts that mean nothing.

In order for man to be satisfied, he needs a world of which he is assured that it is sufficient in itself, that it is a closed whole: energy is enclosed within the system, exactly as for Marx conscience too is a result of the system; it is located within. That this world be closed is the condition for man to have a decisive role in it, for man to realize himself the promises that

---

8. Above all, let us not give in to the simplistic idea according to which commandments of this nature are pure hypocrisy, since no one has observed them! Between having a principle like this one and a certain number of exceptions or transgressions, and not having this moral barrier at all, there is a world of difference. We can say that the moral principle is observed in 99 percent of cases. But in the eyes of our modern despisers, we should destroy this principle because there are exceptions, which is rigorously absurd and catastrophic.

9. This section (pp. 141–51) has already been published in *Mélanges André Neher* [note by F. Rognon].

seem to be made to the "human species" (and that perhaps man made to himself), and above all that man have the guarantee of being able to perfect it himself, that is, to carry it to its point of perfection, or else, and perhaps at the same time, to its endpoint. Finally, that the world be closed and sufficient by itself is the condition for a judgment to be brought, be it one of efficiency or of values, on this world and on the work of man, and a judgment that, as a work of man, would thus not be uncertain: that is, that he be assured of his premises (set by man) and of his conclusions (perfected by man). The need to be assured that the world is indeed closed thus answers at once a vital and an intellectual necessity.

There is no need to look for the origin of this need, for if modern science reinforces it, and seems to justify it, it was powerfully present well before the sixteenth century! In order to realize the importance of this need, it is enough to consider the violence of accusations of pessimism as soon as one claims that the world has no reason in itself, that value judgments are made uncertain by the existence of a potential value beyond our graspings, that the promises will not be fulfilled by man's effort, and that the outcome of history is not the work of this man. This is generally considered either nonsense or blasphemy; if it is not man who gives meaning, who brings all things to perfection, who fulfills the positive work of his raising, then you are a pessimist!

Now, what is very remarkable is that such a judgment was also made from the beginning by many Christian intellectuals and theologians whose main work was to include God within the world, to make him a condition for the existence or the persistence of this world, in any case a God at the service of this history. The Death of God theology affair is but another episode, with nothing new about it, of this permanent *quest*. And of course, it was somewhat facile to enter this false way, since through the Incarnation in Jesus Christ God is *henceforth within* the world. It was so easy to add that that he was now *only* in the world, and that we know *nothing* of an *extra* God, and it is enough to consider, to contemplate the *ad intra* God. This happily filled the distortion and made it possible to reconcile the need for a closed world with the presence to man of a God of love.

But this need for a closed world finds itself in direct opposition to the idea of creation. The latter, biblically, is not the appearance of a something, at point 0+1, from nothing, no more than it is the organization of an order that would function on its own with a mechanism that is included. Creation is not the imposition of a rule nor the designing of a nature, but the institution of the relation between the Created and the Creator, the situating of the Created in relation to the Creator. In any case, the affirmation that the Created is not in itself, nor at the origin nor at any moment of its development.

The Creator is outside the Created. The latter thus always remains inconstant, the Creator being ceaselessly the one who can intervene.

The creation is thus an open concept: it is always neither completed, nor closed, nor self-sufficient. It only exists according to a project that is not inscribed in it, that has its origin elsewhere and leads again elsewhere. The creation is a house whose very door and window is open onto that elsewhere, and through all of which run drafts the inhabitant cannot control. Events therefore keep occurring that depend on these drafts, and man has little tolerance for this indecision, this unpredictability, this nonpossession of the world. One cannot be assured of anything if the assurance rests on a word that comes from the outside, if the fulfillment of promises and works is given by one who intervenes, if the dialectical play is not included *in* the factors of the world, but implies a *tertium movens,* if the fulfillment must at the same time come from the outside and be situated outside our home.[10]

Man finds himself dispossessed of all that he views as his sovereignty; the idea of creation is perfectly intolerable, not because it posits a certain origin (this is not an inconvenience, as we shall see), but because it institutes a certain present status of the created, and it introduces an irreducible indeterminacy.

To shield themselves from this unbearable situation, theologians have adopted the idea of Nature. This was the *great heresy.* God created—yes—but what? A Nature, which is to say, precisely a closed and self-sufficient system. He set down some laws, and these work in his place. (To be sure, until the eighteenth century, people are willing to hold that God is not bound by his laws, and that he can transgress them, but this was then seen as a useless obstruction, which was finally gotten rid of.) He instituted man as director and manager of this creation. And then he withdrew from it. Nature thus corresponds to what man desires: to be a master in his own house.

One can live with not having set the beginning. But there can be no question of relinquishing the slightest prerogative of self-sufficiency. Nature is again a closed concept that is dependent on a *past,* since it is according to what has been that whatever will be will be. (This is a radical opposition with creation, an open concept established according to a project.) With this invention of a nature, tied up with a falsification of creation, man was finally at peace. He had been able to close doors and windows; the drafts were disturbing the laws of Nature. He had been able to shut away God within a role and to assign him a limited function which did not introduce any contingency in the system.

10. *Tertium movens:* literally, a *third mover.* An allusion to the philosophy of Aristotle and the theology of Saint Thomas Aquinas, for whom God is the *primum movens,* the "prime mover" [note by the family].

Of course, biblically, there were three stumbling blocks: the creation narrative taken literally, the allusion to the immutable course of the stars and the seasons, and the ordering established by Wisdom. But in order to construe them in this way, these texts needed to be read through the Greek code of the *phusis*. Already the biblical concept of "Wisdom" introduced an element of disorder in this interpretation, but it too was equated with Greek philosophical wisdom. The laws of Nature stopped being plays of regulation and became the good. To allow these rules to play themselves out meant ensuring not that things worked, but the good. Obeying Nature was identical with doing the Good (based always on the premise that Nature was made by God).

To be sure, this eliminated the whole theology of the Word. But what a gain! To know what the good was, one was no longer given over to the uncertainty of a Word that could be said, or not, and that always risked being surprising since it issued from an unknowable; it was enough to look at Nature and to obey it. The will of God was implicitly written there, fixed, immutable, and at the same time graspable, readable by the effort of man—alone. Nature as such ends up being the index of the Good, and what is more, mediating with respect to the deity. All that was needed from that point was a slight operation of eradication in order to be rid at last of this God, reduced to the status of a "figurehead," a "stopgap," a "starting point," etc.

Why should we want to keep gazing at any cost at an uncertain origin? Science will no doubt make it certain for us sooner or later. And, since this moment, we are strangely enough witnessing a constant return to this Nature, which a superficial view wants to confine to the eighteenth century. It is true that then more than ever was affirmed the excellence of the State of Nature, of the laws of Nature (which it is enough to allow to play out in order to obtain for instance the best possible economic situation: liberalism), but if there was such a heavy insistence, it was because it was the time of the "eradication," of the rupture of the perverse linkage between Creation and Nature. Self-satisfied man closed upon himself the hatch of his submarine and finally found himself alone in a system of his own.

Despite all protests to the contrary, we all obey this conviction about Nature being good. We can only transpose from the Nature around us to that of man. Humanism is one aspect of it; anarchism and socialism display some other ones. Everywhere is the conviction that man is sufficient and good by nature, were it not for accidents. To make but a few allusions, let us recall that Behaviorism too (even though it claims to have nothing to do with any philosophical stance) is a naturalism, conceiving obedience to nature as the only possible way.[11] Marx transposes what had previously been said of Nature to Society, which itself becomes Nature, and this is the new factor of our time. Man is but the network of his relations; actually, the notion of "human condition" that Marx substitutes to that of "human Nature" claims to bring the possibility of an opening, of a future and of an invention, but one must not forget that this is immediately negated by the ruthless immanence of dialectics. Marx's world is just as closed as that of eighteenth-century Naturalists; and just as dependent on the past.

Nowadays we constantly see this appeal to the excellence of Nature, be it in the debate on sexuality (since it is natural, why limit it?), or in the negation, by the youth protest movement, of any basis for morality, which, it is perfectly true, relying in the final analysis on a convention internal to the system, has no more reason to be evident than any other. It is just as much the return to the excellence of Nature in *Summerhill: A Radical Approach to Child Rearing*;[12] again recently, we see in as sophisticated a man as Edgar Morin this return to human nature, which, with great verve, is still but another iteration of this constant quest.[13] It is imperative that this closed Nature, alone fulfilling because it is closed, have its reason and its meaning, not just its being. The immense effort of thought and science ends up in greater closure. This appears to be the only satisfactory way.

We must therefore accept the idea that creation is "Counter-Nature," not only because the concept of nature arose as "Counter-Creation," but much more in that, if there is a human nature, it is expressed and inscribed first in the glorious assertion "*Uomo farà da sé*."[14] There is no need of any help. It is useless to lift up my eyes to the mountains.[15] We are indeed alone in the world, and the sky is empty. This is what we wanted. The concept of Creation (the biblical one which, let us recall without dwelling on it, has nothing to do with genetic myths, be they Assyro-Babylonian or

---

11. Behaviorism: a psychological approach that arose in the early twentieth century, centered on observable behavior, viewed as a response to the subject's environment [note by the family].

12. Neill, *Summerhill*.

13. Morin, *Le Paradigme perdu*.

14. Literally: Man will do on his own. The expression is used by Mounier, *Be Not Afraid*, 102: mankind claims a divine attribute, and in support of which, he quotes Genesis 3:5 (*You will be as gods if . . .*) [note by the family].

15. An allusion to Psalm 121:1.

Greek—the divergences are glaring for any unpreconceived reading!) is thus truly against Nature.

And this becomes even more striking when we understand that the Creation expresses a type of relation that is perfectly alien to Nature: grace and gratuitousness. For creation is either the ever-renewed act of the love of God, who gives himself another to love, and who institutes the only possible relation with him, that of love, or the ever-renewed act of the freedom of God (a freedom that is never in any way arbitrariness!), who constantly sets a "*Novum,*" a point of departure, a beginning, an *Archè*.

Now, to be sure, Love and Freedom are two expressions of the same truth, and cannot be dissociated. Together they exactly signify the grace bestowed by God to his creation and to man within his creation. But, of course, Nature is exclusive of any grace that might be granted to it, if it is the measure of the good. There is never in the concept of Nature anything gratuitous; it is not possible; it cannot be imagined. Nothing is lost; nothing is created. There is no conceivable place in the concept of Nature for a *Novum*, an absolutely new beginning, and without origin, no more than there is for a Love that would not have its source in the erotic relation. Thus all that which Nature means, all that which man has put and wanted to put in this concept, is not only exclusive of Creation, but also of Grace.

Biblical grace, like election, is against Nature. How many times do we not see, throughout Israel's History, that election is against nature, be it the election of patriarchs or that of the people? Absolutely nothing, from the biblical standpoint, can support the idea so often held by theologians that grace is a crowning of Nature, a kind of Super-Nature. But neither is there anything that might allow us to declare that if grace is against Nature, it is because Nature (in itself, and also that of man!) is *bad*. Nature is a concept that is added on. All that we can say is that this concept is false in biblical terms! That is to say, the intellectual (as well as existential) attitude that leads one to develop this concept is not metaphysically false, but simply unacceptable from the standpoint of the Revelation that is in the Bible.

This obviously leads us to view the situation that this Revelation presents as being that of man: he in no way belongs to Nature. He does not obey a nature that would be intrinsic to him and preordained. Biblically, there is no such thing as human nature, only a certain relation between man and God. He himself presents the features which we have recognized as those of creation. He is himself created, which means that he is not "let loose in himself," left on his own, "thrown into the world," but no more is he subject to laws and mechanisms, those of animality, or of *Natura Naturans*, or of Society. He is only as a creature tied to creation.

But I do not believe that biblical texts allow us to say that he belongs to creation. (It is one of the meanings of the story where Adam is called to give a name to the animals.) He has reflective power over this creation, not so much on the object (which constantly attracts our attention and is today taken to be what matters most), but on the fact that this object is *created*. He knows, he reflects and thus finds himself in a special relation to the Creator and thus with creation. His situation is therefore specific, and comparable to the very situation of the Creator, but he is as a created being, inasmuch as this incomparable relation with creation is given to him. He is put in creation as a kind of counterpoint to it, but he is not forced to accept a predefined role; precisely because he is an independent factor of creation in his possibility of reflection, he contains within himself a share of indeterminacy. Otherwise, he could never play his role as a dialectical counterpart of the whole of the world. And in relation to God, he is also the point of consciousness, that is, of knowledge of what the act of creation entails as grace.

Man therefore does not appear, if we accept this interpretation of creation, as a fixed given, constant and closed. As the creation is not the setting in motion of a closed world defined once and for all, so man as created is not ordained to a role nor to a "nature."

Here, however, certain precautions need to be taken. The idea has often been maintained in recent years that man (and creation) was created unfinished, incomplete, that he was only a kind of embryo, and that he then developed himself, that he had to make himself. Likewise, it is he who, by his work and his technique, perfects creation.

I believe that this interpretation, insofar as it mostly seeks to justify and validate the whole technical and scientific enterprise, is incorrect. Creation was created perfect and complete. All that God had done was seen by God as good. There is nothing to add to it. That man *uses* creation, and in so doing transforms it, this is another matter, and in accordance with biblical thought. But for him to make it attain a higher level, for him to be by his own effort more than the first Adam, does not seem possible to me with respect to biblical thought, from which alone the concept of creation is drawn.

But, created perfect, he is created, as we were saying, as a counterpoint, with an indeterminacy, with a possibility of self-affirmation, and not just of being affirmed by another. This man, while being a creature of this God, in this situation, is called to *declare* himself, that is to say, to set himself as conscience and reflection in relation to creation (and not as a nature within Nature). This is much less satisfying than the naturalistic interpretation, much less reassuring. For he must then set himself as a kind of "counter-Nature." It is by being a counter-nature (like grace) that he is man. He therefore is man only, precisely and among other things, by escaping the "natural given" that he deems is found within him.

But to affirm oneself against nature is not to testify to the imperfection of creation, but to rise against the inanity of the concept of Nature. For this very act is the testimony within creation of grace, of the gratuitousness of love. It is precisely the share of freedom that God sets apart for man by love and for love. Thus, as we have said above, man only affirms himself at once as man and as creature when he invents and declares an order such as "Thou shalt not kill."

Formerly, people have wanted to characterize man as *Sapiens*, and as we know, this definition, deemed too imprecise, has been replaced by that of *Homo faber*. The tool would then be the mark of humanity. But this is only one aspect of this relation to the created, which has only become so important because we situate it in relation to "Nature." It seems to me on the contrary that the true attestation of man only exists when he clearly affirms himself as giving himself a rule against nature. "Nature" entails that the animal will destroy and kill. The natural inclination, since creation has become Nature, by man's rupture with God, is aggression; to attack and kill is the normal expression of what lives in this nature. But for man it is the mark, the sign that he is not distinct from it. He is not playing his role then, not the one that the Creator expects.

It is when he discovers, invents disobedience "to natural drives," that he is man. It is not by unleashing desire and sexuality and, in so doing, obeying a supposed nature, with physiological needs, that he is man; it is, on the contrary, by taking a decision against nature, which is to master this instinct and to sublimate it. It is not by engaging in violence or in "the authenticity" of the natural brutality of relations that he is man, but on the contrary, by taking the decision, against nature, of formalizing them, of limiting them, of establishing between men a set of screens that enable a sophisticated relation, be it that of law, or that of courtesy or that of self-mastery. It is then, and only then, that he fulfills his role as Creature, and not just as natural animal. Mankind then testifies to God's grace, even without knowing it, without wanting it, by taking that distance in relation to what is complacently described as the "Natural."

This attitude and decision are in no way explained by some behavioristic ritualization. Actually, we face the impossibility of understanding what happened as long as we stop at the concept of Nature, for what happened was a phenomenon against nature! Evidently, one cannot claim that Non-Violence belongs to man's Nature. And this is why we abandon this decision as a feature of Being-Man. It is so much more reassuring and more explainable to start with the tools! By contrast, everything finds an explanation with the idea of the creation of man, where everything rests on the twofold relation to the created and to the Creator. But to be sure, this situation is uncomfortable, and man, if he is a creature in a dialectic with the rest of creation, is not placed in a restful situation; this indeterminacy is disquieting. Kierkegaard says just this in *The Sickness Unto Death*: "Whence then comes despair? From the relation wherein the synthesis relates itself to itself, in that God who made man a relationship lets this go as it were out of His hand, that is, in the fact that the relation relates itself to itself."[16]

Thus, man's ability to be man by himself, since he was created as a relation where the synthesis relates to itself, opens to man what is often called the possibility of humanization, but at the same time that of despair; but this is just the exact counterpart of his created being.

To be man is to be against Nature. But this entails a whole set of dangers. For if we posit the concept of Nature, and man within it, that means that by obeying the laws of Nature, he does well, or again that he is not wrong. He has a knowledge kit that allows him to orient himself. What is more, he is subjected to drives which, being natural, are good. He meets with obstacles which, being natural, are indications to follow. Now, this is particularly essential if one accepts the idea of a rupture of man with his creator.

As long as there is communion, the created knows how to become man by receiving from the Creator grace, the attestation of love, but also the power to take his decision to be man. This has nothing to do with the mechanical application of a commandment, of a compelling order. God's will never replaces man's will. The relation with God only establishes a possibility for man to affirm himself for what he is, but he invents his own ways and means. There is a regulation, but it comes from within man, from his awareness of being a creature, that the world in which he lives is creation, that is to say, that it belongs first and foremost to the Creator. There is in this way a regulation of the man-World relation, ensured from within man, because he has this unique relation with God. If he declares, "Thou shalt not kill," it is on the basis of his acknowledgment of his created being, as grace and love, and not on the basis of a will that crushes, dominates, and coerces him.

---

16. Kierkegaard, *Sickness unto Death*, 149.

In the rupture with God, man keeps his role with respect to creation, but not this regulation anymore. He no longer knows where the inspiration is for becoming man. He no longer has any measure. He can do everything, but as the covenant with Noah recalls, in violence, by spreading fear all around him. He can do everything and does not know how to choose living, created being within a free creation. He then strives to define this creation in relation to him and not in relation to the creator. He imposes upon it the status of Nature. And this gives him a regulation for his action, which will either be "automatic," when he sets the rule of obeying what he discovers in himself as his own nature, or exterior to him, when he sets the rules of Nature. The regulation is therefore no longer the expression of grace, but obedience to a *fatum*.

What we discover is that this obedience, which is indeed a regulation from a certain standpoint, is on the contrary unfettered unleashing from another standpoint. It is precisely what has been discovered for instance with the laws of liberalism; there is indeed an obedience to a set of natural rules, for instance from the economic standpoint, which, being in conformity with what man has posited as nature, produces efficient results in its area. Economic laws make it possible to obtain the best possible economic result. "Economic Nature," when we obey its structure, answers precisely. But just what happens to characterize this Nature is its fragmentation. There is no point at which it would be gathered together.

In the nineteenth century, Nature was represented in a personification that led one to believe that it was a unity. But since this is, on the contrary, a human invention deriving from the discoveries man makes in each specialized sector of his activity, Nature appears on the contrary not as a full and symbolic given, but as a puzzle put together from disparate pieces. There is no complete natural reality, for this given can only be such from outside itself. It is a gaze that embraces the whole that can lead to an original view. But this assumes Creation and not nature.

The biologist and the physicist who refine their research on matter/energy or on living beings each give us, despite their pretensions, renewed in the modern era, not a synthetic view of Nature, but a tiny sector, however vast and complex it may be. And we find no connection from one sector to the next. We should not be hoping that this is going to change with the progress of knowledge; it is the very origin of the concept of Nature that forbids it, and this is well confirmed by the evolution of sciences over the last century.

Therefore, the result of obedience to the "laws of Nature" is necessarily the transgression of the laws of said nature, defined in a related sector, but not coordinated. We only have the choice between piecemeal obedience and piecemeal transgression. There is no global regulation to be expected from the concept of Nature with respect to man's behavior. It is lucky enough if these instances of obedience do not lead to a destruction of man, due to negligence toward him stemming from our own impotence to find again a meaning to this life. Thus, obedience to the economic natural laws that produce economic expansion also produces the greatest exploitation of man by man and the greatest injustice. This simply because the relation of the created to the creator has been broken, and the substitute "Nature" cannot include grace and love as crucial elements of being man.

Of course, I am in no way saying that these laws discovered by the Sciences do not exist—on the contrary! I am saying that the observance of these laws is not necessarily "good." The concept of Nature is useless with respect to goodness or meaning. It is only if the laws of Nature are set anew within the globality of creation, situated in relation to a creator, and within a proper relation of the created to the created, of man and his environment, that they find meaning. Eliminate creation, and obedience to the laws of Nature becomes a disorder.

But from an altogether different standpoint, when man no longer knows his place in creation, he still continues to keep his power to act against nature, still obeys his calling as created being. He lays hold of its possibility, and this will therefore produce a disastrous situation, well characterized by contradictory discourse: for it is the same ones who proclaim for instance the urgency of liberating sexuality, since it is Natural, and it is very good to behave according to physiological drives, who demand at the same time the universalization of abortion and the pill (which are perfectly against nature) in the name of the mastery that man must exercise over nature, man affirming himself as master and dominator and no longer as obedient toward the "natural given."

This contradiction at the level of justificatory discourses can be generalized and is highly typical of the impossible relation between created man, who as such can only be a transgressor of Nature, and man as inventor of Nature, which he gives himself as a rule, so that he need not know anything of his creator. He then lays hold of his situation toward this Nature and proclaims himself free to act toward it as he pleases. Then begin the abuses against Nature (sexuality "against nature" for instance) which are not disastrous as such, but are so because they no longer express created man's relation to the creation that is given to him in relation to the creator; for if we live this way, then sadism, masochism, homosexuality indeed become not "against nature," but simply impossible. Being man against nature is expressed not in unleashing, but in the acknowledgment of the sole relation of grace, gratuitousness, and love (*agape*) which is the only liberation possible.

It is exactly the same problem with technical expansion. From the moment when the concept of creation is rejected in favor of the concept of Nature, the environment can only be given over to the excessiveness of the means of exploitation, in which, once again, man fulfills his calling as transgressor of Nature, but from now on without any meaning, without any reference. Since this reference could only be exterior to the field of his action, and through the concept of Nature, he has eliminated this outside, taking the very order of Nature as sole reference.

Thus is unleashed the "plunder of the planet." It cannot be otherwise, because of the combination between the condition of created being (thus necessarily of transgressor) and that of creator of Nature (made to be "given over," without any possible control). We thus see the true implicit and hidden meaning of the substitution of Nature for Creation: it is the invention of what allows the will to power (which has absolutely nothing to do with freedom) to be unleashed, including at the same time its own justification, whatever happens. In other words, and up to now, we have arrived at one result by different paths according to which one can say that man determines for himself his own limits, this belongs to his nonnatural universe, this world that he creates for himself, but he establishes them in a closed universe, whose limits he also determines himself, and where he wants to be alone.

It is here that Judeo-Christianity comes into play and puts into question the totality of this construction—as we have just seen with the idea of creation, which we are now going to find again.

3. JUDEO-CHRISTIANITY AS THE NEGATION OF LIMITS

As is well-known, without any need to dwell on it further, Judeo-Christianity has caused a twofold crisis in this universe.

First of all, it is the crisis of desacralization, which people are talking about so much today. Let us say in a word (since we will find it again while critiquing Amery's book) that Judeo-Christianity has destroyed the sacred which man had set in nature and in so doing has destroyed the respect invested in nature by pagans. From then on, the world is simply natural, made up of things and not of gods. There are no taboos, no holy things, no religious fear of a mountain or a spring. Things are things; the God who created them is in heaven. Man therefore need not observe these limits; he can grasp everything, do everything, use everything. Nor is there an equilibrium between a spiritual and a material that interpenetrate each other; the sacred no longer has any meaning, but as a result as well, the world no longer has any meaning in itself. However, this desacralization also includes another aspect: the destruction of gods and religions. Judaism and Christianity did not claim they were superior to other religions, but on the contrary, they destroyed Religion *in itself*. God, the God of Israel and of Jesus Christ, is not the greatest of gods, he is strictly the only one and happens to be a god who does not want religious forms of worship or knowledge. He establishes another relation with his faithful. He recuses all religions (including the one people claim to institute for him) because religion is a product of man, a means for laying hold of God in the final analysis. The God of Israel is an absolute without any compromise, but therefore, this destroys the order of the world that man had instituted, the equilibrium of the world, and by affirming an absolute Transcendent, this forbids any possibility of a conjunction between "heaven and earth."

Thus this radicalism throws man back toward an earth where he no longer finds any meaning nor any value that is not recused. He is also oriented toward a treatment without respect of this earth and withdrawn into himself. This simplistic view of things calls for two remarks:

- The first one is that this acknowledgment had a positive connotation at the time when it was deemed that thanks to this desacralization, Christianity had enabled the rise of thought; Christianity had freed man of his fantasies, made the rise of science possible. Today, as we are experiencing the questioning of Science and Technique, the connotation is turning negative: it is Christianity that is responsible for the appalling modern tragedy, the tragedy of the infinite multiplication of means, of an unlimited power, of the absence of belief in an absolute limit. The mortal and universal danger resulting from the Hydrogen Bomb or the ecological disaster is born of Christianity. Let us not discuss this now.

- The second remark is that, even so, we have to realize that the movement toward the elimination of the sacred, of religion, which is indeed at the heart of Revelation, has largely failed; the sacred instantly took over Judaism and Christianity again, as they instantly became in the hands of men producers of sacred objects. And likewise, people managed to turn them into religions again. Christianity became a "monotheistic religion," or even Religion *itself*. And this always shocks people when one attempts to remove the religious aspects of this Christianity. In other words, the power that creates sacredness and religion, which man invented perhaps two million years ago, is so considerable, so innate, that it is almost impossible to root it out in man.

This being said, was there no more to Judeo-Christianity than to place man in a neutral world and endow him with a wonderful freedom of indifference? Obviously not. Without any doubt, we are indeed dealing with a negation of the limits and the order that man has instituted. And then one plays the freedom card. The God is the liberator. He resituates man in a situation of freedom. He recuses service to other gods, for it is always slavery, and he recuses limits *a priori*, because it is always the limitation of the being that he wants to be free. And yet it is not an incoherence and limitlessness. There are from the start two basic givens: that of creation and that of covenant. But we must avoid misconstruing creation; for instance, the Genesis story is not there to give us a description of what happened, nor an explanation of the world's origin. This was superimposed on this story by positivistic minds; it is given to attest to the presence of a creator. With the twofold recusal of the world being a product of chance, of a blind combination, and of the world being a theogony of the kind known in the Mediterranean Orient (and elsewhere) with fabulous mythical tales.

We are here in the presence of the Creator, who remains that: ever present to his creation, ever faithful to this creation, having a constant disposition. That is to say that this creation, as the fruit of his love, is still the object of his love, and this creation, mirroring his decision, is ever his glory. He is not a fickle, weird God, indulging fancy or passion. He is not a God vested with human passions or a God who is absent after having left to chance the fruit of one of his acts. He is not a perverse and mean God. The creator is the faithful God, ever-present and caring at once for the freedom of the one he wished to be his free counterpart at the center of this creation and for the latter's conservation. The creator's presence is the limit itself.

But it is not an external limit that this creator is going to impose like that of the "garden of Eden," for instance. It is a simple speech limit, which assumes an understanding, an acknowledgment, an obedience. The God does not set objective and immutable limits, no more than he creates in man a Nature that would contain in itself its own limits. It is to a discovery of limits within the relation with this creator that man is called. And he is at the same time called to be accountable, he is made responsible.

There is only one thing which he cannot escape, which is, at one time or another, the question—a question that God puts to him, and that makes him responsible, meaning compelled to answer. Adam, *where* are you? Cain, what have you done? etc. Thus a personal and dialogical relation, necessarily proceeding by trial and error, is substituted for an abstract, ritualized, mythologized, and, in one way or another, objectified relation. Man is thus called by this God to take his own decisions in a space of considerable freedom, but faced with a responsibility. As a result, man is going to consciously set himself these limits with respect to this creator. He is going to create limits within himself. That is where they are born.

The other aspect of the origin of limits is the covenant. But here again we must be careful; this covenant has been interpreted as a kind of blank check given to man. The latter is chosen by man. He is put at the summit of creation, has this creation at his disposal by divine order; the covenant with Adam in particular puts in his hands all that exists, and there is no limit. This is strictly incorrect. The covenant, each covenant, is made up of the act of election, of grace, of liberation set by God, but also and immediately, of the Law of the covenant, that is of God's will, which man is called to obey. Here, it is no longer the Creator's presence that induces man to seek his way of action and his limits; it is the direct expression of a will, which may be, as we know very well from the five books of Moses, quite detailed, but never objectified, immovable, dead.

Once again, this is not about a network of insuperable and absolute limits, but about conditions for life to be possible. It then clearly appears here that, for instance, not all means are possible. Sometimes there are commandments that seem weird to us: those about the mix of species, the prohibition on cooking the kid in its mother's milk, on weaving their textiles with fibers of different kinds, on not using such and such wood or not using scissors for such and such a building, etc. But each time, it is about telling us that not all means are good; thus the covenant that does indeed put man in this eminent situation at the same time situates him in a network of commandments, of orientations, that are never cast in stone, but the experience of a living will, the point being not to follow its directions down to every minute detail, but to seek its meaning and permanent value (even when the agri-pastoral stage has been left).

This being the case, we therefore have limits that are explicitly formulated in the covenant, in the Torah. But these are not objective limits, i.e., received as a law inscribed in Nature, nor permanent. It is not enough to apply them as they are to be in order. In reality, we must not forget that they are said by the creator, who manifests as such, and who as a result calls man to creation, generates him, provokes him. These commandments are the expression here and now of this will within a given set of circumstances. The point is, and this is man's freedom: to receive them at once indeed as a (personal) commandment of God, but also as one whose substance must be interpreted in order to find out what they might mean (and not executed without seeking their meaning: this is what Jesus constantly reminded people of).

It seems to me that we then see two kinds of limits make their appearance in the Bible: those that are indeed explicitly given as a commandment whose meaning must be sought, and those that are gradually discovered by man in the exercise of his responsible freedom.

As far as "commandment limits" are concerned, we find two orientations for them in the Old Testament. There are those included in the Torah that are explicitly aimed at reducing the potential of man's means to save him or to save the environment of Nature. Then there are those that are meant to reduce human means to allow God's power to appear.

As far as the first order is concerned, we have everything that has to do with the Sabbath. This Sabbath is, among other things and when it comes to what interests us here, the suspension not just of human work, as enslavement, but also the suspension of all the technical uses, the elimination of the search for efficiency, the return to worship and contemplation. In other words, the restoration of a genuine right relation with God, which implies a relation of relaxation and liberation with the natural world, the environment that ceases to be exploited. This right relation with God is recreated by God, beyond the rupture and its consequences. In other words, the Sabbath is a grace that is granted by God and in no way a complex ritualization of obligatory commandments. The "condemnation" is lifted, the obligation suspended, the compulsion of fate eliminated, reconciliation proclaimed. For one must always remember that it is in terms of this condemnation, of this obligation, of this compulsion, of these conflicts that man develops his techniques, his means, his power, his efficiency, as a response to it and as compensation for it. Where there is no more condemnation, where reconciliation is given, if Nature no longer produces thorns, then there is no more technique. The Sabbath is the possibility for man to suspend his technical obsession. It is the opening of a new understanding, of another choice for life.

The point is not to say that Technique is bad or outside the will of God, but to manifest that it is only a substitute for what should have been and that its justification only lies in this distress, of which the Sabbath is for us the present sign that it must have an end by the love of God. This suspension of Technique will be expressed, for instance, by the fact that "Nature," on this day of the Sabbath, continues to give as though it was worked, or that there will be a sufficient production in the preceding days so that people do not lack anything on the day of the Sabbath. This is not said in so many words, but it corresponds on the one hand to what is promised for the Sabbatical Year, and on the other hand to what we are told about the manna (which definitely was not a technical product!).

The suspension of work, and thus of Technique, is made up for by the Lord's gratuitous gift. And it is gratuitousness that is here the sign, the attestation of the lifting of the curse, of the reconciliation, of the possibility of freedom. The Sabbath confirms that Technique is situated in the realm of necessity, of compulsion, of obligation. It never produces freedom. The latter comes from the free act of God that liberates, and from nothing else.

It is quite crucial that this limit is met as a limit between the world of necessity and that of freedom. The Sabbath is the opening, not of an empty time, or of one filled with the obligation to worship, but of a free time, in contrast to the rest of the week that is tied to it. The limit between technique and the gratuitous is that between the world of necessity and the world of freedom.

Thus, the Sabbath is also an elimination of Technique in Time: it is the insertion in the course of life of a non-Technical time (which therefore cannot be legalistic either, legalism being a certain religious or moral technique). The limit to Technique is then set in Time and in meaning. In other words, if we have an attitude of worship, of veneration toward Technique (which of course nobody ever admits to as such!), we cannot have any limit.

But theologically, this attitude of veneration is the one expressed in the theories we have alluded to: Technique liberates man; Technique expresses his demiurgic nature; Technique makes man a collaborator with God for his creation. All this therefore implies that there is no limit to Technique, because it is a negation of the meaning of the Sabbath. Likewise, if we devote our Sunday to using technical things, to living through the use of the car and the TV, we eliminate the limit that consisted in inserting a non-technical free time in the course of compulsory technical time.

If, in Mosaic legislation, it was the Sabbath-Work dyad that was dominant, it was insofar as work was the greatest mark of necessity upon man's life; it was the negation of his freedom. Today on the contrary, even though it is still very important to raise the issue of work and of the compulsion of work, the real problem, absolutely identifiable with the previous one, is that of Technique. It is there that the Necessity/Freedom dilemma appears. It is in relation to it that God's declaration of freedom must be formulated. Thus, the Sabbath is in itself a limit upon Technique. But then one has to realize that this only makes sense if one situates oneself in relation to that God, to the one God of Israel. That is to say, the Sabbath has no meaning in itself. It is not even the kind of institution that might be generalizable for all, but has meaning exactly because we believe that this God of Israel is a God who liberates, that this God is the living God who continues to speak, that this God founds a law that has no meaning in itself but as an instruction coming from this God, that this God leads to life (of which the Sabbath is the sign) and that the commandments he gives are exactly the delimitation of the field within which it is possible for man to live, and to live free. It is thus exactly to the extent that we live in this faith that the Sabbath has a meaning.

It is thus God then that sets the limit to Technique, and not a human institution. Suffice it to recall that the Sabbath only has fullness in the worship of God. This is what gives a meaning to the Sabbath. Remove the worship and the Sabbath (Sunday) is nothing more than empty, meaningless time, when one is bored, does not know what to do, fills it with equally empty journeys, and feels sick to have to face oneself and others. But it is on the other hand obvious that worship cannot exist without a genuine faith relationship with this God—otherwise, either we are going to do a fastidious ritualism like Judaism, or the compulsion of worship and hymns all day like Calvin. Without faith, this also becomes meaningless and boring.

In other words, the Sabbath exists as an objective limit on the one hand, or as signifier of a fundamental limit on the other hand, exactly to the extent that there is a faith relationship with God. Failing that, there is no limit; Technique is destined to cover the whole of time and meaning. But this then leads to non-meaning, since Technique itself does not receive meaning from the obligation resulting from the "condemnation," or from the need man may have experienced to invent it. These explain that Technique exists and that thanks to it, man became man in existence, and bound to the artificial, but all this has no meaning. It receives a meaning, not from a divine origin, from a good image of God because he is creator, but precisely from the moment when it is suspended, from the moment when there is no more Technique, and when, from then on, and from there alone, one can turn back to Technique and contemplate it, and indeed learn what it is from the vantage point of the worship of God. It receives its meaning not from a will prior to God that would have created man so that he be a technician, but on the contrary from the *seventh day*, the one when work was *finished*: "You will do *all* your work . . ." You will do it. You will not leave it out of order. You will not sabotage it. But what now validates work here (the only declaration) is the institution of the ceasing of this work. It is during the creation of the Sabbath that working is said to be legitimate in spite of everything—nowhere else. It is while setting the limit of work that it is said that it is also good for man to work.

And what we say about work, we must also say it about Technique, but by positing the demand for the lifting of Technique one day in seven, for the acceptance of a non-technical time, of a relinquishment of any technique. It is from the vantage point of this relinquishment, and from nowhere else, that Technique is validated. "It is true that, out of necessity, you must use Technique; you cannot do otherwise, or else you would regress to the animal, or you would simply cease to be able to live. But learn to see it only as a hard and painful necessity. Do not find your joy in it, nor your hope, nor your value, nor your truth, nor your strength, nor your security. If you place your trust in it, then it will become deadly and destructive." That is exactly *what* the institution of the Sabbath says.

Thus, Technique receives its place, its validation, and its *meaning*, from the vantage point of this lifting of necessity, of this moment of freedom that God gives man. If we eliminate it, then Technique too loses its meaning, becomes non-sense, and introduces us into a universe of non-sense and of totality at the same time.

Here is then an example of an objective limit set by God to the indefinite development of Technique. We find at least one other example, with provisions about respect for the created world, incidentally also related in part to the Sabbath. Man is not allowed to do just anything, even if he is materially able to do it. Such is the meaning of the following provisions: man strictly cannot behave as an absolute owner, but he must show the same love to the world created by God. We have many testimonies to this in the Old Testament.

The two most important ones have to do on the one hand with the animals. The Sabbath is also instituted for the animals (Exod 23:12): the animal cannot be exploited up to the extreme limit of its strength, be exhausted, or produce until death. The Sabbath is the sign that it enters the Lord's very rest, that it is beloved of its Lord. The animal can be in the service of man. It is even delivered into the hands of man for the latter's survival, but killing an animal still remains on a borderline with murder, hence all the Mosaic legislation about blood, which is not a stupid custom of cultural belief, but here again the limit (and it could have taken another form) that God sets to man's excess.

The legislation about the animal's blood is not primarily the belief that the animal's soul or its life is in its blood and that one must not eat the soul, etc. All this is the superficial aspect. The heart of the problem is that God sets a limit to what man can do with respect to the animal. Man has become a carnivore. Granted. He has introduced terror. Granted. But he still cannot do just everything and anything. He must at some point encounter a radical, absolute limit that compels him to accept that the animals and their life belong to God, that God loves them, that God is the Father to them too. And man must then simply obey this rule set by God to acknowledge that his right of ownership is not absolute, unlimited, that his use is only a permission by God.

What is said about life is also said about work, more strongly still. Man does not have the right to exploit the totality of the animal's strength. There is a fundamental respect for it; now, one should apply this in a modern way, not to the work, since animals are hardly made to work anymore, but for instance to the new fattening methods, to battery farming, which is an awful way of treating animals. It is already difficult to accept murder, but during the lifetime of the calf, of the swine, of chicken, to raise them in a torturing manner, to keep them in "economical" but anti-natural conditions, is just as criminal as the concentration camp.

The Sabbath was made for man and at the same time for the animal. God reminds us at the end of the book of Jonah that if he is sparing Nineveh, it is on account of his love for man *and* for the animals who are there. It is not sentimentality, it is not poetry, that is God's order. The limit set is always the limit so that disorder still be livable. It is not the fact that man may kill the animal that is God's order, but the limit that God sets to this hold of man that is the expression of God's love, a love that is at the same time what allows the whole to survive. The transgression of this limit is death—battery farming is the same thing as the concentration camp. And we do not have the right to say that "the animal has no soul." We do not have the right to think that the animal is nothing but meat, nothing but economic utility. This is the same reasoning that enabled the concentration camp: the Jew is not a man.

What we have to know on the contrary is that the animal is beloved of God (whether or not it has a soul is of no concern!), and it is this love that we negate when we claim unlimited dominion over the animal. We are dealing with the abusive use of property. I say very firmly that all the new farming systems, with their use of chemical products to speed up growth, are explicit sins, making the disorder of the world worse beyond limits that can be accepted by God.

And it is the same for the rest of the natural environment. We find there too a very clear decision by God setting a limit about trees: when you besiege a city, you will not cut down the trees. You may eat of their fruits, you may use them, you may cut down just what is necessary to build battlements or machines, but nothing more.[17] There we are still dealing with this limit of usefulness. We may use nature just and exactly for what is indispensable, but we have no right that would go beyond what is strictly necessary. The tree must be left.

Of course, one can say there too that it is a purely cultural measure, i.e. that in a country where trees were rare, they had to be respected. But it must be noted that if man had accepted this, we would not be in an ecological crisis and facing the fundamental threat in which we find ourselves. There too, we are facing the limit and the recusal of abuse, it is why I will not take this text to be merely utilitarian and confined to Israel's wars, but as globally meaningful and having effectively become the Word of God for his creation.

---

17. Deut 20:19–20.

This happens to be decisively confirmed by the Sabbatical Year (Lev 25).[18]

The text begins with: "When you will have entered the country I am giving you, the Land will rest."[19] The first decision is thus I give the land, but, now that you are the owner, I state that this land is entitled to its rest, i.e. that your ownership is quite limited. The land enters *first* into the Eternal's rest, *before* it is in the service of man! And what follows then rigorously confirms this supremacy of God, to the benefit of his creation. For the order is that man may use this land for six years, and the seventh year will be devoted to the land's rest. We will only be entitled to what the land naturally produces, without working it or making it work.

Turning this into a mere agronomic law is a stupid positivism. The mistake is to think that it is the best technical practice that the Jews then hallowed by putting it in the mouth of God. That is absolutely not the meaning. The reality goes further. It is the declaration of a kind of margin where man is not master. God accepts, tolerates that man should exploit this destroyed, scattered creation, which no longer is what had come out of the creator's hands, but a margin of *freedom* is needed. It is not an agronomic practice; it is the affirmation of a freedom for God that nature be freed from man's yoke, that it too should know the freedom of God, that it too finally be to the glory of God.

But this glory is in no way expressed when nature is tortured, exceeded, squeezed, ravaged by man. The peace of creation, the margin that is given to it to be itself, the limit imposed on man are essential for something alive to still subsist. The same text continues very strictly: if you respect these laws, the Sabbatical Year and the Jubilee Year, then you will live in freedom in the country. Man's security is very exactly tied here to respect for the world in which he finds himself.[20]

This did not really appear, at that time, to pertain to some "natural" mechanism; it did not go without saying that nature's rest conditioned man's necessity. In order for this to be, God had to take on the relation with and

---

18. It has often been said that the system of the Sabbatical Year and the Jubilee Year had never been actually applied. It is very difficult to know if it has. But I would say that, as far as we are concerned, this does not matter at all. It is not the observance by the Jews of this part of the law, or its nonobservance, that makes it a commandment of God! It is recognized by Israel as Word of God, and this alone is what matters to us—taking into consideration that, with Israelite rigorism, it was rather difficult to leave in parentheses such an important text. In reality, if doubt has been cast on the application of the text, it is because it was inconvenient for positivistic historians of the late nineteenth and early twentieth centuries!

19. Lev 25:1. [Translator's note: actually Lev 25:2.]

20. Lev 25:18–19.

the protection of his creation against the one who could always become the destroyer, and man's security. And that could then only be situated within the covenant, within a relation of faith and hope, which that same text contains in its conclusion: lest you worry about what you will eat the seventh year, I will be granting you my blessing the sixth year, and the earth will give products for three years . . .[21] We are almost coming back to the Sermon on the Mount.[22]

All this is warning us that above and beyond the property relation, the possibility for man of exploiting the earth, there is this commandment of love, and the protection God grants to this creation. But, once more, when man exceeds the domain that God grants him, when he crosses this limit, then there is not a brutal intervention by the God who sanctions, condemns, and damns, but God allows the logic of things to proceed: man situates himself outside of God's protection, and by a kind of mechanical conditioning (necessity becoming destiny, fate), man's insecurity and the putting into question of man are direct results of his transgression, of his abuse.

This is our current situation in the "environmental tragedy." We have unleashed our power, have exploited to death, by destroying species, riches, possibilities, natural equilibria, cycles, products. We have been squandering them at an incredible pace. All those who deny the possibility of an exhaustion of riches have as their argument: there are so many billion tons of chemical elements of all kinds in the oceans; exploit the oceans (that is in reality: destroy seawater), and mankind can continue at this same pace for centuries. The monstrosity is precisely the willingness, for questionable uses, to unhesitatingly consider the total destruction of basic elements. Then man's security is indeed no longer assured. It is man's behavior toward creation that destroys his own security. This is exactly the point that we are at.[23]

⁂

But the same remark needs to be made about these limits as about the Sabbath: it is exclusively to the extent of faith in this God who asserts these limits that they may be taken seriously. Outside of that, they have no value

---

21. According to Lev 25:20–21.
22. Matt 5–7.
23. Pages 158–62 have already been published in a more expansive article, "Le rapport de l'homme à la création selon la Bible," *Foi et Vie*, 73 nos. 5–6 (Dec 1974) 137–55 (only pages 146–50 are also found here) [note by F. Rognon].

in themselves. It is enough to see today the futility, the perfectly ineffective character of calls to reason, of the anxious unemployed, of all those who see the environmental disaster. It is not enough to tell man that he is sawing the branch on which he is sitting, to explain that we are headed toward the end of the world; what planet are we going to leave to our children? These rational and scientific arguments may interest people and even scare them a little, but this has never prompted any conversion, any deep change of life. A very radical motivation is needed, and I firmly believe that only faith in that God can bring people to take nature seriously enough to change our behavior, if it turns out that this is indeed God's will.

Let us clarify that this is no apologetic argument. I am not saying: "Convert to save Nature or else if you want to save creation." By no means. I am saying (to repeat): "In order to radically change one's lifestyle, a very deep motivation is needed. I know of no deeper motivation than faith in God (experience shows that all others are insufficient). It happens that this God has as his sole designation love, of which man is the mirror at the same time as the image of God in this creation. This God cannot suffer it to be brought back to nothingness. Faith in this God must therefore change our technical behavior by accepting a whole set of limits . . ." Such is my discourse.

One must thus try to understand what these biblical instructions, openly limiting of technical totalitarianism, might mean for our time. Technique allows one to do anything, but you will stop there. We have until now talked about objective limits because they are explicitly pointed out as such in the Bible, expressed and made known as coming from God, without leaving us any other choice than to interpret them for the present time (and not to take them literally).

And we must recall in this respect that these decisions of God are not obsolete. This has a double meaning. We cannot get rid of them by following traditional theological discourse whereby certain purely social, and not moral, laws are abolished by the reign of Grace. Due to Grace we have entered, as Paul has perfectly showed us, into a new world; we are no longer under the law (at a pinch, one is willing, like Calvin, to keep the Moral law, but not the rest, introducing into the law an arbitrary division that was not there).

I would respond by recalling two arguments that I have often developed elsewhere.[24] First: Everything is permitted (in and through grace), to be sure. But not Anything. And the law is there precisely to spare us this inconsistency of the "Anything." Then: Grace frees us from the law to do more

---

24. See in particular Ellul, *Ethics of Freedom*.

and better than the law (what Jesus shows in the Sermon on the Mount!), but if we are not able to do *more and better*, then we are still *under* the law, and keep this law as a precious thing which wondrously tells us what we are unable to do by ourselves! Then if our faith in the God of Jesus Christ leads us to find the genuine and fundamental limits to Technique, no need to look at the law. But since experience shows us the opposite, let us humbly put ourselves under this law that at least clarifies our misbehavior for us and opens us a path.

Secondly, this law is not obsolete either, despite the argument of new theologies that want to reduce it to something purely cultural: laws had their value in that culture, but they are no longer anything today. It is true that the law on fruit trees no longer has much meaning in a world where fruit is superabundant, so that thousands of tons of fruit are thrown in the garbage. But we must be well aware that this famous cultural argument that people harp about with respect to everything and anything is based on a literalism. It only comes into play if one sticks to the letter of the text (and this is funny when you think that these theologians are the most rigorous anti-fundamentalists!), without in the least seeking its meaning in relation to the global situation of man in society, in the natural environment, etc. If we are invited to seek its meaning, we must proceed as follows: what meaning did this prohibition have in and for the environment in which it was formulated? This (deep, spiritual, permanent) meaning may still be relevant for today. Which commandment today, in our own environment and in relation to it, finds the same meaning again? That is the work to be done.

Aside from these objective, explicit limits, we find a second order of limits that are stranger for us, perhaps because they are not from the realm of rules, of law, but from that of our relation to God here and now.

I will take the example of Gideon to help us understand clearly a situation that occurs fairly often. Gideon is going to battle the Midianites, and of course, as a good war leader, he prepares his battle from a technical standpoint. He gathers his men, arms them, prepares them for war, and his preparation is also, let us say, psychological, since it is accompanied by miracles, on the one hand, and on the other hand by the famous decision to send back home everyone who is afraid. He wants to create an élite troop.

But then things change, and we are totally getting out of the technical with the story of the men who drink by bringing the water to their mouth with their hand and those who kneel to drink.[25] This is obviously not a criterion of technical discrimination to separate the good and valiant fighters from the others. And there is a reduction of the number of combatants

---

25. Judg 7.

to three hundred, thus, in fact, an exclusion of normal technical means to wage a war. Finally, instead of arming these three hundred with swords, javelins, spears, he has them take lamps, jugs, and trumpets, and so they leave for war without any adequate technical means.

The meaning of this elimination of any technique is clearly given in the text: "The people that you have with you is too numerous for me to deliver Midian into your hands, lest they vaunt themselves against me, saying, 'My own hand has saved me.'" In other words, God wants to attest that he is indeed the God of Israel, that he is indeed the Lord of Lords, that it is he and he alone who delivers his people, that he is its true fortress, its true power. And to attest it, it is necessary to eliminate technical means to allow the sole will of God to act, so that there be no confusing roles, so that one cannot say, "Of course, God did help us a little and added to what we did, but without our means . . . heaven helps those who help themselves." From there, one goes on to, "We did not need God's action; our military means were amply sufficient." Let us note that here we are already coming across the argument we take to be modern: "God of the gaps" (we use God as resource when we do not know how to do otherwise, hence today we do not need this God).

The story of Gideon, and of many others, is there to counter this attitude. It is not a God to whom one resorts when one lacks the means to act on one's own, not a God who is *made to* act in our place. It is a God who *sometimes* explicitly asks us to abandon our means, incidentally sufficient and efficient, so that his glory shines forth. In other words, the accumulation of Means, of Techniques, eliminates the glory of God, prevents us from seeing it. Now, we have to recall that this glory is the revelation of his will, which is a will to *life*, to *freedom*. When we say that by our technical means we ensure life, we prolong, we develop our freedom, etc., we are erasing the expression of the will of God. For if we take a text like this one seriously (as with countless others), they are not about prolonging the action of God by our techniques nor about expressing God's will by our techniques. It is an "either/or"; either the victory is secured by Gideon's military techniques, or it is given by God. But when it is necessary that God's glory appear, we must totally erase our techniques.

A limit that may appear abstract and theoretical, but which can actually be terribly constraining, is thus that of the glory of God. It is only once the result (decided by God) is the product of a pure gift of God, that the will of God as he wants to reveal it appears. Paul already explains this to us clearly in the First Epistle to the Corinthians when he explains at length that he has used no intellectual stratagem, no oratory technique, etc., to preach Jesus Christ, since confusion might have been possible; to convince someone by persuasive discourses means not leaving any room for the action of the Spirit. And he explains perfectly that God has chosen the weak things of the world to confound the strong ones so that no flesh can glorify itself before him (1 Cor 1 and 2).

The opposition is thus very clear. If we act by technical means, if we use our efficiency "in the service of God," then unfailingly we give the whole importance, the whole weight, the whole meaning to our technical means, i.e., we attribute our victory to the efficiency of our techniques. If Gideon had kept his army, he would have been viewed as a brilliant war leader, and the victory would normally have been attributed by man to man and his means.

We see can see how, accordingly, in our era of multiplication of means, we cease to contemplate the glory of God and to ascribe successes to him. We on the other hand manufacture other religions and divinities that are consonant with our technical means. If the glory of God is to appear, this assumes the dispelling of our means of efficiency, hence of Techniques. To claim to serve God by our means (for instance by doing evangelization in the manner of Billy Graham) is in reality to manifest man's glory and in no way that of God. Eliminating the glory of God in this way is at the same time causing knowledge of his will to disappear. Confidence in our means eliminates the possibility of discerning God's will, of which we have said that it was Liberation, Life, and Peace. But when there is no possibility of knowing it, of discerning it, there is no reality of this will either.

We have often said that the will of God is not some kind of objective machine that unfolds independently of us and determines destinies, organizations, produces events without us! The will of God (at least in the Revelation in Jesus Christ that is our concern and over the course of our history) only has any place for a man who receives it, acknowledges it, and lives from it. Thus, the absence of the glory of God, which means the absence of knowledge of his will that is no longer revealed, implies the disappearance as well of the aim or the content of that will, that is, the effective disappearance of what God wants for man: Freedom, Peace, Life. Thus, the absolute, exclusive trust we have in our technical means, our refusal (currently implicit!) to set a limit to techniques so that the will of God may be manifested, produces as a real, effective consequence the absence of peace, of freedom among men and the destruction of Life.

We are here in the presence of a radical judgment over our means, not in themselves, but to the precise extent that, being perfectly efficient, they produce, and it could not be otherwise, the conversion of man to these means, his worship of their efficiency. He attributes to them what should be reserved to God. Such is the situation created by the absence of any limit set to Technique by the glory of God.

But here we must rule out an objection that immediately arises. This being the case, must we always and at all levels eliminate all Technique? Must we recuse medicine, etc., and come back to a natural life? This is, as we all know, the function of "cranks" who, for instance, when someone falls ill, refuse the doctor and pray for the sick person. It might seem that they alone are consistent with what we have just said. In reality, this is not the case at all. To begin with, we have explained at length that there is no natural state of man and that he is always an artificial being. I have not seen that these same sectarians who refuse the doctor also refuse clothes in winter and pray to feel warm, or to go get water at the tap as they wait for an angel to bring it to them. To believe that God answers all our needs by his direct action is in reality to believe that we are already in the Kingdom of God, that the New creation is already a given, that God is already All and in All; it is to accelerate the promise and to purport not to leave God the sovereignty of his choice of the Time and the Moment. One is therefore adding a major spiritual error to basic ignorance.

But if we consider biblical texts a little more closely, we see that the attitude that consists in limiting or even eliminating our technical means to allow the glory of God to manifest is always described as exceptional, outrageous, so prodigious that it must be related. On the one hand, the story of Gideon is not repeated; the people of Israel will most often fight with its own weapons and its tactics and its techniques (it would often be defeated, incidentally). It is thus in no way a situation that can be taken for granted. The kings of Israel will not repeat at every war Gideon's experience. Sometimes, exceptionally, we are indeed told of an intervention by God: Moses who holds his arm raised above the battle,[26] or again in the fight between David and Goliath, David's refusal to wear body armor, a shield, a sword, but he still keeps a technical means of combat: his slingshot.[27] So it has not become a normal and permanent attitude. And conversely, if we are told in detail about events, rare and spread out over several centuries, where the concern for God's glory produces a limit to Technique, it is because it is and must remain *exceptional*. There would be no manifestation of this glory if prayer healing became automatic.

Finally, we also see that in all cases we are dealing with an explicit order from God. It is not man who decides he is going to eliminate his Technique to allow God to act, but, in the case of Gideon and Moses, a strict

26. Exod 17.
27. 1 Sam 17.

order from God. In David's case, it is as it were a technical choice made by David himself (who feels impeded, hampered, in the king's weapons), but which, being the choice of what appear to be means of non-power, leaves the glory of God all the room to manifest itself. Trust in God, prayer, the call for his glory to become manifest (but we are actually asking for the manifestation of his power! Hence we are in a sense recycling the technical spirit!) should not become in their turn a technical trick to have greater efficiency, even that of God!

For when this glory effectively appears, it is never anything other than a *sign* given to *witness* to the reality and the truth of God's will! A sign, and not a permanent, redundant discourse; a witness, and not a definitive situation, taken for granted and repetitive. And when God gives this sign that tends to bring man to believe that God's will is indeed good and perfect, a will that is Peace, Freedom, Life, this nourishes hope, love and faith and does not at first produce any efficiency. Jesus underlines: "Which is easier: to say to this paralyzed man, 'Your sins are forgiven,' or to say, 'Get up, take your mat and walk'?"[28] We therefore clearly see that the Bible's lesson is in no way a pure and simple rejection of all Technique.

But conversely, we have to know that the acceptance of all techniques, especially in the technical system, is exclusive of the glory of God. In other words, the first limit that appears here is never to yield to the Dionysiac giddiness of Technique or to the spirit of power, but to constantly maintain the question: is the use of Technique legitimate in this situation? When must it cease? What limit should I impose on it so that I may at least possibly hear the commandment of God, so that the glory of God may possibly manifest itself and that men may recognize God as such?—something they are radically incapable of doing in the technical universe invaded by, jammed with techniques. What is the needful sobriety? Not in order for God to manifest his greater efficiency, but so that his word may make itself heard in its exclusive humility, so that his glory may appear in the choice of his non-power: there is the criterion of our choice of limit to Technique.

We are thus called upon to take decisions and to exercise our autonomy, if not our freedom! But we can see that we have imperceptibly slipped from the objective limits of which examples are given to us in the Old Testament to what we might call subjective limits, in that they are based on a coming to awareness, a choice, an individual decision. Man (but we are necessarily always talking of the one who recognizes the God of Jesus Christ as his!—outside of this, there are hardly any options for conceivable limits) is called to draw limits on his own, to invent them as it were.

28. Mark 2:9.

Can we say that there are, in a global, general and situational way, prior, predetermined limits to scientific research or to technical action? For instance, is there a forbidden realm, where man may not enter? A sacred realm? To be sure, biblically, there is indeed such a realm, where man may not and will never be able to enter, and it is Eden, the return by man in the situation of creation, the return by man to a face-to-face relation with God. This is radically excluded, whatever the path and the means taken by man. But this is also not what he pretends to be doing when he enters the technical path. However, this must alert us to the fact that, whatever the progress of society, of science, of means and powers, whatever the improvement of techniques and the increase in happiness, this will never lead to the kingdom of God anyway. The continuity established by Teilhard is radically false, theologically and biblically false.

It is then very important to point out that this forbidden realm is not a question of "must" (a realm where man could, but should not, enter, out of respect, out of reverence, out of obedience), but a question of "non-power": he will simply never be able to "cross to the other side of the mirror." We thus need not view this as a limit that we would have to accept. The only point of underlining this is, as it were, a recurrent judgment we have to pass over Techniques: that the pretension to attain the full development of mankind is false. It is dangerous; it must be destroyed. It is one of the factors of the dangers of Technique that is thus eliminated—no more, but still no less. Man would not prize it so passionately, would not be ready to agree to such great sacrifices, if he did not, when it comes down to it, believe in the possibility of a return to Eden by that path. This being said, let us recall that there is not in this creation any realm that is *a priori* closed to man, no realm that would be reserved to God, as God's share; there is no sacred realm. We have already said it, no need to come back to it, only to recall that the desacralization of the world by the Revelation of the biblical God is the very guarantee and the point of departure of freedom, of any freedom, with of course the hazards that go with this.

But when we say there is no reserved realm, it is not quite the issue of limits that is raised. The limit would be the fact that *in every realm*, be it of action, of life, of thought, there would be a point not to go beyond—as though, as it were (and this is indeed what has often been formulated by Christian philosophers), man could search or act up to a certain point, but not beyond.

For instance, in our time, we may ask ourselves that question as follows: is man allowed to put his hands on the very structure of matter, on what constitutes the very world in which he lives? That he should come to know the "secret" of matter, why not, but that he start to use it, with the disintegration of the atom and the liberation of Energy, is that not a forbidden realm, is that not the very secret of God, does this not in itself carry with it a curse? We must not be too quick to answer.

Likewise, and it is, I think, the other great problem: is there not a prohibition on control over the origin of life, over the artificial manufacture of living beings (the test-tube baby)—there too, we can take up the same questioning. The knowledge, perhaps, the proceeding to action, to practice, the "creation" of life, is that not a prohibition, does that not entail a curse in itself?

And I could ask the third great question with the environmental equilibrium, which is less clear, here it is only a question, without knowing where the limit runs: but is there no limit? May man manipulate all that constitutes his environment, without any reservation, is there no prohibition? Is man not committing evil when he transgresses those limits?

Here we are forced to recall two catechism items which, despite many contradictions, remain strictly biblical! The first one is that man, all of man and any man, is a sinner. In other words, it is not by doing such and such a thing that he does evil; he is in evil, is a born evil-producer, and there is not within a limit a realm of the licit, where man would be good and would do good, and beyond a realm where man would do evil. In all things, he produces evil. This does not mean that he must cease to act. Certainly not! But he must know that in everything, evil is mixed in what he produces. Thus, it is not by producing the hydrogen bomb that he does more evil (from the spiritual standpoint) than in producing a *pebble*:[29] he can simply do more evil!

After this first assertion, one must never forget the second one (which incidentally is actually more like the first one, the other being subordinated to it): namely, that in Jesus Christ, any sin is forgiven (except the one against the Holy Spirit), all of evil assumed by God, and as a result, full freedom of action is given to man. There again, there is no limit. However, as we have seen above, there are indeed in the Bible prohibitions against doing this and that, and what is more, we must take them very seriously and attempt to understand what that means for us today.

To succeed in understanding this problem of limits (for there are some!) and get out of the dilemma caused by the idea of a "realm reserved to God," we must make a detour. It is a reflection on the very process of the biblical message, as it stands out from the historical studies of the last twenty years. For a very long time, we have no longer believed in a message that would have been dictated by God, letter by letter, and as far as we

---

29. Translator's note: in English in the original.

are concerned, we cannot conceive the material historicity of the narrative through which God gives Moses the Tables of the law. Let us note, however, that after all, this is not impossible if God is God, of course! But aside from historical reasons, there are two theological reasons that weigh against it: first, God's respect for human independence, and then, the Incarnation, that makes God enter man's journey and does not force him from outside. Let us also note that we are not talking about the *material* historicity of the fact; the "how did it happen" is not the goal of the biblical text. But without any doubt, it does relate the event's spiritual reality.

This being said, and at the other extreme, Christian historians no longer believe either in a purely human origin of this book, of this law, as the mere manufacture by a series of "legislators," synthesized under the reign of King Josiah, of laws and rules stemming from the conditions of life and government in Israel from the seventh to the fourth centuries BC. Things are more complex. There thus is not a divine law, falling from heaven ready-made and dividing the good from evil, with predetermined limits to action. Neither are there laws that might be compared to any law of any people.

It seems that things may be conceived as follows. Certain men, in the people of Israel, a people *chosen* by God to carry among men his covenant and the witness of his will, examining this people's experiences, be they historical, political, social as well as religious, being inspired by God, reflect the Word of God unto these experiences. They are the judges, the kings, the prophets, and also the priests, but never by function and social status, always by inspiration and election. The Word of God is not given as is; it is reflected, as by a mirror, on the chosen people's experience as it is effectively known.

We thus see that there are four stages: the concrete historical experience of this people, which is already a unique experience since it is that of the people chosen by God; the election by God within this people of particular men, entrusted with a unique task; the effective knowledge of the reality of the people; and finally, the projection of the Word of God onto this reality. And it is then at the end point of this movement that these men discover, and by themselves (but *after* the experience has been had), that there was a limit there, that there *was* the point of no return, of the unacceptable, of the irreparable; that one should have stopped there.

Now, it appears that this judgment is generally made according to two criteria, which we can extract from most of these texts. The first one, which is very simple, is a life-and-death criterion: finally what was forbidden was what produced the death of man, of "nature," of the chosen people, that is to say, anything akin to a counter-creation, to a deconstruction of creation in any realm at all. And one discovers each time that there was the limit not to be crossed. Once again, it is not a metaphysical principle, nor a general and abstract one that I have just formulated; it is only legible in concrete and specific cases.

The other criterion is more complex. It arises from the constantly repeated question: has this experience, this undertaking separated us from God, from the revealed God, from the God of the covenant? Did it lead us to a non-glorification of this God? It is in this concrete relation that the prophets discover that what they had heard, what had appeared to them as a word of God, what was a proclamation, was thus indeed truly (given that experience) a word of God. In other words, their experience is appraised in the comparison between this proclaimed word and the fruits of experience. This is what leads them to draw a limit amidst what man may undertake.

We thus have here a central point: it is not the origin of the Word that guarantees its divinity—which is to say that it is not because an official prophet says it that it is the Word of God—and, one degree upstream, it is not because the prophet has the feeling or the impression that it comes from God that it is a word of God. The distinction that the whole of biblical history manifests to us between the true and the false prophet is not a distinction about the origin of the Word that was uttered. It is perfectly accepted and acknowledged that God can send a spirit of deceit in a man. When there is a competition between two prophets, as we see several times, God's seer always proclaims: "They will see that what I am saying will happen." This is the realization, the execution, the inscription within a lived experience that authenticates this word.

But this is the comparison between this word and reality that is significant and that produces the idea of a limit which one should not have crossed. Now, this is particularly clear from the very fact of the relation between prophets, on the one hand, and the people, kings, clergy on the other hand: the prophets are never recognized, accepted, heard in advance as such. It is neither when Jeremiah nor when Micah starts to talk that the people or the king discern in what they say a word of God. There is no other objective or external criterion that would allow one to discern the true and the false prophet. There is no agreement between what the people or the king thinks, feels, etc., and then what the prophet says. Very generally, we may say, on the contrary, that the situation is quite the reverse: the prophet is rejected, condemned by everyone. The people rises against him, priests accuse him, the king condemns him. But what is most strange, most surprising, is that it is nevertheless what that prophet says that is finally welcomed, gathered, and transmitted, thus *after* the fulfillment, *after* it has been recognized that this prophet was right. It is after this experience that the people recognize that what had been announced there *was* indeed a word of God.

We will never insist enough on the surprising and perfectly abnormal character of this situation: it is the message of these men who condemn the kings, who accuse them at all levels, even political, who are rejected and themselves condemned by these same kings, that is in the end gathered and transmitted, *by these kings and these scribes*, for it is obvious that if kings and priests had wanted to have these men and their words vanish, we would never have heard about them. This historical strangeness leads one to dispel two statements, common "rules of interpretation." The first one has to do with the so-called class struggle in Israel, Kings and Priests on one hand, Prophets and the common people on the other (the common people often detest these prophets). The other principle of interpretation has to do with the dating of texts. It has been accepted (and still is, alas!) that when a prophecy is not fulfilled in actuality, concretely, it indeed has the date presented by the sources, but when a "prophecy" is fulfilled, it has been written "*post eventum*"—because, quite obviously, the prophet could not have been announcing what was going to happen! (Thus again, in the New Testament, people do not hesitate to declare texts mentioning the destruction of Jerusalem to be posterior to Jesus Christ.)

This exegetical rule (a very childish one to say the truth!) is scientifically false. For we have seen that the prophetic Word is uttered, but never recognized as the Word of God, by anyone, as such, at the moment it is said. On the contrary, it is only recognized as a word of God, appropriated by the chosen people, and taken seriously after and because there has been an event, a fulfillment (from the scientific standpoint, one must simply distinguish here the date the prophecy was issued and the date it was written down and preserved, which takes place when the Word of God has been discerned on account of its fulfillment).

Thus, we do not have limits that impose themselves *a priori*, but starting from the Word of God, as we recognize it (and which is the equivalent of the announced prophecy). We must examine the experiences that we have in all areas and discover in this comparison what was the limit to observe. This then means that one can undertake or participate in any number of technical actions, but on the condition of not allowing ourselves to be dominated by them, and of submitting them to a constant judgment with reference to the Word of God.

No doubt, this process that thus corresponds to that of the production of the prophecy, presents an extreme weakness: one can discern the limit and draw the limit only *afterward*, hence once it is too late! One can only then say: one should not have done that! What is the use of that Word of God under these conditions? Before the action and the undertaking, it is only a warning, and never a limit. It is clear enough as a caution and announces what is going to happen. If we are willing to *read* it, we can perfectly well find in it all the necessary forecasts having to do with our technical enterprise. But never an obligatory law: it is up to us to formulate the latter and we indeed can only do it after the experience and its results.

And this is also the condition for us to have a true responsibility in this business! When we discover what the limits were and have to be, it is no longer an obstacle outside us, a repression that is initiated; it is a conscious creation, coming from within us and that we can then effectively take seriously. But for this, someone (and that should be the role of the Church) should utter the word of God, as a prophecy, in a way that is sufficiently clear. That is just what seems to me to be happening today. But the serious question that is being put to us is that indeed, the experience we are going to have, that we are already having in part, is liable to be the last one. It is all the more urgent that the warning be clear and rigorous. Failing which, the historical process of the creation of limits in relation to the Word of God would be interrupted, since there would be no continuation of history to insert within it the understanding of new limits.

Now, among many other ones, we may perhaps take two examples of this analysis, done by Christians, of these limits. One is the analysis by Illich about thresholds and limits.[30] The first point, a well-known one, is that growth, in all areas, ends up reaching a point where its effects start becoming the reverse of what they were before. After a certain stage, more compulsory schooling produces more ignorant and unintelligent people. More physicians produce more sick people. For a very long time, mankind knew a threshold below growth, under which nothing was possible for man. Currently, we are over the upper threshold beyond which there is no point in continuing along the path of technical progress, because its effects are becoming negative: "The institution," writes Illich, "first turns against its own end, then threatens the entire social body with destruction." "This second threshold is reached," writes Verne, "when the marginal utility of 'more specialization' and 'more expenses' starts to decrease. It is crossed when the marginal dis-utility, these unwished-for secondary effects, added to increasing productivity costs, start to increase at the same time as the development of the institution translates as more frustration, more suffering for more people."[31]

30. See Illich, *Tools for Conviviality* [note by the family].

31. This may be Etienne Verne, an education researcher, who co-wrote with Illich an article and a book: "Le piège de l'Ecole à vie" and *Imprisoned in the Global Classroom* [note by the family].

We are dealing here with a perfectly correct analysis of a correct ascertainment, but which takes on the appearance of a prophetic word by its radicalness. And the argument that people have not failed to make is that, indeed, the estimation of thresholds can only be done *a posteriori*. This is perfectly true, as we have seen. But the problem is then to know if the warning, the discovery of thresholds and limits, are sufficient to produce a turnaround not just of awareness, but also of practice and institutional structure. Therein lies the true risk, the true challenge we are facing.

The second example may be taken from the already cited study by Dorfles.[32] He tells us that the limit of artificiality is met when "it *counterfeits* and *taints* the most intimate elements of authentic human nature." What is brought up in this short formula is a three-tiered problem:

- First, globally, that the artificial world of Technique becomes for us Nature, our natural environment.[33] There is no longer here any possibility for man to discern the least rule of conduct.

- Then, the artificial counterfeits the Natural, *i.e.*, claims to be the natural, and here we have of, course, all the endeavors to create new bodies, or a new psyche (with perhaps a questioning of psychoanalysis!).

- Finally, there is a tainting of the elements, that is, a diversion of their "normal" course, of their end, of their meaning, but also a dissociation of the factors constituting them, and which, as a result, lose all meaning. Whatever the objections that can be raised against the idea of Nature, of normalness, of end, we have to take quite seriously such a diagnosis, that indeed shows what limits faith can suggest, totally outside simple moral criteria. It is no longer a question of morals, but of life or death.

This, in the perspective of a biblical theology, limits can only appear once the Revelation is taken completely seriously in Scripture and within the man who is going to formulate them, to invent them. A twofold question then arises.

The first one is that obviously, such limits can be recognized, accepted by Christian and Jews, not by others, who have no reason to accept them in the first place, and who then cannot have them imposed on them from

---

32. Dorfles, "Intenzionalità e mitopoiesi nelle tecniche odierne" and "Mythe de la naturalité et les transformations fruitives"; see note 9, p. 106.

33. See my study *Technological System*.

outside.[34] In other words, these limits, even though they concern the whole of society, even though they have to do with objective and collective phenomena, can only appear in these singular groups (and even then, on the condition that these groups be conscious of their role, which they generally have not been for three centuries). Is this not then totally pointless?

This takes us on another path: how do we make the existence of these limits known, heard, accepted? It is certainly not by a discourse, by arguments and doctrinal pronouncements; it can only be by an intervention that is expressed in experience. In other words, it is those Judeo-Christians who have themselves to live first and foremost this demand, this discovery of limits; they must be the first to take this truth upon themselves. And it can only be the exemplariness of their conduct that might give weight and meaning to the discovery of limits. It is exactly to the extent that men will see what Christians live and do with respect to technical madness that they will be able to take seriously what Christians have to say about limits.

But it is obvious that if Christians behave like anyone (for instance simply with respect to the car, pollution, non-respect of the environment, etc.) or again if having discovered the importance of limits and trying to get people around them to understand it, they carefully hide the fact that they are Christians (which is frequent: many of those who in today's world have launched this issue of limits are Christians, and it is as Christians that they have heard the question, but they avoid declaring themselves to be Christians), then it is obvious that their words are devoid of any kind of authority.

We must go further: it is not only as an individual that the Christian can draw attention to limits; it is the Church that must do it. But yet again, not by a Message or by an Encyclical; by her very being, it is the Church which, as a body and together, is called first to be the limit, herself, as a group representing a certain force and playing its role among the other groups of which society is made. If the Church is not the limit to technical giddiness, then all the limits we have been talking about can only be proposals and timid doctrinal elaborations. But in order for this to be so, it would first be necessary that the Church *be*, as a Church, and that she had become aware in her authorities and in her adherents (which we do alas have to call thus!) of the importance, of the urgency of limits.

Now, neither one nor the other of these two conditions are met by any of the Churches I know, in the situation of decrepitude, of enervation,

---

34. In case one would be dealing with a State claiming to be Christian, I have often written that the major error of States claiming to be Christian had been not only to claim to impose Christianity from outside but above all to impose it, for all that could be imposed was a Christian conduct, a Christian morality, which implied the enormous heresy of dissociating ethics from faith.

of theological and moral uncertainty in which we all find ourselves. The Church is perfectly conformed to this world. We must therefore carry out this reflection about limits, knowing that, concretely, we do not have any practical outlet. But tomorrow...

This obviously leads us to the second question: it is obvious that insofar as Christianity has ruined the equilibrium of the "natural" edifice, where everything had to be replaced by the complete and filial relation to the Father, and by the individual decision-making of man once he has recovered freedom in Jesus Christ, we find ourselves facing a completely unpredictable situation: man, everyone, is made perfectly able in Jesus Christ to fulfill this role in the world, to recover toward his environment the right position of creation. But if the relation to Jesus Christ is broken, the objective negative work of Christianity appears; if man refuses the revelation of his salvation in relation to this sin that is expressed (here in what concerns us) in Technique, if man confuses once more his true freedom coming from his emancipation by Christ with his autonomy in relation to God, if he wants a freedom without responsibility and pretends to attain to power without accepting the power of God the Father, then it is certain that this turns into a catastrophe: none of the limits gradually invented by man hold anymore, because they have been broken at their base by the truth of revelation, and none of the limits internalized by faith come into play anymore, because they have been recused by the spirit of the times, by what had been admirably formulated as early as the first Christian generation as "the concupiscence of the flesh, the concupiscence of the eyes, and the pride of life," which are the three roots, not of Technique, but of the technical unlimited, of technical hubris.

The problem is thus essentially, I would like to say exclusively, spiritual in nature. And in the possible evolution, there are only four[35] ways out in front of us:

- either catastrophe, in annihilation, by one of the forms that can already be entertained now, nuclear war, total pollution;
- either exponential demographic growth, producing in each case penultimate chaos;
- or the establishment of a totalitarianism (secretly yearned for by those who speak of organization to settle the technical problem, or of world government, or of communism, etc.), and this would be taking to its

---

35. Ellul says three ways out; we have corrected the number [suggestion by F. Rognon, note by the French publisher].

extreme the technical unlimited: Technique will have to be total and to be God;

- or the call of limits that assumes a recognition of the status of *creation*, the relation to the *creator*, the *identity* between the creator and love, preserving the creation and responding to man's anxiety, the Transcendence of the Father, the identification with the Son. These are the convictions needed in order for the discernment of limits be possible.

Furthermore, hoping and believing in that revelation is the only motivation strong enough to enable us to want those limits (while knowing the price to be paid!) and to keep the conviction that everything is still possible. Outside of that, there is nothing to be attempted.

4

Technique and Eschatology

To impose limits—very well—but in the name of what? Or more precisely, what is the motivation to be had to go in that direction? Here we find the problem of Eschatology. And first of all in a very elementary sense, one that can be summed up as follows: insofar as the current dangers of Technique (nuclear danger, pollution, exponential population growth) entail an absolute and *final* risk, as we do not know if this danger is real, but that its eventuality is, that is enough, thanks to a dawning awareness of this fact, to motivate the search for and the establishment of limits to research and to application—for if the dreaded effect is realized, it will be the end of history. It is enough that this risk exists as a *serious* eventuality for the necessity and motivation for limits to be found. I had written this quite a while ago about the Hydrogen Bomb. Hans Jonas has studied this and put it thus: "In the face of the quasi eschatological possibilities of our technical progress, remaining unaware of its final implications becomes in itself a reason to impose limits on it."[1] Eschatology thus merely has here the sense of "final event," end of the world!

But indeed, if we understand correctly this reflection's general value, this does not pertain to Christian eschatology and reflection on the *eschaton*. We must however keep this first reflection, for it introduces us, whether

---

1. Jonas, "Technology and Responsibility," 182. These positions were taken up again and developed in Jonas, *Imperative of Responsibility*. [Note by the family, completed by F. Rognon.] There is a risk of misconstruing this text because of the verb "ignorer." Jonas means that the fact of not having certain knowledge about final implications is enough to have to impose limits. [Translator's note: In light of this clarification, the English verb "ignore" has been avoided in translation because it is limited to the other sense (deliberately failing to acknowledge) of the ambivalent French verb whose first meaning is simply a neutral "not knowing."]

we like it or not, within the perspective of final events and forces us to take eschatology seriously, simply due to the fact of the presence of techniques and of their effects. This being said, in this area, we come across two orientations of traditional theological reflection that we can confine ourselves to bringing up; we have in any case already come across them in the introduction. In one case, it has to do with an emphasis on judgment, in the other, with the preparation of the Kingdom of God, orientations that express what could be considered half a century ago as Protestant theology and Catholic theology.

For the first, one starts from the "fall," and the condition of sinful man. The latter being said to be essentially evil, his work, all his work is steeped in sin, and if God loves man enough to want to forgive, if he gave his Son as an expiatory victim for sin, if the man who explicitly believes (and that one alone) is saved, it is indeed man alone who is saved—which is to say that his work, fundamentally evil, is destined to disappear, but it is here that a distinction will be introduced between holy works (worship, priesthood,[2] faith itself, the works of love, that used to be called charity, and "good works," all having a moral character, expressing morals, the attitude of faith) that partake of salvation, but that can never be considered to have any reality of their own, and then profane works, the trade or various activities, of play, travel, politics, etc., that absolutely do not deserve to be preserved, having besides an objectivity that detaches them from man—a startling attitude as consequences of a theology that, following Luther, had recognized a "calling" in the exercise of a trade, and accepted that the man who works prays. But in the end, it was indeed the general orientation, with the particular problem that it made works of art and science into a difficulty. Many were those who held that they were the direct expression of the evil one, while others ascribed to them an ambiguous eschatological status. It goes without saying that, in this theological orientation, Technique was purely and simply annihilated.

This general orientation brought with it two consequences that people often neglected to put forward. The first one is that entrance into "eternity" was an annihilation of human History, even, in the final analysis, of biblical history. A great stroke was made across the thousands of centuries of human effort, and the incomparable joy of communion with God, of meeting God face-to-face, produced powder and ash over this History. And conversely, nothing of the *global* work of man could subsist; individual man alone was saved, and mankind as a whole was nothing next to God's

---

2. Hypothetical; the word is hardly legible [note by the family].

awesome greatness; thus the eschatological putting in perspective produced a reduction, contempt, and suspicion toward Technique.

It is in that perspective that the distinction lies between consequent Eschatology and realized Eschatology, but this does not help very much with our problem (which incidentally goes to show to what extent this great debate was an abstract debate of theologians!), for in the final analysis, realized Eschatology only refers to the spiritual dimension of the Kingdom of God, and carries no actualizable ethical consequence, thus no modification with respect to Technique.

The reverse theological stance is no less well-known. It is the schema of the preparation of the Kingdom of God by the work of man and a certain continuity between what man institutes on earth and the Kingdom. We have already recalled the broad outline of Teilhardian theology; let us say a few words about classic Catholic theology.

The work of man accomplishes Nature; it is crowned with a supernature, which gives it at once its fulfillment and its meaning. Man realizes in the course of his life and of his history a set of works, objectively discernible, other than the subject who accomplishes them: works, institutions, that live on beyond their creation. The judgment is also made over these works. Some of them prepare the kingdom of God, others not. Some are endowed with a transhistorical value. There is then a progress in History, and through successive approximations, either an approach of that final goal that is the Kingdom, or an accumulation of good works that are perfected over the course of history to serve as an introduction to that kingdom. Thus, the works of the man who does the will of God are a definitive gain, and the works of the man who obeys Nature, who accomplishes Nature, correspond to an obedience to this will of God. There is thus in History a good and a bad work of man; the first one is a preparation for the Kingdom. We will therefore have the Nation or the State, but Claudel will be able to show as well in his *Christophe Colomb* that the discovery of America is a necessary condition for the possibility of the coming of the Kingdom.[3]

In these classical theologies, it is not very difficult to introduce art and Science. The latter seems a direct preparation; art, held in more suspicion, is saved if it is "religious." As for Technique, its existence had not yet been noticed; it had no status, but it does not take much effort to see what would be its place. There again, there had to be a good and a bad technique, a good and a bad use of Technique.

These inveterate ideas (which have completely skewed the study of the technical phenomenon) had their root in this eschatology. Now, in

---

3. Claudel, *Book of Christopher Columbus*.

reality, these two great orientations of eschatological reflections appear to be wholly challenged by a new understanding of history, by a deepening of the subject of eschatology, but also by the enormity of the obvious fact of Technique that can no longer be treated as a small appendage, a craftsman's *technè*, of man's activities.

1. ITINERARIES

A conference was held in Strasbourg in 1971 on the theme "Technique and Eschatology," and we may say that the eminent contributions of the participants have indeed crisscrossed the whole field, and practically exhausted the question.[4] I will only retain the orientations indicated by five of them, which have seemed to me the most suggestive. And we will be called upon to see that in the final analysis, the conclusions of each one depend on his conception of eschatology, and that there are very different ones.

In the first place, I will try to summarize Vahanian's contributions to this debate. It seems to me that we may start in his case from two basic conceptions: first, eschatology is defined not so much as the final fulfilment of man's possibilities, but by the fact that God, and him alone, is all in all. This comes down to saying that eschatology is not to be conceived as a final stage of some process either of nature, or of history, or again of culture.

To be sure, that God alone must be all in all cannot exclude either the Promised Land or the new City, or even Utopia, any more than Paradise lost. But eschatology would not be eschatology if it was enough to construct it only in terms of the past or the future. In order for God to be All and in All, eschatology must be conceived not so much in terms of a rupture between time and eternity, between here and the beyond, between the natural and the supernatural. It must first be conceived as an iconoclasm of "nature" and history as much as of "culture."

The other point of departure of Vahanian's thought in this area is his conviction that Technique nowadays allows man to realize, to fulfill man's Utopias. But there are here two branches: on the one hand, the utopias of the human past are now reality; on the other hand, Technique induces utopia. Thus, on the one hand, we will be able to say that there is genuine utopia only where imagination makes possible and achievable the anticipation of a new world, and consequently generates a technique, and on the other hand that, due to the very fact of technical development, due to this expansion of possibilities, man becomes utopian. There is thus a close relation between

---

4. The proceedings of this conference have not been published.

utopianism and Technique. The first one is, one could say, the intellectual construct of the second, or again its "ideology."

Vahanian then shows that we can see three stages: a stage of integration of man in the natural environment, with the ideology of Nature; a stage of integration of man in the social environment, with the ideology of history; and now a new stage, of the technoscientific environment, producing the ideology of Utopia, with the result, of course, that the utopianism of Technique destroys Nature and History. But the other side of Utopianism is that, in the final analysis, any human project tends toward the *eschaton*, toward final realization, but that in the night in which we are, this human project will be formulated in a utopia, so that the latter appears as an ersatz of the *eschaton*, and that, of necessity, the Kingdom of God begins where Utopia stops. We thus have here what I believe to be the twofold foundation of Vahanian's thinking about this issue of Technique and Eschatology—but it is a matter of seeing how these two components play out.

We need to introduce here an essential concept of Vahanian's thought, which is that of *Novum*. God in acting each time produces, in a situation, be it individual or collective, a *Novum*, which is refused by Nature or History. The *Novum* happens in the present, and it is expressed in a work of man who is put by God in conditions such that everything can indeed be started anew from the beginning; the *Novum* is God's decision to set a new beginning, already in the present course of human life.

There thus arises a dialectic between this *Novum* and eschatology, a dialectic which is different from that between consequent and realized eschatology. It is this dialectic which makes it possible to free eschatology from History (knowing whether there is a radical rupture between History and the Kingdom or a continuity), but so as to restore eschatology's central import in Theology. For Vahanian does provide a set of impressive views, refusing that eschatology be the shamefaced appendage of dogmatics treatises.

He gives it a trinitarian structure. To the work of the Father corresponds an Eschatology of Nature, having its origin in creation and expressed in vocation. The *Eschaton* is the principle of creation. Eschatology is Nature's *a priori*; faith in creation is thus the *Novum* of nature. To the work of the Son corresponds an Eschatology of History, having its origin in the Incarnation and finally expressed in Redemption. The *Eschaton* is the principle of Redemption. Eschatology is History's *a priori*, and Redemption appears as the *Novum* in that history (that which in any case history could never have produced on its own). Finally, to the work of the Spirit corresponds an eschatology of Utopia, having its origin in the New Birth (and the Church?), and having its end point in the Pleroma (God All in

All, but also the recapitulation of all things in Christ). The *Eschaton* is the principle of the Pleroma. Eschatology is Utopia's *a priori* and the Pleroma is the *Novum* of Utopia.

But here we would expect a new stage in that we would see a convergence between the *Eschaton* and the *Novum* due to Utopia, which, let us not forget, is thus closely expressive of Technique and its possibilities. For Utopia is the vector that drives Technique in the direction of a humanization. And in this sense, incidentally, the Utopianism of Technique is different from all other Utopianisms that have occurred until now. And it is the first time in human history that Utopianism has its true place, because it comes out of a pure imaginary, of a play without reason. Vahanian can then situate this Utopianism of Technique in a strict relation to the kingdom, for according to the trinitarian analysis we have seen above, we can indeed say that Utopia is to the kingdom what Nature is to creation, what History is to Redemption, what the body is to the Spirit. But with the limit that this assumes: for creation starts where Nature stops, Redemption starts where History stops, and the Kingdom starts where Utopia stops. There is thus neither confusion, nor continuity, nor rupture.

But in all cases, the thought of Eschatology can only translate as iconoclasm: the destruction of any realized ideology—Eschatology is thus in its current presence an iconoclasm of Nature, as of History, as of Utopia—which means there is no reason to expect a kind of final judgment, no more than there is any reason to currently substitute ourselves to this judgment. This iconoclasm, if it is radical and present, makes it possible to prevent eschatology's evaporation in the supernatural, or its sublimation in ideology, or its foundering in the blissful futurism of our most desperately silly hopes. But if it is important that the *eschaton* not be driven back to an indefinitely postponed future, it is also important to underline that it can only meet with the present insofar as this present depends neither on the past nor on the future. This eschatic present is that of the fullness of the times: eternity differs from it neither by its absence, nor by its presence, but by its *otherness*. Such is indeed the limit of the technical operation.

We thus see that, for the issue raised, eschatology in reality ends up in a behavior. And despite the subtlety of Vahanian's theological construction, and the firmness of the relation he establishes between Technique and Eschatology, everything ends up translating as that iconoclasm, which belongs to Ethics! We have here an incomparable gain that we will find again.

TECHNIQUE AND ESCHATOLOGY

෮

With Gadamer, we move on to a radically different way of putting the issue; we enter into a new problematic.[5] The center is hermeneutics, and the aim is self-understanding. The *Eschaton* is thought first as a danger for philosophy; eschatology formulates the rupture, the catastrophe even, of the philosophical enterprise. For it means there is something "outside" that invades our whole understanding of ourselves. Grace, which manifests in the *eschaton*, present, current, makes us lose our intelligibility of practical reason. Now, the conflict worsens, the opposition deepens when we raise the issue of the relation between Technique and Eschatology, for with Technique we are leaving our self-understanding by integrating into a system that is in the final analysis autonomous, or at any rate independent of our choice, and that negates our freedom.

Technique thus assumes the disappearance of self-understanding, and finds itself opposing, on the one hand philosophy's rationality, on the other hand the eschatological intervention of grace. But if it is so, it is because the reality of Technique has completely changed; thus, in Aristotle, it is always subordinated to politics, whereas today what should be self-evident has disappeared. And we must keep in mind that there is a redoubtable relation between Theory and Practice, so that we are also oriented, by the change of concept of Truth and of practice of Technique, to a new grasp of the *Eschaton*. The latter formulates the provocation to our self-understanding, but then, is there anything of the manifestation of our self-understanding in our technical action?

It is essential to realize that the truth of action is a revelation of our social situation by "virtue." Gadamer takes this word not in a moral sense or the sense for instance of an example to be followed, but in the Greek conception of an attitude grounded in man's existence. Virtue is a form of manifestation of human being; there is a truth or a falsehood depending on whether man appears as consistent with himself or not. That is what determines Technique, for this practice encompasses not only Technique, but also any human attitude, and Theory as well. If Practice is so wide-ranging, then it is Speech which reveals the whole, for it is in Speech that our own experience of life and of the world is developed. Speech is constituted by the sedimentation of experience, and it expresses our self-understanding. It is not a mere sign. It encompasses the field of Nature and of Art; it implies the freedom to take an interest, existentially, in what is non-efficient and useless *par excellence*. For if we examine the experience of a practice encompassing

---

5. Hans-Georg Gadamer, German philosopher (1900–2002). Best-known work: *Truth and Method* [note by the family].

all of human activity and not just Technique, then we necessarily come across a moment of rupture and assumption, the *kairos*, that is not a manifestation of History, but the moment of moral decision. Christianity has rejected founding truth solely on practice, for instance, in the commandment of love. We have here a decisive and decision-related reference to the *Eschaton*.

But at the other end of the chain, and situating us in current times, Technique has caused a mutation of the relations between Culture and Nature, and yet it cannot remain "in mid-air"; it has to somehow become reintegrated in culture—which also assumes Nature. Gadamer strongly formulates what we were indicating at the beginning, that there is no such thing as an intact nature on the one hand and a cultural world on the other that alone would be thrown off course by Technique. There is a complete affinity between Nature and Culture, an affinity that must all the more be safeguarded as man feels more threatened by Technique.

Thus, the effort to be undertaken right now is the attempt to reintegrate Technique in culture; it is a practical responsibility of modern man, which reinforces the importance to be given to the *kairos*. We must recuse our ease of repetition of the Technical to attain the *"moment"* of practical decision and our full attainment of historical and final responsibility. Then Technique may appear as a non-eternal return to a humanized nature. We see in short that now still, this investigation on eschatology leads us to a stance that, in the final analysis, is going to be ethical in nature, the one that is founded in the *Kairos*.

❦

We take another vantage point by following Faessler.[6] To be sure, we are finding again here Gadamer's orientation, according to which we must attempt to establish the relation between Technique and Eschatology through a hermeneutics of meaning. But already, the conception of eschatology marks a singularity. It is, for Faessler, a theological locus around which the discourse of faith strives to say the ultimate; it is not a science of the last things. This crucial opposition is very important.

We can then take note of a *prophetic breakthrough* of eschatology, and then of an *apocalyptic interpretation*, which entails on the one hand a universalization of eschatology, with the problem of the unity of history and of its meaning, and finally the eschatological *fulfillment* in Christ's advent. In any case, eschatology is not situated outside history; it is not a leap into a

---

6. See Faessler, *L'Evangile et le politique*.

beyond. The Apocalypse of John itself shows us that the Kingdom and the *Eschaton* are situated within History.

But this unique, exceptional event is a setting in motion of history toward its realization. Eschatology is thus a current presence, but as a limit where freedom is ordained to Transcendence to constitute the historical horizon of any human life. This implies that man is always already rooted in the transcendence that gives him being, and then eschatology is the discovery, the revelation that manifests as being the fullness of "human Being." It is thus at once the possibility of this human being and the certainty of its fulfillment, since there is, here and now, a setting in motion of history; the horizon that is accessible is that of Hope, because it is ultimate, final, decisive, and because what is promised will be fulfilled.

This being the case, we must view Technique in relation to this certainty. We must not appraise it in terms of its origins nor even of its sociological reality. Technique belongs to the process of advance toward the horizon of creation of human Being. And consequently, the current restrictions that we may see cannot prevail against the possibilities of liberation that Eschatology attests and that are in man, and that Technique *can* express, this Technique being incidentally only considered as equipment at man's disposal. Technique makes it possible to satisfy and plan man's needs, acts which are already an actualization of the *Eschaton*, as is incidentally the redistribution of power among all men. We can therefore see that Faessler holds, on the one hand, that Technique is subordinated to politics, on the other hand, that political action is a factor (if not *the* factor) of the realization of human Being. It is by way of politics that Technique is brought to play its role toward the *Eschaton*. Must we then conclude that there is a perfect concordance between the two? To be sure, there is indeed, in biblical Eschatology, a factor of protest and division, but what Eschatology struggles against is in no way a reality of Technique, but the human fantasy that perverts it, particularly the dream of a power that is satisfied with itself.

We will not undertake a critique, no more than with the previous ones, but we will simply note two things: to begin with, what is this Technique that would be pure, all in all, and only tainted by a human fantasy? But where is its wellspring if not precisely there? And how can they be dissociated? Next, with this analysis, we are at risk of falling back into the long-discarded platitude that it all comes down to a good use of Technique. This observation brings us to a conclusion that is comparable to that of the other authors: Technique is not really situated in Eschatology, but last, immediately toward a practice. Here, the political practice is crucial, with liberation, the redistribution of powers, etc.

THEOLOGY AND TECHNIQUE

❧

We have just seen that Faessler introduces Hope in the Eschatology-Technique relation, and this immediately brings us to the paper by Desroche, who, he announces, situates himself on this side of Eschatology and on this side of Technique. We then explicitly leave the ground of Christian Eschatology to make a vast journey through religions, or at least "first-hand religions," origins.

And Desroche ascertains from the start that the collective imagination, in expectation, is looking, not for a beyond, but for a beyond in *this world*, a presence of the heavens on earth, and not a flight from earth toward heaven. It is thus indeed something on this side of Eschatology. But it is also something on this side of Technique, for these phenomena appear in natural environments under attack by Technique. These phenomena of hope and expectation are even a response, a retort to Technique's attacks. It is thus the study of the appearance of what later on supports Eschatology, and of the religious relation to the explosive appearance of Technique. Thus, the first phenomenon is Hope, on which is built Eschatology, and which is necessarily in relation with Technique. The two are therefore correlative.

Desroche then makes a particularly astute study of the possibilities of hope, but of a purely human hope, which, to be sure, is still well-defined: hope against all hope, but about which one fails to see in what it is rooted, in what it is founded, if one understands how it can be born and develop.[7] Desroche distinguishes the full and the empty areas of hope, the realities and the lacks.[8] There are four "full areas" of Hope, four certain realities:

- The first one is the waking dream (in hot societies, there is an analogy with possession cults, and messianic movements at the collective level. In both cases, it is an oneiric layer, of a dream personality, of a god who dreams himself the social dream as dreamed in a messianic personality which seems more real than factual reality).

- Then hope may be viewed as a collective ideation (which corresponds to the analysis of the religious phenomenon in Durkheim).

- Then there is agitated Expectation which, incidentally, may just as well be exhilarating as inhibitive: which is to say, in the latter case, that the fact of awaiting with the most extreme intensity blocks any action. It is useless to undertake anything, since "it" is coming. This agitated

---

7. Desroche, *Sociology of Hope*. See also Desroche, *Les religions de contrebande* [note by the family].

8. Desroche, *Sociology of Hope*, chapter 1: "*Hope: its peaks and its troughs*" [note by the family].

expectation can then be expressed as an extreme technical activity, or else, on the contrary, will totally block it.

- Finally, the last full area of Hope is, according to Desroche, generalized Utopia. This is a concept of Utopia whose model he finds in Gramsci, Utopia being the imaginary project of an alternative society.[9] Imaginary must be taken in the strong sense of the imaginary in Laplantine or Castoriadis (and not that of fabulous, phantasmatic, or illusory).[10] It is a constitutive imagination, a major expression of Hope, with its challenge to the present, to affirm the other to be fulfilled. And of course, it is here that we see the eschatological and the Technical appear on the horizon!

But opposite these full areas, these possible fulfillments, there are what Desroche calls the empty areas of hope. The empty areas in this context are any situation of failed hope, which may be the case of many millenarian hopes that may be agitated, but do not meet the necessary conditions for their survival, their maintenance, or their expansion. Then come the empty areas of springboards for hope: the situation of hope emptied out. The collective imagination carried by hope becomes empty in the absence of an echo in collective memory and a support in the collective consciousness; the past must come back in a future. For lack of an echo of the past and of an actualized coming to consciousness, hope becomes empty of any content.

Then, and this is the third empty area, there is the empty area of the plateaus[11] of hope, what Desroche calls trapped Hope. Hope translates as two strategies aimed at a certain seizure of power, minimalist or maximalist: on the one hand a distancing from society (one asks for the minimum in order to inscribe oneself outside of it); on the other, one pretends to transform society (one asks for the maximum in order to change it from top to bottom). But this strategy is actually a trap for hope, for in inscribing oneself within a will for alterity (alternation, altercation, alternative), hope gets caught in concrete historical-political complications that most often translate into alienation.

Finally, there may be the empty area of the essence of hope: it is the desperate hope in which one acknowledges (and it is the point to which

---

9. Gramsci, *Selections from Political Writings, 1910–1920*; *Selections from Political Writings, 1921–1926*; *Prison Notebooks* [note by the family].

10. Laplantine, *Les trois voix de l'imaginaire* (see note 7, p. 70); Cornelius Castoriadis, philosopher, economist and psychoanalyst; his first book was *Imaginary Institution of Society* [note by the family].

11. [Translator's note: Ellul is deemed to have written "*palier*," the word for a landing in a staircase.] Hypothetical reading of this word [note by the family].

we are led by the preceding case) that when hope succeeds, it is then that it fails as hope. And Desroche has a nice formula to characterize this exile, in which one dreams of the kingdom, but in the kingdom, there is no longer any exile: "mirages set the caravan in motion, but no caravan has reached its mirage or else, vice versa, no caravan has ever reached its mirage, and yet, it is the mirage that sets the caravan in motion."

We thus see that in this study whose critique I will no more undertake than that of the preceding ones, there are very few issues relevant to Technique, at least as we know it, but that it appears just beneath the surface in all the empty areas of hope. On the other hand, the takeaway is that once again, it seems that there is a tremendous difficulty in setting in relation eschatology and Technique; once again, we are thrown back to this side of history, and if we think of eschatology, it is the "here and now"[12] that is kept in mind much more than the final event. And if we think of Technique, it is the relation to a behavior, namely for Desroche, the basic attitude of current hope.

And so we are led to the most rigorous and intransigent attitude: that of Ladrière.[13] He poses the question of knowing to what extent one can raise the question of an Eschatology *of* Technique. And he takes up again a specific concept of Eschatology, which must be a singular *moment*, marking the end of time (consequently, there is no longer here a dissolution of history into space, nor an avoidance of the problem of knowing whether or not there is an end of time, a very frequent avoidance these days, when philosophers and theologians vie in skillfulness to manage not to put the problem of the beginning and that of the end, the passage from a time 0 to a time 0 + 1, and that of a passage from 0 + n to infinity). This moment must at once be homogeneous with time, and yet since it marks an end, and, let us not forget, in any consistent eschatology, not a passage into nothingness, but to the absolute new, it belongs to another dimension. It is not the last term of a series that is completed by a final event that completes the series, but an impact against a power, an obstacle that we bump against. This end is thus a moment that assumes not a stop, but the fulfillment of which all

---

12. [Translator's note: For once, Ellul uses the French "ici et maintenant" rather than the Latin phrase *hic et nunc* (with its French Barthian baggage).]

13. Jean Ladrière, Belgian philosopher and logician (1921–2007). Wrote, among other things, "Technique et eschatologie terrestre" [note by the family].

that has gone before was but an anticipation, as a prelude, a preparation, a givenness.

But this end is not necessarily the consequence of the normal unfolding of a succession of events; it is in the nature of conditions, and not of the conditioned. It is not conditioned by precedents but is unconditioned.[14] A genuine event—*e-ventus*—is of course, according to the oft-repeated formula, at the same time an advent. But much more, it is in the nature of conditions—that is to say that it is what conditions the rest, the preceding series for instance. The end is necessary so that history can unfold, and much more, so that there can be a beginning! It is, as we were saying, an event, and a temporal event, since it comes from time, but inevitably too, a "Non-Event" since it destroys the very possibility of the event.

We can then say that "the end is a temporal event frozen by a transcendental event," the *eschaton* is the negation of what makes it possible, and in relation to this end, time is only ever nothing but the maturing of its own suppression, but it does not produce it; it is not a natural effect of the flow of time; it is not an addition of moments that comes to an end when we have gotten through all the numbers! The event that is an advent cannot be produced directly by this succession of times. It is not by its own virtue that time produces this advent. In reality, it comes up against a power that checks time itself (how could we fail to underline here the radical difference between this Christian thinking and the Greek conception of a Time that is the ultimate reality, in relation to the gods?). This power, which is not manifest, manifests through this abolition of time. It is wholly other, and it penetrates time with its alterity.

Under these conditions, Technique, which is wholly in the nature of the temporal, has no eschatological dimension: there is practically no relation between the two terms. Not only can there be no eschatology of Technique, but it can also be stated that Technique is negated by eschatology. This strongly articulated rupture makes it possible to avoid the various traps we have noticed in passing in these itineraries around the question.

2. HISTORY OF GOD, HISTORY OF MAN

We have tried to very briefly review some of the most original reflections on this difficult problem. Each one of these explanations, of these theories, has its value, brings a fragment of truth. And when I say that, there can be no question of attempting a synthesis of these various studies, nor of conjoining them, still less of endorsing one of them as alone representing the truth.

14. And consequently, in Tillich's perspective, it truly is in the nature of the divine.

THEOLOGY AND TECHNIQUE

I will begin by adding a few elements to this already complex survey. In relation to Technique, it may be fitting to begin, from a biblical standpoint, by stating an opposition between the origin and the beginning. God set a beginning in his creation—and we know how difficult it is to translate this correctly; André Chouraqui refuses to speak of beginning, putting "Heading of the days . . ."[15] But be that as it may, we then see man, in Cain, give himself an origin (Enoch) through the city and Technique, that is to say that he creates for himself, for him alone, an independent world and finds his origin in himself.[16]

The problem is then that of a twofold history: not exactly a profane history and a sacred history (including God's secret action within general history). Some theologians have protested a lot over the last decades against this idea of a "Holy History": God is in all of history; it is the peoples who make history, who express God's action (we can recognize a theme of liberation theologies). Human History is not neutral, independent, indifferent; it is that whole history that is holy.

We will not enter this debate, but we must recognize that this conception, which is very generous, is not biblical. There is indeed, in the Bible, including the New Testament ("my kingdom is not of this world"),[17] a holy history, and the act of God is not performed "per Francos" nor by revolutionaries, but by the saints and the prophets who are perfectly aware of being the envoys of this God who explicitly chose them.[18] The rest is romanticism.

There is a history that comes from the "beginning" inaugurated by God, and a history that unfolds from the origin set by man. And Technique appears as being the absolute face, the hardest, and at the same time the driver, of the second. It is its most complete expression, impermeable to any outside influence, inaccessible to a change that would be imposed to it out of another history. But precisely, under these conditions, how could the relation be established?

At the opposite end, we also have another dyad: *Telos* and *Eschaton*. The first, which is at once the goal and the end, is exactly reached by the

---

15. "En-tête" ("heading") is the title given by Chouraqui to the book of Genesis, following an etymological translation of Genesis 1:1: *be-re'shit* (in-a beginning), the word *re'shit* being derived from *ro'sh*, the head. Chouraqui, *La Bible traduite et présentée par A. Chouraqui* [note by the family].

16. I have shown this at length in *Meaning of the City* and am confining myself to mentioning it here.

17. John 18:36.

18. This is an allusion to the title given by Guibert de Nogent to his chronicle of the first crusade, *Gesta Dei per Francos*. The idea that France is entrusted by God with protecting the Church and spreading the Catholic faith goes back to the preaching of saint Remigius at the baptism of Clovis, king of the Franks [note by the family].

normal development of Technique. On the one hand, this whole history goes toward its end, but it is at the same time like a goal to reach. It is not only a passive end, a decrepitude, an obsolescence. Technique in its evolution produces results; it is even exactly made for this, and this alone, and we may say that in a certain sense it reaches a goal. But it is a kind of linear movement that reaches this goal by a cumulative progression, in the flow of time.

And there can be here two interpretations, well-known ones which we will quickly recall.

- We may hold that there is a predetermined *Telos*, given in advance, existing in itself, an end of history toward which mankind advances. It is a goal such as the one aimed at by the arrow. It is generally idealistic thought that expresses itself in this way.

- If not that the *Telos* is simply going to be the result of successive results reached by Technique. It is an accumulation, not in view of an end, but without an end-term, through the simple putting together of preexisting data, reproducing in history an equivalent of "Chance and Necessity" (but here there is neither chance nor necessity!!).[19] This causes any idealistic aim to disappear, and we know that it is indeed in this way that technical procession is characterized. There is no great objective that mankind seeks to attain. Technique occurs according to its own possibility, in an exclusively causal process, by a combination of instantaneous possibilities with self-produced self-surpassing.[20]

We are thus advancing, step by step, as in a night that is only lit for each step, the next one being at once probable and unpredictable. To be sure, there are possible forecasts in terms of what has already been secured, already been realized. There are also wishes and hopes. Finally, there are programs, intentions, projects, but there is never a great global aim of History—or rather, every time that men have given themselves such a great aim, the outcome was a laughable failure. We can only ever discover a *meaning* to what has already been realized, and attempt to determine the next immediate step, no more, and without being able to give ourselves a

---

19. Translator's note: Monod, *Chance and Necessity*, interprets the processes of evolution to show that life is only the result of natural processes by "pure chance." According to the introduction the book's title was inspired by a line attributed to Democritus, "Everything existing in the universe is the fruit of chance and necessity" (Wikipedia, s.v. "*Chance and Necessity*," para. 2).

20. About all this, I refer the reader to *Technological Society* and *Technological System*.

THEOLOGY AND TECHNIQUE

direction, nor to trace a path on a map, nor to have a magnetic pole, whose orientation we would know by a historical compass.

Now, the *Eschaton* does not correspond to either of the two faces of the *Telos*. It is not a Paradise established as a place toward which we are walking. Nor is it a product of the accumulation of our history. It is a power that is coming, that intervenes (and here we especially concur with Ladrière's very beautiful developments).

It is possible to establish a relation between this *eschaton* and the current step we are in the middle of taking in technical development, but this eludes our customary human means. For there is no final projection of the current step we are in the midst of taking, no extrapolation of an *eschaton* from what is already realized; it is rather an intervention of the final end in the current movement, between the completed step and the one we are taking. And this intervention produces three possible (not compulsory!) effects. On the one hand, it allows us to perform the critique of what is currently being done; then, to give it a meaning (with, of course, the twofold aspect, signification and orientation, which thus means that there is no global orientation to be drawn from some idealism of Ends, but a possible orientation to be discovered in our history when, but only *when* the *eschaton* intervenes); and, finally, it may be that this is going to inscribe this product of our history in the whole movement of God's History. This relation thus turns the penultimate situation into a final situation (the Kingdom *is* currently in your midst), and the penultimate work into a final work, but at every step of our history, this final takes place. It is not the equivalent of a final like the final breath at the end of a life. It is not a moment added to the others and after which there are no more—"Time is fulfilled"; "this is the end time."

We are thus in the movement of a flow of time and of a power that comes from the End, the *Eschaton*, and which penetrates this time, that pries it open in order to make a place for itself within it, which upsets the reality conditioned by Techniques, politics, work, production, etc., and reaches man starting from the point of the expectation of God, in its historical reality that includes a twofold becoming.

Two remarks then need to be made here. The first one, quite clearly, is that the *Eschaton* intervenes neither constantly, nor automatically, nor on demand. We are not dealing with a piece of a system that would be added to all the other components of human history to make it more complete, more satisfying, etc. It is not a necessary and bound historical factor. There is no normalized (therefore constant) presence of the *Eschaton*. We have talked about intervention, which implies a coming, an irruption, but it is *always* and *every time* a coming, an irruption; it is not something that has broken into the world once, and since then, that's it! It must not be confused with the Incarnation: Jesus once came on earth, and since then, he is the Lord ruling in heaven. It can be said this way, provided we can conceive that it is not the historical Jesus who is always continuously present on Earth, and that this Reign of Christ is not a situation we may take for granted, fulfilled, *stabilized*. God is in everything power to create, that is, Creator of an ever-renewed New, never settled. This is also what it means that God is Love. Thus, the *Eschaton*, a force of intervention, does not inscribe itself as a driver in history. It is the unexpected provoking a newness every time, introducing an independent and perfectly unpredictable variable. And it is no more at our whim, at our choice, according to our desire, our wish, our prayer, that the "Last" intervenes: neither in the place we would want nor in the way we would wish. There is the margin of total, but not absolute, unpredictability in that God speaks, reveals himself, gives himself to be known, announces—as in Jesus Christ just as well the deed is done. Nevertheless, the last is not permanent here, nor at our whim. We do not have something we could take for granted; we are feeling the impact of an earthquake or a tidal wave.

The second remark is that we can then see a kind of reversal of the traditional position about history, according to which there would be a history of men, the one described by historians, within which a holy history would proceed. The twofold mistake here is, first, the "within"; second, to view this history of God among men in the same mode and on the same model as historical history. This is very generally done when precisely what is (or mostly *was!*) written is a Holy History with the content and the concatenation of the facts that one is trying to give to our history, something that neither the Old Testament nor the Gospel have done (reducing the Gospel to a Life of Jesus . . .), and which the Apocalypse radically denies.

It therefore seems on the contrary that, first, human history is included, encompassed, situated within a history of God that is its alpha and its omega, but without a coincidence between the alpha, the beginning, and the origin, nor between the omega, *eschaton*, and the *Telos*. Then, in the history of men, there bursts the one-time illumination of something fulfilled, of a final meaning, that one may call divine, absolute, eternal, etc., but which in any case never adds up with the preceding ones, no more than the light of a rocket in fireworks is added to the previous ones, and never determines the one that follows. This God which, to be sure, is always the same one never acts in an identical way in history, and the *eschaton* that comes toward us is always creative of something new from that end.

If one conceives eschatology in this way, one understands that the movement of Technique cannot, theologically, be situated in relation to its origin; it is not what determines, marks, and denotes Technique. This is why this origin, which it has not been useless to recall according to the Old Testament, is not a kind of *nota infamiae* put on Technique, but it is, practically, the infinitely precious warning not to allow oneself to be overcome by technical giddiness, by the Dionysiac explosion of technical power.

Technique is not "bad" because it has this origin. But because it has it, it cannot fulfill man's hope; it is the *deceiver* of life. And of course, there can no more be any question of believing that this Technique can be justified by an origin (we have already seen the mistake there is in believing that man obeys a divine calling in becoming a Technician). It is not a logical derivative of a calling, but a destiny that man has given himself.

Technique therefore can only be situated in relation to the end, and it may take on a positive or a negative meaning in the current moment in terms of a current intervention of the *eschaton* (carried, taken up, proclaimed, by the responsible people whom God chooses, to whom he addresses a call to do it). It receives its qualification, positive or negative, from its ability (or its inability) to integrate in the work already fulfilled by God. It finds itself justified (or not) by the possibility for the *eschaton* to manifest in the technical structure (or not). But we must constantly keep in mind that the movement of the *eschaton* that we have described is rigorously the reverse of and contradictory to the movement of these techniques. On the one hand, there is the coming from the end toward the current, on the other a strictly causal procession. We can then say that from *this standpoint*, there is never any technical progress; there is constantly a questioning of technical accumulation, each time brought back to zero (what would it serve a man to win the world . . .), and this is what explains the contradiction so often acknowledged nowadays between growth (the quantitative that is a product of technical accumulation) and development (the human qualitative of civilization). This is a contradiction that strictly cannot be resolved; the *eschaton* is a contradiction of Technique. And the event of the intervention of this *eschaton* in history is the ever-renewed possibility of a final questioning. There is no possible point nor synthesis, nor dialectic, nor conciliation, nor equilibrium between the Technical Movement and the movement of the *Eschaton*.

❧

This being said, we have to recognize that this does not take us very far. We have already been able to acknowledge with Ladrière that, when it comes down to it, the big question tackled here may be a false question.

TECHNIQUE AND ESCHATOLOGY

We have also ascertained, by succinctly summarizing four other bodies of thought on this issue, that each time there was a drift toward ethical questions, and that in reality, eschatological reflection seemed here to be only a preamble, an introduction to an ethical investigation. We must then reflect on these two conclusions.

As a matter of fact, every time people talk of eschatology (despite Vahanian's effort, which is specifically aimed at escaping this criticism) about Technique, it seems that we are inevitably led to what has so often been held against dogmatics: the latter describes for us the work of God, the incarnation, the revelation, etc., in such a way that we have the impression of some sort of frozen, unchanging panorama. There is a rational, if not scientific, objectivation, and we never find again the living movement of the Word of God, even when talking about a theology of the Word! One constantly gets the impression of an outside, uninvolved view. This is most specifically the case for eschatology when it is described as a kind of external phenomenon, a final point of our adventure. And this is even more strongly to be found about Technique: it gets as it were a status, a role, a destiny foisted upon itself; people foist upon it a certain definition, a history and an end point, perfectly alien to Technique itself, only corresponding to the need of the eschatological view one gives oneself. It is then like an object which the theologian sets without himself being involved, as though he could abstain from taking part in technical society. Given this, what we call technique has very little to do with technical reality, and what is more, one realizes that the theologian very quickly comes up short; he has very few things to say, because the fact is that he cannot manage to integrate this technique within the eschatological procession.

But it now comes about that those who view Technique as a basic reality today, who put the problem in non-objectifying new terms, immediately end up in a how to *be* in relation to Technique. This "being in relation" is the locus where *eschaton* comes into play. It is this being that is altered as a result of what he knows about the *eschaton*, or about its eschatological apprehension, and since, incidentally, he is effectively immersed in the technical environment, this may be perfectly real, new, and the object of an investigation. But one realizes that one is no longer dealing with a pure eschatology, but actually with an ethic in relation to eschatological knowledge.

※

We have secured a few certainties. Technique has to do neither with the origin nor with the final end. It ends with the end of our history; it may (and this is what we are so afraid of!) bring this history to an end, be the occasion of this end, but one which, as we have seen, is not the equivalent of the *Eschaton*. It is thus exactly circumscribed in human History. It does not have to do with final ends nor final things and situations, but only with penultimate ones. And in this closing that it can effect, Technique is incapable of assuming a way out of this closure. There is no "sequel," no other way out in the closing of history than the assumption of the work of man by God, the recapitulation of all things in Christ.

Consequently, we must say that there is no eschatological problem proper about Technique. It does not raise the issue of final ends. Thus, it is indeed correct to say that "Technique and Eschatology" as such is a false problem. All that remains is the question of behavior toward Technique, of the Christian's specific behavior in relation to this new environment, or to this destiny that man has made for himself. There is no other "problem" facing us. It is already daunting enough.

Now, this investigation of behavior, the "how to be," and the "what to do," is indeed of an ethical order, but we have already emphasized several times that this order cannot be instituted starting from a point of departure of originary commandments, of a law buried in the past, of a memory, or else of a permanent nature that would have laws whose observation would give us the content of the moral and spiritual Law, but starting from the promise and its fulfillment; in other words, starting from the actuality of final ends. Ethics is strictly speaking this work of actualization, not through an intellectual updating effort, but by an apprehension in view of this day of the *Eschaton*'s effective work: what favors or prevents it; what makes the kingdom of heaven exist or sterilizes it.

It is thus the presence of revealed (and I would go so far as saying doubly revealed, in the Father's merciful design, present in the Lordship of the immolated lamb, who never changes and can always be known as this constant, and then revealed in the kingdom's work here and now that we must apprehend as God's *Novum*) final realities, that must entail a certain way of being toward Technique, and hence a certain ethic. It is the presence of final things *for faith* and *for hope* that is meant to inspire a certain behavior toward Technique, but nothing more. Here we have a possibility for a new encounter and of influencing this new environment. The rest is pontification.

5

Ethical Mediation

WE MEET HERE WITH a frequent difficulty. From where and how is a Christian ethic to be produced? Obviously, I will not take up anew what I have explained at length elsewhere, namely, that there cannot be Christian morals, and that nevertheless we strictly cannot do without developing one, ever to be challenged (at once by the Word of God to which it is necessarily unfaithful and by the course of Time), and ever to be begun anew every generation.[1]

But there is a common mistake: once one has posited a few theological givens, one pretends to directly and immediately draw from them ethical consequences, thus in behavior, in practice, detailed, concrete, to be applied as is, precepts and commandments that can be multiplied to infinity. Now, it does not seem that this is possible. It is neither from the biblical text nor from a theological construction that one can instantly reach the concrete. There is necessarily a detour through being. It is what Jesus reminds us of when he says that the good tree cannot bear bad fruits, nor the bad tree bear good fruits. This is what needs to be changed: the root of being.

Paul shows us concretely the play of this intermediate stage when, going on to the ethical stage, to the parenetic part of the Epistle to the Romans, he starts, at the beginning of chapter 12, with this twofold orientation that makes the junction between the theological development and the ethical consequence: "I beseech you, therefore . . . Do not conform . . . but be transformed," then: "present your bodies as a sacrifice, which is your reasonable service" (Rom 12:1-2). In other words, there is a mediation between the Theological and the Ethical, a seam in relation to a "gap" (there is a world

---

1. About all this, see Part One of *To Will and To Do*.

of difference between Revelation and Behavior), a reconciliation (in truth, Ethics is the opposite of the Gospel!). But we are generally so thirsty for action, so concerned about immediate realities that we easily leave aside this intermediate link, so that we develop an ethic without any relation to the theological understanding of the Revelation.

This Bonhoeffer has perfectly seen, and in his wonderful *Ethics*,[2] he has precisely treated what I call Ethical Mediation. But it is true that he then displays the opposite flaw: he remains at that, and does not go on to the practical consequence, leaving each one to draw his own consequences for himself, but it does not seem that we can be content with this mirror effect! Jesus also gave very precise commandments (but which must all be put back within the relation to the change of being), as did Paul, of course. This must consistently remind us that there is no contradictory and exclusive opposition between Being–Doing–Having, but only a hierarchy and a determination of the latter two by the first.

In this chapter, we will thus be trying to sketch what the specific ethical mediation about Technique might be, in terms of what we have already said. And this seems to me to feature three givens: the choice of a negative theology (but not in the sense in which this term is understood in classical theology), the recognition of Technique as the new sacred, and the discernment of spirits.

Before doing this, I still have to clear our path of two kinds of platitudes. It is obvious that I do not need to write only to repeat what is of the nature of all and sundry and of the assumed platitude. I recall them for review, and having acknowledged them, move on to something else. I am referring to the humanist platitude and the structuralist platitude, which obviously have nothing specifically Christian, which can be received as truth, to be sure, but the result of which is not very satisfying in relation to the technical world.[3]

The humanist platitude is the one that proceeds through affirmation to sketch an action program in relation to Technique. The idea is for man to regain his hold on Technique and to master it: to orient it as he wishes, to impose ends on it, and to have something added to our soul to do this. Everyone seems to agree on this fine program, but people simply neglect to say what they are talking about and how to go about it.

---

2. Dietrich Bonhoeffer, *Ethics* (Minneapolis: Fortress, 2005).

3. Just so people do not have me say what I am not saying: I am not saying that humanism or structuralism *are* platitudes in themselves! That is not my problem here. It is only their position toward Technique that I am calling a platitude.

- What are we talking about? What does it mean, concretely, to Master Technique? What is the soul in question? What end is to be imposed on it (please, let us leave aside Happiness, Peace or Justice)? What is the Technique people talk about in this discourse?

- How do we go about it? Between the situation in which we live and the ideal moment when Technique will be mastered like a runaway horse, when man as a good driver will have negotiated a difficult roadway, but will remain fully the master of the car carrying him, there is a passage, a gap, and no one is coming forward to tell us how this passage is effected, what are its means and its stages. Let us note the misleading character of this simile that is so often used. The man in his car is dealing with a car, but here is a road on which it rides, and which ensures arrival at a goal. With Technique, there is no road. The situation is about as follows: atop a chariot he cannot stop, man would need on the one hand to plot his course toward an end that he chooses on a map, which actually has not been charted, and should also be able to constantly get out to *make the road* on which the car will go, but the car does not stop! In other words, we remain within an inoperative, wholly irresponsible discourse. There is no need of a theological reflection to end up there, no more than those who hold this discourse, who are content with these nice catchphrases, are in need of a theological investigation that can only put them in an awkward position. Hence, let us leave all this aside.

The other strain of platitudes is the one I would call structuralist triumphalism, not structuralism in itself, but its fairground exhibition. We acknowledge the disappearance of the subject, of independent will, of historicity, and of the possibility of an initiative. That is all well and good, that is wonderful, for it allows a truly scientific understanding. And this tallies with the erasure of man, who has really nothing to do either in history or in society, to leave all the room to structures that come into play wholly objectively with each other, wonderful parts of a wonderful clockwork.

Technique under these conditions? There is simply no problem—none—since what it challenges, what it causes to disappear, what it cancels, is precisely what structuralism shows to be mere vanity, illusion, meaningless ideological construct. Pure Technique corresponds to structuralist purity. It executes in modern concreteness the blueprint drawn from societies that may no longer be called primitive. It verifies the correctness of structuralist thought.

We will have to study later whether this triumphal chant is not in reality the pure and simple ideological translation of the objective situation created by Technique. For the moment, we will limit ourselves to ascertaining that structuralism, by stating the death of the subject, is formulating a platitude that is experienced every day and in millions of specimens by man in this technical environment.

1. THE CHOICE OF A THEOLOGICAL ORIENTATION

The first ethical mediation resides precisely here. For it is certain that ethics can only be elucidated from a theological foundation. And the problem here seems to me twofold. The first aspect consists in the option for a social Ethic or an individual Ethic, for a theology of the Cosmos (and of creation), or a theology of Salvation. In recent years, very strong stress has been put on the error of Protestantism in having emphasized individual salvation, the forgiveness of sins, personal resurrection. It has been argued that the individual, me, is not all that important, that the resurrection is general, that the aim is not the salvation of a soul, but the new creation, while there has been a stress on the already now collective nature of Christ's work, on the communitarian aspects at a minimum, and ultimately on the revolutionary globality of the message. Revolution theologies and liberation theologies that have replaced previous political theologies have immersed us in this general dimension, making us go back to the preeminence of Christ *pantocrator* and the traditional Catholic orientation of the organization of society on the basis of the Gospel message.

All that is true, provided we do not lose sight of what had been gained at the individual level. I have stressed often enough myself the importance of God's universal design in Jesus Christ not to come back to it, but I repeat: provided, even for political, social problems, etc., we do not lose the rest! And we have exactly an example of that here.

With respect to Technique, can there be an ethic other than one of individual decision? It may perhaps appear astounding and incredible that I would ask this question precisely about an eminently general problem of society, of civilization. I of course do not intend to raise here the question of the possibility (or not) of a Christian social Ethic. I am still aiming at the situation here and now, as it presents itself. We have had occasion to demonstrate elsewhere that a different political or economic organization of society will not change anything about the process of the technical system. The latter has such a power, such a specificity, such a structure that it is neither by way of politics, nor of economics, nor of organization, etc., that it can be changed, dominated, oriented, taking into account in addition that Christians in these areas are in a worse position than anyone. They no

ETHICAL MEDIATION

longer have any model of society to put forward! And it is not their business to do so anyway!

On the other hand, I have been able to show that the real current challenge of Technique is to be found in man himself. It is he who is at stake. If we talk so much of alienation, it is technical alienation that is the center. Technique possesses man from the inside, proceeds by seduction and psychic assimilation, changes the being of man, and everything else is secondary. The recovery can only be done from within man, and I would say from within the inner man. We are talking about a real conversion to be done, a change of path. Nothing else than man in his entirety is being challenged by Technique. There is no other starting point for a challenging of Technique than the "heart" of man, and of everyone, of the individual, not of course of Man in himself (who as such cannot convert!), or of humanism.

If, instead of looking for an ethic for all times, all societies, etc., we want an *ad hoc* ethic, specifically established for this given situation, that of man in this society, toward current Technique, there is nothing else but an individual ethic, but all the more demanding, rigorous, ascetic as, precisely, it is individual. We are talking about the reconstruction of the conviction that everyone, starting with me, has something crucial to do, hence a calling in a very strict sense, and if everyone obeys it, the technical system is changed by this very fact.

But this reconstruction is not an inner affair, not a mere question of soul or of abstract spiritual life; like any Christian ethic, it is a practice. It is in a certain number of outer interventions, of concrete decisions taken, of attitudes that are inscribed in the collective fabric, that this reconstruction can be performed. There is no inner and outer. Inner life only exists because it manifests in a certain lifestyle; outer life is not a *behavior*,[4] but the product and the expression of a deep and personal reality. Be that as it may, if we want to set ourselves in the system as what de-alienates man from this fate and what enables change, it is of a personal ethic that we must speak, contrary to appearances.

And it is not the easy way! But once again, it is not an eternal and universal position that I am adopting; it is rigorously in terms of what Technique currently is in our Western world. In relation to that system, a social ethic has no weight, not a chance, no value, and even no meaning. We must start again from the minimal point (for I certainly do not mean to say that an individual ethic is superior!), from point zero, in order to go on to 0 + 1! I have no other ambition!

---

4. Translator's note: In English in the original.

But at this level, then the theology that is operative is indeed that of Salvation, of Forgiveness, of Conversion, of personal Faith, of Hope (including in one's own resurrection!), of love; there, and *there alone*, I find a sufficiently strong motivation to lead man to stand up in front of his new destiny, and to defy it, to attempt the mad, unreasonable, unrealistic enterprise, devoid of any chance of success, of wanting to defeat the most powerful Behemoth[5] that ever existed.

The issue is one of motivation, much more than of program, but a motivation that would be something other than sentimentality, fleeting elation, or fusion in a collective. And after having examined all that serves as motivation in this enterprise, nothing is finally stronger than faith in the God of Jesus Christ, expressed in a theology of justification and sanctification. Once again, I am not saying that it is better, superior, nor universal and eternal; *in this instance*, it is the most *appropriate* one, when we consider the true rootedness and the true impact of the technical system.

But there is a second step to be taken. We have already spoken of the twofold orientation of Theology with respect to Technique. One holds that the future is, as it were, guaranteed by the implementation of Techniques, by the fact that man is theologically conceived as co-creator with God, and he is simply implementing the order to dominate and use this creation that is merely a locus of possibilities given to man to bring him to his perfection. The other holds that Technique is situated in a world separate from God and finds its origin there, in a fragmented universe, where it only appears after Adam's fall. This orientation holds that the order established in Genesis 1 is replaced by the order of the covenant with Noah (where it is said, let us never cease repeating it, that man will dominate through Terror and Violence!) and that Technique belongs to the means used by man to ensure his power and his autonomy against God (in the course of History).

We must choose between these two orientations. It is, in the final analysis, not a choice between two theological formulations that are consonant to a greater or lesser degree with a stable and preexisting biblical given, but, on the contrary, a choice of an eschatological type, because it has to do with the possibility or the impossibility for man of making his history.

Let us further specify (since structuralism compels us to constantly specify this sort of thing!) that when I say "man," I am referring neither to the entity, nor to the species, nor to mankind, nor to Man in himself, nor what was constructed in the eighteenth and nineteenth centuries as being

---

5. Monster of both earth and sea, well-known to ancient Egyptians. Its description (see Job 40:15–24) makes it possible to identify it with the hippopotamus of the Nile. But as a mythological monster, it symbolizes the Brute *par excellence*, powerful and tyrannical [note by the family].

man, but rather to the concrete individuals living today in our society. It is in the end a theological choice between a negation of man and an affirmation of man, between an eschatological possibility and an impasse.

But here we must be very careful; the appearance, the obvious, is the opposite of reality. In appearance, saying that man is a worker with God, developing science and Technique, simply obeying God's order, seems to be affirming the possibility of man, the possibility of history and a legitimacy of that enterprise, and vice versa. Now (and I believe that this is pretty generally consonant with the biblical model!), the truth is quite the opposite: what is the true negation of man is what affirms him as legitimated before God, and reciprocally. It is the business of the Pharisee who, scrupulously obeying all of God's orders, appears as just before God while his endeavors appear as legitimate. But it is not the Pharisee who is in the dialectics of grace; he is precisely sidelined! In today's adventure, which goes far beyond all political, economic, and social problems that have arisen for man up to the present, only the dialectics of grace are relevant.

From that moment on, the actually negative Theology, that is, the one that gives no future, no possibility of history, no fulcrum for the recovery of man in order to start anew, no stable point to allow a rebound beyond this decline and that has no eschatological outcome, is the theology that affirms the positivity of Technique, situates it within God's gracious plan, and which validates it through revelation. It is enough, alas, that the technical process has been favored (as we have seen) by a theological error! But we find ourselves today tempted to persevere in error. To provide a theological justification to Technique is to provoke the final elimination of man. Technique, as we know very well, is gradually, slowly replacing man in all his activities; in the material realm, it is simple. But we know the problem in the intellectual realm. Of course, the machine does not think. The computer, it has often been said, calculates, but it does not know it is calculating. And we fairly often console ourselves by saying that the computer is only replacing man for repetitive chores, translatable only in terms of mathematical logic. However, contrary to what one might think, man is *in this way* gradually dispossessed of his whole meaningful realm.

Let us be very careful: to say that man is freed from lowly chores, repetitive, material, mechanical chores, etc., and that he can then take up the pure joys of creation, of spirituality, of invention, of an unfettered freedom of innovation, is to separate once again the body and the spirit. In Christian theology, that means to deny the Incarnation.

This is fundamental: it is not in vain that man neglects his body nor that he abandons material chores to a mechanical slave; in so doing, he totally sterilizes himself from the intellectual and spiritual standpoint. When

I said that he was abandoning his meaningful realm, I do not mean that he abandons that to which he attributes meaning (of course, he attributes meaning to whatever activity, political, or creative, scientific, artistic, etc., seems "superior" to him), but what gets its meaning from the totality of a life, taken in all its dimensions, from which I cannot exclude the material one! For instance, work is important to the very extent to which it is an expression of the necessity of existence—and not of a "free choice" or of "gratuitousness." An activity which, in the order in which we live, is not tied to the necessity of existence, is meaningless—it is necessity overcome because it has been experienced that gives meaning.

But man cannot hover in a weightless universe, which is his daily experience due to techniques. For them, these necessities inherent in the "human condition" are swept aside, and man has the impression of a freedom, but he enters a new universe of restrictions he no longer knows, that he is subject to in anxiety, while he is immersed in meaninglessness. He is then swept up in a kind of hellish process: every time man abandons an area of his own activity, it is at once invaded by Technique, and he abandons that area every time he sees a replacement technique emerge on the horizon. As a result, man is led to have as his sole locus the useless (all that is useful is performed by something Technical), and the irrational (all that is rational is also performed by something Technical). But with the useful is abandoned whatever has weight, is experiential, experimental, whatever is concrete; with the rational is abandoned whatever is of the nature of the rational. In other words, he abandons the two branches between which meaning is located.

In this dispossession, man consoles himself by asserting that the irrational, the spontaneous, trance are far superior, that the gratuitous, the useless and vanity are what matters, and he foresees a refuge in leisure. In the meantime, he gets settled in the utopia that everyone constructs at his own level, the utopia of the freezer and Club Med for the petty bourgeois, the final utopia for the intellectual or the politician, the utopia of class struggle for the poor and the oppressed; but we are talking in every case of a u-topia, of a No-place, coupled with u-chronia, a No-Time. We take refuge in Utopia when we cannot do anything about the environment in which we find ourselves. Utopia is not a taking charge nor the establishing of ends, but a giving up on defining the real and making history. Utopia, the useless, the fantastical, all this is left to man by the technical system, like the appearance of a determination of ends by politics or philosophy, not because it represents a superiority, but on the contrary because it is devoid of interest, and because one can do that just as well as singing in the rain or catching the wind between one's closed hands. That has no formative value

ETHICAL MEDIATION

of any kind for society. It is mere pleasure one gives oneself of appearing to do something.

Such is the factual situation that the positive Theology of Technique is there to reinforce, complete, justify, and it completes in its turn the wrapping up of the operation by confiscating the theological to the benefit of Technique and by rejecting religious experience into pure irrationality. This theological legitimation is there to finally prohibit the possibility of a correct *praxis* in the technical environment, by breaking the relation between a theory, now become nonexistent (the nonexistence that is certified precisely by the content of that theology), and a practice, which has become purely technical, and which is henceforth justified by this new theological canon.

Thus, we may say that this positive theology toward Technique is at once a negation of man and of a possibility of history, a prohibition with respect to the *Eschaton*. For the only victory, the only recovery that we may win with respect to Technique, in this process of dispossession, is an overcoming of its rationality. Mastery must be asserted not at the level of the soul (something added to the soul), but at that of consciousness and of rationality.

This is why I can assert that the critical theology of Technique is the path of the valid affirmation of man by the critique of his works. Not that, needless to say, I oppose Technique and man, nor that I recuse the fact that Technique is indeed man's major work, nor that I am saying by that that Technique endangers man. For man to gain enough consciousness, he must be able to take a distance from the fact as such; to gain a mastery, he must have the means of establishing himself in confrontation and tension with respect to Technique; to gain a superior rationality (and one that would not be determined by Technique itself), he must be able to undertake a critique of the fact. He must therefore in all three cases, on the one hand, be able to refer to another rationality, not encompassed within the technical one (and this is why in particular structuralist rationality cannot be of use to him to describe it because it is specifically technical), and on the other hand, have an external point of reference from which to proceed. This is what we have tried to show in the first chapter. The only independence that man has toward Technique must be a critical independence, playing within the technical system, but rooted in what is exterior to it.

Theology thus has a crucial role in this possibility of critique. It must be of use to maintain man within rationality (and not to dive into mystical irrationality), to lead toward more consciousness, while keeping him at a distance from this reality by referring to the Transcendent and to the insertion of the Technical between the two poles we have seen: Cain and the Apocalypse.

This demand is nothing but the updated, concretized application of the eschatological Tension, which it is a matter of inscribing in a real history, in a real instant of our human adventure. Thus, the choice of a critical and negative theology with respect to Technique is strictly crucial, radical, for the possibility of a continuation of man; it is not merely the stuff of pedantry or of theological preferences!

2. THE DISCERNMENT OF SPIRITS: THE SPIRIT OF POWER

The second ethical mediation has to do, as I understand it, with the discernment of spirits—what is the spirit that animates Technique (may the reader forgive this substantialist vocabulary and this anthropologism; it is an image, as I will explain).

It may at first seem surprising that the discernment of Spirits should be viewed as a theological operation—people may grant that it is part of a spiritual, mystical attitude, a practice of faith, but theological! However, if indeed we want to know the truth about a human phenomenon, it is from the discernment of spirits that one must start out; if one wants to escape at the same time a subjectivism that is somewhat suspect in this instance, it is by a theological path that one must proceed. But this assumes two remarks:

- First, if we are surprised that the discernment of spirits is a matter of theology, it is because we conceive the latter as an abstract, eternal, permanent, immutable construction—when obviously the spirit that animates such a reality is present, fleeting, concrete. But must theology give up on making judgments about the concrete? Must it be a system tending to immobility? If we accept a theology that forcefully grapples with human daily life, then the discernment of spirits about the realities in which man lives and not a heavenly eternal truth belongs to it.

- The second remark: this discernment is not an abstract and purely intellectual business. It has only one meaning, that is to become involved in a practice, to invent a conduct. We are therefore talking about a theological statement aimed at concretely taking a decision; it is thus an ethical mediation. And, for instance, it corresponds well enough to that theological judgment which Karl Barth had made about Nazism, his being one of the first: it was a discernment of Spirits.[6] I would say as much about the two pontifical Encyclicals of 1936 on Nazism and

---

6. It largely inspired the *Theological Declaration of Barmen*, a declaration of the synod of the German Confessing Church in 1934 [note by the family].

on Stalinism.[7] For it is starting from a factual analysis, under the light of biblical Revelation, that the Spirit that animates this reality appears.

Finally, of course, when I speak of this Spirit, I do not mean to say that there are things like materialized angels or demons, corresponding to medieval iconography for instance, that are located in a heavenly or infernal place, and that come and manipulate our human, historical reality. The spirits in question are indeed inscribed in this reality. They appear as the subsisting "residue" when we have taken away all that is sociological, economic, psychological, etc., scientifically graspable. I have explained myself about this elsewhere. If pressed, I would concede that it is only the human spirit that is involved. But which one? This spirit happens to be defined and determined by its own conditions. But the conditions do not create it; they manifest it. It is not the economic that creates the spirit; an economic structure reveals which is the spirit in question—which could not be any other than what the economic context reveals. But reciprocally, it is not the spirit that itself creates its own conditions of existence; it implies that they exist and is nothing without them. It does not create the Economy or the political structure, for it does not precede it. It is wholly within their reality. Thus there is no production of the Spirit by the play of matter, nor formation of matter by decision of the spirit; but what we may perceive is their mutual conditioning. The Spirit without its conditions of existence, without its incarnation, and since we are talking of Technique, without means, is nothing. But reciprocally, the conditions are not such without the spirit, and the means are nothing without the spirit that animates them: Human Spirit, granted, but endowed with a dimension that exceeds psychology and even psychoanalysis.

This being clarified, it has seemed to us that those spirits which are at the heart of the technical movement are the spirit of power and the spirit of deceit.

The Spirit of power: there is general agreement about making Prometheus the mythical image of Technique. We have seen that, biblically, he is the parallel character, comparable to Cain, who is at the origin, as are the builders of the tower of Babel. There would thus be some kind of constant:

---

7. The reference is to two encyclicals of Pius XI: *Mit brennender Sorge*, of March 14, 1937, against Nazism, and *Divini Redemptoris*, of March 19, 1937, against Communism [note by the family].

the spirit of power expressing itself toward the gods or against men is precisely what Technique produces. But unlike all previous situations, it is a spirit of power that has finally today found a full possibility of manifesting. The myth of Prometheus or of Cain is all the more striking, as it expresses a reality that does not yet exist in its fullness. Today we can know what Technique is really about; it is not the moment to give up the myth, which already denounced the spirit.

This spirit of power of Technique is discerned by two different paths. First, one may consider what Technique achieves in the social body, between ends and means: it produces a total decentering of the end toward the means. Man was always concerned about the end, the last things, the meaning of his life, symbolization, etc. When people were concerned about means, it was always in relation to certain ends; in terms of them, a need was felt to consider that the end justifies (or does not justify) the means, etc., meaning that means were subordinate in any case.

It now comes about that all of that is erased (erased at least in reality, in experience, not in abstract and idealistic discourse). The ends are presupposed, neglected, left to intellectuals; all that captivates nowadays is means. Of what? It matters not. The interest has become totally decentered. The Means is in itself meaning and end.

Now, this shift directly expresses the spirit of power, for the latter *never* expresses itself in the end, if it can be expressed in projects (wanting to conquer the world, accumulating all the wealth, etc.). These projects are "up in the air" if there is not the means. Alexander wants to conquer the world, but he could not do anything, he would not even have this project, if his father had not created the terrible military tactic and the Technique of the phalange. The project arises when the means is there.

Now, the means is exclusively a means of power. If there is not that spirit of power, there is not a search for the means either. This is why it seems to me particularly insane and reckless to proclaim the spirit of power, the will to power, to glorify this superman, a model of man transcending human mediocrity, capable of overcoming, etc., while betraying the most profound contempt for these mechanical instruments, these administrations, these organizations, that one recuses in the name of this man. Sorry, this man only exists insofar as he creates these instruments. And it is those techniques that unveil, express, and glorify the spirit of power. Without those means, the superman will never be anything but a Tarzan superman.[8]

---

8. Translator's note: In this single instance, "superman" appears in English—albeit without italics or a capital S—in the original, suggesting a reference to the comic strip hero rather than to Nietzsche.

ETHICAL MEDIATION

I know that there is nowadays a will to rehabilitate the spirit of power, and a return to Nietzsche (once again probably on the basis of a misconstrual), but we must not forget that the hero today is not the mobilizer of the inner powers of the man who dominates his condition, but the charioteer and the astronaut: a man in engines of power. There is no other power than that of means, and it is indeed to express his spirit of power that man makes this gigantic effort of creation of the means. The fact that everything is now oriented toward these means points to the enhancement of this spirit of power.

If now we consider Technique in itself, in its features, we readily find in it the features that express this: for any technique is dominated by a will to efficiency—a will to domination—a will to use.

Efficiency, with its many guises, of efficiency, of productivity, etc., is the very raison d'être of Technique; outside of this, there is no Technique. This efficiency sought before anything else is quite clearly power. The discrimination of means is always done according to their criterion of effectiveness (the likelihood of bringing about the desired results, hence a "realized possibility," which means power).

Domination is also inseparable from Technique; with it, it is always a matter of mastering certain forces, of dominating certain areas, of taking possession of new bodies, and in reality, of a kind of extension of ownership. It is not the spirit of ownership that is dominant; this is only a consequence of technical possibility. It is when technical means allow it that property takes over and becomes established. But there is not, as a purist Marxism holds, a kind of hijacking of good technique confiscated by the mean spirit of ownership; in reality, it is quite the opposite! There would be no technique at all if there was no will to domination, property being but the posterior expression of this domination ensured by Technique, but strictly included within it. There is a strict contradiction between Technique and the anarchist vision: wherever there is technicization, there is necessarily domination, of man over man, of man over things, etc., hence the creation of a—private or State—capitalism, with property as its only *possible* expression.

And the spirit of power, which causes Technique and inspires it, appears in a third character: *use*. There is no technique without use. We only look for useful instruments, products; this happens to be perfectly consonant with efficiency. Wherever the gratuitous, the useless, the fantastical might reign, there would be no technique anymore. Usefulness has but one orientation: use. The goal of the technical means is to allow us to use what had not yet been used, and this, of course, is interwoven with the theme of domination. All that can be used must be used. Today the ocean's metals . . .

THEOLOGY AND TECHNIQUE

It is scandalous that there are such great unused reserves. Technique's basic objective is to use everything, to make everything usable, that is, to assign a service purpose to what is independent, and to eliminate what exists on its own, in order to make it exist for man's *profit*. The utilitarian spirit, that of profit, is the exact double of Technique.

This trinity—efficiency, domination, use—expresses the totality of the spirit of power. For the latter is not expressed in the clouds; it is not a metaphysics. If there is power, it is not for fun that this power exists in itself; it must manifest itself, and this will be done toward someone or something that must then be subdued, tamed, dominated. The spirit of power assumes slaves, and the slave must be used for . . . We come back to our three aspects. Now, they are exactly brought to their maximum by Technique. It is thus not untrue to bring back the Spirit of power, in this modern world, to Technique, due[9] to the conjunction between this expression of the spirit of power in efficiency, domination, use, and the realization of the latter by Technique *alone*.

We will therefore refrain from attempting to describe here the consequences of this spirit of power. Let us confine ourselves to briefly recalling two points. The first essential recognition is that power always tends toward the unlimited. From the moment when any power system has been initiated, power is always insufficient for itself. That is to say, on the one hand, that power which one had always deemed unfit to realize the great objectives one pursued must always be increased in the conviction that, tomorrow, one will at last have the means of realizing the initial plan (man faced with his failures never accuses anything but a lack of power). But on the other hand, power, which has increased in the immediate past, cannot slow down its own growth; on the contrary, it demands the continuation of movement. The accumulation of previous power is the condition, but also the demand, for the acquisition of future power. For instance, people will explain that when an economic system has a growth of 5 percent per year for ten years, it is materially impossible to attain zero growth; one is condemned, economically and technically, to continue growth for a fairly long time.

The principle of growth is thus to tend toward the unlimited. There is no other limit for power than what it *can* effectively achieve at the present time, but it will not let up in its will to go beyond that purely factual limit of pure temporal "impotence," in order to finally be able to achieve what was still out of its reach. Now, this principle of unlimited growth raises a crucial problem: can there still be values in a society that is subordinated to this growth?

9. Illegible word; a possible reading according to the context [note by the family].

ETHICAL MEDIATION

I will recall Talleyrand's famous dictum: "All power corrupts, absolute power corrupts absolutely,"[10] and likewise, Jünger's profound analysis in *The Glass Bees* in which he shows how the growth of power is necessarily, inevitably destructive of values.[11] Values, in order to exist, need recognition. Outside of power, there is a domain that remains inaccessible, not for lack of power, but by nature. Not only that, much more, we have to admit that on the basis of this preserved domain, a judgment can be exercised on power. These are obviously two conditions without which there are no values, but they are precisely the conditions that power (whatever it be, money, State, Science, Technique) cannot tolerate. How could there be a domain in which power had no part? It is precisely that one which it wants to hold and control, precisely the source of values and their development that interest all power, for a power is never content to exist as such. It also needs proof, a declaration, the recognition that it is right and fitting. It is in the nature of powers to want to be loved. They are never content just to be wielded.

And given this, how would it be possible to admit that independent values could be used to judge power? The latter cannot tolerate any judgment, for that would assume the existence of a power outside itself, and what is more, of a power that would be higher, in that from it would issue a judgment. For power and all power-bearers cannot interpret phenomena in any other way but in terms of power: That is to say, if someone judges someone else, for the one who is dedicated to Power, it can only be because he has a higher power. Thus, the mechanism of power's growth is inevitably destructive of moral, spiritual values, in any group, in any society.[12]

But we need to view the problem from another angle. Power necessarily implies the subordination of man. This power is perforce always brought to bear not only on Nature or on things, but on men and human groups. Men wield powers, but it cannot fail to be the case that this power is also applied to other men. And it matters little that it be the minority that oppresses the majority or the reverse. Tocqueville has perfectly shown that the dictatorship of the majority is just as awful as the other.[13] It is he who is right against Marx. The dictatorship of the proletariat is not legitimated by

---

10. Translator's note: Ellul is obviously misattributing to the French statesman liberal Catholic historian Lord Acton's famous quote.

11. Jünger, *Glass Bees*.

12. See the wonderful book by Heinrich Böll, *Le sacrement du Taureau*. [This is no doubt *Billiards at Half-Past Nine*, that depicts "the sacrament of the buffalo"; note by the family.]

13. See Tocqueville, *Democracy in America* [note by the family].

Number. The Mass, the Crowd that wield power are as radically bad as the Dictator. The demon's name is "legion."[14]

Now, when power is brought to bear on a man, it inevitably produces a radical effect: man becomes an object; he is reified (which is something different from alienation). Man is viewed by power as the object on which it is brought to bear, if he can then be led, manipulated, transformed; he is stripped of his human quality in order to become a function, at best a parameter of power. It is thanks to reified man that the latter will be able to reach its full potential. There can be no power that is respectful of man. This would be a contradiction in terms. A power that would view everyone as an individual case, that would seek his worth and the meaning of his life, would thereby renounce being a power and even exerting it. Since psychology and psychoanalysis have invaded courtrooms, courts have in reality given up on judging. From the moment when the accused becomes more of a unique, singular human being, whose behavior can be explained and whose face is the expression of a complex story, it is impossible to condemn him. Power loses its very reality. For the reality of power is the absence of humanity of the one who exercises this power, but also of those upon which it is brought to bear. It is the tragedy of Hegel's Master and Slave.[15]

Of course, in this relation between Technique and the Spirit of power, we may raise the question: could Technique have been oriented otherwise? And from there: can Technique be oriented otherwise? Can it not remain itself, with a wholly other spirit, a wholly other inspiration?

I would reply radically: No. Everything, each time Technique is involved, always comes back to the deployment of a power, the establishment of a power. Of course, when I speak of the modern world's Technique, it cannot be pried apart from power, the search for power, hence the spirit of power. Without it, it is simply no longer itself, it is no more. But the thing must be measured: this means that all the gains obtained by Technique are then called into question and even recused. For in one way or another, by one path or another, *all* are forms and expressions of the spirit of power: increase in quantities, in consumption, in speed, in distance, etc. All quests for power today are channeled by technical means (political power, the power of money, or physical power for sport, etc.), and conversely, one strictly

---

14. Mark 5:9.

15. This dialectic is developed in *Phenomenology of Spirit* [note by the family completed by F. Rognon].

ETHICAL MEDIATION

cannot imagine what modern Technique can mean if dissociated from the will to power; it has no more reason for being, it no longer has a motivation.

And there is a crushing concordance between the creator of Technique, who seeks to increase power, Technique itself which is nothing but the development of means of power (and nothing else!), and the user (everyone) of Technique who finds in it always and in every intervention the possibility of expressing his spirit of power. It is enough to look at the car driver with his foot to the floor, the motorcyclist who makes his engine roar by making it produce maximum noise, the bulldozer driver who destroys everything in his path in order to have clearance to maneuver, the holder of a psychological, medical, administrative technique who encloses himself in hermeticism out of a spirit of power: everyone and at every level.

It is this conjunction between the *three* factors that makes it possible to decide the true dimension of the Spirit of power, and that it is indeed a spirit. For, it must be said once again, it goes without saying that man (user) already had this instinct of domination, this will to power, but he did not have the means, or very few, to enact them, to express them. What is proper, specific, to Technique is precisely the creation of those means, of means perfectly adapted to the will to power, and that are even only that. In other words, man is seduced, seized by passion, and can only be drawn by those means that correspond so well to what is deepest, most central in him.

As a result, since Technique is not without man, and man without Technique, and the agreement between the two takes place exactly on this point of the spirit of power, one fails to understand what Technique could be under a different orientation. One needs to become aware that, on the one hand, man would not be interested in it; on the other hand, that Technique would simply cease to be. If it did not end up in the most efficient organization, if it was not oriented toward a growth of power and domination, if it lost its concordance with the will to "always more" in man, insatiable as it is, it would lose its very rationale: that is to say, nobody would seek to use it nor to promote it. There would be a regression to the period before the seventeenth century, where there were in fact technical operations to which no great importance was assigned, with middling successes that were never ensured, and vast areas of life in which Technique had not penetrated. There was there no spirit of power of Technique (man's spirit of power was inscribed elsewhere: in war, the domination of slaves, etc.), but there was no Technique either. Wherever it exists as such, that is, as something autonomous and specific, it always becomes (and China is already in the process of proving it: there will be no revolution in China in this respect) an independent process producing a growth of power. Its spirit is indeed the spirit of power.

This is why there painfully arises the problem of soft Techniques, instead of the use of Technique transformed by the advent of an anarchist society (I am thinking in particular of Bookchin's investigations).[16] Do not current Techniques admit of a new use, without the thorough exploitation of things and of men? And people quote examples, of course, of such "Technologies." But what people fail to understand is that this fails to interest modern man: offer him a car that goes faster or a nonpolluting car, he chooses the first one, etc.

People will tell me that it is only a matter of education. Fair enough. But we have to realize that this attacks one of the most central points of man's psyche and that the education in question will take centuries and alter his whole being. One must also wonder: this education—how will it be conducted? Through pedagogical means and a use of audiovisual resources—hence of techniques aimed at altering man. And who will be doing it? Those who have a "good" model, of man as he should be, so that soft technologies predominate, and who are going to train others. But this means precisely that they are going to mold them, to dominate them, and that once again we will have a will to domination (for the good, to be sure) associated to efficient technical means.

Otherwise, how would soft technologies be made to predominate? By counting on man's reason? The game is already played out at this stage! By causing fear and panic in the face of the extent of the dangers, but is that not again a spirit of power? Who can believe that man is spontaneously going to choose the less efficient, the less profitable, the less fast, the less perfect, the less powerful—to allow for the free birth of what is alive? This is a deception[17]—just as it is perfectly childish and idealistic to be convinced that it is capitalism that has made of Technique a means of power. Yet it is only that, and it is what has turned the Soviet revolution into an apparatus of power and domination. As long as soft Technologies will be competing with others, they will necessarily be eliminated, and it is not a change of regime that is going to alter this relationship, if this regime seeks to become settled, to grow, simply to last! It would indeed be a change of the very spirit that animates Technique, of the human spirit, by a spiritual subversion. I must say that, in my eyes, it is the only one that matters nowadays.

Once more, it is not an objective transformation of frameworks, of structures that can change anything. It is not a matter of deciding that the computer *can* be used for decentralization, liberation, etc. It is a matter of

---

16. Murray Bookchin (1921–2006), American essay writer and anarcho-communist activist, author of *Post-Scarcity Anarchism* [note by the family].

17. Wholly hypothetical; illegible word [note by the family].

seeing that everywhere and without exception, the computer is used for centralization, control, and discrimination between the holders of a hierarchical power and the others. It is not a matter of putting an end to the class struggle by the victory of the proletariat; the sheer existence of means of technical power necessarily reproduces new divisions between the dominant and the dominated, indefinitely. But I hasten to add once more that it is not either one or the other, either the spirit of man or means; it is as a result of their conjunction that the soul of Technique is the will to power, without which there is simply no Technique anymore.

3. THE DISCERNMENT OF SPIRITS: THE SPIRIT OF DECEIT

The second spirit that is at the heart of Technique is the spirit of deceit. This may seem surprising and unacceptable. Does not Technique spring from science, and does not the latter have truth as its aim, and does it not indeed provide certain truths? Or again: is not Technique a practice, and is it not practice that is the only acceptable test of truth, forcing us to divest ourselves of a deceptive idealism and to face reality? Here we cannot cheat; we are pushed against the wall. Technique is honesty itself, that of performances. We can nowadays make this speed, this building, this operation; no bluff is possible—it is either yes or no—what could be more honest! And yet, we are going to see that the other inspiration for Technique is indeed the spirit of deceit, but with these two preliminary remarks:

- The first is that we must reject the distinction between the technical operation (and it is here that we may speak of Technique's compulsory honesty!), and then the environment, the technical system, taken in its globality, its complexity, *its* interactions, and it is here that we see that everything is based on, as well as productive of, deceit.[18]

- But as for the spirit of power, and this is our second preliminary remark, this spirit exists through the conjunction, the seamless bond, the intertwining between the spirit, man's will, and then the development of means as a system, not the one without the other. Man with his will to self-justification, his duplicity, the diversity of his sincerities, his structure in contradictory layers, his false consciousness (what

---

18. And we must always remember that Technique being a system, every technical element, every operation, however, belongs to this system and receives from it its true connotation.

Judeo-Christianity had denounced[19] a few centuries before Marx, his hypocrisy), etc., a lie that is in no way a matter of morals, but that seems tied to the very structure of the psyche, combines with the other factor, Technique developed as a system, to produce a rigorously illusory and deceptive universe.

I could say that this permanent process of Technique's development consists in being taken for what it is not. Once again, let us specify that with this formula we are not talking of an anthropologism, endowing Technique with a will or a conscience, but the fact is identical. The play of the structures of the technical system produces a representation of this system that is the reverse of what it is in the reality of its effects. It is man who receives this representation, and it is he, as an accomplice, who develops this system's luminous superstructure, all too happy to take part in this lie, for he cannot tolerate an indictment of the work of his hands. It is this relationship that is the spirit of deceit.

Deceit, and not negativity: it is one of the basic aspects. The spirit of Technique is not the negative spirit, the classic Mephisto. On the contrary, it is doubly positive. It is at first positive in that it refuses to get lost in daydreams, fancies, illusions, hopes, and any idealism (and in this structuralism as well as Leninism exactly belong to it, just as much as bourgeois political or economic realism). It is positive in the second place in that it constantly proceeds by affirmation, by positive demonstration (and the crude psychologism that demands that you always display positive attitudes expresses it well). Technique is innovative; it overcomes without negating, without disowning; it always brings something positive: products, possibilities, solutions; everything in it is positivity. This is how it is experienced. And that is its first lie: for it destroys as much as it produces, but the enormous technical negative is totally papered over, veiled, in such a way that nobody realizes it, unless it be through systematic and in-depth study. Technique is now before anything else a set of positive appearances aimed at erasing, hiding, or erasing from memory the negative, the annihilating, the dissolving, the destructive that it is in its practice. The spirit of deceit appears as soon as Technique is evaluated in terms of positivity.

But we must analyze this more closely. We will find three positions:

- Technique passes for nature, whereas it changes artificiality into counterfactivity.[20]
- Technique passes for manifestation, whereas it is veiling and diversion.

19. Probable meaning; illegible word [note by the family].
20. See on these paths: Dorfles, "Intenzionalità e mitopoiesi nelle tecniche odierne."

- Technique passes for creative of myths and symbols, whereas it destroys the possibility of symbolization.

As far as the first point is concerned, I will not come back to the problem of Technique's (legitimate and healthy) artificiality. It is not because it is artificial, as are its products, that it can be put into question. But on the one hand, it passes for a new nature, it becomes true Nature for modern man;[21] on the other hand, it becomes, through the disappearance of any end point, the "myth of itself" (Dorfles), the object of growing fetishism, and as a result, brings about a falsification and a production of counterfeits. Today's Marxists, so eager to discover fetishism everywhere in our society, have failed to notice that the only true fetish for modern man is Technique, which encompasses, covers, and conditions all other fetishisms (of money, of power, of class, etc.).

Of course, to the very extent that it has become this fetish, Technique is not acknowledged, recognized by man as the new nature. It is, and he experiences it as such; he cannot accept another "natural," but he fetishizes it, and does the same move as when he refused to see in "nature" a mere living environment in order to sacralize it. Technique has become normative in everything, but it is precisely to the extent that it passes for something other than what it is; only mythicization and fetishization make it normative. Technique necessarily substitutes, albeit without genuine usefulness, artificial products for equivalent or superior natural products. But the play of Technique demands that the artificial product should win out; it is judged, proclaimed, advertised, and received as the best, not because a comparison has taken place, but because it invests the maximum of technical activities. The more there is technicity in a product, the more it is judged to be superior. The more "abstract" it is, i.e., the further from any naturalness, as a pure product of technical operations, shorn of any organic transformation, the more it is endowed with qualities. And as a result, this total artifice displays the features required to live in a world of artifice and without responding to the prompting of the technical environment.

Thus, Technique constantly creates as well objects and events that totally leave the realm of any naturalness, that are, in their very constitution, "counterfeit." This is not only true of industrial products; it is the same thing in artistic, literary "creation," with the keynote of communication (of

---

21. On these problems of Technique as a new nature, a natural environment and all the consequences that go with it, see Ellul, *Technological System* and also Ellul, *Empire of Non-Sense*, both forthcoming in 1967–1968. [Actually, *Le Système Technicien* was published by Calmann-Lévy in 1977 and *L'empire du non-sens: L'art et la société technicienne* by Presses universitaires de France in 1980; note by the family.]

nothing), of expression (also of nothing!). "Products are no longer even artificial, but counterfeit, i.e. used for what they are not." The evil here is not that there are artificial products, but that we no longer know that they are and that they are experienced as the natural. For from the moment when Technique makes us live in an *illusory* universe, we are incapable, as the modern intellectual movement demonstrates, of discerning the vital and the spectacular. All that the technical system provides is illusory in nature: illusory satisfactions of needs produced by the system itself (I will refrain from making the distinction that is rejected today between natural and artificial needs!). It makes us confuse reality with its representation, as it annexes for purely technological ends the most spontaneous forces.

We have pointed out that, to the extent that it is fetishized, Technique becomes normative. It passes in our society for the superior norm—*Norma normans*—that produces the normative whole, and the originary producer of norms, albeit not itself a norm having its own norm. It has even become in our society the only effective norm, i.e., everything is measured by Technique, according to the effects and criteria of Technique, as the norm of conducts and of value judgments, even as it excludes any other norm.

It is incidentally this very specific and easily ascertainable fact that explains the debate that has started about anomie in our society. For on the one hand, there are many sociologists who deem our society to be anomic,[22] and who explain most of this society's difficulties and dysfunctions in this way. But on the other hand, other sociologists acknowledge the innumerable restrictions and rules of our societies, and besides, the spontaneous reaction of the citizen, or of the young especially, is a kind of rebellion against the rigidity of regimentation, the universality of rules and norms.

However, both things are correct. We can ascertain moral anomie when we think of the destructuring of natural groups or of the so-called conquest of a so-called freedom (a sexual one for instance), amidst complete laxity; but at the same time, the restrictions weighing on a participant in society are ever more crushing. At one level, there is the disappearance of rules of a moral, legal, relational type, and the disappearance of "conscience." At another level, there is the reinforcement of all regulations and demands of a technical nature.

---

22. We need to remember that this term, which has become fashionable, comes from Durkheim, and that it has two meanings: one that corresponds to its etymology, the absence of rules; the other, that is a more psychological meaning, refers to the gap that exists between the needs of the individual, ever-growing (with consumerism, publicity, etc.), and the possibilities of satisfying these needs. This causes psychological and moral anomie: the consumer is so driven and so repressed that he chucks the rules and prohibitions preventing him from satisfying his needs and desires.

ETHICAL MEDIATION

We have seen, for instance, with psychoanalysis, the destruction of the foundation of any moral precept and of any traditional behavior, but with their replacement by the purely external imperative of technical norms, which, for their part, having no foundation in the heart of man nor in the tradition of the social group, impose themselves through their sheer effectiveness, their sheer power. They are rigorous and absolute, but perfectly deceitful: for how could Technique really be a norm for life, a norm for interpersonal behavior? It pretends to be; it teaches us techniques to make friends or to raise children; but the lie already resides in the fact that, between two people, there is the screen of the Technique used. There always remains the fact that the one who knows the Technique has superiority and that human relationships are more fundamentally skewed in this way than by previous unconditional moral imperatives.

Technique claims to be the norm of all action. It is not consciously received as such. To state it as I do necessarily triggers a negative reaction, but it is deep within us; we have no other common operator, no common denominator, no reference point other than this one. We explicitly refuse that it be so, but in our daily dealings, in our appraisals and judgments, in our hopes for success, it is always Technique that is decisive; it is by it that we measure everything.

I am writing this during the Olympic Games, and I admire the enthusiasm, the disappointment, the admiration, the appraisals proffered around me by all those who otherwise have never practiced any sport. Now, all this is about pure technique. Sportsmen are perfect and rigorous technicians, nothing more, but with whatever is necessary, of course, to practice a Technique well: abnegation, self-forgetfulness and self-sacrifice, will, doggedness, perseverance, rectification of errors (which means that I undertake the critique of my behavior on the basis of technical rules and effects, until I make myself perfectly submissive to technical rigor). For such is the situation, and not the one expressed in the oft-used phrase, "perfectly mastering his Technique." Well, no! Technique is the one that is master and the body the one being mastered. Now, this is what is being invested with emotional powers, a relation with national greatness, political charge, etc., and values appraised according to the technical norm.

But this norm happens to be deceptive. Technique cannot be a true norm because it has no other validity than to produce an efficiency. That is all. And this is indeed the situation of deception and contradiction to which we are driven: efficiency having become the only value, Technique having become the norm of any behavior, but man who obeys it cannot be satisfied with it, he cannot help but feel the falsehood of this pretension. But he does not yet dare question (for challenges to it are weak and miss their aim because they do not dare to look clearly at what the price to be paid for an effective questioning of this normativity might entail), because he has been seduced by this appearance, produced by the spirit of deceit and mystification that characterizes it.

We must broach a second realm of this spirit of deceit that inspires Technique, a more specifically Christian realm. A few years ago, I heard a remarkable lecture by Paul Ricoeur on the hermeneutics of the sacred.[23] He began by a phenomenology of the manifestation of the sacred, which he brought down to five features:

- The sacred as it manifests is potency, power, force.
- The hierophany displays the manifestation of a structure; it has a nonverbal articulate character.
- There exists a close link between the symbolism of the sacred and rite.
- Sacred symbolism is a symbolism that is tied, adhesive; it is an adherence to the real that shows itself.
- Finally, there is a logic of meaning in the sacred Universe.

Now, I have clearly seen that the five themes singled out to elucidate the manifestation of the Sacred would now perfectly elucidate the manifestation of Technique: manifestation of power, of an articulate, ritualized structure, adherence to the real, logic of meaning. All that gives the phenomenology of Technique and happens to confirm the analysis I have carried out elsewhere according to which Technique is an aspect of the new sacred in our society.[24]

We are now adding that it is indeed a *manifest* sacred. Manifestation is indeed the very essence of Technique; it simply does not exist without manifestation, and it is made only of manifestation. And it is here that we detect in this realm a spirit of deceit. For Technique is in no way sacred; it pretends to be and passes for it (here again man consciously refuses that it be so, but he constantly behaves with reference to the technical sacred). It is the only remaining sacred, playing exactly the role and the function of the sacred, but it is not, only a parody of it, a counterfeit, an artifice of the sacred.

---

23. Ricoeur, "Manifestation and Proclamation" [note by F. Rognon].
24. See a long study on the Sacred of Technique in Ellul, *New Demons*.

ETHICAL MEDIATION

It does, however manifest as such; but if its essence is indeed manifestation, it manifests *Nothing*, and therein lies our trouble, our difficulty in entering this hierophany. There is indeed a self-discovery, but of nothing other than itself; it refers to nothing other. It manifests itself, forever a signifier without any signified. There is nothing beyond it or behind it, no truth, no other power. It is the manifestation of its own power, of its own structure, of its own meaning. Manifestation is in itself the whole. There is nothing else to seek. Everything is given in this sensory obviousness; everything is exhausted, but we are seized as though we really were in a sacred universe.

Now this parody (and this is fundamental: it is not the artificiality of Technique that expresses the spirit of deceit, but the fact that it becomes parodic) extends to almost all qualifications of Christian Theology. It is obvious that Technique is now the holder of truth. I do say Technique, and no longer Science (still less philosophy), for we have seen that the criterion of truth is its effectiveness, and that there is nothing to distinguish the correctness or the falsehood of a thought save its confrontation with the real, and its *success* with respect to this real. It is the famous "this side" of the thought of Marx. And the triumph of the "materialist" thought of Marx, of which we are all convinced, marks the triumph of Technique, for technique *alone* is endowed with this power.

Thus, the debate over truth that was carried out for so many centuries—the debate of Theology for or against Philosophy, then the debate of Theology for or against Science—has come to a close. Now, there could be a debate in either case, because one remained in an identical realm. Now, it is Technique that remains the sole attestation of truth, and there can no longer be any debate; technical efficiency is self-demonstrated, and all reasons or theological truths can do nothing about it. There is no possible conciliation (for which Technique has no use) nor synthesis, only the effacement of a (theological) thought that cannot translate into Technique, and so proves thereby that it is not true. The deception consists here in having been gradually led to identify reality and truth. Only the real is true. Nothing exists outside of it anymore. And a thought only has truth inasmuch as it can inform the real. It is this deception that reveals the spirit of Technique, for it is it, and it alone, that has caused this identification to be accepted. It is in no way a philosophical operation; materialist philosophers may loudly triumph on this theme, but they have lost like all others. For it is not on account of the truth of their thought that their triumph is assured, but because of the obviousness of the Technical in the eyes of all men of this society. Their thought was able to be accepted as accounting for this identification, or more correctly, as giving man back his pride, his superiority, his dignity. It would have been too sad if man had been reduced to being Technique's puppet, but, fortunately, everything is saved; man has made a philosophy that, in full agreement with this situation, attests that he is still able to define the Truth! He has not lost anything. But we see the radical opposition; the Truth that is Jesus Christ alone has nothing to do with this substitution of used Reality, replacing Truth.

Likewise, Technique points to the only possible path. It gives the only future for man; it is creative of myths of the future—"insofar as it puts forward this power of man that gives us something to think about and that makes us dream, and that orients us toward all kinds of mythical representations of the future" (R. Mehl).[25] This plays out at all levels, from the blind trust that Technique will in the future resolve all problems, from the development of plans that define our future, from the obvious fact that the future of the peoples of the Third World is exclusively tied to the acquisition and the development of Techniques, down to the conviction of the more critical (and me!), considering that it is radically impossible to go back to a pretechnical stage, and that the only possible way out is "more technique will resolve current technical problems . . ." In other words, if there is a future that is still thinkable, if there is another way out than chaos, it is more Technique. And we come back to B. Charbonneau's formula: system or chaos.[26] It is the only alternative. But there is no future nor history in chaos, so for a future to be, an improvement of Technique is needed.

Now, we have to realize that it is Technique itself that has trapped us in this dilemma. It is what produced the chaos; it is what ensures that, by now, no return to "Nature" is possible any more; it is what is putting us before this option: "Me, always more—or Nothing." There is thus no other way, no other history, no other possibility. This now excludes the declaration of Jesus: *I am the way*.[27] No, he no longer is the way to anything—or, more precisely, the obviousness of the fact that our only future is Technique makes it impossible for us to take any other way into account. In that, Mehl was right to say that this Technique is provocative of the *myths* of the future. But it thereby reveals its spirit of deceit, for it is not the future *of man* that is evoked, provoked, that is put into *his* hands. It is not a way for man that is open before us, but the future of Technique itself, it is its own

---

25. We have not found this quotation by Roger Mehl (1912–1997), who was professor of ethics and religious sociology at the Faculté de théologie protestante de Strasbourg (1945–1981) and who, in this capacity and in a Barthian perspective, strove to define the condition of the Christian in a society marked by technique: *Images de l'homme*; *Pour une éthique sociale chrétienne*; *Les pouvoirs de l'homme* [note by F. Rognon].

26. Charbonneau, *Le système et le chaos* [note by the family].

27. John 14:6.

development—as though it went without saying that this human development *was* technical development, incidentally, the rigorous conviction of all technicians. Who, in our Western world, is not a technician? We can see the circularity of Technique's deceits.

And finally (if we leave aside the too simple question of power, what God today would have the power of Technique? Who could call himself Pantocrator? To be sure, no longer Christ, but Technique!), finally we see Technique drape itself in soteriology! We have to use theological terms to account for the reality of the properly theological operation performed by Technique! It is a power of salvation, guaranteeing man's salvation, functioning salvifically. For what other salvation than a material one can be hoped for nowadays?

Christians themselves accept more and more that everything takes place on this earth, that there is no beyond, that there is no afterlife, that the resurrection and the Kingdom of God are on this earth. And in so doing they do not progress *theologically*; they confirm what Technique forces them to conceive and adapt to the situation created by it. It alone ensures salvation on this earth; it gives and will give bread and all the rest. It is the true power that will perform the multiplication of loaves and the healing of the sick; the blind see and the lame walk thanks to it. The good news of the kingdom (of the poor) is announced through its medium (MMC)[28] in the entire world, and it is it that is finally going to promote the poor to the ranks of the rich.

Technique features precisely all aspects of eschatology, including forgiveness—or rather the elimination of sins. The only sins left are the ones against Technique, since it replaces in all realms the old demand and action that were attributed to God (and in one of his books, François de Closets very aptly talked about the Sins against Technique!).[29] And only Technique can cover sins against it, or rather overcome them by its own development. If, in today's world, man believes in a salvation, it is very often, explicitly, a salvation through politics (class struggle, etc.), but implicitly, at the level of his real life and not in illusory dreams, it is salvation through Technique that is alone internalized. Once more, we must take up Marx's distinction between real life and fantasy life. He had already seen to what extent the political was fantastical. That is still so (and far more nowadays), but salvation in the concrete is only hoped from, expected from technical progress.

---

28. Multi Media Communication [note by the family]. Jacques Ellul is talking about Cultural Mass Media (see p. 84).

29. François de Closets wrote two books connected to the topic: *En danger de progrès* and *Le bonheur en plus* [note by the family].

Thus, Technique covers practically all the traditional realms of Theology, and this is going to be confirmed by the Theologians with the formulation of Death of God theology, which ratifies the substitution of the Technical Sacred for the traditional Sacred. (Once more and without pressing the point, when Christianity has so often been accused of having destroyed the old Sacred order, let us acknowledge that it is in fact Technique that has destroyed it and which has reversed what was a transubstantiation.)

We must not register this Death of God theology as a progress in the understanding of Revelation, nor as a conquest of truth (unless it be the truth of Technique, where one performs the confusion between reality and truth, and this is exactly what this theology responds to). Nor is it the apogee of a Christianity pried loose of the accretions of religion, for it is a jettisoning of the spiritual, of the Transcendent considered as a category of the religious. But who has thus jettisoned the transcendent? It is not even Science, which currently, in one way or another, would seem to cautiously open up to it; it is Technique, it alone that has rejected among inefficient and therefore useless things this God, in tune with[30] the experience of the efficient Technical.

Death of God theology is but the other side of that positive Theology which, in fact (needless to say without expressing it thus), confers upon Technique what previously used to be referred to God. In particular, God is no longer the Almighty, because it is Technique that is almighty; God is derided as the Gap-Filler (of our shortcomings and our powerlessness), because technical efficiency has filled all these deficiencies; there is no more need to put one's assurance in God, when the Technique of insurance absolutely guarantees you against anything that might happen.

And within this Death of God theology, liberation theologies are quite typical of this situation; the liberation of man no longer needs to be the gift of God, the consequence of the decision and work of God. Man is managing very well on his own; it is political action, thanks to adequately used technical power, that alone can liberate, emancipate man. And that remains a theology, because, hats off by the way, one assumes that in doing so, man realizes God's liberating intention. This is quite significant: God, when people still dare to use the word, is reduced to being the locus of intentions, and of course it is man who fulfills them. A remarkable reversal with respect to folk theology, pretty good at that, according to which first, it is hell that is paved with good intentions (which means a very wonderful identification between the God of Liberation Theologies and Hell), then, "Man proposes

---

30. Illegible word [note by the family].

ETHICAL MEDIATION

and God disposes"; thanks to Technique and in terms of it, we have reversed this formula.

But if we replace this Death of God theology with a general sociological consideration, we may say that a society becomes aware of the death of its gods when it goes through being overcome by forces its gods can no longer master. Its gods have been built for a certain type of relations, of social structures, of dangers, in terms of certain aspirations and a certain culture; when this social whole is broken up by an excess force, then society, the people of that society, can no longer be content to acknowledge this fact. The crisis is much deeper; it is the gods themselves who are dead (an experience often seen in colonized peoples).

Our Death of God theology is thus the expression by religious intellectuals (and I do say: even though claiming a nonreligious Christianity, it is because they are religious that they are developing this theology!) of the coming to consciousness of a phenomenon that far exceeds the possibility of our beliefs. It is not the true death of God, but the putting into question of the man (and of the society) who believed in this God, through Technique. It is not the attainment by man of adulthood (which allows him to get rid of the tutoring God and Father); it is the exceeding, the upheaval, the annihilation of our ideologies (including political ones!) by Technique, which we express through the catastrophe of the death of God.

We have to reverse the formula often used these days: God is dead, and man necessarily followed him. Actually, it is: man realizes his impotence and his death due to technique, so he proclaims that it is God (he in reality!) who is dead! In other words, Death of God theology has no actual *content*; it is only the ideological reflection of what is happening with the development of the Technical system. It is a cue to a situation of non-mastery with respect to a dominant fact. And as was to be expected, this reflection is always the reverse of the real. That is to say, as it expresses a non-mastery, this theology proclaims the greatness of man, finally become capable of taking charge of his destiny on his own; as it expresses the putting into question of everything by a non-dominated Technique, it proclaims the perfectly domesticated character of said Technique. This Theology, in other words, belongs among well-known compensatory ideologies. It is the last expression of the spirit of deceit, having annexed truth.

☙

Thus, Technique manifests the spirit of power and the spirit of deceit; it is their most complete form. It is wholly inspired by them. I am not formulating that as a judgment against Technique; it is quite fundamental to know what is at its heart. Now, I get there through the conjunction of a biblical reading, a theological reading, and a sociological reading; that is what is significant. And I claim that any so-called positive reading is actually a baseless imagining that can easily be put up to utopia, but that can be of no use because it does not correspond to any reality (*Wirklichkeit*).

Annex to Chapter 5

WE MUST DEVOTE A separate note to the book by Carl Amery that I have quoted several times, because its investigation is relatively close to mine, and because it very felicitously stands out from among the numerous works on current Christian Ethics or the position of Christians toward technical society.[1] I will only be presenting my criticism here, saving the acknowledgment of convergences for the text itself. I will leave aside the very numerous errors about the history of Christianity and that of Christendom. It is incidentally difficult to speak of its errors, since Amery takes two precautions:

- First of all, he says, the point is in not at all about Christianity in its theology or its message, nor the word of Jesus, nor theological purity, but about the practice of Christians, what Christianity has produced in terms of concrete results at the end of the day; we only want to dwell on the latter and not on intentions.

- Second precaution: we have to approach all this with an outsider's gaze, to adopt

  > the unprejudiced viewpoint that a non-European observer might adopt ... The latter will see in Christianity a driving element of an enterprise of power that is more than aggressive: irresistible, and which has been spreading to the rest of the planet for a few centuries with its missionaries and gunships, its banks, its napalm and its aid to the Third World ... Is such a viewpoint of deviations legitimate? We would rather say that it is indispensable to our purpose. What changes the course of the world ... is not the dogged quarrels in which Rome and Utraquists faced off, or between Stalinists and Trotskyites, but the points they have in common.[2] It is not the followers of this

---

1. Amery, *Fin de la Providence*; see note 2, p. 136.
2. Utraquists: disciples of Jan Hus who, in the early fifteenth century in Bohemia, gave to all the faithful the communion in both species (*sub utraque specie*) [note by the family].

or that confession, of this or that sect, of such an anti-Christian movement who invented the tractor, etc., but the heirs and the protagonists of a common history that, today, at the apogee of its triumphs, threatens to tip over toward final catastrophe.[3]

As a result, any historical criticism will run up against "I am a bird, see my wings; I am a mouse . . ." This is why I will not enter this ground.

But I may begin by recognizing that Amery is part of a twofold fad: his *End of Providence* is actually just an iteration of Death of God Theology. Man must be persuaded that nobody is going to come to his help, that the God on whom he was relying is absent, and that he must manage on his own with the problems he has raised. The other current is the indictment of Christianity, from which comes all the evil of modern Western society. It is Christianity that is the cause of the devastating conquest of the world, of technical expansion, of "planetary revolution." Mainly, Christianity has caused the desacralization of the world; one dreams of this blissful world where, thanks to a well-ordered sacred, Nature was protected. The privileged relation of a chosen man with an Almighty God has destroyed this happy balance that paganism knew. These are the two very common trends that this essay taps into.

But in addition, Amery uses an interpretative key that one might even call Marxist, namely that the total crisis is the result of total success, or again that the victory of Christianity translates as the catastrophe in which the West has involved the world. In other words, Christianity has *succeeded*, far beyond, albeit otherwise, all that one calls its success (conversion, expansion of the Bible or even Christendom), for this success is the conquest of the world, its opening for exploitation, and the development of Technique.

Over the course of the development, there is hardly any mention of anything other than Christianity as inspiration for everything in the West. And for Amery, Christianity is characterized by a spirit of negation (with respect to natural reality and to the cultural reality of the ancient world) that essentially has to do with its contradictory twofold nature that Amery highlights well: it is at once a message and an institution, stability and change, destruction of order and support of order, which makes it only ever progresses from negation to negation (since for Amery, these two contradictory aspects are not synchronous with a dialectical play, but diachronic according to successive historical moments). Christianity set out on a quest for the final Kingdom and only ends up in a general conquest of the world. It bears perfectly contradictory assertions, and currently it is the one that has led to such a total mastery of nature that it causes environmental danger.

3. Amery, *Fin de la Providence*, 15.

ANNEX TO CHAPTER 5

Over the course of this history, the Church, which represents a betrayal of the initial Gospel, was necessarily Machiavellian, an institution forced to constantly contradict itself, because of the contradiction between the message and the continuity, between the Gospel and the practice of the apparatus, because it cannot completely jettison the Gospel! Of course, Amery relies heavily of the thesis, banal since Troeltsch, that the Parousia having failed to occur, one had to perdure.[4] All of Christianity's misfortunes come from this. Continuity, fear of the Parousia, management of salvation, spiritualization of the Gospel, enclosure of truth within the individual, and at the same time, destruction of Nature religions, profanation of the pagan sacred, end of ethnic myths and ethnic priesthoods, dualism between politics and religion—these are a whole series of catastrophes from which today's world stems. In the establishment of the institution and the exercise of authority, the Church, a mistress of deceit and lies, organizing her power, has never practiced self-reflection until recent years when the apparatus lost its power...[5]

The general orientations we are drawing out appear in Amery's book as the *result* of a reading of the history of Christianity, and they claim to explain the situation in which we find ourselves, with ethical consequences (which we will examine later). But in reality, Amery reconstitutes a history of Christianity as he pleases. He has warned that he would leave aside what has not brought about concrete consequences, refusing a pure and spiritual Christianity, to see only its effects—taking into account incidentally that he also uses theoretical and theological data when they can used as proof of his demonstration and that he leaves aside historically ascertainable facts when they go against it.

In reality, Amery's whole work process is perfectly legible. *He starts from a question and an assumption that he does not admit to and which actually inspire all the rest:*

- the question: starting from the current situation, with the triumph of Technique and the environmental danger, how did we manage to end up here?

- the assumption: it is that our society is Christian; Christianity has inspired everything that was done in the Western world, so Christianity is the cause of the current situation.[6]

---

4. Ernst Troeltsch (1865–1923), German philosopher and Protestant theologian. See "Eschatologie," in *Die Religion in Geschichte und Gegenwart* [note by the family].

5. Amery, *Fin de la Providence*, 111.

6. Ellul is implicitly wading into—and in a very stimulating way at that—the debate about Lynn White's thesis concerning the responsibilities of the Judeo-Christian

Starting from there, Amery is going to reconstruct a (somewhat startling if truth be told) history of Judeo-Christianity. He draws from certain Judeo-Christian data and assertions consequences that he can assert because he knows our current situation, but that are blatantly false from a historical standpoint. I must say that it sometimes appears rather far-fetched. As for the suppression of pagan religions, forgetting that Catholicism has for the most part picked them up and integrated them, and that the pagan sacred has survived under a Christian guise, it is important; but there are a hundred others in this imaginary history of Christianity. Surprising, for instance, is the refusal to consider that Christianity has not been the current that he shows, but that there have always been dozens of currents, many of which were perfectly concrete, that aroused populations and informed people's lives, and were strictly opposite to everything Amery says.

This makes it possible to point out a very obvious flaw in Amery's method: he chooses within the Judeo-Christian set what appears to him to have had an historical effect, what appears to him to have caused the current situation, and on that basis, then he says: "This *is* Christianity." He leaves aside a great many other factors, contrary ones, that have *also* had historical effects (which, for instance, Biondo Biondi or Jean Servier have highlighted),[7] but that just do not interest Amery. He should at least start by explaining (if it is true that this particular orientation of Judeo-Christianity has indeed triggered the forces of modern society) why it is *this* orientation, that one and not the others, that has had this influence. For it hardly goes without saying. And the choice of this or that trend within Christianity often appears to me to be *a posteriori* and not *a priori*; that is to say, that Technique has developed very little under the influence of such and such a Christian factor, but within a highly manifold complex of conditions, and afterwards one has spotted within Christianity whatever could seemingly either justify it or explain it.

To be sure, Amery admits that there is a diversity of currents (whose history he surveys in a more than cavalier manner!), but on the one hand in his eyes they do not reflect the dualism, the basic ambiguity that Christianity entertained in its way of being and acting, the contradiction between institution and promise, and on the other hand they are currents that have

---

tradition in the environmental crisis, to which a recent publication was again dedicated (Bourg and Roch, eds., *Crise écologique, crise des valeurs?*) [note by F. Rognon].

7. Biondo Biondi (1888–1966), professor of Roman law in Perugia, Catania and Milan. In *Giustiniano primo, principe e legislatore cattolico*, he counters the customary thesis of historians according to which Justinian's laws were the basis for Cesaro-Papism and were the first source of canon law. Servier, *Les forges d'Hiram ou la Genèse de l'Occident* (Paris: Grasset, 1976) [note by the family].

failed anyway since they have not survived until today, which leads him to say, "If I look ... at the *current* situation, nothing is left of them." This is just what we were saying: he starts from the current situation to identify what is responsible for it within Christianity, and it matters little that contrary currents have lived many centuries, have nurtured the lives of tens of thousands of people ...

But then he is completely wrong to go back so far: it is not the ideas of the tenth century before Christ that have dictated our conduct, not the concept of covenant and the conviction that man is master of nature by virtue of creation, not the certainty of reigning absolutely that have been the crucial inspirations, but much more recent modernist ideas. And I would only point to the following as proof: the Judeo-Christian ideas and practices that Amery singles out date from between the seventh century before Christ and the first century after Christ; now, they have not had *any* consequence, none of those consequences on which Amery dwells (absolute domination over Nature, etc.) until the seventeenth century. Why? Why is it that for sixteen hundred years Christianity remained wholly without effect on conquest, on Technique, on the use of Nature?

As for saying, as we noted, that Christianity has been the engine of a worldwide conquering civilization, it is needless to recall that there have been a few world-conquerors (Genghis Khan) outside of Christianity. More importantly, what Amery seems totally unaware of, is that until the fifteenth century, it was the West that never stopped being invaded, conquered, by Germans, Huns, Hungarians, Normans, Arabs, Turks, etc. Until the reversal of the situation in the fifteenth century, the West is a fortress under siege, and *never* conquering; the crusades are a release operation in the face of a super-threatening adversary at the limits. So then, where is this spirit of conquest coming from Christianity?

This is all the more interesting if one takes the two breaks I have just indicated (fifteenth century for the beginning of the expansion, seventeenth for the beginning of technical domination), for we then easily see that that is the moment when Christianity ceases to dominate minds, politics, and mores. It is the moment when it no longer models intelligence and is no longer embodied in a culture. Declaring that modern science is a fruit of Christianity may be overhasty. It is interesting to note that Foucault in his epistemology strictly never speaks of Christianity, which, of course, in his eyes, has played no role![8]

Amery refuses to consider that strictly non-Christian factors are *also* at the origin of the Western world. It is a bit facile to make of Christianity

---

8. Foucault, *Order of Things* [note by the family].

the engine of this whole scientific, technical, political, dominating history, when even Greek thought, pagan mores, Roman institutions have contributed at least as much to making up this West people call Christian. It is not Christianity that has invented the State, the institutional system, centralizing authoritarianism and the primacy of the political. I would even say that the Church, in its structures as well, has struggled against that as much as it could! Likewise, Amery refuses to consider that in the successive breaks of the sixteenth, seventeenth, eighteenth centuries, it is rigorously anti-Christian elements that were at play. It is certainly interesting to recall that Marxism exactly reproduces all the traits of Christianity, and that it is an avatar of it, as we have long known, but this does not take away from the fact that it misses two dimensions that have always been crucial in Christianity: grace and Transcendence! And there, it was not theory or dogma: it was indeed the center of lived Christianity.

And, as for saying that when sciences and techniques developed, this was a return to the oldest categories of the Promise, "to the covenant between the God of the chosen and the God of creation, to the granting of total sovereignty over this Creation, and to the guarantee of environmental plenitude, as Noah had received it—to a limitless exploitation,"[9] we certainly do not see that the scientists of the eighteenth and nineteenth centuries would have needed to resort to these notions. It is rather (an optical illusion typical of Amery) the Christians of 1950, feeling totally out of step, outrun in the face of Technique, who have recalled all this to prove that they too (after the period of refusal) were faithful servants of Science and Technique!

There is no need to underline Amery's countless factual errors about Christianity. It is rather comical to come and declare that, within the lived Christianity of the first generation, there was no concern for individual salvation (but only for Christ's return) and that it is only little by little that this concern came to dominate. On the contrary, any account of Christianity's oldest writings is centered on the "You are saved." But that hardly matters . . .

I would just want to raise a final question: what is the point today of this indictment of Christianity? Amery, in his final pages, seems to believe that by calling on Christians and socialists, by deciphering the Christian vices that are at the origin of all the ills of our society, we will be able to change the latter's course. And that reveals Amery's last two errors: believing that Christians still have some weight in this society, that if they changed, much would be changed, believing that this society is still inspired by Christianity. I am willing to admit that one may continue to live from this fragile illusion in Germany and the United States, but how can we fail

---

9. Amery, *Fin de la Providence*, 74.

to see that there too, Christianity is only a façade and the call can only be addressed to tiny minorities, which it is useful to awaken, but an indictment of sociological Christianity is totally behind the times.

In other words, this book, in my opinion, confirms things we had known for a long time and for the rest in no way throws light on the relation between the technical modern world and Christianity. One is all the more severe when comparing it to Servier's wonderful book, *Les forges d'Hiram ou la Genèse de l'Occident*.[10] One finds treated in it the same theme of the influence of Judeo-Christianity on the introduction of the idea of progress, with its consequences, but balancing this with the taking into account of individual conscience, the positiveness of History, the search for freedom. Servier does not reduce Christianity to its disastrous effects producing the modern world, this reverse apologetics that is no truer than the one which, in the seventeenth century or in the nineteenth century, saw in Christianity, the Bible, and the West the source of all there had been of good, just, and positive in History!

And to finish, I would like to make a remark about the inopportuneness of Amery's book, since I am dealing with a panic-stricken, dumbstruck West and a post-Christian man who lives without hope, in anguish, in the shadow of death. What could be the use of driving him deeper, of telling him no one will come to his help? "I lift up my eyes to the mountains—where does my help come from?"[11] No, Amery says, nothing nor nobody. It is man alone who must manage. Now, I say that without hope and without the certainty of a Transcendence, the situation in which we are can only lead to suicide. Amery, with his book, seems to me to hasten the temptation of collective suicide. And what he puts forward as an ethic, to which I readily subscribe, has no chance of being born for lack of a *positive* motivation.

---

10. Servier, *Les forges d'Hiram ou la Genèse de l'Occident*.
11. Ps 121:1.

6

Ethical Repercussions

Before entering the heart of the matter, we must recall two basic givens. The first one has to do with social Ethics. I do not believe that Christians need to formulate an ethic valid for all, nor present a collective model of society. We hit against a twofold difficulty: do those who intend to promote a new ethic consonant with the technical world, to develop new human codes of conduct that may serve as guide in an age when Technique is everywhere present, believe that one can thus artificially manufacture ethics? Is it going to be adopted by a society? Is what a thinker or a group has created going to be anything other than a rhetorical exercise? The statement of pious wishes? In this matter, I fail to see anything other than individual decision, persuasion, personal conviction that would lead to the discovery or embrace a new ethic. There is no other way. This being the case, it entails its expansion by osmosis radiating out from those who have understood and accepted this ethic and who are motivated enough to present it as exemplary. Any other mode of progression necessarily goes through Technique (that of MMC), enters the system, and can only promote the Ethic that conforms to the system. In other words, nothing has progressed in this essential realm since Jesus chose his disciples.

The second difficulty has to do with the fact that any collective or social ethical model cannot be specifically Christian. But, as any morals, having a purely useful goal (which is quite respectable in faith; what is useful is what allows man and mankind to continue to live—which is indeed God's will—and to live in a more just way), it must lend itself to being shared by all. We could take up to summarize this point two paragraphs from the Technion declaration:

ETHICAL REPERCUSSIONS

Every technological undertaking must respect basic human rights and cherish human dignity. We must not gamble with human survival. We must not degrade people into things used by machines; every technological innovation must be judged by its contributions to the development of genuinely free and creative *persons*.

The "developed" and the "developing" nations have different priorities but an ultimate convergence of shared interests:

For the developed nations: rejection of expansion at all costs and the selfish satisfaction of ever-multiplying desires and adoption of policies of principled restraint—with unstinting assistance to the unfortunate and the underprivileged.

For the developing nations: complementary but appropriately modified policies of principled restraint, especially in population growth, and a determination to avoid repeating the excesses and follies of the more "developed" economies.

Absolute priority should be given to the relief of human misery, the eradication of hunger and disease, the abolition of social injustice, and the achievement of lasting peace.

This agenda calls for sustained work on three distinct but connected tasks: the development of "guardian disciplines" for watching, modifying, improving, and restraining the human consequences of technology (a special but not exclusive responsibility of the scientists and technologists who originate technological innovations); the confluence of varying moral codes in common action; and the creation of improved educational and social institutions.[1]

We have here one of the best texts on the question. But we see that this double movement concerning the relation between developed countries and the Third World, the creation of "guardian disciplines," concerns us all. What is then the role of Christians in this? I could simply say that they ought to be more clear-sighted on the one hand, more selfless on the other hand, and be more motivated than anybody else to enter this path with others or urge them to enter it. For we must constantly repeat that if we are facing decisions that can only be individual, they lead one to get involved in a global action that is a bearer of the new ethic.

Let us be wary here of any spiritualization of Christianity (which did disappear between 1944 and 1970, but to which we are again liable!).

---

1. Technion, March 1975, *Declaration on Technology and Moral Responsibility released on Mount Carmel*, §§ 6–7, 10; see note 11, p. 51. [Translator's note: The emphasis on *persons* is Ellul's own.]

Any spiritualism means that the Christian will model himself on society. The Christian faith is not a spiritualism, but an action of the Living in the concreteness of our life—which is currently made particularly difficult by technical success and by its refusal of anything that can judge Technique. There is no faith without works, and these works today are inscribed exactly in that world. It is an incarnation of existence.

But it is not enough to participate in this common work, nor even to help promote it. It is what I would for instance hold against the texts of the World Council of Churches, which, so as to be concrete, express what in the final analysis can be thought or sought by any person of good faith who is concerned about the fate of mankind. It is necessary to participate in these programs, to bring to them new motivations and energy (and provided they are not totally driven or contaminated by the technical system itself! Which is often the case!), but that does not seem sufficient to me. There is what Christians are alone to be able to take on in this game—taking this into account: when I say that Christians have a role, a function, a specific calling, that must not drive them away from common investigations and that must not be understood as "in the interest, or for the profit of Christians alone." If they are called to fulfill a unique role, it is exactly *for all*, and to facilitate the birth of an ethic that is livable for all. This ethical role, which we will need to examine, and which belongs to Christian *existence*, leads us to go beyond the common ethic and at the same time to facilitate moving on to the collective.

The second difficulty is, for its part, purely formal. In what follows, we will quite obviously find indications that I have had occasion to give in other works. But there is no repetition, because here I am taking the problem from another angle, in another perspective. I have been able to present such an ethical orientation as the result of a sociological analysis, and this seemed to me valid for all. Since here the foundation is different, this leads to a differentiated behavior: it is a matter of what I might call "cross-investigation."

One example: I ended my study on *The Political Illusion* by an analysis of Tension as the only possibility of effecting political renewal.[2] Here, I will come back again to the necessity of Tension, but no longer starting from a sociopolitical analysis, starting from the theological conflict between the Already and the Not Yet. Though they mesh, they are not identical. If we care to compare, we will realize what I would say is specific to Christian ethics.

---

2. Ellul, *Political Illusion* [note by the family].

With respect to the technical system very specifically, I believe that Christian ethics will be characterized by critical non-power, by Rupture and immediatized Hope. In all three cases, this involves an ethical radicalization.

It is quite essential to understand that in this situation, ethics can only be radical. This does not mean more intransigent, nor does it involve an element of hostility (in the sense in which young left-wing politicos mean radical, when they talk of radicalizing the class struggle, of attaining a harsher struggle, a more decisive hatred). We have to take it first in Marx's sense: looking for the root in every given situation! But one must also look for the root of ethical embedding. In other words, first situating Ethics at the root of the situation, we must make our way back to the point of birth, where the situation arose, where it formed, to the point of origin, to the point of causality, to use an obsolete vocabulary, not considering the consequences but the source. Traditional Ethics is especially powerless, because it never considers anything but consequences and deals with things in an itemized way: in such and such a case here is such and such a situation, which means nothing. Now, we hold that the root is never found in the objective, in the system itself, the institution, the structure, but in the spirit that causes or drives it. In doing our investigation on the discernment of spirits, we have radicalized the question of the realm in which Ethics must apply.

On the other hand, radicalization applies to Ethics itself. There too, it is a matter of finding the point where ethics originates, its possibility for getting back in touch with its source. How is it going to appear, and when? Here again, it is not a matter of listing rules, precepts, commands, prohibitions; this small change means nothing. This is what Jesus recalls a hundred times when he tells us that it is from the abundance of the heart that the mouth speaks, or that it is the roots of the tree that must be changed and not the fruits, etc. Now, it is very difficult to understand that Ethics can only have its source in a conversion of the heart and not in an alteration of behavior. This is, once again, what, for instance, the World Council of Churches fails to understand, by listing problems to be solved and solutions to bring (especially in the conclusions of the Nairobi assembly).[3] This purports to be concrete; in reality, that is absolutely useless. For there are only two ways out and experience enables us to know them since quite a while:

- If we create programs, they are necessarily going to be reintegrated in the technical system (in the extreme and to deliberately take an example that is going to scandalize the reader: a program of help to countries struggling against colonialism is a program actually aimed at integrating them within the system).

3. World Council of Churches, General Assembly, 1975.

- If we present a list of concrete issues to be solved, as something to which ethics should apply, that simply means that we fail to acknowledge this basic law of the technical system, that every issue is tied to all others within the system and receives its scope, its character from the system: one can of course give one's opinion on abortion, on the way of treating immigrant workers, on racism, on the death penalty; that matters not, since these facts only exist in their relation to the technical system (the problem of the death penalty, of violence, of war, of abortion *is not the same* before and after the technical institution).

As a result, one can understand nothing about it and say nothing about it at an ethical level. We have to find the root and act at that level. Concrete consequences will come on their own when the central point will have been altered. It is no use taking sweet plums, removing acid fruits from a wild plum tree, and hanging the sweet plums on said plum tree. This is exactly what is being done in all ethics; this is what people call "concrete" stuff, practical stuff, and not getting lost in the clouds. Now, this "practical stuff" merely leads to the rotting of the sweet plums, no more, which is what we indeed see in all these ethical efforts. The only correct attitude is to graft the plum tree, but it is only going to bear fruit a year later. What graft can one do? And in relation to what global situation? That is the only radical and practical question!

1. CRITICAL NON-POWER

The first path to take is, of course, for the Christians of the Church, the relinquishing of the Spirit of Power. Here I find myself in agreement with Amery when he shows that it is the securities acquired in faith that are the first morals: ceasing to trust in the earthly successes of the Gospel, and ceasing to view our success as a guarantee, or revealed truth as our property: creation destined to be fulfilled, man having a privileged relation to his creator, the future being ensured by the resurrection and Parousia, and by and large, what he calls Providence. This certainty, this security that gives man the guarantee that everything is attributable to a providence on which one can count so that one can then do anything, this equivalent certainty that the ocean is infinite and that we can safely pollute it, etc.: all that must be put into question. As he nicely puts it, we have to lose what we have found. We have succeeded, and it is first the price of this success that we must count, and then when we have to acknowledge that this success is our failure. On these points I am in full agreement.

Likewise, I am in agreement when he shows that the reinterpretation that needs to be done of basic theological givens. The promise of election must be widened to humanity, and no longer be a privilege or a superiority. The mandate of sovereignty must be rethought in terms of complete solidarity with the natural world, and "it is because we are the first that we are one with the entire world of our biosphere." Finally, the dogma of original sin must be the locus of recusal of any domination, of aggressiveness, and lead us to a theology of Nature. All that is well and good. But I think Amery still misses the crux of the matter. He is far too preoccupied with current topics such as inequality between developed peoples and the others, or the risk of annihilation of our world: essentially true and basic problems, but coming from a more basic core—the spirit of power, as we have said.

In the face of the Spirit of power, there cannot be a competition for power. As soon as we enter any quest for power, efficiency, domination whatsoever, there is instantly a triumph of the technical system and a recusal of the truth of the incarnation. But the refusal of power does not entail powerlessness. It is fundamentally critical toward everything we can hold against Technique: it is even the *only* possible critique. When I talk about critique, I do not mean a critique of domination by the one who wants to be right in his negative approach against the one who holds the opposite, or against contrary works, for that is *still* a power-based approach: wanting to show one is right.

But I say that the choice of non-argumentation, of non-power is in itself the critique, and the only one possible, but oh so active, efficient, of all that is aimed at power. It is exactly there that whatever is a quest for power fails, no longer knows how to dominate, for there is nothing to dominate. We must constantly take up again the example of Jesus, who recused all means of power, and who *thereby* has dealt the hardest blow both to the power of political authority and to the power of religious authority. In a world aimed at power by Technique, only the spirit and the behavior of non-power are the critique.

It is therefore not a matter of refusing the technical object, the use of this or that technique, but of existentially recusing what they mean and induce. It is a perfectly decisive reversal: it is a matter of knowing if conviction is an ideology produced by "productive forces," or if the latter may be, not dominated or oriented, which is the permanent dream of idealism, but subjected to such a critique that their spirit (at once their meaning and their capacity to induce) having been reduced to nothing, they are themselves put into question.

I mean by this that if we perform the negation of the spirit of power by the very presence of non-power as a life choice, the critique of means, the critique of all technical apparatuses, of the entire technical system necessarily follows in such a way that a large number of elements of the technical *become* pointless, devoid of interest, devoid of value, meaningless, and can thus be abandoned—but not otherwise nor by another way. Only non-power takes away the meaning attributed to the technical system. It does not fight it directly, and it does not *try* to do a critique, but it takes away its power and its imperative, particularly through the fact that what counts as normal shifts from that very moment.

The choice of non-power, and that one alone, situates us on a scale of values where Technique no longer has anything to do. The latter ceases to be normative and, as a result, as we have seen, loses its self-evidence. Non-power becomes the criterion of the "Good"; this is where the crossroads is taken between several life orientations.

Moreover, there is no denying that the conflict is extraordinarily difficult. One need only recall that, for instance, Buddhism used to be oriented toward non-power. Now, what has been particularly impressive over the last two decades has been to see Buddhism suddenly involved in the technical race. I do not mean that Buddhists are technicians, but the tipping over occurred when Buddhists, bonzes, got deeply involved in the political problem of the Vietnam War and subscribed to Communism. Communism is a technical ideology, and commitment in a modern political conflict is nothing more than the first step in the building of a technical society. The reversal occurred on that occasion, but it is done; in other words, the technical system won its victory with respect to this great movement of non-power.

The technical system strictly cannot stand a life attitude of non-power, which would spell its ruin. It is enough to think that one would no longer choose to consume what is quickest, most efficient, most advanced. I am not saying that one would systematically choose the *least* quick, the *least* efficient, etc., but simply that one ceases to be interested in these qualities. One is indifferent—one is worth as much as the other. Hence one ruins both the infatuation for advertising, and above all, the motivation for research.

But this assumes that one fully understands what is involved. Non-power is not Powerlessness, as we succinctly put it. This is fundamental: Powerlessness means not being able on account of factual circumstances, on account of the limitations of our nature, on account of our condition. We come across realms where we *cannot* penetrate, actions we cannot do; we lack the means or knowledge, etc. Non-power means being able and not being willing to do it. It is choosing not to exercise domination, efficiency, choosing not to rush toward success. It is relinquishing power. It is then attesting that the dimension of power and success *does not* have the final word, does not have the right to judge human life, *is not* the final word of our human condition. Now let us note, and this is crucial, that this choice, as such, is exactly that of Jesus. If there is an imitation of Jesus to accept, it is strictly here that it is situated. At the moment of the Temptation, what is offered to him is three times the manifestation of his power: changing stones into bread, jumping from the top of the Temple to attest that the angels are at this service, exercising power over all the kingdoms of the Earth.[4] Three times Jesus, who has this power, refuses to manifest it, refuses to use it. Most especially, he refuses power over the kingdoms, political power.

Likewise, he refuses to do the miracles people ask him for when it is a matter of expressing his power. His miracles are the fruit of love and a response to faith, hence strictly neither a manifestation of power nor a will to domination; when they risk becoming that, Jesus refuses them. Likewise, at the moment of his arrest, he refuses to use the means that would allow him to escape. Whether it be the human means of material combat or the means of manifesting God by having "twelve legions of angels" intervene, he explicitly says he does not want that.[5] Finally, on the cross, once again, he refuses to manifest his power, when he is provoked by those who call him to do it by telling him to get off the cross (and that they still believe in him), to save himself (physician, heal thyself).[6] The choice of this non-power in any circumstance is probably what is most unacceptable for modern man.

Now, we were indeed saying in any circumstance, for it is quite obvious that it is, as these examples show, when the moment is crucial and assumes an effectivity that the choice is to be done, not at another moment, when in fact there would be no need to display power! It is when someone attacks and enters the path of power that there is call to be non-powerful (so that the theological theory of revolution or of participation in political power, on the one hand, and of legitimate self-defense, on the other hand, is untenable!). It is when we are called upon to use power that it means anything to refuse!

We must in particular underline that it is not a purely interior, spiritual and religious attitude. One strictly cannot say "I am totally for the imitation of Jesus, for entering the path of non-power, of humility, of love of the enemy, of service, etc." and then at the same time buy the car that goes fastest, or join the most efficient political party (or the one that uses the most proven means of power; a good political criterion is refusing the one that uses means of power, whatever its justifications might be). The root of

---

4. Matt 4:3, 6–9.
5. Matt 26:53–54.
6. Matt 27:40–42.

everything, in the technical system, is precisely that the man who *can* do refuses to do, accepts not using the huge means at his disposal.

Now, as we have seen, there is no longer any outer obstacle to the use of the totality of those means and to their expansion: neither values, nor reason, nor divine law, nor nature—not even fear. It is very typical that as much as man may be terrorized by the hydrogen bomb or by pollution, he continues as before to promote technical progress and to rush toward Technique's best products. We must therefore tackle the inside and assert the impossibility of living *together* and even of *living* at all if one does not practice an ethic of non-power. It is the basic option. As long as man is going to be oriented by the spirit of power and toward the acquisition of power, nothing is possible; or rather, only one thing is certain: the end of the world.

We are talking about a systematic search for non-power, which certainly does not mean the acceptance of fate, or passivity. On this issue, I would make two remarks:

- First of all, the argument that would consist precisely in saying that it is passivity fails to take into account the reality in which we are: we are obviously not in any danger of that!! A century from now, if the Ethic of non-power were to triumph in the Western world and risked leading to passivity, it would be time to rethink the situation. Currently, this is a stupid argument.

- The second is that choosing non-power is not passivity; it is choosing a lifestyle that has gone beyond the need for power. It is precisely stripping fate of what is implacable about it; one foils the forces of history through non-power. One foils the logic of situations because one devalues the stakes through this choice. It is no longer worth it.

But then, people will say, this is leaving all the room to the violent, to the powerful, to those who hold the means of power. I ask: "*What room?*" the one at any rate where I am no longer. Of course, that assumes renouncing the conquering of their room, and thus not considering the present life as the All and the ultimate. "I lay down my life; no one takes it from me"[7]; "I am sending you out like sheep among wolves."[8] It is a matter of choosing to be sheep. "Do not be afraid of those who kill the body . . ."[9] It is not leaving fate a free rein, it is taking away the meaning of all that is done through power. It is this devaluation (much more than the imaginary vision

7. John 10:17–18.
8. Matt 10:16.
9. Matt 10:28.

ETHICAL REPERCUSSIONS

currently in fashion of a Jesus as political rebel) that was intolerable for the powerful of his day.

Thus, as a first distinction to be made, non-power is the product of a choice, and strictly not of powerlessness. Where we are powerless, we need not find glory in it by saying that we subscribe to an ethic of non-power. If I am materially stronger than the one who slaps me, and if I give him my left cheek, that is non-power; if I am materially less strong, that is powerlessness, and I need not find glory in not having fought.

The second distinction to be made is that between non-power and non-violence. The latter is obviously included in the former, but is not identical with it. For people have wanted to make nonviolence a strategy or a tactic to win a political struggle. There again, we are facing a triumph of the technical spirit: bringing the nonviolent to justify themselves by proving that nonviolence is efficient and can earn successes. That may be legitimated at a political level, but one must be aware that this is subscribing to the technical system. It is admitting that what does not succeed is not efficient, has no value! Hence the fragility of the position: if, to obtain a given result, nonviolence pays, we use it; if not, we enter violence. And this concern for efficiency is always what brings about a crisis in nonviolent movements and ends up with the nonviolent group being overtaken by a violent wing.

If we try to show, thanks to Gandhi, that we succeed in defeating the adversary, we bring back nonviolence to a technique among others (a soft one to be sure!) that must therefore obey the technical spirit of success and efficiency. It is admitting that we cannot convince the men of our society otherwise than through a proof of efficiency, and that telling them "Of course, it is not efficient (so what?), but it is good, just and true," has no value! It is indeed entering the technical system whose spirit of power is the *norm* and the criterion of the values recognized by all.

Thus, non-power puts an end to all these misunderstandings. It is true that it is not efficient, and for that very reason it is the only path that is critical of the technical system. All the rest is idle playthings.[10] The choice is manifested at all levels: first in the orientation of values, then in global decisions, finally in concrete decisions. As for values, that entails the recusal of all the values on which our society is founded, values of success, of growth, of efficiency, of domination, of use, of maximization, etc., in favor of basing one's life on values of conviviality, of service, of amiability, of transparency, of friendship, of generosity, of nonpossession, etc.

---

10. And let us recall that the technical system is, without any possible reform, State totalitarianism, pollution and ecological catastrophe, the negation of the individual, the triumph of the strongest in all areas, etc., with also, of course, the well-known advantages, about consumption, health, etc.; see my analysis of the technical system.

Now, these two sets of values are incompatible. We must not hope to have at once maximum efficiency and to live in friendly relaxation with others. Efficiency necessarily and always entails competition with others (and whether it be in a capitalist or a socialist system, it comes down to the same!), hence the fact that we view the other as someone to vanquish and to surpass (this kind of problem is known in all Communist parties); no friendship can exist. In this kind of society, a relationship with people with whom one does not need to do anything would be gratuitous, hence meaningless. We are once more brought back to the technical dichotomy: human values as a supplement, a luxury, an ornament, contrasted with "serious" values, technical ones, that exclude the human.

Starting from this decision about non-power, normally the whole hierarchy of human values unfolds. And this ethic of non-power, from there, inscribes itself at all levels: thus in the use of technical means, the way we use devices that may be "of power"; not seeking to surpass others, to be the first, to drive one's car at maximum speed; not to have one's TV or stereo blare; and not to seek to constantly profit and to dominate others by the function one exercises, through apparatuses, etc. But it is also within institutions that we must attempt to insert it: all institutions that tend to develop power, placing competition at the basis of social organization, are to be rejected. Here, we could briefly list all the institutions of the so-called developed world: as much the economic system of free competition (saying "let the best one win" is to encourage the spirit of power, and it is of course on this basis that Technique developed!), as socialist planning that imposes annual growth objectives, 5, 6, 8 percent . . . and also institutes a competition of efficiency between team members or factories (socialist emulation); as much the Olympic Games as most pedagogical methods (contest-based). Every time, it is a matter of proving efficiency, and as a result, of cultivating power in terms of the technical system, and the devaluation of any possible morals.

But it is also in scientific research itself that the ethics of non-power plays out. For instance, what Illich calls radical research is what should provide the criteria that make it possible to determine the harmfulness threshold of a product, an organization, a system, and to judge them to be unacceptable. But this is obviously just the opposite of what people call fundamental scientific research!

It is finally in politics that this ethic can inscribe itself: penalization in all areas of the rich and the powerful, *a priori* protection of the weak, the exploited, the oppressed, of minorities, of the excluded (without trying to find out first if they are right or if they are more just), renunciation of possessions, which obviously leads to a sharing of wealth (for instance with the

Third World), renunciation of domination (for instance colonies, etc.). But let us be very careful: this is not about a political program, nor about voting for a party that would adopt these objectives in theory, since this party too only seeks to win, to prevail over others. It too is a bearer of the spirit of power; it will establish its dictatorship to obtain such good results, and we will not get out of the technical system. It is only a matter of permanently testifying through lived experience that what we have just indicated is the putting into question of all politics, of whatever kind. But the mention of the "political party" opens another topic of reflection.

We have to understand that all these practical elements, and we could multiply them, are not objectives to be attained, of which non-power would be the means, but that they are *consequences* of a basic attitude that alone crucially matters. And this reversal is alone consistent with a theology of grace.

It is a matter of taking up once again, on new bases, the seemingly exhausted topic of ends and means. I begin by recalling the classical theological position according to which theology's role is to define *ends*. No need to insist. I will then recall a current of thought, to which I belong, according to which means must be consistent with ends; the end never justifies the means, because the means determine and define the end, and if they are evil, they irreparably corrupt the best of ends. I will finally recall my personal position, according to which the *only* problem that arises in our society (as a problem) is that of means. This is for two reasons. First, about ends, everyone agrees. Then, because Technique is a set of means and the debate can only be about that, the ends therefore no longer matter.

We have to start from these three givens: Technique forces us to situate ourselves at the level of means, but indeed a biblically faithful theology can only be interested in that. There are no ends in the Bible (contrary to philosophy). Everything that is at the level of the End, of the *Eschaton*, of Salvation, of eternal life—all that is *given*; it is already done, an act of grace, thus not a possible end for any action nor for a theological reflection. We need not wonder about "what end?" nor about its possibility, nor about the ends to be put before Christian action. It is already granted, already present in the kingdom of heaven. The only theological question is "how to live in terms of this end given by grace?" It is thus a question of means. We need not do a theological investigation into the ends we could put before Technique. What is remarkable is the reversal we must perform: on the one hand, Technique is only a set of means, and now it pretends to assign ends, to unveil ends, to ordain everything to an end, itself worked out in terms of means. On the other hand, Theology has too often been a science of ends, has talked of justice, of freedom, of love, as ends to be realized, to attain—and it usually left aside the how.

Now, we need to perform a twofold reversal: the radical reduction of technical finalism to bring back Technique to being no more than what it is—means, systems, ultimately: tricks!—without pretending to assign it ends, which is useless, tearing away its pretension to determine them itself. As for Theology, we must[11] be aware that it has nothing to say about ends, for everything is already said by God on this topic. On the other hand, Theology is a science of means, and can only be that, the means of faith, of hope, of charity, the means of the word and the consolation, the means of the covenant and the Church, the how of manifesting the Lordship of Jesus Christ.

But if Theology is the science of means, it is not a matter of means to reach these objectives, but simply at the level of the conduct of life, and that is why it cannot fail to come up against Technique. Non-power is thus not a Means to obtain some satisfactory end; it is a whole lifestyle that puts everything at stake and into question, but it is a means in that (and that alone) it situates itself as the opposite of means of technical power. It places them in a situation of radical critique.

Thus, everything comes down to a problem of Spirit: on the one hand, a Spirit of power, that pretends to order and animate our whole society and to finalize our lives; on the other, a life inspired by another Spirit, which can only be that of non-power. It is in the use of such and such a means, in the critique of such and such, that such Spirit is manifested, revealed and, properly speaking, exists. We never discern it any other way than at the level of means. It is technical means that have made us understand that the technical Spirit is the spirit of power; it must be the choice of means by the Christian that at the same time manifests the imitation of Jesus Christ, in a spirit of non-power, and as a result places Technique in a critical situation: not at the level of an intellectual critique, but of an existential one, not at the level of the ad hoc, but of the permanent.

It is quite obvious that an ethic of non-power is going to bring with it the establishment of limits. And it is here that we can solve the difficult problem of these limits. We need not return to it, but only show what they are rooted in. However, we may perhaps simply recall that when, in the face of the technical explosion, the spirit of non-power formulates limits, this is neither a negative position, nor a withdrawal position, nor one of timidity, but of a service we are doing the whole of society as Christians: the category of services (such as the questioning of indefinite growth, the critique of the political, etc.) that Christians should understand as their *only* effective, and

---

11. Suggestion; illegible word [note by the family].

deep, service, for the setting of limits is always constitutive of society. It is at the moment when limits are set that society appears as such. The unlimited is the negation of the human, as of culture. There is no human group that can exist as human in the unlimited, whichever it be, whether this unlimited is that of absolute regulation, of unbridled political power, or on the contrary, the unlimited is the pretension to live without any rule, without regulation, without institution; whether the unlimited is unbridled technical rush, in the belief that all possibilities are within reach—or the refusal of all technique to come back to a "state of nature."

The setting of limits is the human act par excellence. It is rigorously the one in which his freedom is expressed. It is when man has become (or becomes) free that he at the same time (and it is the first sign of his freedom!) becomes able to limit himself. Limitless consumption is just as much of a negation of freedom as is absolute famine. When the spirit of non-power leads one to counter technical expansion with limits, by a fundamental critique of power, it makes possible the continuance of society and culture that is negated by the indefinite expansion of Technique.

It is thus not a kind of Christian withdrawal in a refuge, nor an idealist position, nor a spiritual egotism; it is a service rendered to the social body as a whole, a far more important service than any that the totality of research laboratories and human sciences combined could render. It is a necessarily misunderstood service, intolerable in a sense, in any case since it counters hubris, the thirst for power, wealth, domination. But these impulses are only ever expressions of the passion for death (an expression which I favor over death drive). The Spirit of non-power is the concrete manifestation of the Spirit of life. But, it bears repeating, it cannot be accepted joyfully, for it is quite obvious that it at the same time creates tensions and conflicts within the social body. Here again we are dealing with an essential feature of ethics in a technical society.

Technique [tends to demand a synchronization, a unity. It is unifying, and this disappearance of conflicts is presented as a virtue. But we know that human groups in which tensions and conflicts disappear are groups that become sclerotic, losing their ability to change and to resist aggressions, as well as that to evolve.

We are here dealing with a basic issue. It is the substitution of technical progress (with its uniform and linear mode) to the older type of human progress (which always occurred in a conflictual fashion). Now, technical progress is disastrous for the human group as such, because the sclerotic effect (not the entropic one yet) necessarily continues to take place.

If we want human groups to continue existing, and man to have a specific part to play in a human environment, we have to call upon a conflictual ethic and to question the universality of the large units, of the large organizations produced and required by and for technical progress. The conflictual is a survival value for the whole of mankind.

But we are obviously talking about a negotiated, mastered conflict, that does not tend toward the group's destruction pure and simple, to its falling apart. We are not talking about a nihilism, but about the production of calculated tensions within human groups so that these cannot close themselves, become self-enclosed, perfected (any perfected society is dead), but may recover an ability to evolve on their own and without reference to[12] the evolution of Technique.][13]

This conflict does not primarily arise at the level of structures and facts, but at the level of inwardness and behaviors. There is not a pre-established model expressing the choice of non-power (making a program of this kind would only be to fall back into technical programming!). This stance cannot be viewed as a system, a set of means; it is an ever-renewed decision-making, purely personal, but reaching the collective, because the tension produced by non-power is expressed and felt everywhere. It is thus not collective stuff situated within an attack organism, but, due to the social organism, put into question. And yet again, this confronting, this questioning cannot be understood as a negation: the contradiction implies a possibility of change, a hope of evolution. In other words, non-power cannot be an asceticism, an escapism.[14] The relation with the social body must be maintained, but a relation that tends to modify the situation. And if there is a radical critique of the spirit of power, it can only be *against* technical society, not against the man of this society, but *for* them.[15] This questioning is the very condition of the possibility of an evolution for them, of a *genuine* change, because this questioning has to do with technical society's closure, produced *among other things* by the spirit of power (since it implies the negation and the assimilation of all that is exterior to it, hence no possibility of anything new, unless it is an extreme development of technical potentialities).

We have already shown elsewhere that any purely closed, rigid, and repetitive society is an endangered society, practically dead. A society only evolves, that is, is only alive, if it remains unfinished, if it holds within itself

12. Proposed correction; the document has: without referring the evolution of Technique [note by the family].

13. The passage between brackets no doubt comes from a document used elsewhere [note by the family].

14. [Translator's note: written *escapisme* in the original French.] From the English: *to escape*. Refers to a stance of withdrawal from the world and from civic life [note by the family].

15. Translator's note: *sic*.

ETHICAL REPERCUSSIONS

flaws and contradictions that compel it to continue on its path, a disequilibrium that prevents entropy; but for that is needed a genuine tension, namely that produced by a radically alien factor, questioning and new. It is exactly that which non-power represents.[16]

But there remains one final fundamental issue: it is certain that a very strong motivation is needed to make this choice: the imitation of Jesus Christ, we were saying. What is needed is the absolute certainty that what is not within reach of human power is nonetheless realized. We cannot have in mind a kind of magical operation by virtue of which non-power on its own would produce a wonderful reversal. No more can we, as I have shown above, demonstrate that non-power is an efficient means of getting a result. We must therefore have the certainty that there is another way in, another way out, that there is an answer that will be given to this choice of non-power, but an answer that is not of a mechanical nature (stimulation/response . . . reflex!), that there is a fulfillment of promises made, and in terms of which we will choose non-power ("I am with you always, even unto the end of the world"),[17] that there is thus another power at play, a power that is neither mine, nor at my disposal, that does not display the features of the spirit of human power, nor of Technique, that tends neither to domination nor to enslavement, that is autonomous and relative to pure grace and that has already manifested that it is no different than Love. It is in the absolute certainty of this power that the only motivation of the choice of non-power is found. It is exactly the only human possibility that is left to us, outside of Nihilism.

If we want neither suicide (by denying technical society's growth process without any other hope) nor pure and simple integration in the power process, we are necessarily led to the acknowledgment of this Transcendence.

But then we meet with two objections. The first is that this spirit of non-power, which I have shown to be truly free and without valid aim for itself, is therefore not unconditioned, since in the final analysis it refers to the power of God and thus has no merit. The answer is easy: to be sure, it is obviously not unconditioned, since nothing human is; God alone is unconditioned. To claim to be unconditioned is deceit and pride. It is only that this spirit of non-power is not conditioned by the technical system. As for merit, of course there is no merit, but nor is it in order to acquire merits that one enters this path. The choice of non-power by man testifies to the

---

16. About tension, and the positivity of this seemingly negative stance, all developments are in Ellul, *Political Illusion* and *Ethics of Freedom*.

17. Matt 28:20.

fact that the Power of God in which we believe is expressed in the choice by God of his own non-power in Jesus. But this power exists—and it is the one that has raised Christ from the dead.

The second objection is more modern: "Since you do count on the power of God to settle issues, non-power is nothing more than abandonment, giving up on settling issues yourself. You throw back to a God entrusted with Providence, or with doing miracles, that which should be done by you, and which is incumbent upon you. You are reconstituting the God of the gaps, or yet the God Feuerbach shot down so utterly."[18] Indeed, the choice of non-power entails renouncing the spirit of technical power, and the conceit of our theologians who sing the praises of technical greatness, becoming enthused over man's power and the wonders of Science and Technique, so superior to the wondrous of the Gospel, and so much more serious.

I would then simply want, not to answer to this triumphalism, but to underline that we are here indeed dealing with a crucial choice. There is no illusion to be had; either it is this referral to the biblical God, in *all* the dimensions that Revelation shows us (including free fulfillment through his power), or it is in no way, as a disembodied philosophy claims, the full[19] liberation and autonomy of man, but his total subordination to, and insertion within, the technical system. There is no middle way between power, the spirit of power, the will to power, actualized today exclusively by Technique, and the choice of non-power which is the imitation of Jesus Christ (in his faithfulness to his Almighty Father!). There is no half-power, or regularization of power, or moralization; there is not a possibility of finding a way out through a political path, or by institutional transformation on the basis of a horizontal theology. The only ultimate choice today is between the acknowledgment of the Transcendence of God, with everything this entails, and the total enslavement of man, bound hand and foot, to the technical system, with, we must not forget, the fact that the more this system becomes absolute, the more it simultaneously causes chaos.

---

18. Ludwig Feuerbach (1804–1872) was a German philosopher, a disciple and critic of Hegel, considered to be the leader of the materialist current and the father of modern atheism. He performs a radical critique of religion in *Thoughts on Death and Immortality*; *Essence of Christianity*; and *Essence of Religion*. For him, man created God in his own image; belief in God is therefore a sign of man's alienation [note by the family].

19. Proposal; the word is hard to read [note by the family].

2. THE ETHIC OF RUPTURE

What we have just said leads to a second great axis of this ethic, Rupture. But here it is a matter of taking up again the ethical journey; in other words, it is not a philosophical analysis of the rupture that we are called upon to perform. Rupture with respect to the process of technical development happens by a shock effect of a radically different behavior. And we must then note the insufficiency of Amery's proposals in that area. For him, it is a matter of totally rethinking the old ethic and with it the current ethic of production and consumption. I quite agree.

But what he puts forward is an ethic of responsibility, as an indictment of man's carelessness with respect to the looting of the planet, an understanding that we are not owners, but that we only ever possess the usufruct of what exists in the world. Such are the principles, of which he says that they have the merit of being simple, allowing us to see clearly what is good and what is bad (what is good is what enables survival). We only need to know the causality; the fault is not a matter of complicated relationships with an invisible principle. It is the obvious: everybody's harmful behavior toward the biosphere. This responsibility assumes a (simple) consciousness-raising in all, and a rehumanization of human behavior toward the environment (with a nice catchphrase: it is by humanizing the world that we have dehumanized it) that will be recognized as other in relation to us. With all that I can easily agree.

But I would make two objections to it. The first one is that it in no way makes it possible to attack the technical system on which the exploitation of the world actually depends. One remains at the periphery. Of course, this orientation, non-radical and limited, is however quite useful, but Amery seems to believe that it can succeed on its own. Now, we come here to the second criticism, as we already have proof that this is not the case. For what Amery is putting forward is well-known; he brings nothing new. In 1945, Barthian circles were developing a theology of stewardship that exactly matches what Amery is saying. We have everywhere, in Christian circles, explicated this idea that man, according to Revelation, is absolutely not the owner of the world, but a steward and can only enjoy a usufruct. From there, the World Council, starting in 1948, has developed a theology and an ethic of responsibility. I can say that, from 1948 to 1955, it was the constant and general theme, tiresome on account of being repeated so often: a responsible society, a responsible man with all the implications, as much in the political or the economic realm as in what was not yet called the environmental one. There was the responsibility of man toward man, but also toward the natural environment. All this has been said time and again with a great many more details than what Amery can put forward. All this has been spread in all the Churches and has had strictly zero effect. It is exactly during this period that the exploitation of the world developed. I do not see how Amery's proposal would have an effect today.

I believe we have to head toward a point of rupture, again an All or Nothing, because such is indeed the situation. The ethical decision in this area will be the expression of a coming-to-consciousness of this All or Nothing, that such is indeed the objective situation. This coming to consciousness then expresses how the situation comes under control again, the insertion of freedom, that is, total reversal. The situation is objectively such that it is All or Nothing, but now I choose a behavior that manifests it, and things turn out this way as a result of my choice and no longer as a result of my situation.

This rupture can only originate in a will to destroy the ideological superstructure of the phenomenon and in the insertion of an independent value in the process. I have thereby referred to iconoclasm and witness. The two terms show from the outset how far we are from a traditional morality. With respect to Technique, it is no longer a matter of knowing how to use it well, nor what virtues we need to have in order to live fully in a technical world, etc. Yet again, it is much more radical, for we are here talking about the destruction of the technical world's Spirit of deceit. It is the act, the behavior, the lifestyle that produces the unveiling and the destruction of something unreal that gets itself taken for the only reality, of an image that is but an image, but that gets itself taken for very substance, of a representation that is in the final analysis the representation of nothing.

We have just recalled a few aspects of this seduction of (current) Technique that allow it to subjugate the whole of man and prevent him from finding himself again, as well as from becoming "responsible." And it is exactly to this that the twofold behavior of iconoclasm and witness corresponds.

Iconoclasm. We agree here with Vahanian's position. It can be summed up in the idea that faith in Jesus Christ is destructive of images, the image being the counterfeit of God. Here, as far as we are concerned, it implies not a rupture with respect to Technique, not a refusal of Technique, but a destruction of the image, the imaginary concerning Technique, the ideological superstructure, the soteriological representation, indeed, the idol. The transformation of Technique, a material means expressed in an idol, is a

ETHICAL REPERCUSSIONS

condition for the appearance of the technical system, but also an inevitable product of this system.

When the icon of Technique is put into question, it is the very basis of our world that is hit. It is just this which is at stake. Disillusion and desacralization are the two sides of iconoclasm. Disillusion means destruction of illusions by return to the authentic real.[20] The latter is two-dimensional: the vital real as it were, what Marx called the social man, the vital real which is that of effective (and not imaginary, dreamed, believed, etc.) life conditions, with consequences for the surroundings—and the spiritual real, the reference to the other side of the real, without which the first one is nothing and cannot be recognized, the real of a certain order of values, which for the Christian boils down to the God of Jesus Christ. Christian ethics implies the destruction of illusions; the incarnation is this destruction. Jesus Christ brings us back to this real that is irrefutable for having wandered the roads of Judea and having died. There is no philosophical discussion around this real; there is no scattering in a maze of communication, of subjectivities. It is all very nice to say that what we believe to be real is only an interpretation of our senses, a *cultural* image. It is also very nice to say that what we take to be real is only such at a certain level of scientific analysis, but that a deeper analysis shows something else altogether. Even these two negations of the real are correct. The fact still remains that the torture of a man, as illusory or as "one-leveled" as it may be, remains the torture of a man; he *suffers* (even if this is cultural, or even if this is a simple chemical reaction), and there is one who makes him suffer. I know that for refined intellectuals and for scientists, what I am saying is idiotic, but I accept precisely this characterization by holding that this real is more real than the Freudo[21]-structuralist or physical-chemical demonstration. There is a considerable distance between this real and illusions, the fantasies that adorn it with altogether different colors, and it is this distance that I would accuse modern intellectual analyses of erasing, becoming thereby complicit in man's dissolution in the technical system—and only that.

It is this distance that iconoclasm is called upon to harshly reinstate, given the extent to which the technical system draws its life from a set of illusions that make it their idol. These include: the illusion that Technique is neutral, that man is its master; the illusion of that the material and the spiritual coincide, that if we raise the standard of living, we will make man good and intelligent; the illusion that through Technique we attain happiness; the illusion that Technique resolves all problems; the illusion that Technique is

---

20. I refer the reader to the study of Christian Realism in *Ethics of Freedom*.
21. Or: pseudo (?) [note by the family].

scientific and rational, the illusion that we can have and hold concurrently all advantages (virtue and power or wealth, for instance); the illusion that means of communication create genuine relationships between men, that the multiplicity of information produces an informed type of man, present to the world, and that globalization translates as the creation of an open and liberal mind; the illusion of indefinite growth, of the natural environment's potential for limitless recovery, of that environment's infinite wealth, of the possibility for man to grow indefinitely, and that there will always be room; and finally, the illusion of progress. We need not repeat these.

Now, it is this accumulation of illusions that prevents people from seeing what is real. This blindness exists only to the extent that there is a kind of idolatry of the means, of Technique, guaranteeing us that these fantasies are indeed the actual reality. If we bother to look at these illusions one by one, we will see that each one is produced by a blind trust, a faith in Technique viewed as a kind of helpful and infinitely rich divinity, with inexhaustible potential. Such is thus a first side of this iconoclasm.

The other one comes down to what we have already come across, desacralization. But, while until now Christianity had desacralized the natural environment, now, it is with respect to the new environment, the technical environment, that desacralization must take place. It is starting from the acknowledgment that Technique is the new sacred (contrary to what Bonhoeffer could say, this world is not secular),[22] that man invests Technique with his hope and his trust, that it takes on a religious meaning,[23] that one engages in iconoclastic struggle with the sacral forms of technical objects. It is simply a matter of showing that they are merely things. And we find again the great polemical text of Isaiah when he mocks this man who, having a tree trunk, takes one piece to make himself a table, another he burns to make some fire and cook over it, and the last piece he carves, raises, and makes for himself a god before which he prostrates himself.[24] With all that belongs to the realm of Technique, we are dealing with the same behavior.

Iconoclasm, in its desacralizing aspect, must desecrate what man holds to be religious, namely, here, Technique. It is a matter of showing that it is all only about "things." To be sure, Technique provides us with things that are useful, worthwhile, not to be looked down on, not to be condemned as such, but still things. (And I am again very sorry for triumphal modern philosophical trends; there remains a difference between these things and man, despite the ponderous demonstrations that the subject does not exist.)

22. Bonhoeffer, *Letters and Papers from Prison*, 362–67, 425–28.
23. On this point, I refer the reader to *New Demons*.
24. Isa 44:15–18.

ETHICAL REPERCUSSIONS

That is to say, technique provides nothing that would be worth, for instance, sacrificing people to it (to produce these things), nothing that would be worth mutually exterminating each other (it is the spirit of deceit that leads us to that). The products of technique never show us truth (but by making us take their specificity for reality as such, and confuse reality with truth). They also do not reveal to us anything more than what we have put into them. They are nothing, truly nothing but devices and instruments, but that means that we put a stop to all hopes and extrapolations (civilization of leisure, mass culture, etc.).

They are only things, but things that lead to the creation around man of a universe of invasive things, determinative because it is a universe, a process of thingification, of reification of man. We must then destroy with rigor this whole universe. We must recuse "Totality," "Totalization" (which also means Globalization, or the hope in a Universal State, as Savior finally). The technical universe pretends to be a closed universe wherein all things fit together and complete each other (but a universe from which the presence of God is necessarily excluded), which secretes its systems and its philosophies, confirming the character of this total world. Instead of that, iconoclasm must show that Technique merely creates a society made of bits and pieces, a broken world, a false civilization that never manages to be one! We must make evident that Totality is just a fantasy, that it is added onto this chaotic system out of sheer ideology.

I have just said, "We must." Actually, this conversion should take place on its own, starting from the faith in Jesus Christ. Man's movement in God cannot be one of acceptance of this totality imposed by the coherence and the multiplication of things that comes from outside the human; it is instead one of accepting the totality that is created by God, within man and which, from there, goes outward in society.

This confrontation, this iconoclasm obviously do not happen at the level of structures and facts, but at the level of behaviors and inwardness. It is not in word or doctrine, nor in organizational changes that this is done. Behaviors are specific, *ad hoc*,[25] ever invented and questioned anew. It is not in words that one desacralizes money, but by giving it. The same thing goes for Technique. It is the redirecting of the use, the distortion of usage that can destroy the illusion.[26] It is irony, humor, the polemical that can reduce Technique to a thing pure and simple with no other value than use value.

25. Translator's note: Latin expression in italics in the original.

26. Translator's note: Ellul is borrowing here a key concept of the Situationists, with whose leader Guy Debord, author of *Society of the Spectacle*, he was in contact in the 1960s. Détournement has been defined more recently as "turning expressions of the capitalist system and its media culture against itself." Holt and Cameron, *Cultural Strategy*, 252.

But then we instantly come into conflict with the great works, the exploration of the moon, or the fictitious universe of TV. For iconoclasm cannot leave intact the system of objects. From the moment when the idol is destroyed, the temple and the institutions that only existed in terms of the idol fall into ruin. In the same way, if this radical questioning of illusion and the technical sacred comes about, this will have repercussions with the things themselves, producing a refusal, a conscientious objection against devoting one's life to producing these wonderful contraptions and finding joy in their consumption. Attacking at this level is not leaving the universe of techniques and its products intact. But this will only happen from inside. It is the great difference from an asceticism or a puritan ethic. This is not about declaring prohibitions, judgments about good and evil, nor about outlining a geography of the permissible and the forbidden, nor again about seeking to reduce consumption for the sake of reducing it.

Let us just say that, from the moment when the ideological construct is destroyed, its vector loses its splendor, its attraction, its appeal; ascesis comes on its own when we no longer think we can gain salvation and life through what one was doing. A detachment is bound to set in, stemming from weariness and the loss of trust. If we succeed in the iconoclasm of Technique, a reasonable and healthy ascesis is guaranteed to come out of it, without throwing ourselves in an antitechnical rapture nor a return to a "wild and primitive natural state."

Witness: it may seem surprising to include witness in an ethical investigation, about the Christian attitude toward Technique, and what is more, in an ethic of rupture. This surprise is due to misunderstandings, received ideas about witness. We have reduced the latter to pronouncements about God, about Jesus—at best an attempt to make the word of God more topical. Witness is either about stating a dogmatic truth or about reporting a personal experience of relation to God. And no doubt that is not untrue, but we ought to become aware of the terrible reduction this amounts to with respect to the dimension of witness in the Bible.

We should already be given pause by the extreme importance Jesus grants to this act, to this attitude. When the last utterance reported (hope in the community of the primitive Church, of course) is: "you will be my witnesses to the ends of the earth,"[27] we cannot view this as trivial. When finally all of God's demand comes down to that, when we also see that in the Old

---

27. Acts 1:8.

Testament the Witness is the equivalent of the *goël* who is a defender who substitutes for the accused and takes up any condemnation in his stead, can we seriously think that this somehow corresponds to the mediocrity of what we usually mean by witness?

[. . .][28]

3. IMMEDIATIZED HOPE

Technique's spirit of power is answered by the choice of non-power. Technique's spirit of deceit is answered by the decision of rupture. But there remains a third orientation of this ethic. The technical system, as we have seen, tends to close upon itself, precisely because it is a system; it tends to exclude whatever is not a factor of its own functioning and to prevent the appearance of something new, whatever it may be. To be sure, it does evolve and very quickly at that, but only as a system. A thousand new processes may appear, but that amounts to no change, nothing fundamentally New: hence the extreme weariness of all the studies dealing with this "rapid change." A car may go at 100 km/hour, but its engine is still the same and functions in the same way at 20 or 150 km/hour. Now, we have seen that the biblical God is the one who creates the New, and there too it cannot be otherwise! In concordance with this feature of Technique, we associate the existence of an ever more glaring kind of objective discourse, which certain philosophical schools and even some theologians rejoice over, of a subjectless discourse, of a play of structures that functions on its own—with nobody to make it function. It is a discourse that exists on its own as it were and whose speaker is but an incidental vector.

The idea of this objective, preexisting discourse is but the expression of the concrete situation in which Technique throws us with the development of cultural mass media; no philosopher nor theologian had this idea before this technical structure ever spread. It is thus merely a result of the technical system, and not a deepening of our knowledge of man, Freud and Nietzsche being called upon there only as ideological cover for the immanent real.

We know, and this represents the biblical Revelation, that God is Subject, and that he speaks, not an objective discourse, but on the contrary a perfectly personalized one. Here again, therefore, the contradiction is quite radical. Finally, another aspect of the same reality, Technique, has become the universal mediator, not only because it is the environment within which

---

28. In the manuscript, pages 226–29 are missing here, amounting to four pages; it bears the following note: "write the Witness." Have these pages been written and lost? [Note by the family.]

man lives, but also because, as a system of means, and conceived as a means, it has everywhere prevailed. Any "medium" is then viewed as being in itself, and conversely any medium is viewed as being part of Technique. In our (technical) world, there can no longer be any mediation but a technical one.[29]

We know that in the Revelation Jesus Christ is the mediator, the only (obviously nontechnical), mediator and that his mediation is absolutely not of the same quality as that of the technical operation. This is a new formulation of the same contradiction. But in this society, one quickly realizes that it is not a matter of opposing one mediation to another, and that it would be easy to get rid of Jesus Christ if that mediation were equivalent to Technique, or if one could (which is the case, constantly rediscovered!) confine it to a spiritual or religious mediation, i.e., one that is nonexistent in the eyes of the technical.

While the true mediation is performed by Technique, on the contrary, what is at stake here in the human context, in the world at our level, is the possibility of recovering an immediacy, an existence without mediation. It is the great effort of the ever so important movements within youth that express the search for spontaneity or authenticity:

- The spontaneous, as much in human relationships, in politics (spontaneity of the masses), in art (spontaneous creation) obviously has no value on its own and its critique is easily done. It takes little effort to show to what extent political spontaneity is weak. The important thing is this will for something immediate, the refusal of indefinite mediatizations, without ever finding a gap in the system.

- The concern for authenticity has exactly the same origin. For young people, what is authentic (with all that is vague and hazy about this term!) is what is immediately given from one to the other, without masks, without intermediaries, without prior conditionings, without any tactic, without any veil; the authentic is what is unveiled outside the possibilities of expression, of the play of technical devices, always deceitful, always preventing one from knowing the other, from meeting him. Hence the naïve protests: for instance, politeness (as the technique of human relations) and law are inauthentic, and nudism expresses this need, clothing (as a technical mediation) being a lie.

Obviously, this only attacks the problem of mediation at its lowest and least significant level, but it does express discontent about the mediatization of everything.

29. On these three points, see the demonstration in Ellul, *Technological System*.

ETHICAL REPERCUSSIONS

In the Christian perspective, this set of features of the technical system and of the human relations that happen to be included in it and deformed by them is put into question in its very essence by Hope (the introduction of the *Novum*) and immediatized hope (i.e. on the one hand not pushed back to the end of time, on the other hand expressing itself in its fullness in a direct way). The Ethic we observe is an ethic of freedom founded in hope.

Let us note furthermore that in the three preceding cases, the schematically presented ethic is not chosen because it is in contradiction with the world in which we find ourselves. It is not because this world is deemed evil that Christian ethic comes to put forward the opposite. This is in no way the process we have been following. Indeed, insofar as man finds himself either negated, or imprisoned in the development of this society, ethics is what allows us to at once take a distance and live in spite of everything in this world (and not elsewhere). If it appears contradictory, it is only on account of this society's totalitarian character. Hence hope.

And now there arises the problem of the relation between a critical ethic and an ethic of hope. Now, at the moment when we were writing this, there appeared a book of which one chapter bore the same title.[30] It is enough to allude to it to show how distant are realities that can be put under the same heading. The book, resolutely inspired by Nietzsche primarily, by Freud and Marx secondarily, situates itself within a horizontal, immanentist theology of "service of man." In its author's eyes, the discovery of Human sciences has made utterly obsolete the theology of two thousand years. This is not the place to discuss it in a general way. But in his eyes, what constitutes critique and hope, what constitutes the relation between the two, what makes them "consonant," is the existence of "desire." "It is desire itself that speaks and that remains silent in critique. Critique is nothing but an elaboration of desire. It is desire coming back upon itself, the cusp, the endless coil that is as the very play . . . of this plastic power that is desire. Hope is also play, plasticity, expansion of the spring. Critique, in its work of liberation of the negative, is unleashing, launching, taking to the waves . . . Hope, as the love of what is distant, begins, allows in, celebrates the neighbor . . . Innerspring of desire. Critique coils the spring, stretches it and contracts it at once. Hope enlarges it, makes it take all the breadth, all the space it can . . ."[31]

And of course, the author performs the critique of what he very conveniently calls (along with the whole school to which he belongs, incidentally) "idealist," without having any idea of the complexity of orientations.

---

30. Le Gal, *Question(s) à la théologie chrétienne*, 109.
31. Le Gal, *Question(s) à la théologie chrétienne*, 105–6.

"Idealist critique was a mode of relationship to the past. Hope idealizes a mode of relationship to the future. These two categories operated on the same substratum: a temporal continuity. Now, quite precisely, this support is now broken, continuity has collapsed: we are no longer leaning against a past. But a continuity has collapsed to a lesser extent in the other direction, that of the future: progress is dead . . . history is dead . . ." What remains all in all is therefore desire, man as desiring machine, in which critique and hope fuse.

It is easy to see how facile this position is. It is wholly simplistic to say that indeed desire is the origin of a critique (of what might limit it) and of a hope (for what might realize it). Through a huge "philosophical-theological" rigmarole, we find again oversimplifications. Furthermore, we find ourselves facing pseudo-explanation in the manner of "QED."

Finally, and this is what is most serious here, this invocation, evocation, of desire does not represent anything at all, for one begins by not talking about the actual situation. There are, for instance, in Le Gal's book, many developments about modern philosophy, and allusions to human sciences, but strictly nothing about the actual situation of man in this society; he does not have any idea of what Technique might be, and that this is what has changed everything.

He therefore cannot understand that this famous desire that explains everything and, since Lacan and Derrida, becomes the veritable abracadabra of our modern alchemists, is purely and simply and totally conditioned by Technique. Desire is in no way an originary, fundamental force, always bringing man back to a possibility for something new. It is remarkably manipulated, restructured, deformed; it has become secondary and a product, no longer primary and productive, due to the technical environment and the impact of techniques on man's innermost being. In the Western world, in our technical society, desire is but the vibrating wall that receives shock waves from the technical and retransmits them. Nothing more.

Therefore, the whole excited poem that Le Gal writes to prove that nobody knew what theology was until he came along means nothing but one more instance of submission (of which he is quite unaware) to the technical imperative. It is witness to the fact that the quest for an immanent foundation is condemned to serve only Technique and to give up on any way out of the system. Desire being integrated, there is by the same token no longer any critique nor any hope (which incidentally Le Gal's book goes to show in the manner of a wonderful parable).

The only possibility of a critique and of a hope, and their indissoluble bond, their relationship, is the action of a Transcendent. It is the reality of a present Elsewhere, of a Wholly Other who reveals himself. It is starting from there that critique is radical, as it is starting from there that hope is possible. Nothing else. Any other is a pure tautology. And the relationship between critique and hope is then situated as between the obverse and the reverse. Critique by the very presence of the choice of non-power implies, as we have said, the already present reality of hope, of an independent incommensurate power. Conversely, hope, which is rupture, can only come into play if one has opted for non-power. Without this option, plenty of human hopes will be raised (and be perfectly normal and legitimate by the way, as man could not live without producing these hopes), but they almost instantly prove to be deceptive and short-lived. But this relationship only exists in the truth of a Wholly Other.[32]

This ethic of hope, on this point, appears under two aspects: the insertion of the impossible and prophecy.

The insertion of the impossible: There is hope only where nothing is possible anymore. As long as there is an expected, realizable, attainable human possible, hope has no place, no value, no reason for being. Just use the means you have at your disposal, and do not get lost in empty dreams. It is at the moment of the absence of means that hope takes place. But then let us be careful not to commit the mistake according to which hope would be an illusory compensation, a mere cry thrown at an empty sky, and having no other value than to express our despair. No, hope is in no way this error. It is the process of the introduction into the concrete situation of an unexpected dimension, of a new force, different in kind from anything that took place heretofore, and of the restoration of a possibility of play. When the chips are down, hope is the dealing of an extra card, unexpected, ab-normal, a-typical, that now upsets both the rules of the game and the deal already done. It is truly the insertion of the impossible, not of the "not yet possible."

We see here the opposition between Technique and hope. For Technique, there is within what we cannot do now a distinction between the real impossible (for instance, seeing God) with which we do not need to bother, and that we are even led to simply deny, and then the vast category of the "not yet possible," but with new technical means: this is going to be possible and even done tomorrow. But that is tomorrow; hope is only interested about today. And this is why it has nothing to do with any technical progress (which tomorrow will make it possible to defeat cancer) nor with any political progress (which sacrifices today's generation in order to enable future generations to attain full happiness). Hope is the introduction of an "impossible-possible," in the situation of now.[33]

---

32. All this has been elaborated on in Ellul, *Hope in Time of Abandonment*.
33. The indications about the impossible were written out when I found with

I cannot fail to mention here the beautiful translation made by D. Lys of a Hebrew word, in Isaiah 9:5, the famous prophecy that is reported at Christmas: "Unto us a child is born . . . he will be called . . . " The usual translations are very weak: "wonderful counselor . . ." Lys shows that to begin with, the two terms (*Péle' Yocets*) are united, but this actually means, "Politics of the Impossible."[34] Summing up his demonstration, we can say: thus, now the very meaning of politics—as the art of the possible—is reversed. If we take seriously the God whom the Bible tells us about, he is precisely the one who does lead a certain politics, only a politics of the impossible, of which the incarnation is the most explosive manifestation. It just so happens that hope is the taking hold of this impossible as fulfilled or carried out. It is the exact correspondence, on man's part, of God's enterprise. It is the insertion, in the present, of this impossible chosen by God.

But we can then understand its import precisely in a technical world, that closes and reproduces itself indefinitely: it is the opening of the system, the rupture of its systematic character through the addition of an unexpected factor: the impossible made present. There is thus by that very fact an impossibility of closure; nothing is ever finished under these conditions, but no less is needed, and this impossible must not only be said, asserted, stated, but carried at the heart of the real by somebody who lives it.

---

interest indications in a similar vein in Le Gal, *Question(s) à la théologie chrétienne*, 165: "An impossibility. And it is that that opens one or more possibilities. Before the impossible, there is no possible. As long as the situation has not become unbearable, the very field of possibilities is closed . . . Before the closure provided by the impossible, there are instances of laziness, dreams of the least cost, reform hypotheses . . . Perhaps the possible is in the end a pseudo-concept. There is the impossible. There is the other, or the others of the impossible, it is what we discover as realized—after the fact. 'They did not know that it was impossible, so they did it.' 'They knew that it was impossible, so they did something possible.'"

And he also gives a good quote from Blanchot: "When everything is impossible, when the future, given over to the fire, burns, when there is no more rest except in the land of midnight, then prophetic speech, which tells of the impossible future, also tells of the 'nonetheless' that breaks the impossible and restores time" (*Book to Come*, 81, quoted in Le Gal, *Question(s) à la théologie chrétienne*, 180).

But Le Gal gets there by a long philosophical detour and seems not to know that it is a constant theological theme since Isaiah. No need for Nietzsche's philosophy: one need only listen . . . to what Le Gal no longer holds to be the Word of God! And I still say that this option is a *pure verbalism* if it is not made possible by the Transcendent.

34. Daniel Lys (1924–2014) was a professor of philosophy and a pastor before teaching in Chicago and then becoming professor of Hebrew and Old Testament at the Montpellier faculty of Protestant theology. He wrote several books of biblical anthropology (Nephesh, the soul; Ruakh, the breath; Basar, the flesh [see the bibliography at the end of this book]), exegetical comments on the Song of Songs and Ecclesiastes, and some popular works. We could not find his translation of Isaiah 9:5, and he himself was not able to give us the reference [note by the family].

The impossible is not a matter of making *feasible*, nor possible; it remains impossible to do, but it is experienced, to be sure experienced as impossible, but taken upon oneself in the present. When it was announced to Abraham, by then 120 years old, that he would have a son, that was impossible. Obviously—and also on account of Sarah, and due to their prior sterility.[35] The impossible is impossible. It is indeed experienced as such by Abraham, but it is experienced in the present, with a fullness of hope such that what remained impossible is realized.

It is not through a human, technical mediation, a mediatization. The impossible, the category of the impossible that is only accessible to hope, thus excludes at once: the closure of the system, technical mediatization, the objectivity of discourse, because this category of the impossible can only be made present in a given person's experience here and now. There is here no participation in a pre-established discourse, in structures, and still less in an ideology. And if this experience has a capacity for transforming the real, it is by the path of the imaginary, in the full force of this term, the imaginary that is able to transform the conditions of each situation, being neither something illusory nor something fantastical, but a power that is creative of a new that exists because men actually believe in the creative power of newness in a situation.[36] The imaginary eludes to a very great extent both this conditioning by something pre-established (be it pre-established on a Marxist pattern or something preordained within a structuralist pattern), and a simple pattern of causal relationship. I obviously do not mean that this imaginary is originary, is conditioned by nothing, etc., but it is an example, situated within psychology, be it individual or social, of a possibility for the expression of hope. The imaginary is the human agent within which the choice for the impossible can be inscribed.

Prophecy: no more than with the imaginary will I pretend to deal here with prophecy. Countless theological, historical, and psychological works are enough.[37] I will limit myself to using very well-known notions for my purposes. For we were saying above that the ethical relationship to technical

---

35. Gen 18:10 11.

36. On this issue, I refer the reader to the quite crucial studies of, on the one hand, Laplantine, *Les trois voix de l'imaginaire*, and, on the other hand, Castoriadis, *Imaginary Institution of Society*, that show both the reality of the fact and the path of a non-technical intervention.

37. See, for instance, André Neher's wonderful work *Prophetic Existence*.

society is established in immediatized Hope. It is prophecy that expresses this immediacy. But to understand what this is about, two preliminary observations are called for.

First of all, prophecy is in no way a matter of foreseeing. It is already at this level that the opposition with the technical world lies. Of course, prophecy in the biblical sense has nothing to do with the phenomena presented in parapsychology, neither clairvoyance, nor dreams, nor divination of the future, of events concerning such and such a person and supposed to happen tomorrow. But neither is it about a forecast or the establishment of futuribles, which establish themselves decisively within the technical system.[38] For what this purports to forecast is the probable (sometimes also introducing a dimension of the desirable) evolution of technical society. Forecasting is based on techniques, relates to technique, and belongs to this whole. It is because the system is under tremendous stress that we now cannot do without some forecast to try to steer evolution, to compensate foreseeable drawbacks and to effect, whenever possible, a choice between the various possible outcomes established by forecasting.

Prophecy is neither in the fancy of seers nor in the technique of forecasters. It is from another dimension. It introduces in the normal circuit of causes and effects an unexpected reality. It is exactly that of the final events, of the extra-historical, that manifests in the present and starting from which a present judgment may be made about the situation. In other words, prophecy is only ever an anticipation of the "final judgement" made present. It totally eludes relations of cause and effect, as well as the illusion of predicting a future. The only future which prophecy takes into account is the inevitable encounter between this world, this society, this social whole, these works, and then the God of Jesus Christ.[39] The future of the whole of

---

38. Futuribles: A neologism that merges the words "future" and "possible." It is borrowed from Bertrand de Jouvenel, who uses it in his works forecasting the changes in the political and social system to refer to "future states whose mode of production from the present state is imaginable and plausible for us." De Jouvenel, *L'Art de la conjecture*. It is also the title of the forecasting review *Futuribles*, created in 1974 by Bertrand de Jouvenel [note by the family].

39. On this topic, we may allude to the question often asked by Christian theologians: inasmuch as all the prophets of the Old Testament prophesied Jesus Christ, as it was his coming and his reality that were the *true* (as opposed to the real) object of prophecy, can there still be prophets since he came? People very often conclude that there can indeed no longer be prophets in Christianity. I think that this is at once true and false, as I have had occasion to show elsewhere. In a word, I could say that, in the Old Testament, what is prophesied is always the judgment of God. But this judgment in the end God takes upon himself in the person of Jesus Christ. So it is indeed true that the prophets only talk about Jesus Christ, but as he is the sacrificial lamb, a victim for the judgment of the world. Their historical role is not to announce the *coming* of Jesus

ETHICAL REPERCUSSIONS

mankind is therefore the judgment of the "*Mene, mene, tekel, upharsin,*"[40] and the prophet will be the one who stands before this society, in this crowd, not only to announce the final encounter, but to actualize this judgment and make it present in the historical givenness of the moment.

It is thus definitely not a frenzied announcement of the end of Time for the next minute, nor a leap into the absolute of judgment "in itself" (as it were), but an appreciation of the effective historical situation, of the forces at work, of injustices and negations of the human, etc., to bring the light of the last judgment on this specific situation (not in an indistinct globality, while being a sinner and condemned!).

If prophecy is the fact of taking up for the present the dimension of the last things, we see that it is in no way an announcement of what is going to happen, a discourse in advance, but a discourse of sense that does also imply a future. Once more, let us recall that "sense" has a twofold value: orientation and meaning, with a close relationship between the two. (Because we see such and such probable orientation of the situation, hence what we experience has such and such a meaning. Because we see the meaning of such and such an event, hence the situation will probably develop that way.) But here the value that gives a sense is thus the final event that we know in Jesus Christ (not in its factual description). The prophet's role is, in the midst of this *eschaton*, to lay his gaze on the concreteness of our moment.

But this therefore implies at the same time the indication of a future, if the prophet is not content with vague and generic discourse, but indeed enters the "politics" of this time! For a discourse of sense also means that we are going toward *that particular* event that currently represents the last judgment. (I am saying judgment, criterion, and not condemnation.) The

---

but the meaning of this coming, so as to already throw light on the historical situation in which the Jewish people finds itself. Now, since the coming of Jesus Christ, we know what the judgment of God is, but we still need prophets, precisely so as to continue to actualize the presence of the final realities: always the judgment of the world in Jesus Christ, but also its recapitulation and its insertion in the new creation.

40. Dan 5:25. King Belshazzar, son of Nebuchadnezzar, gives a feast in the course of which he drinks and offers drinks in the sacred vases robbed from the Temple of Jerusalem. A hand then appears and writes on the palace wall words that no sage nor magician is able to explain. The prophet Daniel is then brought, and he reads and interprets: *mené*: God has measured your kingship (Hebrew: root *mn'*); *teqèl*: you were weighed in the scales (root *tql*); *pharsin*: your kingdom is divided (root *prs*) and given to the Medes and the Persians (vv. 26–28). The same night, the king was assassinated. History bears the judgment of God [note by the family].

prophet is always the one who is going to reintroduce contingency in the normal discourse of causality: "if . . ."

When the last things break into the present, it is not in view of convincing man about an implacable fate, but on the contrary, to call him to change what appears to him as fate, by giving him the certainty that this is possible from now on, because this situation has a *meaning* that it is possible to change, and what is more, because it is already judged (in Jesus Christ) and the salvation that is proclaimed brings play to necessities that we believed inevitable. From the vantage point of actualized last things, the prophet announces: "This is what follows, unless . . ." (it is in a more general and systematic fashion the permanent message: repent, change your behavior, for the end is near). The end taken up by God in Jesus Christ has current repercussions, among which is the destruction of any Destiny, Inevitability, Fatum, etc. But it is not a magical destruction, an objective establishment, of an objectively different situation: man is called to dominate the fate that no longer dominates him. That is to say, if man does nothing, then what comes into play is indeed this fate; if man allows social forces, history, the Economy, the play of causes and effects, the logic or the dialectics of History to play out, then everything unfolds as is, and it is the equivalent of a fate. By the force of things, Things are what operates, and man is nothing.

But what the prophet recalls is that, precisely because of the judgment laid in Jesus Christ, all that is neither fated nor irreparable. Only that also assumes that man decides, gets involved, and "puts himself on the line" a little! It is not a situation of convenience, of softness and of laxity. And it is not a matter of getting involved any which way, but (and here I am sorry to appear sectarian!) from the exclusive revelation of judgment in Jesus Christ, of the last things, of the sense given by that God. We constantly see people getting excited and getting involved even unto death, without that having any effect nor the slightest interest. Whether one gets involved with Marxism or with liberalism, in politics or the technical path, in class struggle or national greatness, etc., that can lead strictly nowhere, and [can] only reinforce the technical system and the force of things, that is to say, increase submission to destiny, which happens to be what structuralism preaches.

But the situation is tragic in this: those who get involved do so outside the final sense because they fail to hear in anything a prophetic message; those who might receive a prophetic message (Christians) stubbornly refuse it, either by withdrawing to a spiritualist personal piety, or by getting involved in other people's political activities and losing any possibility of understanding meaning (which they seek in Marxism, for instance).

Finally, as a last aspect of prophecy as immediatized hope: it is not for the prophet to establish a purpose. It is not his business to say: "In such and such a situation, here is the purpose we must pursue"; he is not a programmer. He has no business playing the supertechnician by showing solutions that others would then have to implement. He shows with one hand God's design, his reality, his aim; with the other, he shows the current meaning and the sense of this engagement with the historical present, in its totality, its complexity, and then he is forced to say: "It's up to you." You have all the cards—in both senses:[41] the cards of the game, and also the geographical chart of the grounds with the outline of your past and probable path.

But it is neither God who is going to intervene to upset the situation nor me who is going to become leader, shepherd, *Führer*, etc. The prophet having announced, it is men who have heard that must, on the one hand, set their own purpose (from the prophecy), and on the other hand, get involved to realize it. That too is a constant motion in prophecy: "Such is my design in Jesus Christ, says God, and now draw its consequences." Thus, prophecy totally leaves behind the normal concatenation of causes and effects at the same time as it causes an act of freedom.

All that we have just said is of the most extreme importance for the technical system. We are thus no longer dealing with an irreparable inevitability in its evolution; we are facing a possibility of giving back a sense to this whole adventure, no longer being caught in a system in the strict sense, since the insertion of final values prevents its closure (as does witness). But for that to happen, there first needs to be a prophet who speaks! Everything depends on this event. And the prophet cannot speak of his own initiative, at his own whim, according to his own opinions. The Old Testament prophet (as in Judges) speaks according to what God tells him at the moment. It is probably now here that the situation has changed. In Christianity, the prophet is not called upon to be the translator of a word of God here and now,[42] because this word has been said once and for all in Jesus Christ, and it is in him at once eternal, unchangeable, and present.

But it should then be the Church itself that plays this prophetic role. And as it happens, if it remains silent, and more often—for it never stops speaking indiscriminately—if it errs, no individual prophet can wholly make up for it. It will only ever be an individual word, necessarily expressing what will be taken to be a personal opinion. For three centuries, the Church has proven, and this in all its bodies, its total inability to play this prophetic role. To be sure, Christians have stepped into the breach, but as could be expected, without any prophetic value for the people in society. We are thus caught here in another contradiction. Nevertheless, there is no

---

41. Translator's note: of the single word "carte" in French.
42. Translator's note: See note 8, p. 104.

ground to get discouraged. We have to continue formulating what prophecy represents, the irreplaceable, and then one day, when we are no longer able to tolerate mistakes and lies within the Church, it may become more prone to come out of its talkative silence.

Be that as it may, when prophecy happens, we realize that it immediatizes reality and truth—that is to say, the two dimensions become rigorously present without any intermediary or delay. Prophecy destroys all mediations to place us in a direct relation with God and with what I am in this world as it is. In other words, prophecy is radical non-technicity. Just as, from a "religious" perspective, it short-circuits the function of the priest to directly express to the whole people, without any mediation, the Word of God in its immediacy, without rites, without formulas, without morals, without philosophical digression, so it unveils the final reality of the situation in which we are, without political analysis, without reference to civil authorities, without deferral and without a convincing demonstration. It is self-sufficient as a word (and this was widely known, well before all linguistic studies!).

But as a word, a de-mediatizing one, it is in no way an objective discourse; on the contrary, it does not exist in prior structures, in an expected social discourse. It reduces to nonexistence the whole speech of that group, for what it calls to existence is a reality that has nothing in common with anything we might have known, since it is the insertion of a final reality, from which everything comes clear, is judged and established. In other words, the act of prophecy, when it happens, undertakes the critique (without even wanting to do this critique) of the technical system on these two levels, that of general mediatization and that of the structural objectivity of discourse.

Finally, it reduces to nothing the causal process of the technical system. And it is even rigorously the only act that can have that effect. The ends being insignificant, impossible to establish in any effective way, everything being brought down to the causal approach that absorbs all, nothing less is needed than the actual presence of final ends, in no way dependent on historical unfolding. These do not come at the conclusion of a cumulative or explanatory process, but, on the contrary, have their origin in the end known, recognized, revealed, issuing from that ultimate time and coming into the present, having nothing in common with all experiences. Nothing less than that is needed to elude first assimilation by Technique's causal process, then to blow apart the obviousness of that process's legitimacy.

A simple example: the picture of a catastrophic end of the world, well buried under the optimism of progress, was proclaimed anew following the appearance of the atom bomb. But it is not a prophecy in the sense that people have striven to show that this cataclysmic end became a probability due to the development of nuclear weapons. It is thus still within the realm of demonstration and causality. The prophet has nothing to do with it: the perceptible real is sufficient for this.

However, taking up Matthew 24 again, with the accumulation of signs of the end times (family breakup, increase in political persecutions, insane multiplication of deceit, generalization of sexual and other immorality, constant wars and rumors of war, persecution of Christians, abandonment of the Christian faith by the majority of people) and unveiling, through this proclamation of an end of time, the meaning and truth of what we are experiencing in chaos and apathy *may* be a prophetic act. It is the impact of this coming of an ultimate word against what we are experiencing. But this must translate as the impact against what *produces* what we are experiencing, and which is, in all its aspects, the technical system bursting apart old habits, customs, and traditions. It is then the causal process of technical development that is called into question. But what I am saying there *is not* prophecy; it is an example of what it might be.

We thus have now sketched the outlines of a Christian ethic correlative to the technical system, one that is critical—with, let us recall, the main lines of critique through the choice of non-power, of rupture through iconoclasm and witness, of opening through hope and prophecy. In all cases, it is the disabling of what appears to us as both the fate and the glory of man: modern Technique.

But once more, if Christians entered that path, a difficult one, but that is exactly up to the level of vocation and grace, that demand no less. Otherwise, what does it mean to believe in this incredible event of the incarnation, God who comes here, and [in this][43] other incredible event, of the resurrection, a dead man who ceases to be dead, in all the dimensions of this term (including life—a bodily life despite all the spiritualizations the thing has been made to undergo for the last twenty years!) and in whom all of Death, all deaths are overcome? What does it mean to believe in that if it is to lead the good little life of petty bourgeois who accept the way society goes by tinkering with politics? Can we not see[44] the incommensurability between the two? Therefore, vocation and grace demand no less than this.

---

43. [Addition by the family.]
44. Hypothetical reading; the word is hardly legible [note by the family].

If Christians enter this ethical path, then a mutation of the technical system may take place. Despite the good will of humanists and scientists, I do not think there are any other basic possibilities. If Christians do not assume the role they are called to by Revelation, then

- In the first place that will just confirm what we can easily see every day, namely, that Christianity no longer has any point of contact neither with modern man nor with current society.[45]
- Secondly, the technical system will continue down its path, simultaneously increasing chaos and systematization toward a final entropy.
- Finally, since that development of the system implies a total integration of man in the technical enterprise, it is by that path that the prophecy of the disappearance of the Christian faith can be accomplished.

It is possible for faith to disappear, for the truth of Jesus Christ to be totally clouded over by men. But that will be the exact consequence of the refusal on Christians' part to take on the consequences of faith, of love, of hope in the society in which we are[46] and to have pretended to live in the sky or in politics, as opposed to accepting a revelation that implies the exact recognition of the place God gives us to live.

---

45. And this is the constant foolishness of all current Christian currents in wishing to change Christianity to adapt it to this modern world, the subjectivist Theologies stemming from Bultmann as much as political theologies, in their various incarnations as Marxist Christians, revolutionaries, rationalists, etc. How can they fail to see that, very precisely, it is by adopting this path that they definitively cast Christianity into the mold of that society they question—but which they do not know?

46. Proposal; illegible word, hidden by an ink stain [note by the family].

Bibliography

Amery, Carl. *Fin de la Providence*. Paris: Seuil, 1976. Originally published as *Das Ende der Vorsehung*. Hamburg: Rohwolt, 1972.

Barreau, Abbé Jean-Claude. *The Religious Impulse*. Translated by John George Lynch. New York: Paulist, 1979. Originally published as *Du bon usage de la religion*. Paris: Stock, 1976.

Beauvoir, Simone de. *The Ethics of Ambiguity*. Translated by Bernard Frechtman. New York: Philosophical Library, 1948. Originally published as *Pour une morale de l'ambiguïté*. Paris: Gallimard, 1947.

Beck, Ulrich. *Risk Society: Towards a New Modernity*. Translated by Mark Ritter. London: Sage, 1992. Originally published as *Risikogesellschaft: Auf dem Weg in eine andere Moderne*. Frankfurt: Suhrkamp, 1986.

Belo, Fernando. *A Materialist Reading of the Gospel of Mark*. Translated by Matthew J. O'Connell. Maryknoll, NY: Orbis, 1981. Originally published as *Lecture matérialiste de l'évangile de Marc*. Paris: Cerf, 1974.

Benveniste, Émile. *Problems in General Linguistics*. Translated by Mary Elizabeth Meek. Coral Gables, FL: University of Miami Press, 1971. Originally published as *Problèmes de Linguistique Générale*, vol. 1. Paris: Gallimard, 1966.

Bergson, Henri. *The Two Sources of Morality and Religion*. Translated by R. Ashley Audra and Cloudesley Brereton, with the assistance of W. Horsfall Carter. Reprint of the 1954 edition published by Doubleday. Notre Dame: University of Notre Dame Press, 2013. Originally published as *Les deux sources de la morale et de la religion*. Paris: F. Alcan, 1932.

Bertalanffy, Ludwig von. *General System Theory*. New York: G. Braziller, 1968.

Biondi, Biondo. *Giustiniano primo, principe e legislatore cattolico*. Milan: Vita e pensiero, 1936.

Birch, Charles. "Creation, Technology and Human Survival: Called to Replenish the Earth." *The Ecumenical Review* 28 (1976) 66–79.

Blanchot, Maurice. *The Book to Come*. Translated by Charlotte Mandell. Stanford, CA: Stanford University Press, 2003. Originally published as *Le livre à venir*. Paris: Gallimard, 1959, 1986.

Bloch, Ernst. *The Principle of Hope*. 3 vols. Translated by Neville Plaice, Stephen Plaice, and Paul Knight. Cambridge: MIT Press, 1995. Originally published as *Das Prinzip Hoffnung*. 3 vols. Frankfurt: Suhrkamp, 1954–1959.

Böll, Heinrich. *Billiards at Half-Past Nine*. Translated by Patrick Bowles. London: Weidenfeld & Nicolson, 1961. Originally published as *Billiard um halb zehn*:

Roman. Cologne: Kiepenheuer & Witsch, 1959. Translated into French as *Les deux sacrements: roman* by Solange de Lalène and Georges de Lalène. Paris: Seuil, 1961.

Bonhoeffer, Dietrich, *Ethics*. Edited by Clifford J. Green. Translated by Reinhard Krauss, Charles C. West, and Douglas W. Stott. Dietrich Bonhoeffer Works 6. Minneapolis: Fortress, 2005. Originally published as *Ethik*. Munich: C. Kaiser, 1949.

———. *Letters and Papers from Prison*. Edited by John W. de Gruchy. Translated by Isabel Best et al. Dietrich Bonhoeffer Works 8. Minneapolis: Fortress, 2010. Originally published as *Widerstand und Ergebung: Briefe und Aufzeichunugen aus der Haft*. Stuttgart: Evangelische Buchgemeinde, 1951.

Bookchin, Murray. *Post-Scarcity Anarchism*. San Francisco: Rampart, 1971.

Bourg, Dominique, and Philippe Roch, eds. *Crise écologique, crise des valeurs? Défis pour l'anthropologie et la spiritualité*. Geneva: Labor et Fides, 2010.

Buber-Agassi, Judith. "Morality in Industry." In *Ethics in an Age of Pervasive Technology*, edited by Melvin Kranzberg, 174–76. Boulder, CO: Westview, 1980.

Bunge, Mario. *Ética y ciencia*. Buenos Aires: Ediciones Siglo Veinte, 1960.

———. "Technoethics." In *Ethics in an Age of Pervasive Technology*, edited by Melvin Kranzberg, 139–42. Boulder, CO: Westview, 1980.

Casalis, Georges. *Correct Ideas Don't Fall from the Skies: Elements for an Inductive Theology*. Translated by Sister Jeanne Marie Lyons and Michael Jon. Maryknoll, NY: Orbis, 1984. Originally published as *Les idées justes ne tombent pas du ciel: Eléments de "théologie inductive."* Paris: Cerf, 1977.

Castoriadis, Cornelius. *The Imaginary Institution of Society*. Translated by Kathleen Blamey. Cambridge, UK: Polity, 1997. Originally published as *L'institution imaginaire de la société*. Paris: Seuil, 1975.

Charbonneau, Bernard. *The Green Light: A Self-Critique of the Ecological Movement*. London: Bloomsbury Academic, 2018.

———. *Le système et le chaos: Critique du développement exponentiel*. Paris: Anthropos, 1973; Paris: Economica, 1990; Paris: Sang de la terre, 2012.

———. *Teilhard de Chardin, prophète d'un âge totalitaire*. Paris: Denoël, 1963, 1981.

Chaunu, Pierre. *Histoire quantitative, histoire sérielle*. Paris: Armand Colin, 1978.

Chouraqui, André. *La Bible traduite et présentée par A. Chouraqui*. Paris: Desclée, 1974.

Claudel, Paul. *The Book of Christopher Columbus: A Lyrical Drama in Two Parts*. New Haven: Yale University Press, 1930. French original published as *Le Livre de Christophe Colomb: Drame lyrique en deux parties*. Paris: Gallimard, 1933, 2005.

Closets, François de. *Le bonheur en plus*. Paris: Denoël, 1974.

———. *En danger de progrès*. Paris: Denoël, 1971.

Coates, Joseph F. "What is Technology Assessment?" *Impact Assessment* 1, no. 1 (1982) 20–24.

Coulardeau, Jean. "*Technique et Théologie* de Jacques Ellul (Avertissement)." In *L'Ordinateur, dernière tour de Babel: Analyse critique du rôle de l'ordinateur dans la société* (blog). November 8, 2011. http://tourdebabel.over-blog.org/article-technique-et-theologie-de-jacques-ellul-avertissement-88275867.html.

Cox, Harvey. *The Feast of Fools: A Theological Essay on Festivity and Fantasy*. Cambridge: Harvard University Press, 1969.

———. *The Secular City: Secularization and Urbanization in Theological Perspective*. New York: Macmillan, 1965.

BIBLIOGRAPHY

Cullmann, Oscar. *The Christology of the New Testament*. Translated by Shirley C. Guthrie and Charles A. M. Hall. Philadelphia: Westminster, 1959. Originally published as *Die Christologie des Neuen Testaments*. Tübingen: J. C. B. Mohr (Paul Siebeck), 1957.

Desroche, Henri. *Les religions de contrebande: Essai sur les phénomènes religieux en époques critiques*. Paris: Mâme, 1974.

———. *The Sociology of Hope*. Translated by Carol Martin-Sperry. London: Routledge and Kegan Paul, 1979. Originally published as *Sociologie de l'Espérance*. Paris: Calmann-Lévy, 1973.

Dorfles, Gillo. "Intenzionalità e mitopoiesi nelle tecniche odierne." In *Tecnica e casistica: tecnica, escatologia e casistica: Atti del Colloquio Internazionale sulla demitizzazione, Università di Roma, 7-12 gennaio 1964*, edited by Enrico Castelli, 353–62. Archivio di Filosofia 1964 nos. 1–2. Padua: CEDAM, 1964.

———. "Mythe de la naturalité et les transformations fruitives." In *Démythisation et morale: Actes du colloque organisé par le Centre international d'Études humanistes et par l'Institut d'études philosophiques de Rome, Rome 7-12 janvier 1965*, edited by Enrico Castelli, 227–32. Paris: Aubier-Montaigne, 1965.

Dostoevsky, Fyodor. *The Brothers Karamazov*. Translated by Richard Pevear and Larissa Volokhonsky. New York: Farrar, Straus and Giroux, 2002. Originally published as *Brat'ya Karamazovy*. Serialized in *Russkiy Vestnik*, 1879–1880.

———. *Crime and Punishment*. Translated by Richard Pevear and Larissa Volokhonsky. New York: Knopf, 1993. Originally published as *Prestuplenie i nakazanie*. Serialized in *Russkiy Vestnik*, 1866.

———. *The Eternal Husband and Other Stories*. Translated by Richard Pevear and Larissa Volokhonsky. New York: Modern Library, 2012. Title novella originally published as *Vechny muzh*. In *Zarya*, 1870.

———. *Notes from Underground*. Translated by Boris Jakim. Grand Rapids: Eerdmans, 2009. Originally published as *Zapiski iz Podpol'ya*. Serialized in *Epokha*, 1864.

———. *The Possessed*. Translated by Andrew R. MacAndrew. New York: New American Library, 1980. Originally published as *Besy*. Serialized in *Russkiy Vestnik*, 1871–1872.

Dubois, Jacques-Marcel. "Éthique ancienne, philosophie spiritualiste et technologie." *Revue thomiste* 75 (1975) 418–31.

———. "What Ancient Ethics Can Contribute." In *Ethics in an Age of Pervasive Technology*, edited by Melvin Kranzberg, 78–82. Boulder, CO: Westview, 1980.

Dumas, André. *Prospective et prophétie: Les Églises dans la société industrielle*. Paris: Cerf, 1972.

Dumitriu, Petru. *Incognito*. Translated by Norman Denny. Glasgow: W. Collins Sons and Co., 1978. Originally published in French as *Incognito*. Paris: Seuil, 1962.

Ellul, Jacques. "Aimez-vous Barth? Karl Barth et nous." *Réforme*, no. 2143 (May 10, 1986) 7.

———. *Anarchy and Christianity*. Translated by Geoffrey W. Bromiley. Grand Rapids: Eerdmans, 1991. Originally published as *Anarchie et christianisme*. Lyon: Atelier de création libertaire, 1988; Paris: La Table Ronde, 1998.

———. *Autopsy of Revolution*. Translated by Patricia Wolf. New York: Knopf, 1971; Eugene, OR: Wipf and Stock, 2012. Originally published as *Autopsie de la revolution*. Paris: Calmann-Lévy, 1969; Paris: La Table Ronde, 2008.

———. *Changer de révolution: L'inéluctable prolétariat*. Paris: Seuil, 1982.

———. *Un chrétien pour Israël*. Monaco: Editions du Rocher, 1986. Reissued in *Le défi et le nouveau: Oeuvres théologiques 1948–1991*, 753–936. Paris: La Table Ronde, 2007.

———. *Les classes sociales: Cours de Jacques Ellul à l'Institut d'Études politiques de Bordeaux, 1966/1967*. Edited by Michel Hourcade, Jean-Pierre Jézéquel, and Gérard Paul. Talence: Institut d'études politiques, 1998.

———. *Déviances et déviants dans notre société intolérante*. Toulouse: Erès, 1992, 2013.

———. *The Empire of Non-Sense: Art in the Technological Society*. Translated by Michael Johnson and David Lovekin. Winterbourne, Berkshire, UK: Papadakis, 2014. Originally published as *L'empire du non-sens: L'art et la société technicienne*. Paris: Presses Universitaires de France, 1980.

———. *The Ethics of Freedom*. Translated and edited by Geoffrey W. Bromiley. Grand Rapids: Eerdmans, 1976. (A translation of volume 1 and an early draft of part of volume 3.) Originally published as *Éthique de la liberté*. V. 1–2, Paris: Librairie Protestante; Geneva: Labor et Fides, 1973–1974. V. 3 (*Les Combats de la liberté*), Paris: Centurion; Geneva; Labor et Fides, 1984.

———. *Hope in Time of Abandonment*. Translated by C. Edward Hopkin. New York: Seabury, 1973; Eugene, OR: Wipf and Stock, 2012. Originally published as *L'Espérance oubliée*. Paris: Gallimard, 1972; Paris: La Table Ronde, 2004.

———. *The Humiliation of the Word*. Translated by Joyce Main Hanks. Grand Rapids: Eerdmans, 1985. Originally published as *La parole humiliée*. Paris: Seuil, 1981; Paris: La Table Ronde, 2014.

———. *If You Are the Son of God: The Sufferings and Temptations of Jesus*. Translated by Anne-Marie Andreasson-Hogg. Eugene, OR: Cascade, 2014. Originally published as *Si tu es le fils de Dieu: Souffrances et tentations de Jésus*. Paris: Le Centurion; Zurich: EBV, 1991. Reissued in *Le défi et le nouveau: Oeuvres théologiques 1948–1991*, 937–1016. Paris: La Table Ronde, 2007.

———. "Intermezzo instinctif et non-scientifique (inédit de *Technique et Théologie*)." *Foi et Vie* 111, no. 2 (June 2012) 5–13.

———. *Islam et judéo-christianisme*. Paris: Presses Universitaires de France, 2004, 2006.

———. *Israël, chance de civilisation: Articles de journaux et de revues 1967–1992*. Paris: Editions Première Partie, 2008.

———. *Jesus and Marx: From Gospel to Ideology*. Translated by Joyce Main Hanks. Grand Rapids: Eerdmans, 1988; Eugene, OR: Wipf and Stock, 2012. Originally published as *L'idéologie marxiste chrétienne: Que fait-on de l'Evangile?* Paris: Le Centurion, 1979; Paris: La Table Ronde, 2006.

———. *Living Faith: Belief and Doubt in a Perilous World*. Translated by Peter Heinegg. New York: Harper and Row, 1983; Eugene, OR: Wipf and Stock, 2012. Originally published as *La Foi au prix du doute: "encore quarante jours . . ."* Paris: Hachette, 1980; Paris: La Table Ronde, 2006.

———. *The Meaning of the City*. Translated by Dennis Pardee. Grand Rapids: Eerdmans, 1970; Eugene, OR: Wipf and Stock, 2011. French original published as *Sans feu ni lieu: signification biblique de la grande ville*. Paris: Gallimard, 1975; Paris: La Table Ronde, 2003.

———. *The New Demons*. Translated by C. Edward Hopkin. New York: Seabury, 1975; London: Mowbrays, 1975. Originally published as *Les Nouveaux Possédés*. Paris: Fayard, 1973; Paris: Mille et une nuits, 2003.

BIBLIOGRAPHY

———. *On Freedom, Love, and Power*. Compiled, edited, and translated by Willem H. Vanderburg. Toronto: University of Toronto Press, 2008.

———. *La pensée marxiste: Cours professé à l'Institut d'études politiques de Bordeaux de 1947 à 1979*. Edited by Michel Hourcade, Jean-Pierre Jézéquel, and Gérard Paul. Paris: La Table Ronde, 2003, 2012.

———. *The Political Illusion*. Translated by Konrad Kellen. New York: Knopf, 1967; New York: Random, 1972; Eugene, OR: Wipf & Stock, 2015. Originally published as *L'Illusion politique*. Paris: Robert Laffont, 1965; Paris: Pluriel-Le Livre de Poche, 1977; Rev. ed., Paris: Librairie Générale Française, 1977; Paris: La Table Ronde, 2004, 2012.

———. *Presence in the Modern World*. Translated by Lisa Richmond. Eugene, OR: Cascade, 2016. Previously translated as *The Presence of the Kingdom*. Translated by Olive Wyon. New York: Seabury, 1967; Colorado Springs: Helmers & Howard, 1989. Originally published as *Présence au monde moderne*. Geneva: Roulet, 1948. Reissued in *Le défi et le nouveau: Oeuvres théologiques 1948–1991*, 19–116. Paris: La Table Ronde, 2007.

———. *Reason for Being: A Meditation on Ecclesiastes*. Translated by Joyce Main Hanks. Grand Rapids: Eerdmans, 1990. Originally published as *La raison d'être: Méditation sur l'Ecclésiaste*. Paris: Seuil, 1987, 2007.

———. "Recherche pour une éthique dans une société technicienne." In *Éthique et technique*, edited by Jacques Sojcher and Gilbert Hottois, 7–20. Annales de l'Institut de philosophie et de sciences morales, Université Libre de Bruxelles. Brussels: Editions de l'Université de Bruxelles, 1983.

———. "The Relationship between Man and Creation in the Bible." In *Theology and Technology: Essays in Christian Analysis and Exegesis*, edited by Carl Mitcham and Jim Grote, 139–55. Lanham, MD: University Press of America, 1984.

———. "Le Sacré dans le monde moderne." *Le Semeur* 61, no. 2 (1963) 24–36.

———. "Signification actuelle de la Réforme." In *Protestantisme français*, edited by Marc Boegner and André Siegfried, 137–65. Paris: Plon, 1945.

———. *Les successeurs de Marx: Cours professé à l'Institut d'études politiques de Bordeaux*. Edited by Michel Hourcade, Jean-Pierre Jézéquel, and Gérard Paul. Paris: La Table Ronde, 2007.

———. "Technique and the Opening Chapters of Genesis." In *Theology and Technology: Essays in Christian Analysis and Exegesis*, edited by Carl Mitcham and Jim Grote, 123–37. Lanham, MD: University Press of America, 1984.

———. *The Technological Bluff*. Translated by Geoffrey W. Bromiley. Grand Rapids: Eerdmans, 1990. Originally published as *Le Bluff technologique*. Paris: Hachette, 1988, 2004, 2012.

———. *The Technological Society*. Translated by John Wilkinson. New York: Knopf, 1964; London: Jonathan Cape, 1965; Rev. ed., New York: Knopf, 1967. Originally published as *La Technique ou l'enjeu du siècle*. Paris: Armand Colin, 1954; Paris: Economica, 1990, 2008.

———. *The Technological System*. Translated by Joachim Neugroschel. New York: Continuum, 1980; Eugene, OR: Wipf and Stock, 2018. Originally published as *Le Système technicien*. Paris: Calmann-Lévy, 1977; Paris: Le Cherche midi, 2004, 2012.

———. *To Will and to Do: An Ethical Research for Christians*. Translated by C. Edward Hopkin. Philadelphia: Pilgrim, 1969. Originally published as *Le Vouloir et le Faire*:

BIBLIOGRAPHY

Recherches éthiques pour les chrétiens. Geneva: Labor et Fides, 1964, 2013; Paris: Librairie Protestante, 1964, 2013; Volumes 1 & 2, Eugene, OR: Wipf & Stock, 2020, 2021 (translated by Jacob Marques Rollison). The original translation was just vol. 1.

———. *An Unjust God? A Christian Theology of Israel in Light of Romans 9-11*. Translated by Anne-Marie Andreasson-Hogg. Eugene, OR: Cascade, 2012. Originally published as *Ce Dieu injuste . . . ? Théologie chrétienne pour le peuple d'Israël*. Paris: Arléa, 1991.

Ellul, Jacques, with Patrick Chastenet. *Jacques Ellul on Politics, Technology, and Christianity: Conversations with Patrick Troude-Chastenet*. Translated by Joan Mendès France. Eugene, OR: Wipf & Stock, 2005. Originally published as *Entretiens avec Jacques Ellul*. Paris: La Table Ronde, 1994.

Ellul, Jacques, with Jean-Claude Guillebaud. "Jacques Ellul ou la passion d'un sceptique: Entretien avec Jean-Claude Guillebaud." *Le Nouvel Observateur*, July 17, 1982, 12–16.

Ellul, Jacques, with Didier Nordon. *L'homme à lui-même: correspondance*. Paris: Editions du Félin, 1992.

Faessler, Marc. *L'Évangile et le politique; la technique et l'eschatologique*. Bulletin du Centre protestant d'études 1974 1–2. Geneva: Centre protestant d'études, 1974.

Feuerbach, Ludwig. *The Essence of Christianity*. Translated by George Eliot. New York: Harper, 1957. Originally published as *Das Wesen des Christentums*. Leipzig: Otto Wigand, 1841.

———. *The Essence of Religion*. Translated by Alexander Loos. New York: Asa K. Butts and Co., 1873. Originally published as *Das Wesen der Religion*. Leipzig: Otto Wigand, 1845.

———. *Thoughts on Death and Immortality: From the Papers of a Thinker, along with an Appendix of Theological-Satirical Epigrams*. Translated by James A. Massey. Berkeley: University of California Press, 1980. Originally published as *Gedanken über Tod und Unsterblichkeit aus den Papieren eines Denkers, nebst einem Anhang theologisch-satyrischer Xenien*. Nuremberg: Stein, 1830.

Foucault, Michel. *The Order of Things: An Archaeology of the Human Sciences*. London: Tavistock, 1970. Originally published as *Les Mots et les Choses*. Paris: Gallimard, 1966.

Fourastié, Jean. *Essais de morale prospective*. Paris: Gonthier, 1966.

———. *Le grand espoir du XXe siècle: Progrès technique, progrès économique, progrès social*. Paris: Presses Universitaires de France, 1949.

Francis, John, and Paul Abrecht, eds. "Facing Up to Nuclear Power." *Anticipation: Christian Social Thought in a Future Perspective*, no. 20, 1975. Geneva: World Council of Churches, Department on Church and Society.

Friedmann, Georges P. *The Anatomy of Work: The Implications of Specialization*. Translated by Wyatt Rawson. London: Heinemann, 1961. Originally published as *Le travail en miettes*. Paris: Gallimard, 1956.

———. *La crise du progrès: esquisse d'histoire des idées, 1895–1935*. Paris: Gallimard, 1936.

———. *Industrial Society: The Emergence of the Human Problems of Automation*. Edited by Harold L. Sheppard. Glencoe, IL: Free Press, 1955. Originally published as *Problèmes humains du machinisme industriel*. Paris: Gallimard, 1946.

———. *La puissance et la sagesse*. Paris: Galllimard, 1971.

———. *Sept études sur l'homme et la technique*. Paris: Gonthier, 1966.
Gadamer, Hans-Georg. *Truth and Method*. Translated by Joel Weinsheimer and Donald G. Marshall. London: Bloomsbury Academic, 2014. Originally published as *Wahrheit und Methode: Grundzüge einer philosophischen Hermeneutik*. Tübingen: J. C. B. Mohr, 1960.
Gilkey, Langdon B. "Technology, History and Liberation." *Anticipation*, no. 16 (1974) 14–19. Included as an annex in "The Technological Understanding of Humanity and Nature in a Technological Era." In *Reaping the Whirlwind: A Christian Interpretation of History*, 319–22. New York: Seabury, 1976.
Gill, David M. *From Here to Where? Technology, Faith and the Future of Man: Report on an Exploratory Conference, Geneva, June 28–July 4, 1970*. Geneva: World Council of Churches, 1970.
Gill, David W. "A Conversation with René Girard." In "René Girard and Jacques Ellul," special issue, *Ellul Forum*, no. 35 (Spring 2005) 19–20.
Girard, René. *Resurrection from the Underground: Feodor Dostoevsky*. Edited and translated by James G. Williams. East Lansing, MI: Michigan State University Press, 2012. Originally published as *Dostoïevski: Du double à l'unité*. Paris: Plon, 1963. Also published in *Critique dans un souterrain*. Lausanne: L'Age d'Homme, 1976.
———. *Violence and the Sacred*. Translated by Patrick Gregory. London: Bloomsbury Academic, 2017. Originally published as *La Violence et le Sacré*. Paris: Hachette, 1972.
Gordis, Robert. "Science, Natural Law and Ethics, a Jewish Perspective." In *Ethics in an Age of Pervasive Technology*, edited by Melvin Kranzberg, 83–106. Boulder, CO: Westview, 1980.
Gramsci, Antonio. *Prison Notebooks*. 3 vols. Edited by Joseph A. Buttigieg. Translated by Joseph A. Buttigieg and Antonio Callari. New York: Columbia University Press, 1992–2007. Originally published as *Quaderni del Carcere*. Edited by Valentino Gerratana. 4 vols. Turin: Einaudi, 1975.
———. *Selections from Political Writings*. 2 vols. Edited and translated by Quintin Hoare. Translated by John Mathews. London: Lawrence and Wishart; Minneapolis: University of Minnesota Press, 1977–1978. Originally published as *Scritti politici*. 3 vols. Edited by Paolo Spriano. Rome: Editori riuniti, 1973.
Gruson, Claude. "Theological problems raised by technological options: the confessions of an economist." *Anticipation*, no. 15 (1973) 22–29.
Guillebaud, Jean-Claude. *Comment je suis redevenu chrétien*. Paris: Albin Michel, 2007.
———. "Mort de Jacques Ellul: Un précurseur impénitent." *Le Monde*, May 21, 1994, 17.
Hall, Cameron P., ed. *Human Values and Advancing Technology: A New Agenda for the Church in Mission*. New York: Friendship, 1967.
Hegel, Georg W. F. *Hegel's Philosophy of Right*. Translated by Thomas Malcolm Knox. Oxford: Clarendon, 1952. Originally published as *Grundlinien der Philosophie des Rechts*. Berlin: Nicolai, 1820.
———. *The Phenomenology of Spirit*. Translated by Peter Fuss and John Dobbins. Notre Dame: University of Notre Dame Press, 2019. Originally published as *Die Phänomenologie des Geistes*. Bamberg: Joseph Anton Goebhardt, 1807.
Holt, Douglas, and Douglas Cameron. *Cultural Strategy: Using Innovative Ideologies to Build Breakthrough Brands*. Oxford: Oxford University Press, 2010.

BIBLIOGRAPHY

Horney, Karen. *The Neurotic Personality of Our Time*. New York: Norton, 1937.

Howe, Günter, and Heinz E. Todt. "Peace in the Scientific and Technical Age." World Council of Churches, *Background information for Church and Society*, no. 35-36 (1966).

Illich, Ivan. *Tools for Conviviality*. New York: Harper and Row, 1973.

Illich, Ivan, and Étienne Verne. *Imprisoned in the Global Classroom*. London: Pluto, 1976.

———. "Le piège de l'École à vie." *Le Monde de l'Éducation* 2 (January 1975) 11-14.

Jacob, François. "L'évolution sans projet." In *Le Darwinisme aujourd'hui*, interviews of François Chapeville and others conducted by Émile Noël, 145-47. Paris: Seuil, 1979.

———. *The Possible and the Actual*. Seattle: University of Washington Press, 1982. Originally published as *Le Jeu des Possibles: Essai sur la diversité du vivant*. Paris: Fayard, 1981.

Jacquard, Albert. *Endangered by Science?* Translated by Margaret M. Moriarty. New York: Columbia University Press, 1985. Originally published as *Au péril de la science: Interrogations d'un généticien*. Paris: Seuil, 1982.

Jonas, Hans. "The Heuristics of Fear." In *Ethics in an Age of Pervasive Technology*, edited by Melvin Kranzberg, 213-21. Boulder, CO: Westview, 1980.

———. *The Imperative of Responsibility: In Search of an Ethics for the Technological Age*. Translated by Hans Jonas and David Herr. Chicago: University of Chicago Press, 1984. Originally published as *Das Prinzip Verantwortung: Versuch einer Ethik für die technologische Zivilisation*. Frankfurt: Insel-Verlag, 1980.

———. "Technology and Responsibility: Reflections on the New Task of Ethics." In *The Humanizing of Man*, edited by James M. Robinson, 3-20. Waterloo, ON: Council on the Study of Religion, 1973.

Jouvenel, Bertrand de. *Arcadie: Essais sur le mieux-vivre*. Paris: S.E.D.E.I.S., 1969.

———. *L'Art de la conjecture*. Paris: S.E.D.E.I.S., 1972.

Jünger, Ernst. *The Glass Bees*. Translated by Louise Bogan and Elizabeth Mayer. New York: Noonday, 1960. Originally published as *Gläserne Bienen*. Stuttgart: E. Klett, 1957.

Kahneman, Daniel. "Human Engineering of Decisions." In *Ethics in an Age of Pervasive Technology*, edited by Melvin Kranzberg, 190-92. Boulder, CO: Westview, 1980.

Kahneman, Daniel, with Amos Tversky. "Prospect Theory: An Analysis of Decision under Risk." *Econometria* 47, no. 2 (March 1979) 263-91.

Kierkegaard, Søren. *Concluding Unscientific Postscript to "Philosophical Fragments."* Translated by Howard V. Hong and Edna H. Hong. Kierkegaard's Writings 12.1. Princeton: Princeton University Press, 1992. Originally published as *Afsluttende uvidenskabelig Efterskrift til de philosophiske Smuler*. Copenhagen: C. A. Reitzel, 1846.

———. *The Sickness unto Death*. In *Fear and Trembling and The Sickness unto Death*. Translated by Walter Lowrie. Garden City, NY: Anchor, 1954. Originally published as *Sygdommen til Døden*. Copenhagen: C. A. Reitzel, 1848.

Kranzberg, Melvin, ed. *Ethics in an Age of Pervasive Technology*. Boulder, CO: Westview, 1980.

Kuhn, Thomas S. *The Structure of Scientific Revolutions*. 2nd, enlarged ed. Chicago: University of Chicago Press, 1970.

BIBLIOGRAPHY

Kurzweil, Zvi. "Why Heteronomous Ethics?" In *Ethics in an Age of Pervasive Technology*, edited by Melvin Kranzberg, 68–71. Boulder, CO: Westview, 1980.

Ladrière, Jean. "Technique et eschatologie terrestre." In *Civilisation technique et humanisme: Colloque de l'Académie internationale de philosophie des sciences*, 211–44. Paris: Beauchesne, 1968.

Laloup, Jean, and Jean Nélis. *Hommes et machines*. 5th ed. Tournai: Casterman, 1959.

Laplantine, François. *Les trois voix de l'imaginaire: le messianisme, la possession et l'utopie: Étude ethnopsychiatrique*. Paris: Éditions Universitaires, 1974.

Le Gal, Yves. *Question(s) à la théologie chrétienne*. Paris: Cerf, 1975.

Leroi-Gourhan, André. *Évolution et techniques*. Vol. 2, *Milieu et techniques*. Paris: Albin Michel, 1945.

Lieberman, David S. "Broadening Engineering Education—The Technological Imperative." In *Ethics in an Age of Pervasive Technology*, edited by Melvin Kranzberg, 160–61. Boulder, CO: Westview, 1980.

Lorenz, Konrad. *On Aggression*. Translated by Marjorie Kerr Wilson. London: Routledge, 2002. Originally published as *Das sogenannte Böse: Zur Naturgeschichte der Aggression*. Vienna: G. Borotha-Schoeler, 1963.

Lys, Daniel. *La chair dans l'Ancien Testament: "Bâsâr."* Paris: Editions Universitaires, 1967.

———. *L'Ecclésiaste: ou Que vaut la vie?* Paris: Letouzey et Ané, 1977.

———. *Nèphèsh: Histoire de l'âme dans la révélation d'Israël au sein des religions proche-orientales*. Paris: Presses Universitaires de France, 1959.

———. *Le plus beau chant de la création: Commentaire du Cantique des cantiques*. Paris: Cerf, 1968.

———. *Ruach: Le souffle dans l 'Ancien Testament: Enquête anthropologique à travers l'histoire théologique d'Israël*. Paris: Presses Universitaires de France, 1962.

Marx, Karl. *Critique of Hegel's Philosophy of Right*. Edited by Joseph O'Malley. Translated by Annette Jolin and Joseph O'Malley. Cambridge: Cambridge University Press, 1970. Originally published as *Kritik des Hegelschen Staatsrechts*, 1843. Published in *Karl Marx/Friedrich Engels/Werke*, edited by the Institut für Marxismus-Leninismus beim Zentralkommittee der Sozialistischen Einheitspartei Deutschlands, vol. 1, 203–333. Berlin: Dietz, 1964.

McLuhan, Marshall. *Understanding Media: The Extensions of Man*. New York: McGraw-Hill, 1964.

Mehl, Roger. *Images of Man*. Translated by James H. Farley. London: SPCK, 1966. Originally published as *Images de l'homme*. Geneva: Labor et Fides, 1953.

———. *Pour une éthique sociale chrétienne*. Neuchâtel: Delachaux et Niestlé, 1967.

———. *Les pouvoirs de l'homme*. Lausanne, L'Âge d'Homme, 1975.

Mehl-Koehnlein, Herrade. *L'homme selon l'apôtre Paul*. Neuchâtel; Paris: Delachaux et Niestlé, 1950.

———. "Travail." In *Vocabulaire biblique*, edited by Jean-Jacques Von Allmen, 298–300. Neuchâtel: Delachaux et Niestlé, 1954.

Moltmann, Jürgen. *Theology of Hope: On the Ground and the Implications of a Christian Eschatology*. Translated by James Waterson Leitch. London: SCM, 1967. Originally published as *Theologie der Hoffnung: Untersuchungen zur Begründung und zu den Konsequenzen einer christlichen Eschatologie*. Munich: Chr. Kaiser, 1964.

Monod, Jacques. *Chance and Necessity: An Essay on the Natural Philosophy of Modern Biology*. Translated by Austryn Wainhouse. New York: Knopf, 1971. Originally published as *Le Hasard et la Nécessité: Essai sur la philosophie naturelle de la biologie moderne*. Paris: Seuil, 1970.

Montgomery, John W. *Computers, Cultural Change and the Christ = Les ordinateurs, l'ordre culturel et le Christ = Komputer, kultureller Wandel und Christus*. Wayne, NJ: Christian Research Institute, 1969.

Morin, Edgar. *Le Paradigme perdu: la nature humaine*. Paris: Seuil, 1973.

Mounier, Emmanuel. *Be Not Afraid: Studies in Personalist Sociology*. Translated by Cynthia Rowland. New York: New York University Press, 1969. Originally published as *La petite peur du XXe siècle*. Neuchâtel: La Baconnière; Paris: Le Seuil, 1948, 1953, 1959.

Mumford, Lewis M. *The Myth of the Machine*. 2 vols. New York: Harcourt Brace Jovanovich, 1967–1970.

———. *Technics and Civilization*. New York: Harcourt, Brace and Co., 1934.

Mushakoji, Kinhide. "Technology and the Cultural Revolution." *Anticipation*, no. 3 (1970) 8–13.

Neher, André. *The Prophetic Existence*. Translated by William Wolf. South Brunswick, NJ: A. S. Barnes, 1969. Originally published as *L'essence du prophétisme*. Paris: Presses Universitaires de France, 1955.

Neill, Alexander S. *Summerhill: A Radical Approach to Child Rearing*. New York: Hart, 1960.

"René Girard and Jacques Ellul." Special issue, *Ellul Forum*, no. 35 (Spring 2005).

Ricoeur, Paul. "Manifestation and Proclamation." In *Figuring the Sacred: Religion, Narrative, and Imagination*, edited by Mark I. Wallace, translated by David Pellauer, 48–67. Minneapolis: Fortress, 1995. Originally published as "Manifestation et proclamation." In *Le Sacré: Études et recherches: Actes du Colloque organisé par le Centre international d'études humanistes et par l'Institut d'études philosophiques de Rome, Rome, 4–9 janvier 1974*, edited by Enrico Castelli, 57–76. Paris: Aubier-Montaigne, 1974.

———. "The Socius and the Neighbor." In *History and Truth*, translated by Charles Andrew Kelbley, 98–109. Evanston, IL: Northwestern University Press, 1965. Originally published as "Le Socius et le Prochain." In *Histoire et Vérité*, 113–27. Paris: Seuil, 1955, 1964.

Rognon, Frédéric. "Bernard Charbonneau et la critique des racines chrétiennes de la Grande Mue." In *Bernard Charbonneau: habiter la terre: Actes du Colloque du 2–4 mai 2011, Université de Pau et des Pays de l'Adour*, edited by Alain Cazenave-Parriot, 108–16. DVD accompanied by a booklet. Pau: Université de Pau et des Pays de l'Adour, 2011. The text of this lecture is available on the Internet: http://web.univ-pau.fr/RECHERCHE/SET/CHARBONNEAU/documents/Actes_colloque_Bernard_CHARBONNEAU_Habiter_la_terre_SET.pdf.

———. *Jacques Ellul: Une pensée en dialogue*. Geneva: Labor et Fides, 2007, 2013.

———. "Les racines personnalistes de l'écologie radicale: Denis de Rougemont, Bernard Charbonneau, Jacques Ellul." *Entropia*, no. 14 (Spring 2013) 187–99.

Rognon, Frédéric, ed. *Générations Ellul: Soixante héritiers de la pensée de Jacques Ellul*. Geneva: Labor et Fides, 2012.

Sahlins, Marshall. *Stone Age Economics*. Chicago: Aldine Atherton, 1972.

Schumacher, Ernst F. *Small Is Beautiful*. New York: Harper & Row, 1973.

Servier, Jean. *Les forges d'Hiram ou la Genèse de l'Occident*. Paris: Grasset, 1976.

———. *Histoire de l'Utopie*. Paris: Gallimard, 1967.

BIBLIOGRAPHY

Simondon, Gilbert. *On the Mode of Existence of Technical Objects*. Translated by Cecile Malaspina and John Rogove. Minneapolis: Univocal, 2016. Originally published as *Du mode d'existence des objets techniques*. Paris: Aubier, 1958.

Skinner, B. F. *Beyond Freedom and Dignity*. London: J. Cape, 1971.

———. *Science and Human Behavior*. New York: Macmillan, 1953.

Sojcher, Jacques, and Gilbert Hottois, eds. *Éthique et technique*. Annales de l'Institut de philosophie et de sciences morales, Université Libre de Bruxelles. Brussels: Editions de l'Université de Bruxelles, 1983.

Steg, Léo. "The Social Responsibility of Scientists." In *Ethics in an Age of Pervasive Technology*, edited by Melvin Kranzberg, 158–59. Boulder, CO: Westview, 1980.

Steg, Léo, ed. "Should We Limit Science and Technology?" *Journal of the Franklin Institute*, September 1975.

Thring, Meredith Wooldridge. "Lost in the Fog." In *Ethics in an Age of Pervasive Technology*, edited by Melvin Kranzberg, 15–16. Boulder, CO: Westview, 1980.

———. "Towards a Creative Society." *Electronics and Power* 19, no. 21 (1973) 522–24.

Tocqueville, Alexis de. *Democracy in America*. Translated by Henry Reeve. Edited, with notes, by Francis Bowen. Mineola, NY: Dover, 2017. Originally published as *De la démocratie en Amérique*. 2 vols. Paris: Librairie de Charles Gosselin, 1835–1840.

Tribe, Lawrence H. "From Environmental Foundations to Constitutional Structures: Learning from Nature's Future." *Yale Law Journal* 84 (1975) 545–56.

———. "Technology Assessment and the Fourth Discontinuity: The Limits of Instrumental Rationality." *Southern California Law Review* 46 (1973) 617–60.

———. "Ways not to Think about Plastic Trees: New Foundations for Environmental Law." *Yale Law Journal* 83, no. 7 (1974) 1330–31.

Troeltsch, Ernst. "Eschatologie." In *Die Religion in Geschichte und Gegenwart*, edited by Friedrich Michael Schiele, vol. 2, col. 630–31. Tübingen: J. C. B. Mohr (P. Siebeck), 1910.

Vacca, Roberto. *The Coming Dark Age*. Translated by J. S. Whale. St. Albans: Panther; Garden City, NY: Anchor, 1974. Originally published as *Il Medioevo prossimo venturo*. Milan: A. Mondadori, 1971.

Vahanian, Gabriel. *The Death of God: The Culture of our Post-Christian Era*. New York: Braziller, 1961.

———. "En ce jour-là: la liturgie en tant que structure eschatologique du temps." In *Temporalité et Aliénation: Actes du Colloque: Rome, 3–8 janvier 1975*, edited by Enrico Castelli, 129–38. Paris: Aubier-Montaigne, 1975.

———. "L'expérience de Dieu." In *La Philosophie de la Religion: l'herméneutique et la philosophie de la religion: Actes du colloque organisé par le Centre international d'études humanistes et par l'Institut d'études philosophiques de Rome, Rome, 3–8 janvier 1977*, edited by Enrico Castelli, 329–36. Paris: Aubier-Montaigne, 1977.

———. *God and Utopia: The Church in a Technological Civilization*. New York: Seabury, 1977.

———. "Idéologie et Eschatologie." In *Démythisation et idéologie: Actes du Colloque organisé par le Centre International d'Etudes Humanistes (Romé) et par l'Institut d'Etudes Philosophiques (Istituto di Studi Filosofici) de Rome: Rome, 4–9 janvier 1973*, edited by Enrico Castelli, 93–101. Paris: Aubier-Montaigne, 1973.

———. "Jacques Ellul, un homme d'amitié." Special issue, "Le siècle de Jacques Ellul," *Foi et Vie* 93, no. 5–6 (December 1994) 1–8.

———. *No Other God*. New York: Braziller, 1966.

BIBLIOGRAPHY

———. "Sécularisation, Sécularisme, Sécularité: la Foi et les choses." In *L'Herméneutique de la sécularisation: Actes du Colloque organisé par le Centre International d'Etudes Humanistes et par l'Institut d'Etudes Philosophiques de Rome: Rome, 3–8 janvier 1976*, edited by Enrico Castelli, 111–20. Paris: Aubier-Montaigne, 1976.

———. *Wait Without Idols*. New York: Braziller, 1964.

Weber, Hans-Ruedi. *Experiments with Man: Report of an Ecumenical Consultation*. Geneva: World Council of Churches, 1969.

———. *Man in his Living Environment: An Ethical Assessment*. London: Church Information Office, 1970.

Wiener, Norbert. *God and Golem, Inc.: A Comment on Certain Points where Cybernetics Impinges on Religion*. Cambridge: MIT Press, 1964.

World Council of Churches. "Science and Technology for Human Development." Report, 1974 World Conference in Bucharest, Romania. *Anticipation*, no. 19 (1974) 8–13.

———. "Report on Nuclear Energy. Ecumenical Hearing on Nuclear Energy: A Report to the Churches, Sigtuna, Sweden, June 24–29, 1975." *Anticipation*, no. 21, 1975.

www.ingramcontent.com/pod-product-compliance
Lightning Source LLC
Chambersburg PA
CBHW021654230426
43668CB00008B/615